Film Feminisms offers a global and updated overview of the history, present-day concerns, and future of feminist film and theory. It introduces frameworks from phenomenology, affect theory, and psychoanalysis to reception studies, new media theories, and critical historiography, as well as engaging with key issues in documentary ethics, genre theory, and star studies.

This new textbook situates feminist film theory within the larger framework of transnational scholarly approaches, as well as decolonial, queer, disability studies, and critical race theories. It offers a much-needed update on pedagogical approaches to feminist film studies, providing discussions of filmmakers and films that have been overlooked in the field, or that are overdue for further analysis.

Each chapter is supported by a variety of pedagogical features including activities, key terms, and case studies. Many of the activities draw on contemporary digital media, such as social media and streaming platforms, to update the field to today's changing media landscape.

Kristin Lené Hole is an Assistant Professor in Film Studies at Portland State University. She is the author of *Towards a Feminist Cinematic Ethics: Claire Denis, Emmanuel Levinas, and Jean-Luc Nancy* (2016) and co-editor of *The Routledge Companion to Cinema and Gender* (with Dijana Jelača, E. Ann Kaplan, and Patrice Petro, 2017).

Dijana Jelača is Adjunct Professor in the Film Department at Brooklyn College. She is the author of *Dislocated Screen Memory: Narrating Trauma in Post-Yugoslav Cinema* (2016).

FILM FEMINISMS

A Global Introduction

Kristin Lené Hole and Dijana Jelača

LONDON AND NEW YORK

First published 2019
by Routledge
2 Park Square, Milton Park, Abingdon, Oxon OX14 4RN

and by Routledge
711 Third Avenue, New York, NY 10017

Routledge is an imprint of the Taylor & Francis Group, an informa business

British Library Cataloguing-in-Publication Data
A catalogue record for this book is available from the British Library

Library of Congress Cataloging-in-Publication Data
Names: Hole, Kristin Lené, author. | Jelača, Dijana, 1979– author.
Title: Film feminisms / Kristin Lené Hole and Dijana Jelača.
Description: London ; New York : Routledge, 2018. | Includes
    bibliographical references and index.
Identifiers: LCCN 2018015389 | ISBN 9781138667891 (hardback :
    alk. paper) | ISBN 9781138667907 (pbk. : alk. paper) |
    ISBN 9781315618845 (ebook)
Subjects: LCSH: Feminism and motion pictures. | Women in motion
    pictures. | Feminist film criticism.
Classification: LCC PN1995.9.W6 H63 2018 | DDC 791.43/6522—dc23
LC record available at https://lccn.loc.gov/2018015389

ISBN: 978-1-138-66789-1 (hbk)
ISBN: 978-1-138-66790-7 (pbk)
ISBN: 978-1-315-61884-5 (ebk)

Typeset in Sabon
by Apex CoVantage, LLC

To our daughters, Pola and Sava

CONTENTS

FIGURES

ACKNOWLEDGEMENTS

We would like to thank our reviewers, both anonymous and named, for their valuable input on this project. Patricia White and Anikó Imre in particular read the book almost in its entirety and helped us to improve the final manuscript. We want to extend extra thanks to Patricia White for her mentorship on this and other projects. Our editor Natalie Foster and her assistants Sheni Kruger and Jennifer Vennall have also been wonderful to work with over the course of writing and the production of this book.

Kristin would like to thank Mia Ferm for her invaluable input and influence on the experimental chapter. Also key in relation to this chapter were conversations with Melinda Kowalska and Julie Perini. Claire Lindsay and Tim Nelson both provided administrative help at various stages of the project. Thank you! For the new media chapter in particular I'd like to thank Jungmin Kwon for sharing resources, teaching me about Korean fandoms, and gossiping with me about BYJ. Thanks also to Shannon Wilson for her aesthetic expertise. I'd also like to thank the students who took my two stardom seminars at Portland State University for helping me to test and explore the material that ended up in the chapter on stars. Finally, thanks to my family, Stephen and Pola, for giving me so much joy and support.

Dijana would like to thank all her friends and colleagues who have supported her work and invited her to present portions of the material developed for the textbook: Meta Mazaj, Aleksandar Bošković, Maša Kolanović, Danijela Lugarić, Tanja Petrović, Barb LeSavoy, Nikolay Karkov and Xhercis Mendez. Warm gratitude also goes to Debra Zimmerman for sharing her invaluable resources and input. My students in St. Petersburg, Russia, and at Brooklyn College have been a wonderful source of feedback and inspiration for this project. Most of all, thank you to my family and special loved ones – you know who you are. Finally, my biggest gratitude goes to Sava and John for your unconditional love.

INTRODUCTION

Questions of gender and sexual equality seem to be omnipresent in today's media landscape. From issues of sexual harassment in the entertainment industry, exemplified by the recent #MeToo and Time's Up movements that have shaken up the establishment from North America to South Korea, to a growing awareness of the lack of opportunities for black and Latina women in Hollywood, to Bollywood's recent "feminist turn," the representation of gender and the opportunities available to women in film and television are prevalent concerns internationally. In the 21st century, many people find it hard to name even five female directors. Most people would have difficulty naming any non-binary directors at all (the Wachowski sisters excepted!). While the fact of a director being female, trans, or from non-dominant racial categories does not guarantee that their work will be politically progressive in any way, questions about the re/production of power and the politics of images – and how they relate to those who make said images – have always been a facet of feminist approaches to thinking about cinema.

Feminist theory was foundational in the establishment of film studies as an academic discipline. *Film Feminisms* centers the ongoing contributions of feminist scholarship to thinking about cinema within a global framework. We draw on postcolonial, transnational, queer, disability studies, and critical race theories in order to illustrate how feminist film studies intersects with and inflects these related intellectual trajectories. The plural use of feminisms in the title refers to the fact that feminism is not a unified political or intellectual perspective. We emphasize the contextually specific ways in which issues of gender, race, class, and nation relate to major concepts in film studies from authorship and spectatorship to documentary practices and genres. In each chapter, the material is organized in a way that integrates issues of transnationality, decoloniality, sexuality, class and race as essential to understanding the topic at hand, rather than as "special" perspectives that are added on as an afterthought once dominant (i.e. white

Western) paradigms have been explicated. We have chosen a diverse range of films, filmmakers and theoretical texts around which to build each chapter, to privilege non-dominant voices and to display the breadth of work that is available to the curious spectator or reader.

While our focus is on film in particular, there is significant overlap with television, as the two forms increasingly converge in the digital media landscape, being accessed and viewed on the same platforms and being adapted into one other. Although we only address television occasionally, many of the paradigms discussed and questions raised are equally applicable to your favorite television series. The eighth and final chapter, in particular, looks at the ways in which film intersects with other media platforms, particularly those most associated with digital culture (aka new media).

Each of the eight chapters is designed to give a comprehensive overview of a prominent area in feminist film studies. The chapters cross-reference one another when relevant, in order to help readers make connections between related themes and recurring concerns. They can be read in any order, since they do not follow a linear progression, except for the final chapter, "Feminism, Film, and New Media," which addresses current and ongoing changes in screen culture that influence our understandings of both cinema and feminism. In each chapter, key terms and concepts are bolded in the main text for easier identification and orientation.

Chapter 1, "Women filmmakers and feminist authorship," interrogates the concept of film authorship and examines how feminist film inquiry has been a useful tool for unpacking some of the unspoken prejudices of film history. In this chapter we distinguish between female filmmakers and feminist forms of address. In discussing auteur theory and its shortcomings, particularly when it comes to women filmmakers, the chapter aims to illustrate how women as film authors have historically been left out of dominant film history. We discuss the more recent historical turn in feminist film studies, and notable women film pioneers across the globe. We also introduce some contemporary feminist filmmakers from around the world and explore the idea of authorship beyond directing, in areas such as screenwriting and cinematography.

Chapter 2, "Spectatorship and reception," explores the feminist foundations of thinking about spectatorship and reception, from psychoanalytic to empirical approaches. Readers are asked to consider how films address particular kinds of viewers and how historical audiences interpret the images they consume. The chapter also explores fandoms and fan practices. Films such as Ousmane Sembene's *Black Girl* (1966, Senegal) and Balu Mehendra's *Julie Ganapathi* (2003, India) are given special focus.

Chapter 3, "Cinema and the body," introduces an often-overlooked area of crucial feminist interventions. It provides a strong basis in contemporary approaches to thinking about the body as it relates to film and how thinking about the body engages with an analysis of categories from gender and sexuality to race and ability. We examine a variety of paradigms, including phenomenological approaches and Deleuzian and affect-based frameworks, and focus on case studies such as *Nénette and Boni* (Claire Denis, 1996, France), *Under the Skin* (Jonathan Glazer, 2013, UK), and *Orlando* (Sally Potter, 1992, UK). Disability studies and trauma theory are introduced to discuss films from *Rust and Bone* (Jacques Audiard, 2012, France/Belgium) to *Pan's Labyrinth* (Guillermo del Toro, 2006, Spain/Mexico).

Chapter 4, "Stars: gendered texts, circulating images," introduces the major terminology and methodological considerations in feminist approaches to star studies. Looking at stars as texts that circulate both nationally and transnationally, we examine the ways that stars embody and negotiate cultural contradictions around class, gender, sexuality, and other categories. We explore issues of race and ethnicity in Hollywood, sexuality and skin color in Bollywood stardom, and transnational Asian masculinities.

Chapters 5 and 6 examine two major modes of filmmaking that often overlap, documentary and experimental film and video. Chapter 5, "Documentary: local realities, (trans)national perspectives," examines feminist perspectives on documentary realism, historiography, and ethnography. As a film mode, documentary is a vital and vibrant outlet for feminist work. We explore how women have used the autobiographical documentary form to articulate experiences that are otherwise invisible in the larger media landscape. The chapter discusses notable and overlooked feminist documentaries, including *Year of the Woman* (Susan Hochman, 1973, US), *Finding Christa* (Camille Billops and James Hatch, 1991, US), *Images from the Corner* (Jasmila Žbanić, 2000, Bosnia-Herzegovina), and *Sonita* (Rokhsareh Ghaem Maghami, 2015, Iran). Some of the key debates addressed in this chapter focus on direct cinema, Third Worldist cinema, and feminist documentary ethics.

Chapter 6, "Feminism and experimental film and video," discusses women's relationship with the historical avant-garde and with experimental film form more broadly. It foregrounds the question of what makes experimental work feminist and introduces some of the reasons why experimental modes of filmmaking have been more conducive to telling non-dominant stories or sharing experiences marginalized by mainstream culture. After exploring major threads within experimental filmmaking, including expressive and structural traditions and the diary film, we highlight several key strategies in feminist experimental filmmaking. These include appropriating and recontextualizing images; rewriting male texts; telling culturally or politically marginalized stories and exploring identities; and, finally, creating histories where official records do not exist. Readers will be introduced to an extensive number of experimental filmmakers and new media video artists, with case studies including Vera Chytilová's *Daisies* (1966, Czechoslovakia) and work by Basma al Sharif and Mounira al Solh.

Chapter 7, "Narrative film: gender and genre," introduces students to key debates within feminist film studies around the uses of realist versus genre modes and film forms, particularly as they relate to ideology and to whose stories are represented and how. Several genres that have continued relevance in feminist film studies – such as melodrama, horror, science fiction, action films, and porn – are discussed in terms of the significant contributions feminist scholars have made to how we think about the interactions between gender and genre in particular. We also explore how genres "travel" internationally, and how a genre like melodrama has been adapted in varying national and historical contexts. Case studies include lesser known genre films such as the Ghanaian melodrama *Sinking Sands* (Leila Djansi, 2011) and the transnational, generically hybrid *A Girl Walks Home Alone at Night* (Ana Lily Amirpour, 2014, US). In the section on porn, we consider the proliferation of new media platforms for feminist, queer, trans, and ethical porn in particular, in terms of production, distribution, and viewership.

Our final chapter, "From film to new media: emergent feminist perspectives," explores the intersections between feminist film studies and new media. It introduces the major questions that feminist media studies asks about digital technologies and cultures, with specific attention to the ways in which digital media both connect with film studies approaches and also diverge from and put pressure on film studies paradigms. Attention is paid to the political implications of the ways that technology and virtual spaces are conceived in theory and on film and to the ways in which digital discourses often reproduce real world inequalities in areas from avatar design to video game discussion boards. We examine how non-dominant groups use various digital spaces and technologies to form community and/or engage in activism. Sections on fandom (from vidding to Korean fanfic), online harassment, and video games are included.

Each chapter includes a range of pedagogical features including:

- A variety of research and viewing activities, many of which incorporate contemporary media platforms and all of which expand on or apply the material covered in the chapter
- Discussion questions designed to facilitate dialogue or to be used as writing prompts on key issues
- Case studies focused on specific films, filmmakers, or related issues, often highlighting important yet overlooked work; case studies also function as viewing suggestions and examples of work that tackles or effectively illustrates the themes discussed in the main body of each chapter

- Bolded key terms to signal the major concepts the chapters introduce
- A list of references that also serve as suggestions for further reading and research

It is our hope that this book introduces you to the complexity and diversity of feminist thinking about cinema and of feminist filmmaking. Feminist scholarship has been and continues to be vital to the development of film studies. As a result, this book can only offer a snapshot of a rapidly expanding field. Some of our readers will themselves undoubtedly contribute to the future of film feminisms in dynamic and generative ways.

Chapter one

WOMEN FILMMAKERS AND FEMINIST AUTHORSHIP

In this chapter, we interrogate the concept of film authorship and examine how feminist film inquiry has been a useful tool for unpacking some of the unspoken prejudices of film history in relation to women filmmakers. By scrutinizing auteur theory (defined later) and its shortcomings, particularly when it comes to women filmmakers, the chapter illustrates how women as film authors have historically been left out of dominant film history. This holds particularly true when it comes to women of color, LGBTQ women or non-binary filmmakers, and women making films outside of their native national contexts. The fixed idea of the nation is often one of the key premises upon which the standing of an auteur rests, and which has frequently privileged Western film industries as sites where auteurs are located. In what follows, we put special focus on recent work in feminist film studies that highlights the ways in which many films are the product of hybrid identities and transnational patterns of displacement and migration that go beyond the nation as a central organizing framework (Wang 2011; White 2015). The chapter also addresses the work of women directors during the silent era and through the studio period, touching on the ways that women exerted significant influence on films in various capacities in classical cinema, including as screenwriters, cinematographers, and editors.

FILM HISTORY AND AUTHORSHIP

Film, as a general rule, is a collaborative art. Unlike a novel or sculpture, which can be seen as the result of a fairly singular creative vision, typically, it takes dozens – if not hundreds – of people working together in order to create a single work of cinema. As film developed as an art form and medium of mass entertainment over the 20th century, the director came to be seen as the author or sole creative force, although this was not the case early on in the development of cinema. The notion of the director being the primary author of a film rose to prominence in the 1950s and 1960s. Director François Truffaut, critic André Bazin, and others writing for the French film journal *Cahiers du Cinéma*, argued that a director's authorial vision should be considered the key creative force shaping a film – an approach to film typically referred to as **auteurism**. Under auteurism, writes Robert Stam, "the director was no longer merely the servant of a preexisting text (novel, screenplay), but a creative artist in his/her own right" (2000: 83). This approach was subsequently developed in the United States by Andrew Sarris, a critic for *The Village Voice*, into what came to be known as **auteur theory**. Auteur theory particularly privileges those directors who are seen as shaping movies according to their unique aesthetic vision and worldview, rather than "merely" restaging existing paradigms of film language. Moreover, the theory also suggests that great movie auteurs typically show visual, aesthetic, and thematic consistencies across their body of work. "Intrinsically strong directors, auteur theory argued, will exhibit over the years a recognizable stylistic and thematic personality, even when they work in Hollywood studios" (Stam: 84). Alfred Hitchcock is a good example, as he fits the pattern of thematic and visual consistency that spans across most, if not all, of his films. Virtually all of his films, regardless of the production context, distinguish themselves through the director's idiosyncratic creation of suspense, use of specific camera angles, dramatic editing, and ingenious utilization of sound (silent films excluded), among other things. Moreover, many of his films carry horror and thriller overtones, with psychologically tortured women as central figures. However, some versions of auteur theory do not presuppose that a film is solely the product of the director's conscious efforts and intended meanings. As Peter Wollen observes, in structuralist auteur theory:

> the structure [that carries across a director's body of work] is associated with a single director, an individual, not because he has played the role of artist, expressing himself or his own vision in the film, but because it is through the force of his preoccupations that an unconscious, unintended meaning can be decoded in the film.
>
> (1972: 144)

7

In other words, the director's stated intentions do not govern the meanings of their films. What may preoccupy a director the least, consciously speaking, may in fact be what gives their films their ideological or thematic consistencies. Claire Johnston used precisely this structuralist approach to develop the concept of women's cinema, which we discuss in subsequent sections.

Yet, as previously discussed, films are typically the product of large teams of workers, which is why it is often inaccurate to attribute film authorship solely to one person. In fact, during cinema's early history, camera operators were considered primary film authors. During Hollywood's studio era (between the 1920s and 1940s), producers were more frequently considered the dominant force behind a film, as they were generally responsible for overseeing a film's production from conception through postproduction and even beyond. Even in the contemporary film scene, the notion of the director as the sole author of a film can be challenged by examining the role of screenwriters, cinematographers, set designers, sound technicians, and actors, which we explore later in the chapter.

In film studies, auteurship and gender have had a fraught and complicated relationship, in large part due to the fact that men have had the opportunity to make films much more often than women. As a result, the concept of auteurship is imbued with a sense of creative authority historically denied to women. The word "genius," for example, tends to conjure up a male image in the mind, as the domain of creative cultural and intellectual production has largely been seen as the purview of men. Moreover, the ability to become a "film auteur" is closely aligned with racial, class, and geopolitical privilege, where non-First World filmmakers have frequently gotten less attention and support for their work, or international recognition as auteurs. And in instances where international directors are indeed recognized – such as India's Satyajit Ray, for example – they are often seen as exceptions that have risen beyond their national contexts to produce higher instances of culture, often through Western influences and/or education.

Related to this, we could also scrutinize auteur theory's investment in the auteur as a representative of national culture – e.g. the French auteur (Truffaut or Godard) or the Swedish auteur (Bergman) – where the nation is taken to be a monolithic and clearly demarcated entity that the auteur, willingly or not, stands and speaks for (or against). The inadequacy of the national model can be clearly observed in the case of Andrei Tarkovsky, who is generally considered an auteur of Soviet cinema even though he made his last few films in exile, outside of the Soviet Union (indeed, Hamid Naficy [2001] considers him an exilic rather than national filmmaker). In the section on transnational paradigms, we will further explore the position of women filmmakers in particular with respect to contemporary national film cultures.

While women filmmakers continue to be outnumbered by men across the globe, the recent "historical turn" in feminist film studies has uncovered an increasing amount of evidence that female authorship (as distinct from "auteurship") was a very lively and broad-ranging occurrence in the early days of cinema (Gaines 2018). We can distinguish authorship from auteurship here by stipulating that auteurship often inherently invites hagiographic celebrations of a filmmaker's artistic achievement, while the concept of authorship is more democratic and less burdened by such demands for high artistic recognition. In other words, an author may be largely responsible for the making of a film without necessarily being considered a visionary genius (i.e. "auteur") as well. While the concept of the "auteur" did not yet exist in cinema's beginnings, in the next section, we look at the work of some early female filmmakers ("authors") in more detail. For a long time largely ignored by standard film history, the women film pioneers discussed ahead have in recent years finally been given their rightful place in the history of the medium.

A BRIEF HISTORY OF WOMEN'S FILM AUTHORSHIP

In this section, we highlight some notable women filmmakers from around the world, who have made significant contributions to cinema throughout film history. And while we discuss a lot of "firsts," it should be noted that the framework of "pioneers" is not meant as a limiting device that narrows the scope or focus of feminist film scholarship. The contributions of many women in film industries from around the globe remain vital even when they are not considered "pioneering" in the classical sense of pertaining only to early cinema. While a woman filmmaker is not necessarily a feminist filmmaker, identifying a lineage of women working in film has been central to the work of feminist film historians, in order to address the invisibility of women in dominant film history accounts and to create an archive of women working in the industry that may serve as inspiration and inheritance for female-identified filmmakers of the present and future.

Women filmmakers of the silent film era

What is today considered **classical feminist film theory** – the focus on spectatorship, psychoanalysis, semiotics and visual pleasure in scholarship of the 1970s and 1980s (which we discuss in Chapter 2) – closely scrutinized the way in which women were depicted on the cinematic screen. During this period, the focus was on representation and spectatorship, more than on other aspects of the film experience such as production, distribution, or historical reception. With the dominant feminist theory focused on the representation of women in the films of major male directors, even classical feminist film theory neglected to take into consideration the fact that many women filmmakers played a key role in the earliest periods of film history. The **historical turn** and the attention to women film pioneers has been a more recent development, prompting Jane Gaines (2004) to pose two related questions: why did women filmmakers largely leave the film industry with the rise of sound, and why did feminist film theory "forget" them? Reflecting the tension between theory and history, Gaines finds the latter question a more complicated one, since it asks feminist film scholars to consider why the active role of women as filmmakers in early cinema remained a blind spot for feminist film studies for a considerable period of time. "To ask why these women were forgotten is to ask why *we* forgot them" (113, emphasis in the text), Gaines pointedly notes. At the same time, if we historicize gender in order to prevent taking "woman" as a trans-historical and unchanging category, we must also consider the dilemma that Monica Dall'Asta summarizes when she asks how we can conceive the research on women film pioneers "at a moment like the present, when the very idea of 'women' no longer appears to describe a unified, unproblematic reality and emerges instead as an intellectual artifact or a sociocultural construction? (2010: 39)." Dall'Asta finds a possible solution in theories such as Iris Marion Young's concept of gender as seriality (1994), which holds that identities are complex and fluid, and "that each individual finds her or himself at the intersection of different, multiple series, such as those formed by class, nationality, ethnicity, sexual orientation etc." (Dall'Asta 2010: 42). Gender and female identity therefore need to be historicized rather than considered an a priori given, in order to enact an effective feminist historiography that draws on the historically specific constellations that have influenced women's role in the history of cinema.

At the turn of the 21st century and with the onset of a renewed interest in silent cinema, early women filmmakers have received long-overdue attention by film historians. The **Women Film Pioneers**[1] project is an online archive of existing information about early women film workers across the globe, and volumes like *A Feminist Reader in Early Cinema* (edited by Jennifer M. Bean and Diane Negra 2002) and *Reclaiming the Archive: Feminism and Film History* (edited by Vicki Callahan 2010) seek to challenge normative film history's erasure of women's roles behind the camera. In the introduction to *A Feminist Reader in Early Cinema*, Jennifer M. Bean poses an important question:

> How might the prominent sign of "woman" in the period, her role in not only the production but also the reception of early film, be taken up in terms beyond those of a gender paradigm that has never been comprehensive enough, never able to account for the production of whiteness or blackness – indeed of race of any kind – much less ethnicity, nationality, and the distinction of class?
>
> (2002: 2)

Feminist approaches to history need to be careful not to privilege gender as a category over and above race and class and thus reproduce the power asymmetries of the larger world within feminist history and theory. Bean notes that, "for contemporary film feminism, the excitement generated by these acts of discovery is inexorably bound to a series of questions concerning the production of historical and disciplinary knowledge" (2002: 2). That is to say, rather than unquestionably celebrating the reclaiming of lost histories of "pioneering" women in cinema, film scholars need to be careful not to romanticize this history or interpret it only through contemporary understandings of gender, womanhood, and film authorship. They also need to avoid the pitfalls of inadvertently reiterating the primacy of whiteness or class privilege, for instance, in constructing the archive of early women film workers.

In discussing women film pioneers, we need to acknowledge that at the time of its emergence, film technology was typically available only to the more privileged members of society, and therefore early film authorship has significant class dimensions (regardless of whether the director was a woman or a man). Moreover, early film technology was more available in the so-called First World than other parts of the globe, which renders the pioneering frameworks that pertain to the era of silent cinema (circa 1894–1929) inadequate for those parts of the world where film technology became more widely available only later. For example, many African film "firsts" did not occur until the 1960s with the advent of decolonization. At the same time, there is evidence that women film pioneers were active in parts of the world not typically placed within the so-called First World – in countries such as Mexico, Argentina, Peru, and the Soviet Union, to name a few.

With all this in mind, it is increasingly clear that women played a major role in early cinema history, and that any such history would be incomplete without an acknowledgment of their contributions. In what follows, we highlight a number of notable women film pioneers in order to illustrate the breadth and depth of their work.

ACTIVITY

Browse the Women Film Pioneers Project website (https://wfpp.cdrs. columbia.edu/) and record your impressions. What did you learn from the online archive? Did you discover any surprising insights into the role of women in early film history?

Alice Guy Blaché (1873–1968)

Any standard film history starts with the French pioneers of cinema, the Lumière brothers, as well as their countryman Georges Méliès, who is considered the father of narrative cinema and sci-fi. While the first films ever projected are claimed to be the works of the Lumière brothers, another French national, Alice Guy Blaché (Figure 1.1), was not far behind – she made her first film, *The Cabbage Fairy* (*La Fée aux Choux*), in 1896. This sixty-second film is widely considered to be the first film made by a woman. Based on an old French folk tale, it depicts a fairy picking babies out of cabbage leaves. Guy Blaché went on to make hundreds of films, including the tongue-in-cheek comedy *The Consequences of Feminism* (*Les Résultats du féminisme*, 1906, France), in which she playfully reverses the social roles of men and women in order to poke fun at gender inequality as such, but also to warn that the feminist project needs to rethink its relationship to power. Notably, this short film treats gender roles as performative social categories rather than biological or natural givens. When they become fed up with how the men are treating them, the women in the film turn the gender roles around, and make men perform the housework and childcare, while the women engage in drinking and socializing. As a result, the men are forced to occupy an oppressed social position typically reserved for women. This satirical short comedy points to the inadequacy of assuming that history (of film and beyond) is comprised of linear progress from a more traditional to a more progressive social existence, since already in the early 20th century, Guy Blaché was making the kinds of provocative interventions about **gender performativity** that would be considered the contribution of late 20th century **queer theory** (notably, after the publication of Judith Butler's *Gender Trouble* in 1990).

Figure 1.1 Alice Guy Blaché

Besides being a director, Guy Blaché was involved in many other aspects of filmmaking, from writing scripts and scouting locations, to owning her own film studio in the United States – Solax. This prompted Alison McMahan to tackle an important dilemma in her book-length study of Guy Blaché's life and work:

> Given the length and breadth of Guy Blaché's career and the variety of roles she played within the industry [. . .], which films do we say

are hers – the films she wrote, the films she directed, the films she produced, or all of the above?

(2002: xxvii)

This question points to the difficulty of pinning film authorship to a single role in the process of filmmaking. But regardless of which aspect of film-making we highlight as indicative of authorship as such, there is no doubt that Alice Guy Blaché is one of the key pioneers of early cinema in general, and women's film authorship in particular.

Germaine Dulac (1882–1942)

Germaine Dulac (Figure 1.2) was a French film director, author, and film theorist, widely considered to be the first feminist filmmaker. She is a pioneer of avant-garde cinema who made impressionistic narrative and abstract works, for which she is best remembered today. Dulac also made docu-mentaries and newsreel films and was a prolific writer and lecturer on cinema. In her book-length study of Dulac's life and work, Tami Williams describes her as a pacifist, feminist, activist and humanist who strongly believed in the "emanci-patory potential of art" (2014: 4).

Figure 1.2 Germaine Dulac

Two of Dulac's most famous works are *The Smiling Madame Beudet* (*La Souriante Madame Beudet*, 1923, France) and *The Seashell and the Clergyman* (*La Coquille et le clergyman*, 1927, France). Even though Luis Buñuel and Salvador Dalí's *Un chien Andalou* (1929, France) is argu-ably the most famous surrealist film ever made, Dulac's surrealist masterpiece *The Seashell and the Clergyman* (scripted by another iconic avant-garde artist, Antonin Artaud) precedes it by at least a year. Moreover, Dulac developed the concepts of "pure cinema" (later taken up by André Bazin) and "expanded cinema." She theorized pure cinema as an art form free of conventions adopted from other arts, such as literature and theater, which captured life in its most microscopic form, and saw the newsreel as the most sincere and pure form of film.

Lois Weber (1879–1939)

Lois Weber is an American filmmaking pioneer who got her early oppor-tunities in the film industry in Alice Guy Blaché's studio, alongside her husband Phillips Smalley. Weber was also a producer, screenwriter, actress, and film company owner. She directed about 125 films, although a significantly smaller number have been preserved. In his book *The Silent Feminists* (1996), Anthony Slide hails Weber as "one of the few genuine auteurs of American cinema" because "she always wrote the films which she directed," and moreover "used the motion picture as a medium for her ideas and philosophy" (viii). As a director, she was a great innovator – for instance, her short film *Suspense* (1913, US) is considered to be one of the earliest films to use split screen to depict parallel action (Figure 1.3).

At one point in her career, Weber was the highest paid director in Hollywood, and moreover, was the first and only female member of the Motion Picture Director's Association (Stamp 2010: 141). In her book-length study of Lois Weber's life and work in early Hollywood, Shelley Stamp argues that Weber's "arsenal of cinematic techniques" was positioned as a pointed critique of "the very institutions upon which cinema's imagined bourgeois viewers depend: heterosexual marriage, feminine propriety and class privilege" (2015: 35). Stamp highlights Weber's film *Eyes That See Not* (1912,

Figure 1.3 One of the earliest uses of split screen to show parallel action (*Suspense*, Lois Weber, 1913)

US), in which a self-centered wealthy woman is transformed after she is confronted with the harsh reality of the living conditions endured by the employees of her husband's mill.

With the advent of sound cinema, and as the film industry became more compartmentalized through guilds and professional associations, the careers of many multi-faceted women filmmakers suffered, and Lois Weber was not an exception. In the last few years of her life, she was constricted to the industry's margins and all but forgotten, only to be rediscovered by feminist film historians in the new millennium.

Zora Neale Hurston (1891–1960)

Better known as a novelist and key figure of the Harlem Renaissance, Zora Neale Hurston (Figure 1.4) is one of the first African-American female directors, along with Eloyce King Patrick Gist, Tressie Souders, Maria P. Williams, and others (Welbon 2001). She made ethnographic films, documenting the everyday life, folklore, and rituals of African-American communities in the South, particularly in Florida, where she grew up. Much of this footage has been lost, and what remains is assembled in the collection *The Fieldwork* (1928, US). The footage includes baptisms, children dancing and playing games, and also recordings of Cudjo Lewis, the final survivor from *The Clotilde*, the last arriving slave ship to America (in 1859). This is the only known film footage of an African person deported to the United States through slave trade, and therefore represents a very important historical document.

Figure 1.4 Zora Neale Hurston

Mimí Derba (1893–1953)

Born Herminia Pérez de León, Mimí Derba was one of the first Mexican female directors (her co-directorial debut was *La tigresa*, 1917, Mexico; Figure 1.5). She was the founder, along with Enrique Rosas, of Azteca Film Company (also in 1917), as well as an actress, writer, and film producer. Subsequently she became disillusioned with the film industry and largely retired, except for occasional acting roles.

Figure 1.5 A still from *La tigresa* (Mimí Derba & Enrique Rosas, 1917)

Alla Nazimova (1875–1945)

A Russian Jewish émigré to the United States, Alla Nazimova was a stage actress who produced and likely directed starring vehicles for her own company. She worked as a director and producer, and was known for reinventing her own image and celebrity persona. Openly lesbian, she was "the founding mother of Sapphic Hollywood" (McLellan 2000: xxiii), and, according to Patricia White, "the most notorious Hollywood lesbian actress of all" (1999: 187) (quoted in Horne 2013). Her best-known work is arguably *Salome* (1923, US), a silent movie based on Oscar Wilde's play and envisioned as an homage to Wilde. The film's directorial credit went to Charles Bryant, even though film historians generally agree that Nazimova was the film's central author. She starred in it as the titular character, and, according to the filmmaker Kenneth Anger, insisted that all other actors employed in the film be gay and lesbian (Horne 2013).

Figure 1.6 Alla Nazimova in *Salome* (Alla Nazimova & Charles Bryant, 1923)

Nowadays, Nazimova continues to be an iconic, cult figure of the hidden history of queer Hollywood (Figure 1.6).

Lotte Reiniger (1899–1981)

Germany's Lotte Reiniger was an inventor of "silhouette animation," in which figures are only visible as black silhouettes (Figure 1.7). Reiniger's technique was inspired by the ancient art of shadow plays. One of her most iconic and influential works is *The Adventures of Prince Achmed* (1926, Germany), the oldest surviving feature-length animated film. The film's story was partially influenced by the Arabic folktales that comprise the *One Thousand and One Nights*. The film is also Reiniger's only feature, since for the rest of her prolific career she focused on shorts. Most of her postwar work was completed in Great Britain. She made around sixty films altogether, but only about forty survive.

Figure 1.7 A still from *The Adventures of Prince Achmed* (Lotte Reiniger, 1926)

CASE STUDY: RETHINKING AUTHORSHIP IN EARLY SOVIET CINEMA

Early Soviet cinema had a large influence on the development of film form, with innovative filmmakers and film theorists such as Sergei

Eisenstein, Lev Kuleshov, Vsevolod Pudovkin, and Dziga Vertov inventing new and groundbreaking film language, and theorizing what came to be known as Soviet montage and Kino-Pravda ("film truth"). Two of the most notable and iconic works of early Soviet cinema are Eisenstein's *Battleship Potemkin* (*Bronenosets Potyomkin*, 1925, USSR) and Vertov's *Man with a Movie Camera* (*Chelovek s kinoaparatom*, 1929, USSR). And while these men deservedly occupy a central place in film history, Soviet women filmmakers are less frequently recognized as important figures during this golden era of Russian cinema, even if historical records indicate that they were unquestionably a significant creative force. Here we highlight several notable women filmmakers of early Soviet film.

Elizaveta Svilova (1900–1975)

While Dziga Vertov is one of the most celebrated pioneers of cinema, it remains less well known that his wife, Elizaveta Svilova, was an active film worker and Vertov's frequent professional partner. She edited all of his best-regarded work, including *Man with a Movie Camera* (Figure 1.8), a film whose groundbreaking editing became its

Figure 1.8 Elizaveta Svilova seen at the editing desk in *Man with a Movie Camera* (Dziga Vertov, 1929)

most iconic trait. Their film collaborations, as part of the collective that called themselves Kinoks, or Kino-oki ("film eyes"), were so integral to Vertov's cinematic output that Svilova is now often considered his co-director on films such as *Three Songs of Lenin* (*Tri pesni o Lenine*, 1934, USSR), for instance. Svilova's lifelong passion was documentary film – she played a historic role in documenting the Red Army's entrance into Auschwitz after the Nazi capitulation in 1945. Gwendolyn Audrey Foster rightfully notes that, "[T]he legacy of Elizaveta Svilova, like that of many women directors whose lives were obscured by their famous husbands, remains to be rediscovered and contextualized" (1995: 350).

Yuliya Solntseva (1901–1989)

Another notable woman film worker in early Soviet cinema was Yulia Solntseva, who was married to iconic Soviet director Alexandr Dovzhenko. As an actress, she played the lead character in what is considered to be the first Soviet sci-fi film – *Aelita, the Queen of Mars* (*Aelita*, Yakov Protazanov, 1924, USSR; Figure 1.9). But she was also

Figure 1.9 Yuliya Solntseva as *Aelita, the Queen of Mars* (Yakov Protazanov, 1924)

engaged in other aspects of the filmmaking process, and together with Dovzhenko co-directed a number of films. However, he remained the more recognized figure of the two during their creative collaborations, and Solntseva gained full recognition as a film director only after 1939, when she started directing her own films.

Esfir Shub (1894–1959)

If Sergei Eisenstein became the name most associated with the virtues of the Soviet montage, historical records show that he learned a great deal about the technique from Esfir Shub (Figure 1.10), another prominent female figure of the Soviet film era who nevertheless remained overshadowed by men. Shub was such a skilled editor that the government hired her in 1922 to re-cut American films in order to make them "more suitable" for Russian audiences. This helped Shub develop the technique of so-called "compilation documentary," in which the filmmaker uses only preexisting visual material collected from archival footage, newsreels, and found footage. Her most famous surviving work is the compilation documentary *The Fall of the Romanov Dynasty* (*Padenie dinastii Romanovykh*, 1927, USSR), commissioned on the occasion of the 10th anniversary of the October Revolution. Shub whittled down hours of documentary and newsreel footage into a feature-length film that shows the firm authorial stamp of its editor.

Figure 1.10 Esfir Shub in Dziga Vertov's *Man with a Movie Camera* (1929)

Alexandra Khokhlova (1897–1985)

Alexandra Khokhlova was the spouse and creative partner of another legendary figure of Soviet cinema, Lev Kuleshov. She was an iconic film actress known for her avant-garde acting style – one of her best-regarded onscreen performances was in Kuleshov's *By the Law*

(*Po zakonu*, 1926, USSR; Figure 1.11). Reflecting on their creative partnership, Kuleshov wrote: "Nearly all that I have done in film directing, in teaching, and in life is connected to [Khokhlova] in terms of ideas and art practice" (quoted in Olenina 2014). Khokhlova directed two silent narrative films – *An Affair of the Clasps* (1929, USSR) and *Sasha* (1930, USSR) – as well as a documentary, *Toys* (1931, USSR), about the history of children's play objects. She ran into problems with Soviet authorities because of her non-proletarian background, and as a result received limited opportunities for work later in her career.

The intellectual premise of the Bolshevik revolution included a firm commitment to gender equality, even if said equality was not fully achieved in practice. As part of the socialist restructuring of society after the 1917 revolution, women entered the workplace in greater numbers, and the Soviet Union's pioneering film industry was no exception. However, while the socialist state's official gender politics were progressive for its time, it remains an open question whether Soviet women filmmakers would consider themselves feminist, even if they were active proponents of equality between the sexes. Importantly, this negative stance towards the term feminism was not necessarily predicated on it being perceived as a Western construct, or

Figure 1.11 Aleksandra Khokhlova in Lev Kuleshov's *By the Law* (1926)

a term inadequate to the Russian context, but rather on first wave feminism (defined mainly by demands for women's suffrage) being seen as a movement that did not recognize the centrality of class struggle in the broader efforts for social and political equality for all. In other words, feminism was perceived as a bourgeois movement, which seemingly strived only to advance the rights of already privileged women (in class terms), and as such, was inadequate for a socialist society declaratively based on the elimination of class differences. Regardless of whether we call them feminist or not, Soviet women film workers were undoubtedly indispensable pioneers in film history more generally, and women's film history in particular.

Watch and discuss: Soviet women film pioneers

1   Some of the Russian women film pioneers' work is in the public domain and can be found on video streaming sites such as YouTube. Watch some of their work and consider whether these female authors could also be considered feminist filmmakers.
2   Do you find in their work any political or social critique relating to gender?
3   Esfir Shub's "compilation documentary" technique of using found and preexisting footage was groundbreaking and innovating for its time. Can you think of examples of similar techniques being used in contemporary cinema?

Expanding the notion of "pioneers"

While the term "women film pioneers" has come to be most closely associated with the silent film era, in some parts of the world, women did not have a chance to become filmmakers until well after the development of sound film. These women are as pioneering in their geographical and historical contexts as their silent film era counterparts in other parts of the world. Therefore, the concept of "women film pioneers" needs to be extended in time and space, in order to be able to account for the different historical circumstances within which women have become filmmakers. For example, some parts of the world, such as colonial French Africa, were virtually denied any access to filmmaking until decolonization. Film historians therefore need to remain mindful of the geopolitical contexts and local complexities that make it possible for women to become filmmakers in the first place. Below we highlight some women film pioneers who made their first films during the sound film era, in the mid- to late 20th century.

Kinuyo Tanaka (1909–1977)

Kinuyo Tanaka (Figure 1.12) was Japan's first female director, who, as an actress, worked with notable Japanese male directors Yasujiro Ozu and Kenji Mizoguchi. Having distinguished herself in the course of a memorable

acting career, Tanaka eventually turned to directing, making her first film, *Love Letter* (*Koibumi*, Japan) in 1953. Her second film, *The Moon Has Risen* (*Tsuki wa noborinu*, 1955, Japan), co-written by Ozu, has distinct feminist overtones in its depiction of the social constraints imposed on a carefree young woman. Her films tackle important social themes affecting women, such as patriarchal control, breast cancer, and sex work. And just as her protagonists often face the reality of women's limited options in a patriarchal society, similarly Tanaka's directing career was short-lived "because of the male-dominated studio system" (Kuhn & Radstone 1990: 399). She

Figure 1.12 Kinuyo Tanaka in *Burden of Life* (*Jinsei no onimotsu*, Heinosuke Gosho, 1935)

nevertheless remains an important and pioneering figure in the context of Japanese and Asian cinema, and in the context of women's cinema as world cinema.

Nam-ok Park (1923–2017)

Nam-ok Park is considered to be the first Korean woman director with *The Widow* (*Mimang-in*, 1955, Korea; Figure 1.13). The film revolves around the desires of a widow of the Korean War, and is presented from a female perspective. Since the film did not do well at the box office, Nam-ok Park decided to leave the male-dominated film industry and moved to the United States, where she spent the rest of her life. The last reel of her film has been lost, leaving the ending abrupt and unclear. The film was recently critically rediscovered when it screened at the first Women's Film Festival in Seoul in 1997, pointing to the continued importance of women's film festivals in showcasing the neglected work of women filmmakers from around the globe.

Figure 1.13 Still from *The Widow* (Nam-ok Park, 1955)

Carmen Santos (1904–1952)

Carmen Santos was an important pioneer of Brazilian cinema who worked as a director, screenwriter, actress, and producer. Made famous by her larger-than-life screen persona, Santos subsequently took even more control of her career by producing films. "A feisty trailblazer" (Shaw & Dennison 2007: 58), she was also a co-founder of Brazil Vox Film in 1934 (later Brasil Vita Filmes). Her films frequently tackled important social and political issues. Her arguably best-known film is *Minas Conspiracy* (*Inconfidência Mineira*, 1948, Brazil), which she wrote, produced, directed and starred in. This film made Santos only the second woman to direct a feature film in Brazil. The film follows a failed anticolonial uprising against the Portuguese in 1789 and at the time of its release had overt contemporary overtones, since it "comments indirectly on the illegitimacy of political power during the Vargas Era (1930–1945)" (Marsh 2012: 94).

Safi Faye (1943–)

Senegalese Safi Faye was the first sub-Saharan African woman filmmaker to direct a commercially distributed feature film – *Letters from My Village* (*Kaddu Beykat*, 1975, Senegal), which gained Faye international recognition. Coming from rural origins, she showed an interest in cinema early in life, and

Figure 1.14 A still from *Mossane* (Safi Faye, 1996)

went on to study filmmaking at the Louis Lumière Film School. She was also an ethnographer and an actress. Having collaborated with Jean Rouch, the pioneer of *cinéma vérité*, she became particularly interested in this mode of realist documentary filmmaking. *Letters from My Village* is a fictionalized documentary that takes inspiration from life in Faye's home village. The film-maker insists that all her films are made primarily for African audiences, whose perspectives are not frequently highlighted on the world cinema stage. To that end, Faye's films avoid self-exoticizing for the sake of foreign audiences and portraying African women as passive victims. She describes her filmmaking as a careful process of not working single-handedly, but "through and with other people." She adds that her films are "collective works in which every-body takes an active part."[2] Her film *Mossane* (1996, Senegal; Figure 1.14) "centers on the female domain, relegating the male characters to a secondary role" (Thackway 2003: 155). Today, Faye lives and works in Paris, France.

THE 20TH CENTURY: WHAT IS WOMEN'S CINEMA? WHAT IS FEMINIST CINEMA?

While auteurship suggests that one's films are marked by a unique authorial stamp, in this section we are more broadly interested in looking at female directors whether or not their work explicitly meets the criterion of authorial consistency, as we move towards a broader discussion of women's cinema and what constitutes a woman's form of address. As historical evidence increasingly shows, and as we discussed in the previous section, women filmmakers were an essential part of the early days of cinema. However, as the cinema became a more established and complex industry, in many contexts the number of women filmmakers diminished, prompting feminist film scholars to ask why. While women have been less recognized and frequently outnumbered by men as film authors throughout most of the 20th century, some notable female filmmakers did enter mainstream cinema and become recognizable, well-regarded names in the industry. They are perhaps exceptions that prove the rule, but are nevertheless central to a discussion of female film authorship.

In the classic Hollywood era, Mae West's stardom made her a powerful figure. Her comedies featured provocative sexual content geared towards building her screen persona as a dominating seductress unafraid to express her sexual desires. West's popularity suffered with the enforcement of The Production Code in 1934, which prohibited explicit sexual content in movies. Filmmakers Dorothy Arzner and Ida Lupino directed numerous films and often had creative control over their work in an otherwise male-dominated industry. Dorothy Arzner was the first woman to be admitted to the Director's Guild of America (DGA), and "the only woman to produce a body of work as a film director in the heyday of the Hollywood studio system in the 1930s and 1940s" (Kuhn & Radstone 1990: 24). Ida Lupino, who began her career as an actress, started her own film company in 1949 and during the 1950s was the only woman working as a director and producer in Hollywood. Upon her death in 1995, Martin Scorsese described her as:

> A woman of extraordinary talents, and one of those talents was directing. Her tough, glowingly emotional work as an actress is well remembered, but her considerable accomplishments as a filmmaker are largely forgotten and they shouldn't be. The five films she directed between 1949 and 1953 are remarkable chamber pieces that deal with challenging subjects in a clear, almost documentary fashion, and they represent a singular achievement in American cinema.[3]

Elsewhere in the world in the mid-20th century, actresses similarly took to directing in order to further their artistic output – for example, Edith Carlmar in Norway, Mai Zetterling in Sweden, Bodil Ipsen in Denmark, and the aforementioned Kinuyo Tanaka in Japan.

The 1960s and 1970s brought about a number of social and political upheavals around the world, from anti-imperialist revolutions to antiwar and women's rights movements, and cinema increasingly became overtly politicized as well. This was reflected in the work of a number of women filmmakers around the world. Venezuela's Margot Benacerraf made the notable documentary *Araya* (1958), which dealt with the diminishing prospects of the laborers extracting salt off the shore of the Araya peninsula in Venezuela. In Colombia, Marta Rodríguez, together with Jorge Silva, took several years to make *The Brickmakers* (*Chircales*, 1972), an influential documentary about labor exploitation and social injustice. In Cuba, Sara Gómez made her mark with *One Way or Another* (*De Cierta Manera*, 1974), mixing documentary and fiction to depict the struggles of poor residents of Havana. Iranian filmmaker Forough Farrokhzad made a poetic and influential documentary that probed social hierarchies and discrimination by depicting life at a leper colony in *The House is Black* (*Khane siah ast*, 1962, Iran). In Western Europe, Agnès Varda was as pivotal to the French New Wave as her male counterparts. Varda's *Cléo from 5 to 7* (*Cléo de 5 à 7*, 1962, France), for instance, probes Western privilege, femininity, vanity, and depression by situating the story of a Paris bohemian, Cléo, against the backdrop of the French-Algerian War, in which Algerians fought for freedom from France's colonial rule. In Eastern Europe, where 1968 saw social upheavals throughout the different countries of the so-called "Socialist Bloc," cinema became a weapon of political subversion. In this climate, Věra Chytilová's *Daisies* (*Sedmikrásky*, 1966, Czechoslovakia) is at least as subversive as the films of her provocative male counterparts (see Chapter 6 on experimental film for a more detailed analysis of *Daisies*). In the Soviet Union, Kira Muratova, Larisa Shepitko and Dinara Asanova made films explicitly or implicitly critical of the existing regime.

Yet to associate women filmmakers exclusively with progressive or subversive filmmaking would be to romanticize the role of female artists. In fact, the range and complexity of women's film work makes evident that female film authorship is not inherently and inevitably feminist, nor aligned with progressive social causes by default (see, for example, the discussion of Leni Riefenstahl in Chapter 5). By extension, feminist films can, and have frequently been made by male directors – examples include work as varied as Carl Theodor Dreyer's *The Passion of Joan of Arc* (*La Passion de Jeanne d'Arc*, 1928, France/Denmark), Kenji Mizoguchi's *The Victory of Women* (*Josei no Shori*, 1946, Japan, starring Kinuyo Tanaka), William Wyler's *The Children's Hour* (1961, US), Ousmane Sembene's *Xala* (1974, Senegal), or Todd Haynes's *Far from Heaven* (2002, US). The 1954 film *Salt of the Earth* (Herbert J. Biberman, US), made by male film workers who were blacklisted in Hollywood as communists during the McCarthy era, presents a landmark work of socialist feminist cinema that offers a materialist critique of the capitalist exploitation of labor, as well as of the capitalist structuring of gender inequality. The film's lead was played by Mexican actress Rosaura Revueltas (Figure 1.15), who was deported during the filming, labeled as a communist, and never worked in the United States again. Films such as *Salt of the Earth* complicate the notion that film authorship – or more precisely, the gender identity of the director – somehow determines the kind of message that a film conveys, and by extension, that feminist films can only be made by

Figure 1.15 Rosaura Revueltas as Esperanza in *Salt of the Earth* (Herbert J. Biberman, 1954)

women. Avoiding assumptions that rely on reductive identity politics keeps the identity of "woman" and the meaning of "feminism" complicated and fluid, as social constructs that are perpetually redefined. Another case in point is Yugoslavia's first woman feature film director, Sofia Soja Jovanović, who, even during the height of the innovative Yugoslav New Film and its particularly subversive strain, the Black Wave, continued to make highly popular, mainstream comedies (only seemingly) devoid of political content.

Feminist film scholarship often draws a distinction between the woman's film and women's cinema. **The woman's film**, closely associated with **melodrama** (which we discuss in Chapter 7 on genre), is a genre of filmmaking that features female-centric narratives (often stereotypically so), and whose target audience is primarily women. These films may focus on mothers and daughters or women and illness, for example. They are also often directed by male directors (in fact, almost exclusively so in the studio era). **Women's cinema**, on the other hand, is typically applied when works of cinema carry a stamp of female authorship, and not just the representation of issues relating to women or gender. Many female directors have rejected the label "woman director," because it implies that their films are somehow lesser or that they appeal only to particular – that is, female – audiences. Terms like woman director may seem to place constricting labels on a director's work, who is then seen as responsible to, or representative of a constituency – in this case, all women. Male directors are rarely saddled with the same expectations or burdens of representation. Important contemporary female authors like Claire Denis and Kelly Reichardt have openly distanced themselves from any alignment of their work with female specificity. This was also the case with Chantal Akerman, whose work is discussed in more detail later. Even though she has an iconic standing in feminist film studies, she famously did not want to be considered a female auteur, but rather just an auteur.

Moreover, there are women filmmakers such as Rakhshan Bani-E'temad, often referred to as "the first lady of Iranian cinema," whose films frequently feature strong female protagonists, but who explicitly refuse the label of feminist filmmaker because it is often interpreted through a Western-centric framework of women's liberation.[4] As noted before, a distinction therefore needs to be made between women filmmakers and feminist filmmakers. Sometimes the two categories overlap, but at the same time, there are many women filmmakers who do not regard themselves as feminist, and male filmmakers who do.

In Claire Johnston's influential essay "Women's Cinema as Counter-Cinema," published in 1973, she uses the semiotic method in order to criticize the notion that culture is monolithic and that it consciously maintains simplistic stereotypes about women. This approach "short-circuits the possibility of a critique which could prove useful for developing a strategy for women's cinema" (32). In other words, positing culture as unchanging and homogenous in its oppression of women denies women the possibility of creatively interacting with and challenging dominant representational codes. At the same time, Johnston notes that movies are not made in a vacuum, and while they develop their own iconography and associate it with particular meanings, "the myths governing the cinema are no different from those governing other cultural products: they relate to a standard value system informing all cultural systems in a given society" (32). In her analysis, stereotypes are cultural myths that become naturalized over time. Pushing against a simplistic binary that sees art cinema as more progressive than mainstream cinema in its depiction of women, Johnston argues that art cinema is often the *more* problematic vehicle because its sexist undertones, although present, are concealed under the protective cloak of art. Art cinema often *seems* less mythologized and melodramatic than mainstream cinema (i.e. less dependent on stereotypes) and draws more on conventions of realism. Its very appearance of realism, however, can hide the ways in which art cinema reinforces myths about femininity and female sexuality. In this context, Johnston embraces auteur theory because it privileges an interpretation of mainstream cinema that does not rest on the norms of Hollywood, but on the idiosyncrasies of particular authors. In mainstream cinema's obviousness, she suggests, there is a greater potential to rearticulate, or reappropriate, the link between the icon and the myth, therefore disrupting the patriarchal premises on which the depiction of women rests. For example, Johnston discusses Arzner's film *Dance Girl, Dance* (1940, US), focusing on a moment when a female dancer refuses to be the object of the gaze and looks directly back at the audience that is laughing at her. In an impassioned speech, she calls out the audience for their voyeurism, embedding a critique of the male gaze and the spectacle of the female body into the film's narrative. Johnston sees this as a reflection of how Arzner inscribes a female gaze into her film and an instance in which she turns mainstream Hollywood against itself.

Johnston takes a Marxist approach to film, arguing that all films "are products of an existing system of economic relations, in the final analysis" (36). Within that understanding, we need to locate possibilities for subversion, infusing art with responsibility to incite change. Scrutinizing the work of Hollywood's women filmmakers, Johnston finds, somewhat controversially, that "the persona of Mae West is entirely consistent with sexist ideology; it in no way subverts existing myths, but reinforces them" (34). On the other hand, Johnston finds that the films of Dorothy Arzner and Ida Lupino manage to subvert sexist ideology from within the text itself, and as such, reflect the potentials of women's cinema. With her focus on these two directors, Johnston suggests that there are possibilities of subversion within Hollywood cinema, and that feminist film scholarship needs to do more to identify them, in order to work towards a better understanding of how women's cinema can act as transformative counter-cinema.

Johnston rejects the idea that the fact of female authorship can, in and of itself, reveal the truth about social conditions – or, by extension function as a feminist critique. Rather, new meanings need to be actively manufactured within the text of the film, by using cinematic tools, which are always steeped in ideology to begin with. To that end, women's cinema cannot simply "record" the objective truth (which is never outside of ideology), but has to intervene into reality and impose new meanings and interpretations. Moreover, it needs to do so by merging entertainment and politics, and not drawing a line between the two. Just as auteur theory expanded the understanding of the director as film artist to include Hollywood directors (and not just their European art cinema counterparts), one of the main contributions of Johnston's essay with respect to feminist authorship was to firmly determine that feminist female directors can be found in the heyday of Hollywood's classical era – a period not typically associated with female authorship or feminist leanings.

In step with the women's liberation movement and the rise of feminist film theory as an influential scholarly field, the 1970s also saw the rise of **cinefeminism** and **the feminist auteur,** most notably in the figure of Chantal Akerman, whose seminal work *Jeanne Dielman, 23, Quai du Commerce, 1080 Bruxelles* (Belgium; Figure 1.16) has left a lasting impact since premiering at the Cannes Film Festival in 1975. During its over-three-hour running time, the film depicts three days in the mundane life of the titular character, who cooks, cleans, fulfills motherly duties, and makes money as a sex worker. Since the concept of women's cinema became an important object around which feminist film scholarship coalesced, it brought forward the question of whether there is such a thing as feminine or female aesthetics, or recognizable visual markers that would indicate a woman's presence behind the camera. Teresa de Lauretis argues that to "ask whether there is a feminine or female aesthetic, or a specific language of women's cinema, is to remain caught in the master's house" (1985: 158). In other words, she asks whether we need to somehow get outside of film language as we know it (i.e. the master's house), in order to look for a space that can truly express feminine subjectivity or experience. She discusses *Jeanne Dielman* as an example of women's cinema that conveys a **pre-aesthetic** by depicting images, gestures and experiences not traditionally coded as cinematic. The aforementioned mundane motifs of everyday boredom, routine, and housework that the film focuses on represent the film's commitment to the pre-aesthetic cinematic depiction of a situation considered so ordinary that it had heretofore not been featured much on the big screen. Importantly, de Lauretis finds that this aesthetic and formal construction addresses the spectator as a woman,

Figure 1.16 A still from *Jeanne Dielman, 23, Quai du Commerce, 1080 Bruxelles* (Chantal Akerman, 1975)

"regardless of the gender of the viewers" (161). This leads de Lauretis to theorize women's cinema not only as cinema *by*, but also *for* women, one that presupposes the primacy of the female spectator, and not just the female filmmaker.

In the 1970s and 1980s, feminist films, and particularly feminist documentaries (some of which we discuss in Chapter 5), became a very important activist aspect of second wave feminism and women's cinema. For example, Lizzie Borden's *Born in Flames* (1983, US) represents a staple of what later became known as **intersectional feminism** – activism that sees gender inequality as a form of discrimination that intersects with other overlapping power structures, including homophobia, racism, and classism. De Lauretis notes that, like *Jeanne Dielman*, *Born in Flames* also addresses the spectator as female, but that it does so in a way that makes us face the differences that are inscribed within the category of "woman" along the lines of race, class and sexuality. *Born in Flames* is a docu-fiction/sci-fi hybrid that envisions an alternative reality in which the United States is a socialist democracy, and where various grassroots feminist and LGBTQ groups engage in activist guerilla endeavors as a way to bring focus to the powerful intersections between patriarchy, heteronormativity, and racism. De Lauretis concludes that the film's fragmentary nature and unresolved ending make us embrace differences between women, "which cannot be collapsed into a fixed identity, a sameness of all women as Woman or a representation of Feminism as a coherent and available image" (168). Amid their frequently allied political interventions, the differences between *Jeanne Dielman* and *Born in Flames* can be used to illustrate how some experiences are ideologically privileged (white, middle class, heterosexual) over others (nonwhite, lower class, queer). As *Born in Flames* suggests, feminist political coalitions continue to struggle with efforts to unlearn such tendencies.

More recently, Alison Butler (2002) has argued that women's cinema increasingly appears as a minor rather than counter-cinema. She develops the concept of **minor cinema** from Deleuze and Guattari's theorizing of minor literature as the literature of a marginalized group written in the language of the dominant majority. With respect to cinema, the term implies that marginalized groups use dominant film language – a language that they did not create – to convey their stories. Butler traces the three major features of minor literature that are also present in women's cinema: displacement, dispossession, and deterritorialization, along with "a sense that everything is political, and a tendency for everything to take on a collective value" (20). Butler argues that this approach avoids basing the concept of women's cinema on essentialist understandings of "woman" as identity because "the communities imagined by women's cinema are as many and varied as the films it comprises, and each is involved in its own historical moment" (21). Minor cinema also helps us to avoid the dichotomies between avant-garde and mainstream cinema, as well as between oppositional and reactionary filmmaking. Understanding women's cinema as minor cinema alleviates its perceived burden of having to conform to oppositional political tendencies where both form and content are concerned.

In the later parts of the 20th century, female authors came to greater cultural prominence. As discussed, Chantal Akerman became an iconic figure in the film world, and Sally Potter made her groundbreaking feminist film *Thriller* in 1979 (UK), and, among others, directed the gender bending *Orlando* (UK) in 1992 (Potter is also discussed in Chapters 3 and 6). Notably, Jane Campion became the first woman director to win the world's most prestigious film award – the Palme d'Or at the Cannes Film Festival – for *The Piano* (1993, New Zealand). During this time, Julie Dash made her most influential work as well – *Illusions* (1982, US) and *Daughters of the Dust* (1991, US). The latter film was the first feature-length film directed by an African-American woman to receive theatrical distribution in the United States, and has more recently come to prominence again as one of the pre-eminent cinematic influences on Beyoncé's visual album *Lemonade* (2016, US; see also Chapter 4).

During this time, Kathryn Bigelow (who, incidentally, makes an appearance in *Born in Flames*) became a lauded filmmaker by directing thrillers and action films such as the stalker-themed *Blue Steel* (1989, US). Her rise to prominence culminated in 2009, when she became the first woman to win an Academy Award for directing with *The Hurt Locker* (US), which also went on to win Best Picture. In other genres, filmmakers such as Nora Ephron made their mark in the 1990s with a popular strain of the woman's film – the so-called chick flick. Her best-known films include *Sleepless in Seattle* (1993, US) and *You've Got Mail* (1998, US).

CASE STUDY: LINA WERTMÜLLER (1928–)

Lina Wertmüller is an extremely prolific Italian screenwriter and director, and the first woman to be nominated for a Best Directing Academy Award for *Seven Beauties* (*Pasqualino Settebellezze*, 1975, Italy). She started her directing career in the 1960s, after working as an assistant on Federico Fellini's *8½* (1963, Italy). But she truly came to international prominence as a director in the 1970s, with films such as the aforementioned *Seven Beauties*, *The Seduction of Mimi* (*Mimì metallurgico ferito nell'onore*, 1972, Italy), *Love and Anarchy* (*Film d'amore e d'anarchia, ovvero 'stamattina alle 10 in via dei Fiori nella nota casa di tolleranza . . . '*, 1973, Italy) and *Swept Away* (*Travolti da un insolito destino nell'azzurro mare d'agosto*, 1974, Italy). She created a uniquely grotesque film style and frequently mixed humor and tragedy, as well as sex and violence, to provocative ends (Figure 1.17).

Figure 1.17 Lina Wertmüller's *Love and Anarchy* (1973)

Apart from gender, Wertmüller's films are frequently infused with a focus on social class, and often probe the relationship between individuals and Marxist/socialist politics (Russo Bullaro 2006). Since many of Wertmüller's films feature grotesque-looking women, this tendency has unsurprisingly garnered attention from feminist critics. While it can be interpreted in many different ways, Claudia Consolati finds that, at least to some extent, "these deformed female characters could be regarded as subversive of the mainstream, patriarchal order and of its limiting and objectifying ideas of femininity" (2013: 40). In *Seven Beauties*, for instance, the story follows an Italian man, Pasquale, who grew up in an all-female household and who is such a ladies' man that his nickname is the titular "Seven Beauties." During World War II, he deserts his unit and ends up in a German concentration camp. The camp is run by a sadistic German woman whom Pasquale tries to seduce in order to survive. Representing a female character who is highly ranked in the Nazi death camp, Wertmüller's film challenges the standard trope of women being perceived solely as passive victims during wartime. Here women actively participate and are fully complicit in the Nazi ideology. They help to carry out its genocidal plan, and in the dynamics between the camp commander and Pasquale, traditional gender roles are fully reversed.

Watch and discuss: the films of Lina Wertmüller

1 How might a figure such as Lina Wertmüller challenge the normative assumptions about auteurism discussed previously?
2 Could her work be considered an example of minor cinema?
3 Should we think of Wertmüller as a feminist filmmaker?
4 Since Wertmüller's groundbreaking best director Oscar nomination in 1977, only four other women have been nominated in the same category (as of 2018). Look them up and find out if you are familiar with their work.

ACTIVITY

Watch *Brief Encounters* (Kira Muratova, 1967, USSR) and *Jeanne Dielman* (Chantal Akerman, 1975, Belgium). These two important films focus on women in two different socio-political settings. Both are made by iconic women filmmakers. What is similar and what is different in the way the films function as women's cinema and represent women's issues? How does each film treat domestic labor and woman's work? What role does film form play with respect to the feminist politics of each film? How are women positioned (or not positioned) as political subjects in the films?

FEMINISM AND AUTHORSHIP IN THE NEW MILLENNIUM

In the new millennium, women's participation in major film industries continues to be stifled by systemic inequality. In Hollywood, as the world's still-dominant film industry, women filmmakers frequently struggle with getting projects funded and green-lit. Yet, even when they do get an opportunity to direct in Hollywood, many women filmmakers are not able to make more than one feature film due to limiting structural and material factors (most notably, the fact that filmmaking is an expensive process). These constraints often work to the detriment of women more so than men, especially minority women. In its survey of the movies released in 2014, the Annenberg School of Communication and Journalism's 2016 report on inclusion and diversity in film and scripted series finds that, within their sample of 109 films, only 3.4% of all directors were female. Moreover, when it comes to race and ethnicity, 87.3% of film directors were white, while 12.7% belonged to an underrepresented group (the report does not cross-pollinate race and gender).[5]

The situation is not very different in the world's other major film industries. For instance, a recent study of Indian cinema found only one in every ten directors to be female.[6] And while Hindi cinema has "a rich history of respected and celebrated female filmmakers", they are still far outnumbered by their male counterparts.[7] In one of the world's most prolific film industries – Nigeria's Nollywood – women directors, while in the minority, have been influential figures. This includes Amaka Igwe, filmmaker and founder of Amaka Igwe Studios, who is largely credited with raising the quality of Nollywood films during the video era, and Sandra Mbanefo Obiago, a filmmaker, activist and founder of Communicating for Change. And in South Korea, Soon-rye Yim, one of the few women to be considered a part of the Korean New Wave, made an important documentary *Keeping the Vision Alive* (2002), about the struggles that women film workers face in Korea's flourishing film industry (the documentary was in part an homage to aforementioned Nam-ok Park, Korea's first woman director).

The late 20th and early 21st centuries' proliferation of critical theories that pertain to gender, sexual difference, sexuality, race, class, ethnicity, and national identity, has brought about new understandings of how these categories interact with cinema. Classical paradigms of feminist film studies – which often inadvertently took white Western womanhood as their central object of inquiry – have therefore been transformed to expand the scope of feminist politics as they pertain to and are reflected on the cinematic screen. For instance, intersectional feminism has sought to identify how gender interacts with race and structural power (or the lack thereof), while **queer theory** challenged the implicit heteronormativity of many feminist projects. An important film that merges both perspectives is Cheryl Dunye's *The Watermelon Woman* (1996, US). Its story and self-reflexive structure offer a poignant critique of film history's whitewashing and heteronormativity. The protagonist, Cheryl, is an African-American lesbian who plans on making a movie about a forgotten Hollywood actress who played the stereotypical role of a "mammy" during the studio era and was only credited as the "watermelon woman." Cheryl's film project, a narrative of making a movie within a movie, is therefore an exercise in intersectional feminist historiography that seeks to recover the subjugated histories of systematically marginalized figures (for more on this film, see Chapter 6).

More recently, **transnational feminism** has problematized the concept of the nation as a limited and limiting category in our increasingly globalized world. In addition to that fact that many people do not live in the nation-state with which they may most identify (due to war, migration, histories of colonialism, or exile), many people find themselves between multiple nations and cultures. In filmmaking, this means that individual films may not best be understood through the idea of the nation or a national cinema. The concept of the transnational can be described as structures and flows of power/knowledge that are situated above national but below global frameworks of interpretation. With respect to authorship, this means that certain categories whose stability was heretofore taken for granted – such as gender, sexual identity, race, or ethnic/national background – have to be rethought and destabilized. "Transnational feminist media studies," claim Marciniak, Imre, and O'Healy, "draws on the interdisciplinarity and intersectionality evidenced in the writing of feminists working in the field of postcolonial theory, similarly concerned with issues of incommensurability, counter-hegemonic interpretation, and modes of address" (2007: 11–12). Beyond not "identifying" with the nation, much transnational feminist work is made by filmmakers whose experiences are not seen as representative of dominant national culture, such as women, racial and sexual minorities, and people with disabilities. In her introduction to *Chinese Women's Cinema*, Lingzhen Wang emphasizes the importance of not "bracketing out" the female filmmaker when discussing her work since, she argues, such bracketing leads "to a universal essentialism deprived of specific socioeconomic and historical experiences of women in the world" (2011: 10). As an alternative, Wang adopts the framework of transnational feminism, which helps us situate the role of feminist projects in our increasingly interconnected, globalized world without losing sight of local specificities and complexities. Such attention to local specificities leads Wang to illustrate how "in postsocialist, mainland China, after thirty years of state-socialist feminism, Western cinefeminism has never played a major role in the development of women's cinema" (16). By extension, such a difference in intellectual tradition needs to be acknowledged when one discusses Chinese women's cinema. For instance, Xiaolu Guo's film *She, a Chinese* (2009, UK/China) cannot be interpreted solely within Western feminist traditions, since it tackles themes endemic to Chinese postsocialism – in particular, the globalizing currents that influence the lives and outlooks of young women, as well as the opportunities that come their way. Transnational approaches to film and feminism can effectively help in avoiding the pitfalls of assuming singular understandings of both feminism and women's (film) histories around the world.

Closely related to the concept of the transnational, is Hamid Naficy's use of the term **accented cinema** (2001; see also Chapter 3) to describe diasporic and exilic filmmaking. If migration, displacement and hybrid ethnic and national identities define the experience of a growing number of people, cinema reflects this tendency as well, whether topically (for instance, in films like *Babel* [Alejandro González Iñárritu, 2006, US]), or with respect to authorship itself. The latter is exemplified by filmmakers who live a diasporic or exilic existence, and often make films that reflect such a perspective on life: examples include Indo-Canadian Deepa Mehta (*Fire* [1996], *Water* [2005]), Indian American Mira Nair (*Mississippi Masala* [1991]), Iranian-Americans Shirin Neshat (*Women Without Men* [2009]) and Ana Lily Amirpour (*A Girl Walks Home Alone at Night* [2014], *The Bad Batch* [2016]), or British-Nigerian Ngozi Onwurah (*Coffee Colored Children* [1988], *The Body Beautiful* [1991]). This framework can also extend to indigenous filmmakers such as Tracey Moffatt, whose films, such as *Nice Coloured Girls* (1987) and *Night Cries: A Rural Tragedy* (1990), address the present-day consequences of Australia's troubled treatment of indigenous peoples and their cultural legacies and traditions (both Moffatt and Onwurah are further discussed in Chapter 6). If film is a language, then these filmmakers literally "speak" film with an accent. That is to say, their films reflect a relationship to the dominant language of film that involves acts of translation, and evince different ways of formally and narratively articulating their concerns.

Accented cinema rose to prominence under the postcolonial paradigm, and often insists on the decolonizing perspectives that seek to undo the dominant Western representations of local non-Western cultures. Some theorists have suggested that postcolonial perspectives, while important, often all too quickly imply that the rule of colonial power is in the past. As Ella Shohat and Robert Stam pointedly note in their influential book *Unthinking Eurocentrism*, "By implying that colonialism is over, 'postcolonial' obscures the deformative traces of colonialism in the present" (1994: 40). Decolonial perspectives, on the other hand, seek to identify these deformative traces and hidden channels of ongoing (neo)colonial power dynamics in the present. **Decolonial feminism** exposes the categorical and hierarchical logic inherent to colonial/capitalist formations of race, sexuality, and gender (Lugones 2010). Under this framework, gender itself is treated as a colonial category imposed by dominant cultures onto the cultures it came to dominate through colonial rule. We have to remain mindful of this when we consider what constitutes feminist film authorship and the different roles and social positions women filmmakers occupy in varied local contexts across the globe. This becomes a particularly sensitive topic when the issue of Islam and women is discussed, for instance. The frameworks of transnational and decolonial feminism help us resist positioning women filmmakers in majority Muslim countries as inherently and unquestionably oppressed, which has been the dominant, simplistic approach to the issue, and one that feeds into Islamophobic biases in the West.

CASE STUDY: *BLACKBOARDS* (SAMIRA MAKHMALBAF, 2000, IRAN)

In her book *Women's Cinema, World Cinema*, Patricia White notes the uneasy alignment between female auteurs and national cinemas. She argues that "[w]omen making films today, whatever their avowed relationship to feminism, are displacing Eurocentrism and Hollywood hegemony, envisioning new relationships among gender, politics, place, and the future" (2015: 27). White's case studies include prominent women filmmakers from around the globe active in cinema since 2000, such as Argentina's Lucrecia Martel and Iran's Samira Makhmalbaf (Figure 1.18). Both women have garnered a considerable amount of artistic recognition internationally, particularly on the film festival circuit, which has become one of the key sites that provides opportunities for global women filmmakers' work to be showcased. Martel's *The Headless Woman* (2008, Argentina), for instance, was shown in the main competition at the Cannes Film

Figure 1.18 Samira Makhmalbaf directing on the set of *Blackboards* (2000) in the documentary *How Samira Made the Blackboard* (Maysam Makhmalbaf, 2000)

Festival and won numerous other international awards, while Makhmalbaf won the Prix du Jury at Cannes twice, for *Blackboards* (2001, Iran) and *At Five in the Afternoon* (2003, Iran). Recognition at A-level international film festivals has established both women as prominent feminist auteurs of the 21st century's world cinema.

Samira Makhmalbaf is one of the most prominent directors in contemporary Iranian cinema. She hails from a filmmaking family. Her father, Mohsen Makhmalbaf, is a prominent director himself, who started a film school in his home when he was unsatisfied with the educational opportunities available to his daughters. Samira's younger sister Hana, as well as her stepmother Marzieh Meshkini, have all produced work under the Makhmalbaf Film House label and all the films worked on under this imprint have involved collective modes of production. At age eighteen, when her debut film *The Apple* (1998, Iran) screened in the *Un Certain Regard* program, Samira Makhmalbaf became one of the youngest ever directors to have their work screened at the Cannes Film Festival. She followed this film with *Blackboards*, a transnational meditation on the nature of borders, home, and human labor. The film, with dialogue entirely in Kurdish, follows a group of Kurdish teachers who travel on foot somewhere in the mountainous borderlands between Iraq and Iran. The statelessness of the refugee group is deeply embedded in the film's narrative, as the teachers wander around the rocky borderland in search of work. The film makes evident the irony of the itinerant teachers trying to force education on to groups of people whose basic needs for shelter and economic security continue to be unmet. For example, one teacher, Reeboir (played by Kurdish-Iranian director Bahman Ghobadi), desperately tries to teach the alphabet to a group of Kurdish children who are working as mules, transporting contraband across the Iran-Iraq border. Their lives constantly in danger, the children have little use for reading and writing. The blackboards of the film's title function as almost anything but tools for education: they are variously camouflaged to hide the teachers from sky border patrols, a wall to create a shelter, a support for hanging laundry, a barrier used in an impromptu marriage ceremony, and at one point broken down to provide a splint for a child's injury. The film's only female character is a woman who travels with her young son and elderly father, and marries one of the teachers out of practical necessity. She is also one of the most headstrong and independent characters in the film. The teacher hopes, in part, that in marrying her he will have found a pupil and persistently attempts to teach her to read the phrase "I love you." Here, the humor creates a tension with the film's dark depiction of a people who lack stability and safety (the Kurds have been historically persecuted, notably in chemical attacks in Iraq, and tend to occupy the border regions that are filled with landmines remaining from international conflicts). After the group that includes the woman is subjected to continued gunfire and chemical bombing, they arrive at a foggy but peaceful spot – a literal and symbolic no man's land – which some of them, possibly under the influence of the chemicals, declare home. The film therefore comments on the virtual impossibility of home for peoples who have been as systematically persecuted as the Kurds.

Watch and discuss: *Blackboards*

1 How does the film address diasporic or stateless identity?
2 Does gender play a role in how the characters relate to one another?
3 What do you think of the film's ending? Is it hopeful or ambiguous about the future of the community? Where is their "home"?
4 Does the concept of transnational feminism help us to analyze a film like *Blackboards*? Why or why not?

TRANS CINEMA AND AUTHORSHIP

Another framework that complicates a simplistic alignment between feminist filmmaking and female authorship is **trans cinema**, which brings into sharper focus the fluidity of gender and sex as categories of identity. "Like queer cinema, which responded to the AIDS crisis and flourished with the advent of more accessible film production technologies," notes Eliza Steinbock, "an increasing number of trans-created audio-visual works appeared in the mid-1980s and 1990s" (2017: 400). Related themes are not new to the cinema, however, nor specifically tied to the new millennium. Laura Horak's work (2016) illustrates that early cinema grappled with the notions of cross-dressing and gender and sexual indeterminacy, as well as the possibility of gender and sexual transition. The figure of the transvestite has long been a fixture of cinema, in both provocative and problematic ways. With respect to the latter, films such as Brian de Palma's *Dressed to Kill* (1980, US) and Jonathan Demme's *The Silence of the Lambs* (1991, US) have been criticized for pathologizing trans identities by making such protagonists into sadistic, psychopathic killers. This is one important reason why in recent years there has been increased demand for trans cinema made by and for trans persons.

In 1999, Kimberly Peirce co-wrote and directed *Boys Don't Cry* (US), based on the true story of Brandon Teena, a youth who was brutally murdered by acquaintances in Nebraska. The role of Brandon Teena was played by Hilary Swank, and the performance earned the actress her first Academy Award, while film critics, as well as scholars such as J. Halberstam (2005), lauded the film as a milestone in transgender representation. For Halberstam (2005), the visual and narrative framework of the film invites a "transgender look" – that is, it addresses the spectator through a lens removed from the normative binary gender frameworks, instead embodying the perspective of trans individuals in a subversive manner that is outside heteronormative polarities.

Another milestone in trans stories reaching mainstream audiences is the film *Hedwig and the Angry Inch* (John Cameron Mitchell, 2001, US), based on the off-Broadway musical by John Cameron Mitchell, a gay, cis-gendered man who both directed the film and played the lead. The offbeat film uses music and humor to tell the story of Hedwig, an immigrant to the United States who was raised as a boy, Hansel, in East Germany during the Cold War. The only way Hansel could fulfill his dream of getting over the Iron Curtain and move to the West was to have a sex-change operation and marry a U.S. solider patrolling the wall. Hedwig's trans identity is therefore complicated by external geopolitical factors and the global flows of power that regulate the mobility of different kinds of bodies. Moreover, when Hedwig makes it to the United States, she is quickly disillusioned with its promise, specifically because the hopes of prosperity are replaced by the reality of living in a trailer park and struggling to make ends meet.

Whereas both *Hedwig* and *Boys Don't Cry* cast cis-gendered actors in roles that we would now consider expressive of trans identities, the recent *Tangerine* (Sean Barker, 2015, US) garnered critical acclaim as a low-fi, small budget film that addresses trans experience *and* features trans actresses in the central roles (see also Chapter 8). The film was shot entirely on iPhones, which exemplifies the ways in which new media technologies have opened up more possibilities for marginalized stories to be told and disseminated. In the wake of these milestones, the demand for trans cinema to be made by trans filmmakers and feature trans actors has increased. Gender and sex non-conformity continues to be an important social and political issue tackled by a variety of film authors across the globe – such as Iran's Negar Azarbayjani, China's Wei Zhang, and Sweden's Ester Martin Bergsmark. In Negar Azarbayjani's *Facing Mirrors* (*Aynehaye Rooberoo*, 2011, Iran), two strangers – a female cab driver

Figure 1.19 An unlikely friendship in *Facing Mirrors* (*Aynehaye Rooberoo*, Negar Azarbay-jani, 2011)

suffering the burdens of patriarchy and tradition, and her transgender passenger facing their own social stigma – meet by chance and, over the course of their trip, bond and find empathy for each other's marginalized positions in society (Figure 1.19).

BEYOND DIRECTING

If we problematize the notion that a film author is always necessarily the director, we can expand film history and interrogate the less visible dimensions of film work. In this context, screenwriting is a particularly critical aspect of women's film work, since it presents a unique opportunity to project a woman's perspective onto the screen. Indeed, women have frequently left their mark on cinema through screenwriting. Jill Nelmes and Jule Selbo's *Women Screenwriters: An International Guide* (2015) presents a global perspective on women writing for film, reflecting on a rich and diverse tradition of female screenwriting in film industries around the world. However, as with women directors (indeed, many women screenwriters referenced in the volume were simultaneously directors as well), early cinema was a prolific ground for their creativity, while the advent of sound cinema made film industries more male-centered. Subsequently, women writers participated in greater numbers in writing for television, which was considered a less elite cultural form, and therefore became more accessible to women's voices.

One of the most renowned female screenwriters in the 20th century Hollywood cinema was Frances Marion, who was the first woman to win an Academy Award for Best Adapted Screenplay for *The Big House* (George W. Hill, 1930, US). After Marion won again for *The Champ* (King Vidor, 1932, US), she became the first screenwriter to win two Oscars. Another prominent screenwriter, June Mathis (*The Four Horseman of the Apocalypse*, Rex Ingram, 1921, US), was also one of the first female executives in Hollywood. And Anita Loos began writing scripts in 1912, contributing a vast number of memorable screenplays over the course of several decades (including *The Women* [George Cukor, 1939, US] and *Gentlemen Prefer Blondes* [Howard Hawks, 1953, US]). In Argentina, actress Niní Marshall, who was a popular screen figure in the 1930s and 1940s, frequently wrote her own dialogue and helped develop the characters she played (without necessarily receiving writing credit). In contemporary film culture, one of the most prominent Argentinian directors, Lucrecia Martel, frequently writes her own screenplays, as does acclaimed Peruvian director Claudia Llosa.

As we mentioned at the beginning of this chapter, under the Hollywood studio system, a producer was often considered the central figure of film authorship. Women stars of the silent film era frequently served as producers of their films, while few women worked in the studio system as producers. Nowadays, women producers and heads of film companies and studios are more commonplace, although they are still far outnumbered by men. In independent production especially, feminist producers can leave consistent and recognizable authorial marks based on the kinds of movies they produce, finance and oversee.

In Hollywood, Megan Ellison and her company, Annapurna Pictures, founded in 2011, have been making their mark in recent years, producing films such as *Zero Dark Thirty* (Kathryn Bigelow, 2012, US), *Her* (Spike Jonze, 2013, US) and *20th Century Women* (Mike Mills, 2016, US). As an example of a female producer who plays an important role in foregrounding underrepresented stories and voices, we can highlight the storied career of independent film producer and co-founder (with Pamela Koffler) of Killer Films, Christine Vachon. Since the 1990s, Vachon has championed groundbreaking LGBTQ and female-driven films, including *Poison* (Todd Haynes, 1991, US), *I Shot Andy Warhol* (Mary Harron, 1996, US), *Boys Don't Cry* (Kimberly Peirce, 1999, US), *Hedwig and the Angry Inch* (John Cameron Mitchell, 2001, US) and *Carol* (Todd Haynes, 2015, US). She has recently reiterated that female-driven films continue to face difficulties in securing financing, noting that the question she often hears from potential investors with respect to such films is: "Who's the guy?"[8]

Women have played an important role as editors, as well. From the early Soviet women pioneers who edited and therefore put their authorial-visual stamp on iconic works of Soviet montage attributed to men, to women editors during the classic Hollywood era (Smyth 2017), to the more recent successes of Scorsese's frequent editor Thelma Schoonmaker, women's editing work has to be recognized as one of the crucial steps in the process of creating a work of cinema – and therefore, a form of film authorship in its own right. To that end, Margaret Sixel is a pertinent recent example: she edited the feminist action blockbuster *Mad Max: Fury Road* (George Miller, 2015, US) and won an Academy Award for her work on the film. The logistics and staging of the action sequences in that film make evident that it is the kind of film that is "made" in the editing room – and as much has been argued by the film's director and Sixel's husband, George Miller. If we look at it from this perspective, we could argue that Sixel is perhaps as much an author of *Fury Road* as her director-screenwriter husband.

In recent years, female cinematographers have also received increased attention. In 2016, an International Collective of Female Cinematographers was formed in order to dispel the notion that female directors of photography (or DPs) are an anomaly.[9] Prominent names of female DPs making an impact in contemporary film include Ellen Kuras, Nausheen Dadabhoy, Tami Reiker, Reed Morano, Agnès Godard, Josée Deshaies, Caroline Champetier, Maryse Alberti, Charlotte Bruus Christensen, Quyen Tran, and Mandy Walker. In 2018, Rachel Morrison became the first woman ever to be nominated for an Academy Award for cinematography for her work in *Mudbound* (Dee Rees, 2017, US).

CASE STUDY: *CAMERAPERSON* (KIRSTEN JOHNSON, 2016, US)

Kirsten Johnson, the director of photography on a number of documentary films, including *Pray the Devil Back to Hell* (Gini Reticker, 2008, US) and *Citizenfour* (Laura Poitras, 2014, US), directed *Cameraperson* (2016), a personal documentary about her own career as a cinematographer. In the film, she combines outtakes from the films she's worked on with her private family videos in order to weave a memoir of her creative, as well as personal, journey. Personal home videos include footage of Johnson's children, but also of her mother suffering from Alzheimer's and slowly losing her memories and her ability to recognize close

Figure 1.20 Kirsten Johnson's ailing mother in *Cameraperson* (2016)

family members (Figure 1.20). Apart from returning to some of the scenes from her professional life (including situations where shooting a film put her and the rest of the crew in harm's way), the film is also about the imprint that the footage she has shot over the years has left on her. In this unique essay film, cinematography directly translates into film authorship, as Johnson's preexisting footage, shot as a DP, now becomes the basis for a movie about herself, but also about film authorship more generally.

Watch and discuss: *Cameraperson*

1 How does *Cameraperson* create a unique mix of personal and professional footage shot by Kirsten Johnson? What purpose does that mixing serve?

2 The documentary is, among other things, a collage of footage from various films that Johnson had previously shot for other directors. Does her use of preexisting footage echo Esfir Shub's technique of "compilation film" and if so, in what ways?

3 In this documentary, the cameraperson becomes the actual author of the film. At the same time, do you see the film suggesting that the cameraperson is always a part of the authorship process, even when they are not directing? Elaborate on your answer.

ACTIVITY

Female cinematographers have worked as DPs on a number of notable films. Find out which women served as DP for the following films: *Eternal Sunshine of the Spotless Mind* (Michel Gondry, 2004, US), *Holy Motors* (Leos Carax, 2012, France), *Beau Travail* (Claire Denis, 1999, France), *Creed* (Ryan Coogler, 2015, US) and *Frozen River* (Courtney Hunt, 2008, US). What other films did they shoot, and what are some of their unique visual traits when it comes to film photography?

DISCUSSION QUESTIONS

1   Should early women filmmakers be regarded as "film pioneers" or as "women film pioneers"? What might be lost or gained in each qualification?
2   What is a feminist auteur today? Is there a necessary correlation between women-made films and feminist auteurs? Are there any male directors working today whose work you see as feminist?
3   How might a feminist director alter the content as well as the form of her work in comparison with dominant cinematic models?
4   Think of a female director whose work you are familiar with. Is she associated with any particular national cinema? How does her work address a particular idea of the nation, or conversely, why is her subject matter *not* considered representative of the national?
5   What should the relationship be between a filmmaker and the subject matter they represent? For example, should only trans filmmakers tell trans stories? If not, what is the responsibility of a non-trans filmmaker to the community that they are representing?
6   Has television offered women more opportunities to be "authors"? Who are some of the feminist voices working in television today?

KEY TERMS

accented cinema

auteurism

auteur theory

cinefeminism

classical feminist film theory

decolonial feminism

the feminist auteur

gender performativity

historical turn

intersectional feminism

melodrama

minor cinema

pre-aesthetic

queer theory

trans cinema

transnational feminism

the woman's film

women film pioneers

women's cinema

NOTES

1 See their website at https://wfpp.cdrs.columbia.edu/

2 Françoise Pfaff, "Safi Faye (1943–), Senegal," www.africanwomenin cinema.org/AFWC/Faye_Pfaff.html

3 Quoted in Christoph Huber, "Mother of all of us: Ida Lupino, the film-maker," *Cinema-Scope*, http://cinema-scope.com/features/mother-of-all-of-us-ida-lupino-the-filmmaker/

4 Milos Stehlik, "Interview," www.firouzanfilms.com/HallOfFame/Inductees/RakhshanBaniEtemad.html

5 Eric Deggans, "Hollywood has a major diversity problem, USC study finds," www.npr.org/sections/thetwo-way/2016/02/22/467665890/hollywood-has-a-major-diversity-problem-usc-study-finds

6 "Only 1 in 10 directors in India are women, finds study on 'Gender representation in Indian films'," www.dnaindia.com/entertainment/report-only-1-in-10-directors-in-india-are-women-finds-study-on-gender-representation-in-indian-films-2178976

7 Mehrotra, S., "Is 2016 the year of the female directors in Bollywood?" www.filminquiry.com/2016-year-female-director-bollywood/

8 Ed Meza, "Producer Christine Vachon discusses LGBT movies, challenges of financing female-driven films," http://variety.com/2016/film/news/christine-vachon-lgbt-movies-female-driven-films-1201708261/

9 You can browse their website at http://icfcfilm.com/

REFERENCES

Bean, J. M., & Negra, D. (Eds.). (2002). *A feminist reader in early cinema.* Durham: Duke University Press.

Butler, A. (2002). *Women's cinema: The contested screen.* London: Wallflower Press.

Butler, J. (1990). *Gender trouble: Feminism and the subversion of identity.* New York: Routledge.

Callahan, V. (Ed.). (2010). *Reclaiming the archive: Feminism and film history.* Detroit: Wayne State University Press.

Consolati, C. (2013). "Grotesque bodies, fragmented selves: Lina Wertmüller's women in *Love and Anarchy* (1973)." In M. Cantini (Ed.), *Italian women filmmakers and the Gendered Screen.* London: Palgrave McMillan, 33–52.

Dall'Asta, M. (2010). "What it means to be a woman: Theorizing feminist film history beyond the essentialism/constructionism divide." In S. Bull & A. Söderbergh Widding (Eds.), *Not so silent: Women in cinema before sound.* Stockholm: Acta Universitatis Stockhomiensis, 39–47.

De Lauretis, T. (1985). "Aesthetic and feminist theory: Rethinking women's cinema." *New German Critique*, (34), 154–175.

Foster, G. A. (1995). *Women film directors: An international bio-critical dictionary.* London: Greenwood Publishing Group.

Gaines, J. M. (2004). "Film history and the two presents of feminist film theory." *Cinema Journal*, 44(1), 113–119.

Gaines, J. M. (2018). *Pink-slipped: What happened to women in the silent film industries?* Urbana: University of Illinois Press.

Halberstam, J. (2005). *In a queer time and place: Transgender bodies, subcultural lives.* New York: NYU Press.

Horak, L. (2016). *Girls will be boys: Cross-dressed women, lesbians, and American cinema, 1908–1934.* New Brunswick: Rutgers University Press.

Horne, J. (2013). "Alla Nazimova." In J. Gaines, R. Vatsal, & M. Dall'Asta, (Eds.), *Women film pioneers project. Center for digital research and scholarship.* New York: Columbia University Libraries, https://wfpp.cdrs.columbia.edu/pioneer/ccp-alla-nazimova/. Last accessed September 10, 2017.

Johnston. C. (1973) [1999]. "Women's cinema as counter-cinema." In S. Thornham (Ed.), *Feminist film theory: A reader*. New York: NYU Press, 31–40.

Kuhn, A., & Radstone, S. (Eds.). (1990). *The women's companion to international film*. Berkeley: University of California Press.

Lugones, M. (2010). "Toward a decolonial feminism." *Hypatia*, 25(4), 742–759.

Marciniak, K., Imre, A., & O'Healy, A. (Eds.). (2007). *Transnational feminism in film and media*. New York: Palgrave MacMillan.

Marsh, L. (2012). *Brazilian women's filmmaking: From dictatorship to democracy*. Urbana: University of Illinois Press.

McLellan, D. (2000). *The girls: Sappho goes to Hollywood*. New York: LA Weekly Books.

McMahan, A. (2002). *Alice Guy Blaché: Lost visionary of the cinema*. New York: Bloomsbury Publishing.

Mehrotra, S. (2016). "Is 2016 the year of the female directors in Bollywood?" *Film Inquiry*, October 21, 2016, www.filminquiry.com/2016-yearfemale-director-bollywood/

Naficy, H. (2001). *An accented cinema: Exilic and diasporic filmmaking*. Princeton: Princeton University Press.

Nelmes, J., & Selbo, J. (Eds.). (2015). *Women screenwriters: An international guide*. London: Palgrave MacMillan.

Olenina, A. (2014). "Aleksandra Khokhlova." In J. Gaines, R. Vatsal, & M. Dall'Asta (Eds.), *Women film pioneers project. Center for Digital Research and Scholarship*. New York: Columbia University Libraries, https://wfpp.cdrs.columbia.edu/pioneer/aleksandra-khokhlova-2/. Last accessed September 10, 2017.

Russo Bullaro, G. (2006). *Man in disorder: The cinema of Lina Wertmüller in the 1970s*. Leicester: Troubadour Publishing Ltd.

Shaw, L., & Dennison, S. (2007). *Brazilian national cinema*. London: Routledge.

Shohat, E., & Stam, R. (1994). *Unthinking Eurocentrism: Multiculturalism and the media*. New York: Routledge.

Slide, A. (1996). *The silent feminists: America's first women directors*. London: Scarecrow Press.

Smyth, J. E. (2017). "Female editors in studio-era Hollywood." In K. Hole, D. Jelača, E. A. Kaplan & P. Petro (Eds.), *The Routledge companion to cinema and gender*. London: Routledge, 279–288.

Stam, R. (2000). *Film theory: An introduction*. Malden, MA: Wiley-Blackwell.

Stamp, S. (2010). "Lois Weber, star maker." In V. Callahan (Ed.), *Reclaiming the archive: Feminism and film history*. Detroit: Wayne State University Press, 131–153.

Stamp, S. (2015). *Lois Weber in early Hollywood*. Oakland: University of California Press.

Steinbock. E. (2017). "Towards trans cinema." In K. Hole, D. Jelača, E. A. Kaplan & P. Petro (Eds.), *The Routledge companion to cinema and gender*. London: Routledge, 395–406.

Thackway, M. (2003). *Africa shoots back: Alternative perspectives in sub-Saharan francophone African film*. Bloomington: Indiana University Press.

Wang, L. (Ed.). (2011). *Chinese women's cinema: Transnational contexts*. New York: Columbia University Press.

Welbon, Y. (2001). *Sisters in Cinema: Case Studies of Three First-Time Achievements Made by African American Women Feature Film Directors in the 1990s*. PhD. Diss. Northwestern University.

White, P. (1999). *Uninvited: Classical Hollywood cinema and lesbian representability*. Bloomington: Indiana University Press.

White, P. (2015). *Women's cinema, world cinema: Projecting contemporary feminisms*. Durham: Duke University Press.

Williams, T. (2014). *Germaine Dulac: A cinema of sensations*. Chicago: University of Illinois Press.

Wollen, P. (1972). *Signs and meaning in the cinema*. London: Secker & Warburg.

Young, I. M. (1994). "Gender as seriality: Thinking about women as a social collective." *Signs*, 19(3), 713–738.

Chapter two
SPECTATORSHIP AND RECEPTION

FEMINISM, SPECTATORSHIP, AND PSYCHOANALYSIS

Film is a visual medium organized primarily around the act of looking, even as senses such as hearing play an important role when we watch a movie. Think back to the experience of watching your favorite film. What emotions and reactions did you experience? How did the film engage you as a spectator and facilitate your identification with the protagonists onscreen? What do we mean when we say that a film has "stayed with us"?

Classical feminist film theory draws on psychoanalytic approaches to cinema that assume that in the act of watching a film, we as spectators engage our conscious and unconscious desires, fears, and impulses. The films we watch, in turn, reflect back to us various tendencies that inform or construct the social psyche more generally and influence individual spectators, without them necessarily being consciously aware of it. Theories that take into consideration not just an individual film as an isolated text, but also the spectatorial experience of viewing in both its material and psychic domains, are typically called theories of **the cinematic apparatus**.

An influential film theorist who contributed to the emergence of psychoanalytic film theory is Christian Metz, whose *Film Language: A Semiotics of the Cinema* (1974) combines structuralist linguistic approaches and psychoanalysis in order to examine the cinematic apparatus. Metz was significantly influenced by French psychoanalyst Jacques Lacan, who identified **the mirror stage** as the defining moment in which a young child acquires subjectivity, or a sense of self, by entering what Lacan called the Imaginary Order (a psychic realm organized around images and the dualism of self and other). It takes place when the child (between six and eighteen months of age) sees their reflection in the mirror and identifies that reflection as an "I" for the first time. At that very moment, however, a crucial *misrecognition* takes place, because the figure in the mirror is not truly oneself, but rather a *reflection* of oneself. The mirror image appears as a unified and coherent whole, with abilities that are beyond the motor coordination of the child herself. The child's visual powers are more mature than its sensory-motor coordination, so it identifies with an image that appears superior to and more in control of itself. As a result, we spend the rest of our life thinking of our own reflections as our "true selves." This misrecognition is a fitting metaphor for cinema, since it can be used to explain some aspects of our affective investment in and identification with the characters onscreen in psychoanalytic terms, as a way of reenacting the mirror stage that ushers in subjectivity, or our sense of identity, in the first place.

As if to mirror this psychoanalytic model, many films overtly call attention to the act of looking by having their protagonists longingly gaze at, spy on, or attempt to visually capture another person. Examples of this are numerous: from *All About Eve* (Joseph L. Mankiewicz, 1950, US), *Rear Window* (Alfred Hitchcock, 1954, US), *Peeping Tom* (Michael Powell, 1960, UK) and *Blow-Up* (Michelangelo Antonioni, 1966, UK/Italy), to more recent films such as *Mulholland Drive* (David Lynch, 2001, US), *Blue Is the Warmest Color* (Abdellatif Kechiche, 2013, France), or *Ex Machina* (Alex Garland, 2015, UK).

Scopophilia is a term used to describe the pleasure of looking. According to the psychoanalytic understanding of scopophilia, looking at others is an inherently pleasurable activity that we are unconsciously drawn to. The act of looking at another person, however, does not occur in a vacuum. On the contrary, it is structured by systems of social power such as patriarchy and heteronormativity. Psychoanalytic feminist film theory has identified these underlying structures in order to change the status quo by making dominant constructions of viewing pleasure conscious and explicit.

There are numerous cinematic examples of men turning their gaze and camera lens longingly towards women (Figure 2.1). However, alternative looking relations can complicate this patriarchal dynamic. For instance, in one scene in *Carol* (Todd Haynes, 2015, US), a film about a lesbian romance set in the 1950s, Therese, who is a photographer, turns her camera lens towards Carol, the woman she desires. She photographs her love interest

Figure 2.1 The male gaze and camera lens turned towards a woman (*Blow-Up*, Michelangelo Antonioni, 1966)

from a distance as Carol buys a Christmas tree (Figure 2.2). In this seemingly simple scene, a significant patriarchal, heteronormative discourse is being challenged: the trope that women onscreen serve as mere objects of the controlling male gaze and desire. In *Carol*, one woman sexually desires and turns her camera lens towards another woman, taking ownership of the viewing apparatus and making space for the female libido outside dominant patriarchal frameworks. By extension, the audience is invited to identify with Therese's gaze and align with her lesbian desire towards Carol – an act of looking that actively undermines the patriarchal and heteronormative sexualizing of women onscreen.

The pervasiveness of the **controlling male gaze** within the cinematic apparatus of classic Hollywood film form was a central object of focus for classical feminist film theory of the 1970s. In particular, using the psychoanalytic approach, Laura Mulvey's landmark 1975 essay "Visual Pleasure and Narrative Cinema" identifies a dominant pattern in classic Hollywood cinema within which women onscreen embody **to-be-looked-at-ness**, and are framed as objects of male desire. That desire is channeled through the gaze of the male protagonist, which is in turn aligned with the movie camera. The point of view of the male protagonist drives the narrative and dominates the frame and, by proxy, the spectator is invited to identify with the male gaze and its desire. Mulvey argues that this gaze is a controlling device that perpetuates the patriarchal framing of women as sexual objects of male desire.

Furthermore, the image of the woman onscreen presents a threat that the psychoanalytic approach theorizes as the threat of castration (or, castration

Figure 2.2 In *Carol* (Todd Haynes, 2015), a woman longingly turns her gaze and camera lens towards another woman

anxiety). While her image is pleasurable, the woman also threatens to remind the male viewer of sexual difference – that is, the fact that he too could lose his phallus, understood as the male position of power and authority in the world. The ensuing castration anxiety, according to Mulvey, is mitigated in classical narrative cinema either through sexual objectification – what she calls **fetishistic scopophilia** – or through punishment rooted in **sadistic voyeurism**. As an example of fetishistic scopophilia, Mulvey uses Josef von Sternberg's *Blue Angel* (1930, Germany), featuring young Marlene Dietrich. Dietrich's characters are often dressed fetishistically, in feathers, veils, tuxedos, or, in one unforgettable and racially loaded instance, a gorilla costume. All of these accessories or sartorial decisions can be read psychoanalytically as stand-ins for the "missing" penis (for the orthodox psychoanalytic account, see Freud's 1927 essay "Fetishism"). The narrative of Sternberg's film often halts altogether to allow Dietrich's character to perform a song or to let the camera linger on a part of Dietrich's body. Her fetishized appearance and framing, according to the psychoanalytic model, enable the viewer to disavow her sexual difference: "I know she doesn't have a penis, but all the same she does" have some power that might stand in for the phallus.

Hitchcock's films, on the other hand, manifest both fetishistic scopophilia and sadistic voyeurism. Mulvey pays particular attention to *Rear Window* (1954, US) and *Vertigo* (1958, US) as manifestations of that interplay. In these scenarios, the woman is an object of investigation and her innocence or guilt is revealed through her interrogation or trial, as if to prove that she deserves her castrated/disempowered status. *Vertigo* is notable in this regard, as the character of Judy/Madeleine is taken to the scene of an earlier crime and aggressively terrorized by the protagonist into confessing her guilt – and her love – for her interrogator. Thus she is, unconsciously, proven guilty for her difference. Her forgiveness precipitates her death (Figure 2.3).

Mulvey's highly influential essay offers many key insights into the psychic positioning of men and women, particularly in and by classic Hollywood films. Yet it is most powerful when read as a polemic – the discussion of these looking relations is framed by a call for an experimental film practice that would position the spectator differently. Mulvey's ideas emerged out of a women's reading group in the 1970s that considered psychoanalytic theory in relation to their own lives. The essay is a political act that is

Figure 2.3 Judy/Madeleine being punished by her controlling lover (*Vertigo*, Alfred Hitchcock, 1958)

directed at particular films in the Hollywood classical narrative tradition. As such, without her overtly saying so, Mulvey's framework is decidedly Western-centric, as psychoanalytic theory more generally often is (for instance, in assuming that the Western forms of patriarchy, gender dynamics, and family structures are universal occurrences). Mulvey, who was herself an experimental filmmaker, does not allow for the possibility of mainstream cinema to embody female pleasure since, according to her, the gaze itself is intrinsically male. This, of course, leaves even Western female viewers in a difficult position – how can we account for the fact that women like to watch films if such films are addressed to a male spectator's unconscious fantasies and fears? A few years later, Mulvey offered a slight revision of her initial theory by acknowledging that female spectators can indeed identify with the male gaze onscreen, but that that identification enacts a form of gender masquerade or "transvestitism" (1981).

A number of theorists challenged Mulvey's proposition that feminine pleasure is categorically denied in mainstream cinema, by arguing that her model overlooks both the possibility of queer readings that challenge her idea of "woman as image; man as bearer of the look," and also of reading against the grain more broadly (recall also our discussion in Chapter 1 of Claire Johnston's suggestion that mainstream cinema is in fact more available to ideological subversion and counter readings than art film). Some theorists looked to female-oriented genres, such as the maternal melodrama, in order to understand how these films address women according to their status as wives and mothers under patriarchy. E. Ann Kaplan notes that "the gaze is not necessarily male (literally), but to own and activate the gaze, given our language and the structure of the unconscious, is to be in the 'masculine' position" (1983: 30). What these critiques of Mulvey suggest is that the speculative spectator (that is, a spectator who is theorized about but not empirically observed) is not as firmly restricted in their desires and identifications by either their own or the film protagonist's gender, sex, sexuality, race and other aspects of identity. In other words, a spectator has the ability to identify with a figure on the screen who is different from them, sometimes drastically so. Moreover, the spectator can interpret a film differently than may have been intended, in accordance with their own idiosyncratic preferences (we discuss various forms of oppositional readings, or reading against the grain, later in this chapter). In her book *Cinema and Spectatorship*, Judith Mayne suggests that, while spectatorship is one of the most vital aspects of studying cinema, it is also one that has been most misunderstood, "largely because of the obsessive preoccupation with dualistic categories of critique versus celebration, or 'critical' versus 'complacent' spectatorship" (1993: 4). That is to say, many scholarly writings on spectatorship have taken a position that viewing practices are either wholly critical or completely negative, rather than making space for the complex mixture of levels at which we psychically engage with the films we watch.

Even the films of a director who is typically considered a textbook case of Mulvey's theoretical insight – Alfred Hitchcock – have been interpreted through oppositional, or more affirmative approaches. Alexander Doty (2011) notes that Hitchcock's films frequently contain queer elements in the framing of both gender and sexuality. For instance, *Rebecca* (1940, US; Figure 2.4) centers on repressed lesbian desire, while *Psycho* (1960, US) prominently features cross-dressing. Both of these films have been put under the scrutiny of feminist film studies numerous times, in ways that offer both affirmative and negative readings, confirming that the work of a filmmaker as complex as Hitchcock lends itself to a variety of interpretations and analytical approaches.

In her book about Hitchcock's female protagonists, Tania Modleski observes that "his films are always in danger of being subverted by females whose power is both fascinating and seemingly limitless" (1988: 1). Similarly, in *Alice Doesn't: Feminism, Semiotics, Cinema* (1984), Teresa de Lauretis uses Hitchcock's *Rebecca* and *Vertigo* in order to theorize **the female spectator** – a departure from Mulvey's suggestion that spectatorship is inevitably male. "If the spectator's identification is engaged and directed in each film by specific cinematic-narrative codes," writes de Lauretis, "it should be possible to work through these codes in order to shift or redirect identification toward

Figure 2.4 Repressed lesbian desire in Hitchcock's *Rebecca* (1940)

the two positionalities of desire that define the female's Oedipal situation" (153). Here, de Lauretis refers to the supposedly incomplete Oedipus complex of the woman, who never fully gives up her desire for the mother in favor of the father. While both the male and female child take their mother as their first love object, the female child (under a heteronormative developmental model), transfers her affection to her father, but never completely renounces the mother either (hence her "two positionalities of desire"). Although the male child must give up the *literal* mother in the **Oedipal scenario**, he keeps a female object of desire (again, in the heteronormative psychoanalytic developmental model), so his relationship to his own desire is less bisexual and ambiguous. De Lauretis finds that the films which center on Oedipal narratives (of women being defined by their phallic envy/ lack), as *Rebecca* and *Vertigo* seemingly do, simultaneously make possible a duplicitous, female-centric reading that sees "the question of desire as precisely enigma, contradiction, difference not reducible to sameness" (157). What this entails is that the projection of the woman onscreen is not identical or entirely reducible to the female spectator in the audience, and this is precisely what allows the female spectator to *not* identify with the objectified position on the screen (see also Bergstrom & Doane 1989).

Mary Ann Doane argues that "for the female spectator there is a certain over-presence of the image – she *is* the image" (1982: 78, emphasis in the text). Complicating Mulvey's contestation that the female spectator enacts transvestitism in identifying with the male protagonist, Doane theorizes female spectatorship vis-à-vis its relationship to the female object on the screen, and argues that the female spectator engages in a masquerade triggered by the excess of femininity represented on the screen. Masquerade "constitutes an acknowledgment that it is femininity itself which is constructed as mask" (81) and therefore allows the female spectator to distance herself from the excessively feminine object onscreen, or rather, to destabilize her image. In other words, the female spectator recognizes the artificiality of the feminine masquerade being presented onscreen, and therefore does not fully internalize it or passively identify with it. This position could be tied back to Claire Johnston's theorizing of women's cinema and the possibilities of reading seemingly reactionary and patriarchal mainstream films in oppositional ways, precisely because their representations of women are so obviously stereotypes.

This stance is evident in the work of artist Cindy Sherman, who, in one of her most lauded projects, *Untitled Film Stills* (1977–1980; Figure 2.5), produced a series of photographic auto-portraits depicting herself in a number of guises evoking the clichés of postwar feminine Hollywood glamor. By enacting such a performance, Sherman echoes Doane's words that masquerade makes us acknowledge that femininity is a constructed mask. In this work, Sherman both embodies widely recognizable cinematic archetypes

Figure 2.5 Cindy Sherman's *Untitled Film Still #43*
Courtesy of the artist and Metro Pictures, New York

of femininity and calls attention to their artifice. "Thus," observes Jackie Stacey, "the conventional visual pleasures of classic icons of femininity are both constructed and deconstructed at the same time" (1994: 7). Feminist cultural workers and scholars have frequently recognized the subversive potential of reappropriating excessive femininity and exposing it as a social construct that can be used to provocative ends.

Some film theorists have challenged the necessity of using Oedipal frameworks to understand spectatorship. Gaylyn Studlar (1984) argues that feminist film theory can broaden its perspective by focusing on the **pre-Oedipal stage**. In psychoanalytic theory, this period of development includes **an oral stage**, which among others, precedes the phallic, Oedipal stage in a child's development that subsequently gives rise to penis envy or castration anxiety. In paying closer attention to the pre-Oedipal stage, according to Studlar, we can better understand the ways in which cinema "may be capable of forming spectatorial pleasures divorced from issues of castration, sexual difference, and feminine lack" (1985: 5). Studlar argues that if our investment in cinema's visual pleasure has its genesis in our infancy, it therefore caters to the infantile modes of sexuality that predate the Oedipal stage. Studlar traces the ways in which mother is the central figure in the pre-Oedipal, pre-phallic phase of a child's development, regardless of the child's biological sex. In this stage, the mother is perceived as an active and powerful figure, rather than a passive afterthought, as the Oedipal frameworks often cast her. Out of this, **masochism** – or deriving pleasure from pain – emerges as a way to channel anxiety caused by the ambivalent relationship with the mother – who is an object of both admiration and separation anxiety. As a result, "the female is mystically idealized as the loving inflictor of punishment" (8). Studlar finds examples of this dynamic in the films of Josef von Sternberg, particularly those starring the iconic Marlene Dietrich. Whereas Mulvey saw Dietrich's function in these films as representing post-Oedipal fetishistic (active) scopophilia, Studlar sees her representation as tapping into pre-Oedipal fantasies that are much more passive, feminized, and masochistic. Studlar's important intervention into psychoanalytic feminist film theory opens up the possibilities of articulating more complicated viewing positions that go beyond active/passive and male/female dichotomies, as they are typically defined through Oedipal frameworks.

Most of these accounts of female spectatorship and the gaze, however, typically stay firmly within the frameworks of whiteness and heteronormative Western cinema largely made in Hollywood and Western Europe. How might these theoretical insights be rendered more complicated, or even revealed to be inadequate, when non-heteronormative, non-Western, and nonwhite perspectives are taken into consideration? In her essay "Pleasurable Negotiations," Christine Gledhill criticizes cine-psychoanalysis for not only rendering (female) spectatorship in starkly negative terms, but also for positioning the textual spectator as a "trans-class construct," which results in the "difficulty in dealing with the female image or spectator in terms of class difference" (2006: 112). Additionally, Jane Gaines (1986) introduces race as an important factor that was frequently rendered invisible by both mainstream cinema and dominant feminist theory of the time. Gaines argues that the incessant focus on male/female divisions in feminist film theory has obfuscated the question of race: "Women of color, like lesbians, have been added to feminist analysis as an afterthought" (65). Importantly, in her analysis of *Mahogany* (Berry Gordy & Tony Richardson, 1975, US), Gaines discusses "the class nature of social antagonisms" (72) as a crucial aspect of the film's framing of black femininity. With this, she offers a Marxist analysis that is grounded in material reality and not just in figurative representation. In some ways, these debates converge on what de Lauretis has called "the paradox of woman" (1990). Namely, feminist theory has, on the one hand, been invested in denaturalizing and deconstructing "woman," considering it as a constructed category rather than a natural, a priori given (recall Simone de Beauvoir's oft cited "One is not born, but rather becomes, a woman"). Yet the deconstruction of "woman" as a discursive identity can easily slip into a form of relativism that negates real-life experiences of oppression. On the other hand, making claims on behalf of "women" can flatten the differences that exist among women, differences based on the locally specific and historically contingent circumstances of their lives.

ACTIVITY

Watch one of the Hitchcock films discussed in this chapter and consider whether it is a critique of patriarchy, or if it upholds traditional views toward women. How would you interpret the film through a psychoanalytic feminist approach?

CASE STUDY: *THE CHILDREN'S HOUR* (WILLIAM WYLER, 1961, US)

While Laura Mulvey argued that classical narrative cinema favors a male gaze, even mid-20th century Hollywood cinema offers numerous examples in which the spectator is invited to identify with female desire onscreen. *The Children's Hour* is one such example: the story revolves around two women, Karen and Martha (played by Audrey Hepburn and Shirley MacLaine), who run a private girls' boarding school (Figure 2.6).

In *The Children's Hour*, the two women share an emotional bond that remains in the realm of friendship, due to the social stigma around same-sex desire. When Karen gets engaged to a local doctor, Martha expresses fits of jealousy that her aunt refers to as "unnatural." The aunt reminds Martha that she's always had this "unnatural" streak, even as a young child. "You are making me sick," replies Martha, with apparent frustration that her feelings are being taken as signs of disease. When a schoolgirl overhears this conversation, she decides to use it as an opportunity to get her grandmother to take her out of the school by implying that Karen and Martha's relationship is a sexual one. The rumor of a romantic relationship between Karen and Martha spreads quickly, and shortly thereafter all the girls are taken out of the school, while the two women become community pariahs.

Figure 2.6 The stigma of same-sex desire in *The Children's Hour* (William Wyler, 1961)

The film frames the community's growing paranoia about the women's sexuality through the perspective of Karen and Martha, inviting the spectator to empathize with them. Lesbian desire is never named in the film, but rather hinted at by various other terms such as the women's "sinful sexual knowledge of one another." After they lose their school and a libel suit, Martha confesses her love to Karen, and notes that in the schoolgirl's lie there was an ounce of truth that made Martha clearly identify her feelings towards Karen for the first time. And although they are exonerated when one student admits to taking part in the lie, Martha takes her own life out of desperation that her love would only continue to make life difficult for Karen. In the end, Karen says her loving goodbye at Martha's grave and defiantly walks past the women's accusers. Her future is uncertain, but she has gained a new understanding of herself through tragedy. And while this film does not avoid the pitfall identified by Vito Russo, of having gay and lesbian characters meet a tragic fate, it is also an important cinematic study of fraught community morals that police (female) sexuality and love.

The film is an adaptation of a hit 1934 Broadway play written by Lillian Hellman. The first film adaptation of the play, adapted for the screen by Hellman herself, was initially blocked in accordance with Hollywood's Production Code (also known as "the Code") that forbade content in the movies deemed improper, particularly of a sexual nature. One of the concessions that the production company was asked to make was to erase overt mentions of lesbianism. This, as Patricia White notes in *UnInvited: Classical Hollywood Cinema and Lesbian Representability*, multiplied "the contradictions of the play: what remained unspoken is declared unspeakable, only to resonate . . . as the loudest whisper. In the case of this adaptation, censorship drew attention to a text that is already *about* the question of lesbian representability" (1999: 21, emphasis in the text). Eventually, the first film adaptation of the play, renamed *These Three* (also directed by William Wyler, in 1936), focused on a heterosexual love triangle involving Martha, Karen, and Karen's fiancé Joe. White suggests that the film is "lying about lesbianism" (28) in order to produce it, or to articulate its existence through the narrative of social stigma and suppression.

It was only in the 1961 movie adaptation of the play – made by the same director and again scripted by Lillian Hellman – that lesbianism returned as a whisper. Indeed, this new version was released in the UK with the title *The Loudest Whisper*. This iteration of the story needs to be historically contextualized as well, having come out in 1961, not long after the end of a decade generally identified as one that cemented conservative family values and gender roles in America. In fact, Hellman herself was a target of the Hollywood blacklist in the postwar period. However, the film also comes out during a period in which formerly taboo subjects became somewhat more available for treatment in film, as the collapse of the studio system in the wake of the 1948 Paramount Decision had rendered the Code ineffectual. In that light, its focusing on women's largely unspoken same-sex desire, and moreover, casting its female protagonists as figures the spectator is *invited to identify with* outside of the framework of the male gaze, presents an important departure for mainstream Hollywood cinema.

"The case of the production and adaptation of *The Children's Hour*," Patricia White pointedly observes, "allows us to scrutinize parameters of lesbian representability across a thirty-year history of commercial mass culture and self-regulation" (24).

Watch and discuss: *The Children's Hour*

1   Do you think the film offers an effective representation of the social policing of female sexuality, or does it cater to stereotypes about doomed lesbian love?
2   Mary Ann Doane argues that "there is always a certain excessiveness, a difficulty associated with women who appropriate the gaze, who insist upon looking" (1982: 83). Can you identify that pattern in *The Children's Hour*? Elaborate on your answer.
3   Can you think of contemporary examples of films in which the male gaze is provided as the only framework of vision, and where the woman is objectified in a problematic way? What about examples of films where women own the gaze?

CRITICAL POSTCOLONIAL PERSPECTIVES ON SPECTATORSHIP

Psychoanalytic approaches are also challenged when geographical, economic or historical contexts are changed, and when the European/Western (male) subject is not the normative frame of reference. In particular, how do feminist interventions politically aligned with **decolonizing approaches** conceptualize female spectatorship differently from classical theories of the gaze?

Key to these discussions is the ongoing impact of (neo)colonialism, which imposes **Eurocentrism** as an ideological expansion of Western values and ways of life as the only markers of civilization and progress. Colonial discursive practices can be traced in many popular cultural figures and tropes – from Tarzan and King Kong, to Robinson Crusoe's companion, Friday – where whiteness is reaffirmed as the source of modernity, enlightenment, and progress, while nonwhite subjects are frequently positioned, literally and symbolically, as animalistic or infantile savages (Figure 2.7). By extension of that logic, colonial ideology justifies itself through claiming that colonized cultures deserved to be colonized because they needed to be

Figure 2.7 King Kong and vulnerable yet seductive white femininity (*King Kong*, Peter Jackson, 2005)

enlightened and modernized according to Eurocentric standards. One of the most influential utilizations of psychoanalysis through the prism of colonialism is Frantz Fanon's *Black Skin, White Masks* (1952). In the book, Fanon, himself an analyst who studied the impact of colonialism on both colonizer and colonized, deploys psychoanalytic interpretations of the power dynamics between white and nonwhite communities in the colonial context, including accounts of the power of the gaze, in order to examine how nonwhite subjects negotiate the psychic inferiority complexes that result from the colonial context and the dominant discourses of white superiority. Fanon's work here represents one of the key texts that utilize psychoanalysis to examine the horrors and devastating long-term psychological effects of systemic oppression.

Cinema's role in both colonialist projects and resistance to colonialism cannot be underestimated. As Ella Shohat and Robert Stam point out, "the beginnings of cinema coincided with the giddy heights of the imperial project, with an epoch where Europe held sway over vast tracts of alien territory and hosts of subjugated peoples" (1994: 100). Consequently, "the cinema, as the world's storyteller par excellence, was ideally suited to relay the projected narratives of nations and empires" (101). Sandra Ponzanesi observes that, "colonial images of gender, race, and class carried ideological connotations that confirmed imperial epistemologies and racial taxonomies, depicting natives – in documentary or fiction films – as savages, primitive, and outside modernity" (2017: 25–26). At the same time, colonized communities were generally denied the ability to represent themselves or to access the often expensive technology required to produce films. In her book *Dark Continents*, Ranjana Khanna (2003) notes that psychoanalysis and colonialism are overtly linked in Freud's infamous designation of women's sexuality as the "dark continent," since the term is so deeply imbued with colonial assumptions about the nonwhite "Other," having frequently been used to demarcate Africa itself. With this, Freud projects "his lack of knowledge about women onto his theory of them" (Khanna 50). Moreover, in gendering the term "dark continent" this way, psychoanalysis elides race at the expense of gendered difference. "This early conflation and the total erasure of black women within that conflation," Khanna points out (48), contributes to the consistent exclusion of black or nonwhite experiences in psychoanalysis, as well as in theorizing about womanhood as a performative or socially constructed function. We could add that it may also be the reason why psychoanalytic theories of spectatorship have been late, if not entirely inadequate, in accounting for racial difference.

Rather than taking for granted psychoanalysis as a deterritorialized, "pure" theory, scholars such as Khanna approach it as an epistemological practice rooted in a specific time, place, and geopolitical context. Namely, she argues that, "if psychoanalysis is read as an ethnography rather than a contextless theory or its opposite, alternative models for the nation-state begin to emerge" (64). Here Khanna refuses to adhere to a strict boundary between the self (and particularly the self's unconscious) and the nation. If we extend this to the psychoanalytic theory of spectatorship, we could add that the textual or speculative spectator is similarly not an ahistorical figure, but rather one rooted in very concrete geopolitical frameworks of history – colonial, national, and otherwise. What this means is that how we conceptualize male or female viewing positions, identification and sexual difference both on the screen and in spectators, is heavily dependent on how transnational colonial and national histories construct "men" and "women" against real and imaginary Others.

An illustration of this is the mechanism of **the oppositional gaze** theorized by influential black feminist thinker bell hooks. Acknowledging the painful history of trauma associated with slave owners frequently punishing slaves simply for the act of looking (too proudly, too defiantly, or otherwise), and examining how that trauma might have influenced generations of black parents in teaching their children to look away, hooks writes about "the ways power as domination reproduces itself in different locations employing similar apparatuses, strategies, and mechanisms of control" (1992: 115). But precisely because the gaze is policed by the more powerful, it also produces a deeper desire to look for those who are in the powerless position – thereby creating what she calls the oppositional gaze enacted by the subjugated.

"Even in the worse circumstances of domination, the ability to manipulate one's gaze in the face of structures of domination that would contain it, opens up the possibility of agency," observes hooks, adding that "the 'gaze' has been and is a site of resistance for colonized black people globally" (116). Here we move starkly away from the gaze being theorized as merely an instrument of patriarchal power. Quite the contrary, critical decolonial approaches theorize the oppositional gaze as a site of subversive opportunity to return the objectifying, colonial gaze and enact resistance, sometimes as the only weapon that subjugated peoples have. This interrogation of the gaze and cinema's technology of vision led to such anticolonial movements as Third Cinema (see Chapters 1 and 5). Here it is important to note that psychoanalysis, too, can be reappropriated as a paradigm through which we can reveal and understand the dynamics of patriarchal and colonial power rather than merely reiterate them.

CASE STUDY: *BLACK GIRL (LA NOIRE DE . . .,* OUSMANE SEMBENE, 1966, SENEGAL)

In *Black Girl* – considered the first feature-length film made by a director from sub-Saharan Africa – legendary Senegalese filmmaker Ousmane Sembene depicts the story of Diouana, a young Senegalese woman who leaves Dakar and goes to the south of France to work as a maid for a well-to-do white French couple. Throughout the film, she is an invisible and mute Other for the French couple – we hear her voice only through her voiceover narration – merely there to provide useful labor, but otherwise not treated as a person in her own right. This is symbolized by a traditional mask that Diouana brings to the couple as a gift from Senegal, and which hangs on their wall as a "tribal" decoration with which they can impress their friends. By the film's end, Diouana sees no way out of her precarious situation and, tragically, commits suicide. Her employer collects her belongings, including the mask, and takes them back to Dakar. There, he finds Diouana's mother, who refuses the money he tries to give her. A young Senegalese boy takes the mask, puts it on and follows the visitor as he returns to his car. Visually evocative of the title of Fanon's book – *Black Skin, White Masks* – the boy with the mask breaks the fourth wall and gazes straight at the camera (Figure 2.8).

In psychoanalytic terms, we could view this as a return of the repressed, whereby whiteness and (neo)colonial power are exposed

Figure 2.8 The return of the repressed in *Black Girl* (Ousmane Sembene, 1966)

in their exploitative privilege, and where the subjugated, silent other returns the gaze as a way to refuse mitigating white guilt. The film is interested in critically highlighting the lasting effects of colonialism even after the oppressive system ends. Indeed, the neocolonial situation that defines Diouana's fate indicates that the cultural, social, and political hegemony of the former colonial powers continues unchallenged – exemplified, for instance, by Diouana's treatment by white French protagonists as an ethnographic object rather than as a person in her own right.

Watch and discuss: *Black Girl*

1   What are some of the formal and narrative devices through which the film offers a decolonial feminist critique?
2   How might a psychoanalytic approach be inadequate for analyzing the underlying structures that inform the meaning of the film?
3   Are there ways in which psychoanalytic frameworks provide insight into the film?

AUDIENCE AND RECEPTION: TAKING BACK THE GAZE

In the late 20th and early 21st centuries, changes ushered by **the digital era** have introduced significant shifts in moviegoing experience, as well as audience reception of cinema. Nowadays, audiences are generally considered to be heterogeneous and active. This is one of the reasons why the study of film and media has increasingly focused on **empirical research** that examines **reception** rather than speculating about possible (abstractly conceived) viewing positions. In her 1993 essay "Early Cinema, Late Cinema: Permutations of the Public Sphere," which reassesses the historical significance of the psychoanalytic notion of the spectator and focuses on cinema's historical role in the public sphere, Miriam Hansen observes that in the latter part of the 20th century, "the classical principle by which reception is controlled by the film as an integral product and commodity is weakened by the social proliferation of film consumption in institutionally less regulated viewing situations" (198). Here Hansen highlights the rise of television and accompanying technologies of video playback and satellite and cable. Starting in the 1950s, television challenged the primacy of cinema going and became the dominant pastime. Hansen ties these shifts from cinema to television and new electronic technologies to the end of a unified mass culture in favor of splintered, heterogeneous audiences. The classical film apparatus whose location was the movie theater was splintered into more privatized viewing situations in domestic spaces. Contemporary mass culture (for instance, cable television) contributes to this splintering by offering "something for everyone" and catering to diverse tastes through varied niche genre movies (Figure 2.9). "Today's postmodern, globalized culture of consumption has developed new, and ever more elusive, technologies of power and commodification, operating through diversification rather than homogenization," notes Hansen, and this, in turn, requires "theories of reception and identification different from those predicated on classical Hollywood cinema and the American model of mass culture" (1993: 199). Hansen here identifies important structural, historical, and cultural shifts that have only accelerated in our digital era, which has seen the rapid proliferation of new ways of making, distributing, and consuming media. Importantly for her, this does not entail that the psychoanalytic theory of spectatorship should be done away with completely, but rather that it needs to be counterbalanced with other approaches – such as reception and audience research – since "thinking of the cinema in terms of the public involves an approach that cuts across theoretical and historical, textual and contextual, modes of inquiry" (206). This approach allows us to account for "multiple and conflicting identities and constituencies" (208) that inform varied viewing positions and our understanding of cinema more broadly.

As we have seen in previous sections, psychoanalytic approaches largely speculate about viewing positions without necessarily rooting them in

Figure 2.9 The female-centric comedy *Bridesmaids* (Paul Feig, 2011) was a huge box-office success, predominantly catering to female audiences

actual practice observed through **ethnography** or **fieldwork**. At the same time, critical postcolonial theorists such as Ranjana Khanna caution against treating psychoanalysis as a "pure" theory devoid of context, effectively dismantling an assumption that psychoanalytic theories are the polar opposites of ethnology. Quite the contrary, Khanna argues that psychoanalysis is "dependent on ethnology, and in fact forms a kind of ethnology suitable for the West, from that form of analysis designed for the Rest" (68). This decolonial stance challenges the fundamental premise of the debates discussed in this section, dedicated to the perceived split between psychoanalytic spectatorship theory on the one hand, and empirical studies of audience and reception on the other.

While psychoanalytic approaches theorized the speculative spectator as influenced by, or constituted through, his/her interaction with the cinematic text, a growing number of feminist film theorists pointed to the gap that this concept creates between the theoretical spectator and the actual living, breathing audience member. This criticism ushered in **empirical audience research** rooted in the fields of communication and cultural studies. Psychoanalytic and empirical frameworks are not mutually exclusive – rather, they give complementary insight into different aspects of the spectatorial process. For instance, while empirical audience research is good at uncovering viewing positions not overtly invited by the text itself yet experienced by some spectators, it cannot fully account for audiences' unconscious drives and motivations since those are, by definition, not something of which individual audience members are consciously aware.

Although not about cinema, Janice Radway's *Reading the Romance* (1984) is a highly influential work within the fields of audience and reception studies of film and media more broadly. In her study, Radway empirically observes and analyzes the reading practices of a group of women who are fans of mass market romance novels. Radway's research relies on numerous methods to understand the reading practices of the women, from interviews to psychoanalytic frameworks. Ultimately, she concludes that no single approach can fully explain the complexity of the phenomenon of women's reading pleasure, but each angle of analysis contributes something to the sense that these reading practices are neither fully oppositional nor fully complicit with the ideology of the genre.

Christine Gledhill distinguishes between the female spectator constructed by the text, and **the female audience**, whose group identity is difficult to essentialize, as it is fractured by various social factors such as class, race, age, sexuality, nationality, ethnicity, and so on. Echoing Claire Johnston, Gledhill argues that "the textual possibilities of resistant or deconstructive reading exist in the processes of the mainstream text" (113). To account for them, she puts forth the concept of **negotiation**, an approach to spectatorship that can bridge "the gap between textual and social subject" (114) and contribute to a more complex understanding of viewing practices that does not categorically jump to either positive or negative conclusions. Understanding spectatorship as a process of negotiation helps us avoid overly deterministic views that typically foreclose some possibilities while excessively focusing on others. Under Gledhill's framework, "meaning is neither imposed, nor passively imbibed, but arises out of a struggle or negotiation between competing frames of reference, motivation and experience" (114). As Gledhill's title suggests, negotiating the intended and often contradictory meanings within a film can in fact be a source of pleasure for the viewer.

In her influential empirical study of female film audiences, *Star Gazing* (1994), Jackie Stacey analyzed written feedback from British women who were fans of 1940s and 1950s Hollywood female stars. In embarking on such an analysis, Stacey is interested in troubling the centrality of the spectator-in-the-text in psychoanalytic feminist film studies, but also in examining "how identities are fixed through particular social and historical discourses and representational practices, outside, as well as inside, the cinema" (31–32). To accomplish this, one needs to account for the social discourses and historical locations within which actual audience members operate, rather than theorize about these audiences in generalized, trans-historical and trans-geographical terms. Stacey finds that so-called cultural studies' approaches to audiences and reception open up more possibility for contextualized analyses than do approaches that exclusively theorize the gaze through psychoanalytic frameworks (Figure 2.10).

Film Studies	Cultural Studies
Spectator positioning	Audience readings
Textual analysis	Ethnographic methods
Meaning as production-led	Meaning as consumption-led
Passive viewer	Active viewer
Unconscious	Conscious
Pessimistic	Optimistic

Figure 2.10 Jackie Stacey's chart of the contrasting paradigms of film studies and cultural studies. From *Star Gazing: Hollywood Cinema and Female Spectatorship* (1994: 24)

Audience and reception studies are traditionally more associated with television, perhaps due to television's cultural status as a more immediate and domestic form of entertainment, one that therefore remains more actively a part of the audiences' everyday life. Yet a growing interest in studying film audiences and reception corresponds with a wider "historical turn" in film studies. Janet Staiger's *Interpreting Films* (1992), for instance, is an influential early work on film reception, offering a materialist historiography that focuses on historical context rather than on audience members' individual psychologies or the spectator constructed by the film text. Importantly, Staiger notes that **reception studies** do not attempt "to construct a generalized, systematic explanation of how individuals might have comprehended texts, and possibly someday will, but rather how they actually have understood them. Additionally, and consequently, reception studies criticized the notion of the ideal reader as ahistorical" (8). Of course, it is difficult to pinpoint how audiences have "actually" understood something for a number of reasons, including the possibility of that understanding changing or shifting over time. Nevertheless, reception studies aim to account for the reactions of real audience members in contextual and situated ways. In contrast to the empirical approaches discussed earlier, Staiger focuses on **discourse analysis**. Rather than interviewing audience members, she examines the media reception of the film to locate a film's meanings in a particular context. Her well-known study of the reception of *The Silence of the Lambs* (Jonathan Demme, 1991, US; Figure 2.11), for example, looked at the homophobic and classed dimensions of the film's representation of a serial killer. She situates the perception of homophobia and what we would now call transphobia in the film in the context of the AIDS crisis, which provided the historical context for the film's release. Staiger argues that the film's star, Jodie Foster, was seen as a strong female image for female audiences, but the gay community viewed Foster as a hypocrite for being a (presumed) closeted lesbian actress acting in a film that was read as homophobic in the context of early-1990s American sexual politics. Foster, at that time quiet about her sexuality, was therefore sacrificially "outed" in the media. Staiger is

Figure 2.11 Buffalo Bill as a gender-bending serial killer in *The Silence of the Lambs* (Jonathan Demme, 1991)

thus interested in the complex and contradictory meanings that circulated around *The Silence of the Lambs* in the specific historical and cultural context in which it was released, as represented through its reception in the media.

One of the most striking examples of reception studies is Jacqueline Bobo's work on the reception of the film *The Color Purple* (Steven Spielberg, 1985, US; Figure 2.12) by black female viewers (1988). The film, an adaptation of Alice Walker's prize-winning 1982 novel, received mixed reviews and garnered controversy because some critics found that its depiction of a Southern black community was overly negative and stereotypical. This charge was rendered more troubling by the fact that the film was directed by Steven Spielberg, a mainstream Hollywood filmmaker and a privileged white man who claimed that the story was not about race. Specifically, there was concern that the explicit gender politics of the book were washed out in the film through its narrative strategies, alterations and omissions. Regardless, black female audiences overwhelmingly embraced the film, which prompted Bobo "to examine the way in which a specific audience creates meaning from a mainstream text and uses the reconstructed meaning to empower themselves and their social group" (93). As part of her research methodology, Bobo conducted a group interview and gauged the ways in which black female viewers enacted oppositional readings of a mainstream Hollywood film depicting racial and gender issues. Bobo deploys Stuart Hall's influential encoding/decoding model of interpretation (1980), which accounts for the different ways in which we can understand

Figure 2.12 Female bonding in *The Color Purple* (Steven Spielberg, 1985)

or decode texts: dominant interpretation (or the one intended by its creators), negotiated (one that takes into account the intended meanings but does not take them for granted) and oppositional readings (which go against the intended interpretative grain). Through this theoretical framework, Bobo dismisses the possibility that black women's positive reception of *The Color Purple* is a simple example "of internalizing negative stereotypes imposed on them by white ideology or 'false consciousness'" (102). Rather, the viewers that Bobo engages with are much more active readers of the text, who are critically aware that their experience "has never been adequately dealt with in the mainstream media" (102).

Viewers are actively engaged in negotiating and reappropriating the subject positions provided by the text, rather than passively submitting to their limitations – the viewing subject does not only receive a film but also creates its meaning anew in the act of viewing. This implies that identity is fluid and malleable, and that a clear-cut alliance between our own identity traits and those of the characters depicted on the screen is not a given, nor the only guarantee of identification. Our identification with figures on the screen does not follow a mirror-like process by which we affectively respond to characters that are most like us. Nor are our own identities as viewers fixed and stable in the world outside of the film. In the following section, we discuss fandom, where processes of identification and cooptation come to the fore in striking ways.

ACTIVITY

Come up with a short survey about a film the class has recently screened and have your peers complete it. Look for 3–5 reviews of the film online and see how the film was received in the media.

Discuss the survey as a group. What information did your survey enable you to glean, and what dimensions of the audience experience did it fail to capture? Would interviewing be a more fruitful approach? Did the survey and group discussions highlight different dimensions of the film's reception than the reviews you read? What might account for these differences?

MEDIA FANDOM AND PARTICIPATORY CULTURE

In this section, we discuss how active fans and cultural activities developed around **fandom** have changed the landscape of spectatorship and reception studies, as well as the ways we understand the role of film and media in our lives. While fandom is not a new phenomenon, nor solely associated with the digital era, digital technologies have raised new questions for thinking about the relationship between the viewer and the screen (for more on fandom, see Chapter 8). We live in an era of what Henry Jenkins has called **convergence culture**, "where old and new media collide, where grassroots and corporate media intersect, where the power of the media producer and the power of the media consumer interact in unpredictable ways" (2006: 2). These collisions have generated **participatory culture**, which Jenkins locates in the blurring of the lines between media producers and media consumers. Jenkins finds that the figure of a **fan** is one of the most interesting contemporary examples of the shift from traditional to participatory culture: a fan is nowadays a person who not only likes and engages with particular media content, but is also someone who often produces new content by reappropriating the original text(s). In participatory culture, the binary opposition between subject and object, meaning-maker and meaning-receiver is blurred if not entirely disposed of. Evidence of this can be found in audience-driven aggregate scores on websites like Rotten Tomatoes, Amazon, or Netflix, as well as in **fan art** and **fanfiction** (or **fanfic**), where the original text – be it a movie, a TV show, or a book – serves as a springboard for the fans' own cultural production, interaction and exchange. And while the initial source of such activities can be mainstream media texts, the bulk of the ensuing fan interactions take place outside of mainstream media pathways, thus circumventing corporate centrality as producers or overseers of cultural content. In many ways, fandom has been the most visible confirmation of the theory that audiences receive texts in varied and often unpredictable ways, and make these texts their own. Fan studies have, as a result, focused on the ways in which fandom challenges the assumption that audiences are passive, and that they receive a text's preferred meanings uncritically.

One of the earliest and best-known forms of media fandom was inspired by the TV series (and subsequent movies) *Star Trek*. The original series began airing in the 1960s and quickly garnered a cult following including a sizable percentage of women. *Star Trek* fandom is associated with the origins of **slash fiction**, fan writing that brought the characters Kirk and Spock together in various romantic and sexual scenarios. Slash fiction gets its name from the slash that fans place between the two characters that are being "paired" in the fiction, in this case "Kirk/Spock," or "K/S." Constance Penley (1997) estimates that the slash genre originally emerged in the first half of the 1970s. Since its appearance, the majority of slash fiction authors have been heterosexual women – Joanna Russ describes it as "pornography by women, for women, with love" (1985: 79). For Penley, the lack of satisfying female characters motivated women to rewrite the narrative using the only characters with whom they could identify – who happened to male. Furthermore, by making Kirk and Spock lovers, but not gay, women slash writers could occupy either position in the relationship, or be a potential observer. That is, they weren't excluded based on the sexual preferences of their protagonists. Penley was thus seeing cross-gender forms of identification at work in the fanfic. Though slash-based *Star Trek* fandom, like its contemporaries, was originally distributed through print fanzines, "by the mid 1990s," observes Sara Gwenllian Jones (2002), "slash had moved onto the web along with much of the rest of fandom, a shift that increased both its visibility and accessibility" (80). Online fandoms helped spread slash fiction centered on female characters – such as Xena and Gabrielle from the show *Xena: Warrior Princess* (Figure 2.13) – referred to as **femslash**. It has also made visible an active demographic of queer female fanfic authors. Jones finds that slash fiction can be better understood if we approach it not merely as a form of subversive reading against the grain, but rather "as an actualization of latent textual elements" (82), meaning that fans often pick up on a show's unspoken subtext and build fan fiction from there. This is possible because "cult television series are already 'queer' in their constructions of fantastic virtual realities that must problematize heterosexuality and erase heterosexual process in order to maintain their integrity and distance from the everyday" (90). Rather than seeing fan fiction as mere reappropriation, then, it may be more useful to see it as an active and open-ended interaction between fans and media content that is circular rather than one-directional. Other notable fandom groups that involve slash fiction include *The X-Files*, *Buffy the Vampire Slayer*, and *Harry Potter*. Nowadays, fandoms

Figure 2.13 Xena and Gabrielle, the inspiration for femslash fanfiction (*Xena: Warrior Princess*)

are mainly organized through online platforms such as social media groups, websites, blogs, and forums, making connectivity easier and less constricted by geographical boundaries. However, this visibility also means that corporations have more access to (and therefore potential to reappropriate or challenge) fan creations.

The rise to cultural prominence of media fandom has important implications for feminist film and media studies, as it opens up new channels for understanding media's impact and influence on female audiences and feminist politics, and conversely, the underrepresented fans' influence on media industries. The study of fandom gives us insight into the bottom-up cultural politics whereby grassroots fan communities increasingly impact mainstream media, rather than being only on the receiving end of product consumption. This is particularly important when it comes to women's, queer, trans, and other underrepresented stories. The name of one online fan archive, *An Archive of Our Own*, suggests these politics of representation in its reference to Virginia Woolf's *A Room of One's Own*. The need for a space to create and express one's (often socially unsanctioned) desires is aided by the anonymity of the internet. Contributors can find both a sense of community through these forums, while also maintaining a level of anonymity that keeps them free from the fears of "real world" repercussions. In Chapter 8, we discuss the internet more broadly, and the ways in which inequalities that exist outside of the digital realm are often reproduced online. Spaces like *An Archive of Our Own* provide subcultural spaces for building community on the web (a space that can often be hostile to non-normative identities). The archive houses thousands of fanfic works, including, notably, works of **transfic** – a more recent genre of fan fiction that features transgender characters, typically those that are not designated as transgender in the original source. Examples of transfic include such popular cultural fixtures as Marvel's Avengers and Peter Parker/Spider-Man envisioned as transgender characters.

An example of the broader cultural influence of fandom is a grassroots initiative for Hollywood to produce a movie starring Rihanna and Lupita Nyong'o. The initiative started when a fan circulated a picture of the two women at a fashion show on Tumblr, envisioning them as stars of a heist movie (Figure 2.14). Eventually both stars embraced the idea on Twitter, which prompted Ava DuVernay to express interest in directing the film, and Issa Rae to agree to write the script. Netflix secured a preliminary deal, demonstrating how participatory culture has permeated the vertical industry structures of Hollywood filmmaking.[1] Moreover, the absence of mainstream movie narratives produced and driven by black women's experiences – or at least films that are not focused on black women solely as victims in need of rescue – makes the case for Rihanna and Lupita Nyong'o's "Twitter movie" all the more urgent and timely. As Kristina Busse notes, "the story of media fandom is one steeped in economic and gender concerns, from the beginning, when women began creating the narratives commercial media

Figure 2.14 Rihanna and Lupita Nyong'o: "Twitter movie" and the power of grassroots fan activity

wouldn't offer" (2009: 105). This can often trigger what Busse calls "a radical politics of digital reappropriation" (106), as fans produce the content that mainstream media has neglected.

Here then, we see how fans can actively generate or inspire content that is otherwise missing in the mainstream culture, calling attention to underrepresented or overlooked experiences in the process. At the same time, fan cultures have been increasingly "industrialized" or incorporated into the decisions made by big media conglomerates, from how new projects generate initial buzz at Comic-Con gatherings, to how fans rate films on Rotten Tomatoes. This prompts Kristina Busse to ask: "When media industries interpellate specific types of fans, what happens to the ones that do not fit?" (2015: 111). Some fan voices are heard and addressed by the dominant media, and others are ignored or excluded. Busse identifies, in her reflections on feminism and fandom, "the new geek hierarchy of positive (white, male, straight, intellectual, apolitical) and negative (person of color, female, queer, embodied, political) fan identities." This hierarchy "creates legal and economic chasms" (114) that may reiterate existing power structures rather than dismantle them. The ways in which objects of cult fandom are often gendered masculine can be seen in the violent reactions of some male fans to recent films like *Mad Max: Fury Road* (George Miller, 2015, US) and *Ghostbusters* (Paul Feig, 2016, US; Figure 2.15). In both cases, the insertion of powerful women who control the narrative arc of the film was perceived by some male fans as a defamation of the original (masculine) cult object.

Figure 2.15 The all-female remake of *Ghostbusters* (Paul Feig, 2016) was targeted with a sustained negative campaign by online trolls from the moment the project was announced

Additionally, fans' love for a media product can be exploited by media industries. Fan labor is treated as "labor of love" rather than as actual (i.e. paid) labor. It may be referenced, cited, and even plagiarized by corporate media without any acknowledgment of the source (fan-created) material. Fan labor is, according to Busse, an important feminist issue since "feminism has long had a central stake in labor theory through its focus on the ways in which reproductive labor tends to be unpaid or underpaid" (113). This is precisely why feminist interventions into fan cultures remain a vital area of both academic study and cultural activity. Moreover, feminist fan studies can avoid the perpetuation of Western-centric approaches to global digital cultures and the dominance of Anglophone content. This can be done, for instance, by paying particular attention to transnational connectivities and trajectories of fandom across geographical and other borders in ways that do not implicitly reaffirm the hegemonic dominance of the West (for more on non-Western fandoms, see Chapter 8).

ACTIVITY

Do some internet research into media fandom (visit websites such as fanfic.net or Ao3.org, *An Archive of our Own*). What are some of the most popular current television series or movies that are the object of slash or trans fiction? What kinds of representations do these stories recognize that are absent from their authorized television sources? Do you find the fiction to be culturally subversive? How does this form of active fandom challenge or expand on theories of spectatorship and/or reception? How are the creators of such work protected by the anonymity of online culture?

CASE STUDY: *MISERY* (ROB REINER, 1990, US) AND *JULIE GANAPATHI* (BALU MEHENDRA, 2003, INDIA)

In the movie *Misery*, a psychological horror film based on Stephen King's novel of the same name, a psychotic female fan, Annie Wilkes, holds a famous writer, Paul Sheldon, hostage and orders him to write another installment in his romance novel series, which previously ended by killing off its female protagonist – the eponymous Misery (Figure 2.16). Annie, a single middle-aged woman living in rural Colorado, is pathologically obsessed with the series, and the thought of the heroine being killed off pushes her into psychosis, contributing to an escalating list of horrors to which the writer is subjected. The film probes the dark limits of the interaction between an author, a text, and a fan, so much so that the roles are often switched and the lines between the author and consumer are blurred – as when Annie, for instance, dislikes a draft of the new novel and orders Paul to write a new one, demanding a particular outcome that would satisfy her as an obsessed fan. As its genre limits dictate, the film does not delve deeper into Annie's mental illness other than staging it as a source of horror and threat. By extension, the stereotype of a lonely and unfulfilled female fan is pushed into the domain of the pathological, as a useful plot device, rather than deconstructed or challenged.

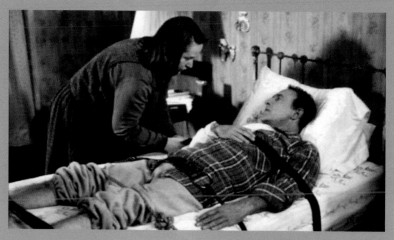

Figure 2.16 A crazed fan in *Misery* (Rob Reiner, 1990)

Stephen King's novel received another film adaptation, this time as an Indian Tamil psychological thriller *Julie Ganapathi* (Figure 2.17). Tamil cinema is one of the largest branches of the Indian film industry, producing films in the Tamil language in the Indian state of Tamil Nadu (this branch of the Indian film industry is sometimes referred to as "Kollywood"). *Julie Ganapathi*, apart from the insertion of song-and-dance numbers that adhere to broader Indian cinema

Figure 2.17 *Julie Ganapathi* (Balu Mehendra, 2003), an Indian Tamil remake of *Misery* (Rob Reiner, 1990)

conventions, is a generally faithful adaptation, with the exception of one important update – the protagonist, Julie, is here an obsessive fan of a TV show called *Manga*, and holds its creator, Tenkasi, hostage in order to get him to write the show in a way that satisfies her. In this cross-cultural adaptation then, fandom is transferred from romance novels to a TV show, while the obsessed fan remains a lonely and unfulfilled, overweight woman whose fandom fills various voids in her life.

In their own way, both films offer insight into the gendered dynamics of media production and reception – as well as female spectatorship in the case of *Julie Ganapathi*. In each film, the focus is on male-created media content designed specifically for female consumers, in the form of romance novels and soap operas. The popularity of the male authors' products pivotally depends on the dedication of their female audiences. Both films explore what happens when fan dedication takes a morbid turn. Yet the male author is not depicted as the entirely sympathetic victim of a crazed woman in either film. Rather, they are clearly identified as the ones who exploit female fandom and reproduce various stereotypes in order to keep their audiences hooked, even when they themselves are skeptical of or look down on the content they create (and implicitly, on the fans of that content as well). In the end, in both films the male author lives to tell the story of his victimization and survival, yet the ambiguity of his own complicity remains.

Watch and discuss: *Misery* and *Julie Ganapathi*

1 How do contemporary ideas of fandom challenge the older stereotypes of fans exemplified in *Misery* and *Julie Ganapathi*?
2 Do you think that male fans are viewed the same way as female fans, culturally speaking?
3 Would the power dynamics and psychological pathologizing seen in *Misery* and *Julie Ganapathi* look different if gender roles were reversed? (See also the discussion of *Fan* in Chapter 4 for a Bollywood film that features a male-male fan-star obsession).

DISCUSSION QUESTIONS

1 Think of the last film you've seen for this class or in general. What does analyzing it through the psychoanalytic theories of spectatorship discussed in this chapter reveal about the film's gender politics? Does the film cater to the "male gaze," or perhaps challenge it?
2 Think of a film whose gender politics you have found troubling or reiterative of stereotypes. What key concepts and intellectual debates discussed in this chapter could help you illuminate and critique the film?
3 What role do film reviews play in your consumption and reception of films? Where do you read about films you want to or have already seen? Who are the major figures in film criticism, and what perspectives on cinema do they espouse?
4 In contemporary film culture, audience reviews on websites like Rotten Tomatoes or Metacritic are arguably more influential than reviews in traditional media. Are crowdsourced ratings for a film skewed along implicit gender biases? Or do these reviews

SPECTATORSHIP AND RECEPTION

contribute to the diversity of the stories being told and supported by the film industry?

5   Digital culture has afforded new ways for audiences to be active participants in cultural production. What are the ways in which you actively participate in contemporary film culture (through fandom, writing online reviews, voting trailers up or down, and so on), and how might they influence what type of content is being produced?

KEY TERMS

the cinematic apparatus

classical feminist film theory

controlling male gaze

convergence culture

decolonizing approaches

the digital era

discourse analysis

empirical audience research

ethnography

Eurocentrism

fan

fan art

fandom

fanfic

femslash

the female audience

the female spectator

fetishistic scopophilia

fieldwork

masochism

the mirror stage

negotiation

Oedipal scenario

the oppositional gaze

oral stage

pre-Oedipal stage

participatory culture

reception studies

sadistic voyeurism

scopophilia

slash fiction

to-be-looked-at-ness

transfic

NOTE

1 Yohana Desta, "That Twitter inspired Rihanna-Lupita heist movie is actually happening," www.vanityfair.com/hollywood/2017/05/rihanna-lupita-movie-netflix

REFERENCES

Bergstrom, J., & Doane, M. A. (1989). "The female spectator: Contexts and directions." *Camera Obscura, 7*(2–3), 5–27.

Bobo, J. (1988). "Black women as cultural readers." In D. Pribram (Ed.), *Female spectators*. London: Verso, 90–109.

Busse, K. (2009). In focus: Fandom and feminism: Gender and the politics of fan production: "Introduction." *Cinema Journal, 48*(4), 104–107.

Busse, K. (2015). "Fan labor and feminism: Capitalizing on the fannish labor of love." *Cinema Journal, 54*(3), 110–115.

De Lauretis, T. (1984). *Alice doesn't: Feminism, semiotics, cinema*. Bloomington: Indiana University Press.

De Lauretis, T. (1990). "Eccentric subjects: Feminist theory and historical consciousness." *Feminist studies, 16*(1), 115–150.

Doane, M. A. (1982). "Film and the masquerade: Theorising the female spectator." *Screen, 23*(3–4), 74–88.

Doty, A. (2011). "Queer Hitchcock." In T. Leitch & l. Poague (Eds.), *A companion to Alfred Hitchcock*. Oxford: Wiley-Blackwell, 473–89.

Fanon, F. (1952). *Black skin, white masks*. New York: Grove Press.

Freud, S. (1927). "Fetishism." In J. Strachey (Ed.), *Miscellaneous Papers, 1888–1938*, Vol.5 of *Collected Papers*. London: Hogarth and Institute of Psycho-Analysis, 198–204.

Gaines, J. (1986). "White privilege and looking relations: Race and gender in feminist film theory." *Cultural Critique*, (4), 59–79.

Gledhill, C. (2006). "Pleasurable negotiations." In J. Storey. (Ed.), *Cultural theory and popular culture: A reader*. Athens: University of Georgia Press, 111–123.

Hall, S. (1980). "Encoding/decoding." In S. Hall, D. Hobson, A. Love & P. Willis (Eds.), *Culture, media, language*. London: Hutchinson, 128–138.

Hansen, M. (1993). "Early cinema, late cinema: Permutations of the public sphere." *Screen*, 34(3), 197–210.

hooks, b. (1992). "The oppositional gaze: Black female spectators." In *Black looks: Race and representation*. Boston: South End Press, 115–131.

Jenkins, H. (2006). *Convergence culture: Where old and new media collide*. New York: NYU Press.

Jones, S. G. (2002). "The sex lives of cult television characters." *Screen*, 43(1), 79–90.

Kaplan, E. A. (1983). *Women & film: Both sides of the camera*. London: Routledge.

Khanna, R. (2003). *Dark continents: Psychoanalysis and colonialism*. Durham: Duke University Press.

Mayne, J. (1993). *Cinema and spectatorship*. London: Routledge.

Metz, C. (1974). *Film language: A semiotics of the cinema*. Chicago: University of Chicago Press.

Modleski, T. (1988). *The women who knew too much: Hitchcock and feminist theory*. London: Routledge.

Mulvey, L. (1975). "Visual pleasure and narrative cinema." *Screen*, 16(3), 6–18.

Mulvey, L. (1981). "Afterthoughts on 'Visual pleasure and narrative cinema' inspired by King Vidor's *Duel in the Sun* (1946)." *Framework*, 15–17, 12–15.

Penley, C. (1997). *NASA/Trek: Popular science and sex in America*. London: Verso.

Ponzanesi, S. (2017). "Postcolonial and transnational approaches to film and feminism." In K. Hole, D. Jelača, E. A. Kaplan & P. Petro (Eds.), *The Routledge companion to cinema and gender*. London: Routledge, 25–35.

Radway, J. A. (1984). *Reading the romance: Women, patriarchy, and popular literature*. Chapel Hill: University of North Carolina Press.

Russ, J. (1985). "Pornography by women, for women, with love." In *Magic mommas, trembling sisters, puritans and perverts: Feminist essays*. Trumansburg: Crossing Press, 79–99.

Shohat, E., & Stam, R. (1994). *Unthinking Eurocentrism: Multiculturalism and the media*. New York: Routledge.

Stacey, J. (1994). *Star gazing: Hollywood cinema and female spectatorship.* London: Routledge.

Staiger, J. (1992). *Interpreting films: Studies in the historical reception of American cinema.* Princeton: Princeton University Press.

Studlar, G. (1984). "Masochism and the perverse pleasures of the cinema." *Quarterly Review of Film Studies,* 9(4), 267–282.

Studlar, G. (1985). "Visual pleasure and the masochistic aesthetic." *Journal of Film and Video,* 37(2), 5–26.

White, P. (1999). *Uninvited: Classical Hollywood cinema and lesbian representability.* Bloomington: Indiana University Press.

Chapter three

CINEMA AND THE BODY

INTRODUCTION

One of the potential shortcomings of the psychoanalytic or semiotic para-digms that were so predominant in the early years of feminist film studies is their lesser ability to account for affect, emotion, and the audience's bodily encounter with films. For example, psychoanalytic theories of the gaze tend to think about the viewing audience in terms of psychic processes of (gen-dered) identification but lack a robust account of how the body experiences cinema. Because women have been associated historically with the body, as opposed to the mind, feminists have had a heightened investment in these questions. A turn to the body, emotion, and affective sensation has been a feminist strategy for correcting a Cartesian tendency to denigrate the (femi-nized) corporeal in favor of the (masculinized) mind, both to revalorize the body as a source of knowledge and meaning and also to undermine a mind/body dualism. As we will illustrate in this chapter, film theorists have often turned to more philosophical traditions to talk about the body in and on film – for example, to the work of phenomenologists or philosophers such as Gilles Deleuze, who has focused on affect in his writing. This turn to the body inserts the physicality of experience into both cinematic represen-tation and film viewing, albeit in a way that does not imply a binary split between mind and body, but rather their mutual inseparability. As we will see in what follows, the body has been used to better understand the cultural work that genres do, to describe the actual phenomenological experience of encountering a film, to understand the work of filmmakers who exist between cultures and identities, and to move towards a posthuman account of the extra-narrative sensory power of film.

BODY GENRES

An influential essay that attempts to create an account of the body as it engages with cinema is Linda Williams' writing on **body genres** (1991). In this article, Williams looks at "gross" genres – namely melodrama (the "woman's picture"), porn, and horror. Typically, these films tend to be thought of as lower cultural forms. Williams links this cultural devaluation with the tendency of these genres to evoke a bodily response in the spectator – crying in the case of the "woman's picture," arousal in the case of porn, and fear and anxiety in the case of horror. Williams goes on to connect these bodily forms of engagement with particular psychic fantasies and with the kind of spectator they address (for example, male or female). In other words, porn, melodrama, and horror each address differently gendered spectators and provide ways to negotiate various fantasies related to sexual development. For example, horror is targeted at adolescent males and deals with the psychic threat of castration; that is to say, the origin of binary sexual difference. Victims are never quite prepared for their death at the hands of the killer, and often the first victims are women engaging in some sort of sexual activity. Body genres also display the female body onscreen in a manner that mimics the bodily response of the spectator. The woman crying in the melodrama is mirrored by the spectator's tears, the woman aroused or in ecstasy in porn mimics the spectator's own physical arousal, and finally, the woman in abject fear in horror mirrors the fear experienced by the audience. Her analysis gets to some of the ways in which genres, then, are gendered. In this way, Williams brought together psychoanalysis (through theories of fantasy), the body of the spectator, and a feminist perspective. As influential as Williams' essay has been, however, it needs to be contextualized as offering a theory of the body and cinema that is tied to Western (or U.S.) cinema. It remains an open question whether this theoretical model can be usefully applied to "bodily" cinematic genres in other cultural contexts (we discuss genre in more detail in Chapter 7).

PHENOMENOLOGY

One of the earliest methodological approaches to theorizing the body of the spectator in relation to film came from the philosophy of **phenomenology**. Phenomenology is based in the viewer's experience of the world around her. It favors what is called **thick description**: that is, phenomenologists are more concerned with describing the conscious and embodied experience or perception of the film than with analyzing the (largely unconscious) psychic processes evoked in film viewing or in understanding the structures or oppositions that give the film's narrative its underlying shape.

Vivian Sobchack has been an influential scholar in developing a phenomenological approach to film, specifically with her book, *The Address of the Eye* (1991). While phenomenology had certainly influenced film theory previously (most notably the work of André Bazin), Sobchack took up phenomenology in a different way – to emphasize the embodiedness and the **intersubjectivity** of the encounter between film and spectator. Intersubjectivity refers to the relationship between two or more consciousnesses (typically two or more humans, although here we see the film itself is given the status of another consciousness). Some major phenomenological philosophers who preceded Sobchack include Edmund Husserl, Martin Heidegger, and Maurice Merleau-Ponty. Terms such as transcendence, consciousness, intentionality, and idealism are often clues that someone is taking up a phenomenological perspective. In phenomenology, the perceiving subject is a **transcendent consciousness**. This consciousness is directed towards a world: one's experience of this world grounds knowledge of the world, and, importantly gives the world meaning. **Intentionality** in this context refers to the consciousness being directed towards (intended toward) an object in the world – for our purposes here, a film. **Idealism** is often associated with phenomenology because the world is given significance in the mind of the spectator, rather than grounded in an external, material empirical reality. Earlier phenomenologists, such as Husserl, often advocated a kind of disembodied transcendent consciousness, which could bracket its preconceived ideas of the world and encounter it objectively. Sobchack, however, drew in particular on the writing of a later thinker, Maurice Merleau-Ponty, who, of all the aforementioned phenomenologists, was the most insistent on the perceiving consciousness's embodiedness and locatedness in a physical, material world. For Merleau-Ponty, perception is necessarily located and embodied. In the *Phenomenology of Perception* he writes, "we are in the world through our body, and in so far as we perceive the world with our body" (1962: 239). From a phenomenological perspective, the encounter with film, or any media object, is therefore intersubjective and based in the conscious and bodily experience of the viewer. Sobchack writes:

> To ask the question, "What is it to see a film?" is to doubly entail the questions: What is it to see? How does seeing exist and mean? Who is seeing being and what is being seen? These questions refer not only to the spectator *of* the film, but also to the film *as* spectator.
>
> (49)

A phenomenological approach often involves describing sensations – how a film *feels* or what sensations it evokes – before being concerned with its thematic meaning or narrative structure. This can be particularly useful in discussing the work of directors who take a more sensory and less explanatory approach to their subject matter.

One example of a filmmaker who privileges sensation and encounter over dialogue and psychological explanation is contemporary French filmmaker Claire Denis (see the case study ahead). Denis's stories are often elliptical and very rarely rely on expository dialogue. They move from one moment to the next according to a different logic, and often expose bodies in motion or evoke smells or tactile sensations. This mode tends to privilege the affective over the cognitive, or forms of knowledge that lie somewhere outside or beyond language.

Because feminist approaches to phenomenology have tended to draw on Merleau-Ponty's phenomenological philosophy, which emphasizes that consciousness is embodied, they are mindful of the fact that an embodied consciousness may experience the world differently based on its social location. That is to say that each viewer has an experience of the world that is shaped by their relationship to categories of race, class, gender, age, and bodily ability, for example. As a result, the way that one person reads an image may be different from someone who occupies different identity categories and/or has had different life experiences. Put differently, our experience of embodiment is historically and culturally specific and inflects how we perceive the world.

For women, this may mean a different awareness of one's body. As Sobchack writes, "the lived-body's transcendence is ambiguous when it is lived as a woman" (153). Before moving on to what a phenomenological approach might do in practice, it is important to consider this notion of the **ambiguous transcendence** of the female body. In Iris Marion Young's canonical essay, "Throwing Like a Girl" (1980), she examines the ways in which women are often socialized to feel more self-aware of their bodies and to not fully utilize their body's full range of motion. Women often feel excessively embodied, as opposed to being a transcendent consciousness that can bracket off their bodily reality. Young takes a study by a phenomenological psychologist as her starting point, which found that girls tended to throw differently than boys – they tended not to use the full range of motion possible, keeping their body relatively immobile, except for the arm, which even then was not fully extended. Young continues, "Reflection on feminine comportment and body movement in other physical activities reveals that these also are frequently characterized, much as in the throwing case, by a failure to make full use of the body's spatial and lateral potentialities" (142). She goes on to note the ways in which women tend to be less open with their bodies in terms of their stride, to take up less space when they sit down, perhaps crossing their legs and arms over their bodies, and they tend to carry objects like books close to their chest. While these observations are now over thirty years old and Young herself claims no universality for her observations, she notes that they offer some evidence of larger tendencies in how women use and inhabit their bodies. She argues that women physically manifest the social injunction that they not take up as much space as men and thus exhibit less unity with their surroundings, an inhibited intentionality (i.e. a less spontaneous and confident projection towards the world), and finally, an ambiguous transcendence. Rather than active conscious phenomenological subjects, women tend to be aware of themselves as both object and subject, not fully inhabiting the phenomenological consciousness of the philosophical subject. Phenomenological approaches then, while treating the film as an embodied encounter between the viewer and the film, must also acknowledge that not all viewers come to the film experience with the same kinds of bodies and bodily relationship to space.

Focusing on the body and phenomenology, Jennifer Barker writes,

> [I]t is through the tactile experience of the film that we come to understand. Through the skin, we gain a clearer picture of ourselves in relation to others and to history, and we come to recognize that relationship as one of mutual permeability.
>
> (2009: 62)

The film, then, becomes an occasion for the phenomenological subject to move towards a greater understanding of her world. Although the spectator is here given a body that haptically engages with the image (where haptic refers to those aspects of experience that relate to the sense of touch), the medium and viewer are seen as two separate entities, which realize their mutual ability to be affected by one another. The idea of a **haptic image** refers to an image that is tactile, that encourages feeling over mastery, or that reveals textures and colors more than easily recognized objects.

For example, in discussing the concept of the film's "skin," Barker looks at Carolee Schneemann's experimental work *Fuses* (1965, US). This film, shot on 16mm, includes imagery of Schneemann and her partner having sex interspersed with images of her cat watching them. Beyond its overtly erotic (and simultaneously mundane) content, Schneemann has physically altered the skin of the film itself, by painting on and scratching the celluloid, where bits of cat hair and fuzz also become part of the final print and the texture of its images (Figures 3.1 and 3.2).

The film itself is treated as a material body with a marked skin. Barker writes:

> The film obscures its object, not prudishly but playfully, using shadows and superimpositions, among other things, to make vision difficult and thus to invite the viewer to feel rather than see the film, to make contact with its skin. And we respond accordingly. . . . Our

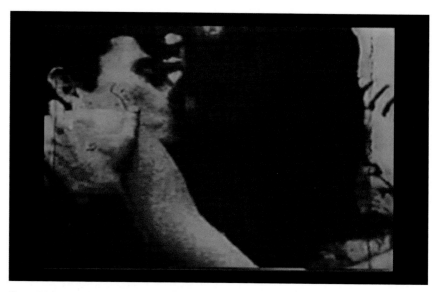

Figure 3.1 Scenes from Carolee Schneemann's *Fuses* (1965)

Figure 3.2 Scenes from Carolee Schneemann's *Fuses* (1965)

eyes skitter over the film, enjoying the textures we can't identify but can only feel; or we squint and try to hold the film in place, try to look past the fluttering specks of dust and cat hair in order to get a clearer view.

(23)

Fuses both insists on the materiality of the image and is also a powerful representation of female desire from a female perspective.

Another way in which images can act haptically is through their representation of space and dimensionality. Compare the following images from *Take Shelter* (Jeff Nichols, 2011, US) and *Friday Night* (Claire Denis, 2002, France) in Figures 3.3 and 3.4:

Figure 3.3 Differing representations of space: *Take Shelter* (Jeff Nichols, 2011)

Figure 3.4 Differing representations of space: *Friday Night* (Claire Denis, 2002)

Whereas the first image draws on the renaissance tradition of conveying depth of physical perspective (as do many films), the second invites us to feel the image – it privileges sensation over understanding or cognition. It asks our eyes to work differently and requires us as spectators to be more open to the image. One of the reasons that feminist thinkers have been interested in haptic vision is that rather than equating vision with mastery and distance, it tunes us in to the dimensions of vision that involve proximity and bodily vulnerability. Seeing, in haptic images, is not possessing the image but rather engaging with it in a way that may not reproduce dominant forms of knowledge.

In her writing, Laura U. Marks has specifically linked tactile haptic images with the work of what she calls "intercultural filmmakers"; that is, filmmakers working between multiple ethnic and cultural identities. In *The Skin of the Film* (2000), she focuses on the relationship between historical and personal memory and the body (see also the "Trauma" section at the end of this chapter). She writes that, "since memory functions multisensorially, a work of cinema, though it only directly engages two senses, activates a memory that necessarily involves all the senses. I suggest that an understanding of the embodied experience of cinema is especially important for representing cultural experiences that are unavailable to vision" (22). Films like Rea Tajiri's *History and Memory: For Akiko and Takashige* (1991, US) and Mona Hatoum's *Measures of Distance* (1988, UK) address issues of the gap between representations and people or events that are inaccessible due to either temporal or geographic displacement.

Tajiri, a Japanese-American whose parents and grandparents were interned in American concentration camps after the bombing of Pearl Harbor, looks for evidence of the past in archives and through conversations with her family members, many of whom can't remember or choose not to remember this period in their lives.

Her film mixes footage from Hollywood films about the war and the Japanese, historical newsreels, images of Tajiri's own pilgrimages to the sites of her family's internment, and reenactments of memories, with voiceover narration, audio interview with family, and the reading of other texts, such as her nephew's review of the film, *Come See the Paradise* (Alan Parker, 1990, US), which treats the subject of the internment of Japanese-Americans. As Marks notes, the film often relies on artifacts – objects that act as repositories of memories – such as the wooden bird her grandmother carved in a camp. Her grandmother did not remember where the bird came from, until Tajiri found a picture of the bird-carving workshop in the national archives and her grandmother was in the photo. The juxtaposition of official footage with these haunting objects and attempts at reconstruction raises key questions about whose story gets told and how power shapes the versions of history we receive. The Japanese-Americans were forbidden radios and cameras in the camps, so there is a significant lack of footage from their perspective. In that vein, the film is punctuated with a reenacted image memory of a woman – Tajiri's mother, played here by Tajiri – filling a canteen with cool water in a dusty and dry environment (the relocation camp). As Marks notes, "Intercultural works redeem these stranded images by bringing them into the very present, even into the body of the viewer" (53). In some of these images, the water is shown flowing through the hands of the woman, as if it itself represents the memory of the internment, felt without being grasped, elusive yet necessary for life (Figure 3.5). For Marks, many of these images are visually "thin," a lack of depth that is explained by their attempt to get at an event that is in some sense inaccessible. This inaccessibility can also be traced to the effects of trauma, which we discuss in a subsequent section. The images lack the sense of fullness that may accompany another type of representation. As Tajiri's voiceover notes, her mother can't remember the camps, but she remembers why she can't remember: her mother's voice enters the soundtrack to recount how one woman who couldn't forget lost her mind as a result.

Figure 3.5 A "thin image" in *History and Memory* (Rea Tajiri, 1991)

Measures of Distance shares with *History and Memory* layered audio and visual tracks, although in Hatoum's film the layering is much more continuous, weaving a dense audio and visual fabric around a series of memories, or distances. Images of Hatoum's naked mother, exiled from Palestine to Lebanon, slowly come into focus underneath layers of Arabic letters written by Hatoum's mother (Figure 3.6). Recorded conversations in Arabic are layered with Hatoum reading the letters in English translation – letters that address the distance between mother and daughter, between mother, daughter and homeland, and issues of sexuality and the body as they relate to the intimate and candid exchange that the women shared around the taking of the photographs. The audio and visual layers multiply the levels of distance between the women, and between the present and the past through photos and letters, themselves markers of an absence – a body that is not there to see or hear in reality. Both of these films, then, use objects to access something that is not fully there – the body of the desiring mother and the history of forced relocation.

Both of these films are also examples of what Hamid Naficy has called **accented cinema** (2001; see also Chapter 1). Like intercultural cinema, accented cinema is a form of transnational (often feminist) cultural production, occurring across and between borders. Accented films are made by and about those living between nations and cultures, due to exile, diasporic

Figure 3.6 "He still nags me about it as if I have given you something that only belongs to him." Hatoum translates her mother's letters from the Arabic in *Measures of Distance* (Mona Hatoum, 1988). Here, her mother discusses her father's reaction to the nude photos Hatoum took of her

resettlement, migration, or being born into multi-ethnic contexts. In our increasingly globalized world, this describes the lived experience of an ever-growing number of people. According to Naficy, one of the features of accented cinema is a tactile optics:

> The dominance of vision . . . is attenuated for the exiles by the prominence of the other senses, which continually and poignantly remind them of their seemingly irrevocable difference, loss, or lack of fit. A particular fragrance on the hillside, a stolen glance in a restaurant, a body brush in a crowded street, a particular posture by a passenger in an elevator, a flash of memory during daily conversations, the sound of familiar words in one's native tongue heard from an adjoining car at a red traffic light – each of these sensory reports activates private memories and intensifies the feeling of *displacement*, a feeling that one may have suppressed in order to get on with life. However, just as frequently and powerfully, these very reports may serve the opposite function of restoration and *emplacement* – by reestablishing connection.
>
> (28)

For Naficy, besides sensory and textural images, tactile optics also manifest themselves in their form, which is often nonlinear and involves montage that collapses or juxtaposes "multiple spaces, times, voices, narratives, and foci" (29). These aesthetics are evident in both Tajiri's and Hatoum's work.

ACTIVITIES

1 Pick a scene from the last film viewed in class that you had a notable bodily response to. Work at describing the scene and the way in which your body experienced the scene. Does what you've written represent something crucial to the experience of the film that would be missed by analyzing the formal elements in relation to the content/themes alone?

2 See a film at a theater that you don't normally visit. Describe how the space in which you viewed the film impacted your experience of it. Were the seats comfortable? What kind of audience were you sharing the space with? Compare this with watching a film at home on your computer.

3 Watch Spike Lee's short film *Mo'ne Davis: Throwing Like a Girl* (2014, US). Does the film challenge or confirm Iris Marion Young's conclusions about feminine motility?

CASE STUDY: *NÉNETTE AND BONI* (CLAIRE DENIS, 1996, FRANCE)

French filmmaker Claire Denis' fourth feature film *Nénette and Boni* moves farther away from narrative than any of her previous work and towards a cinema that privileges the sensory over the cognitive. It tells the story of a teenage girl, Nénette, who runs away from her boarding school to her brother – Boni's – home in Marseille. Boni, himself only nineteen, has inherited their dead mother's apartment and lives there with a group of friends and his pet rabbit. The kitchen is messy with a barren fridge and the apartment feels transitory and uncared for. Boni sells pizza from a truck with his roommate and also dabbles in the black market.

Boni projects fantasies of love and sex onto the character of the baker's wife or boulangère. Boni spends much of the film narrating his aggressive sexual fantasies towards this woman, sometimes with dream-like visual accompaniment spliced in. Nénette, for her part, seems indifferent to sex, despite the revelation that she is pregnant. At times, the film implies that the child's father may be Nénette's own. Boni is estranged from their father, who is linked throughout the film to a criminal underworld and is eventually shot. The film elliptically tracks the siblings' relationship, culminating in the birth of the child "under x" – Nénette has chosen to give her child up anonymously once it is born. Ultimately, Boni takes the child from the hospital at gunpoint, presumably to raise it himself. While the various plot elements such as teen pregnancy, murder, criminality, and kidnapping may seem to suggest a highly dramatic film, the portrayal of events is muted and unmelodramatic. The film creates, through music, editing, and camerawork, a flowing dream-like quality that floats between characters and scenes, privileging smells, colors, sounds, and feelings over linear narrative and dialogue. Dialogue is sparse and becomes almost part of the soundtrack and the mise-en-scène is dominated by close-ups shot with often shaky hand-held camera, and frequent slow pans over faces, bodies, and spaces.

The film's aesthetic and editing create a drifting quality at the formal level that echoes the ways in which both siblings are adrift in the world. The first image of Nénette shows her floating through the water, impassive and ephemeral (Figure 3.7). This is followed by

Figure 3.7 Nénette floating in *Nénette and Boni* (Claire Denis, 1996)

a scene of Boni and his friend driving wildly through the streets of Marseilles, eventually passing the boulangère and shouting vulgarities at her. In its sensual drift, the film explores meanings that are difficult to put into language. The elliptical editing and multisensory non-causal movement between scenes encourage the spectator to experience the film outside of modes of cognition or understanding, exposing her to existence, rather than forcing a meaning or lesson on her.

Often in Claire Denis's films, it is unclear whose dreams we are seeing (A character's? The camera's?), or whether an image is a memory or fantasy. Many image sequences are not meant to explain causality or psychology but to float across the screen, filling it with scents, textures, colors, and affects. At the same time, these images splinter the world of the film, inserting an unmasterable difference into the diegesis. In one scene, Boni wakes up to a trail of brioche leading his way down the hall. As Boni's world has often been filled with fantasy images, we assume this is going to lead to an erotic scenario. Boni picks up a brioche and gently caresses it with a "Bonjour," after which we see him bite into the pastry on his patio. The film then cuts to Boni, back inside and sitting next to his coffee maker, which gurgles and exhales sensually (this machine comprises a very haptic and erotic aspect of the soundtrack) behind a small mountain of brioche, one of which he squeezes rhythmically (Figures 3.8 and 3.9).

Figure 3.8 Boni follows the trail of brioche (*Nénette and Boni*, Claire Denis, 1996)

Figure 3.9 Boni caresses the brioche (*Nénette and Boni*, Claire Denis, 1996)

It is possible that Nénette has purchased and arranged the baked goods after reading Boni's diary, in which he narrates his bakery-related fantasies; however, the film leaves this unclear. Boni's immediate acceptance of the existence of the buns is puzzling if they are not an element of his fantasy life. There is a surreal blurring of dream and reality here that the film's general tone encourages us to accept and float with. It works against direct narrative meaning as it privileges a sensory drift over viewer comprehension.

Although the film deals with broken familial ties and a teen pregnancy, it never judges or moralizes its characters. Its look is curious rather than categorical. As Nénette herself says to the nurse as she goes into labor, "Don't moralize me!" This does not mean that it lacks a politics, per se, but rather that it does not aim to give the viewer a set of maxims or truths that she can walk away from the film feeling self-content about having reaffirmed or gained. The film lacks any moral judgment about Nénette's pregnancy or her attitude towards it – she wants to abort the child but is told that she is too far along. She attempts to abort the baby herself by bathing in a tub of mustard – but is stopped by Boni's intervention. And countering standard narratives about motherhood, she shows no positive emotion towards the child, remaining indifferent to it during ultrasounds, calling the technician a "dumb bitch" and refusing to look at or touch the baby once it is born. Her labor is experienced as an unbearable suffering and Denis does not turn the child's birth into a moment of melodramatic maternal awakening in Nénette. In many ways, Nénette refuses our pity, as much as she obfuscates any understanding. The film encourages an openness to her singularity that must remain sensed rather than cognized. She *exists* before being subsumed under any meaning-giving label, be it that of teenager, girl, or mother.

Boni similarly refuses condemnation or redemption. He is shown engaging in contraband sales and having aggressive and nonconsensual sexual fantasies about the boulangère and other women. (His language is peppered by such colorful imperatives as, "Come here you bitches. Come and eat daddy.") His dreams move into the realm of the real when he approaches the bakery counter and asks the boulangère for a "long French stick." Visibly uncomfortable with the interaction, she calls out for her husband to replenish the baked goods. One could easily assume that a protagonist such as Boni, with his misogynist rants and repressed emotional rage, would be a fairly unsympathetic character in front of a female director's lens. Yet, Denis has expressed her identification with Boni in interviews, and her manner of filming him suggests that his character fascinated rather than repulsed her. He is given full human complexity and not simply dismissed as a category or type. This treatment works to demystify constructs of masculinity and refuses to only shed light on characters we assume self-evidently to be worthy of our gaze. For, ultimately, Boni too occupies a position on the margin from which he struggles to survive. In both the representation of Boni and Nénette then, a feminist ethics is at work. Ethics here refers to a way of relating to the other that works against objectifying or oppressing them. In this case, it is an ethics that refuses to define people primarily in terms of social categories like "woman," "delinquent," or "mother," which can determine and limit people in advance of experiencing who they are in their singularity. Instead, it asks us to be open to experiencing characters as they are – to allow them to keep moving or drifting instead of trying to reduce their complex personhood to simple pre-defined terms.

Watch and discuss: *Nénette and Boni*

1   What about this film makes a phenomenological reading a good methodological choice?
2   How does the film evoke smells, tastes, or other sensations?
3   In your opinion, what is the film *about*? Does its meaning relate more to what we understand happens in the film or to what we feel during the film?
4   How does music function in the film?
5   What is the relationship between identity categories and the realities of the characters onscreen? Do they defy or fulfill our expectations as viewers?

DELEUZIAN APPROACHES

Near the beginning of Leos Carax's film *Holy Motors* (2012, France), a wealthy businessman is seen leaving his modern mansion, calling goodbye to his children, and entering a limousine that awaits him in a large driveway. His chauffer is a well-dressed attractive woman. They exchange pleasantries as she gives the man his first assignment of the day. As he rifles through the folder he is given and makes business calls on his cell phone, an expectation is created that he is headed to an important meeting, negotiation, or interview. Instead, we discover that his assignments involve changing costumes and performing different identities – by the end of the film we realize that even this businessman identity is a performance, and that his "real self" is something we have never seen and therefore have no access to.

Getting into character in the back of the limousine, "Mr. Oscar," as he is sometimes called, changes before our eyes into characters that span different ages, different genders, and even stretch into the world of the fantastic. For his second assignment, he emerges in a black form-fitting suit that covers everything but his face. He enters a warehouse where we see him engage in a thrilling display of acrobatics for a motion capture machine in a large dark room. Points of light emanate from the motion capture suit as he flips over, fights heroically against no one, and runs at top speed on a treadmill shooting a machine gun. He is nothing but a force in the world, light and movement, his identity unknown and obscured by the costume and lighting. Suddenly, a woman enters in red latex. A latex mask covers her face and the two bodies begin to intertwine, erotically moving in unison as they continue to perform balletic poses. They become as one force and one image – again, there is essentially no narrative content to the scene here as the two engage in what seems an anonymous and unrehearsed exchange of intensities and affects.

The soundtrack provides a pulsating, breathing rhythm that accentuates the polymorphous eroticism of the exchange. The camera eventually drifts away to the CGI rendering of the couple's movements – they are rendered as two alien snake-like forms sexually engaged in a barren rocky landscape (Figures 3.10 and 3.11). A continuum is established between human and alien, mammal and reptile, real and animated, bodily and technological. Moreover, in this enactment the film calls attention to the ongoing technical developments of the cinematic medium itself, where CGI images frequently replace "real" places and people.

While it is possible to address this scene – and the film more generally – using perspectives that focus on psychic identifications or narrative and thematic dimensions, these frameworks would miss something crucial about what the scene, and the film as a whole, *does*. The affective power of the images and forces that are put in motion are left unaccounted for if we solely focus on dimensions like character arc, narrative plot, or what the scene means. This is where a Deleuzian approach can account for some of the more bodily and extra-subjective dimensions of the image. **Deleuzian approaches** get their name from the philosopher Gilles Deleuze, who wrote some of his most influential works with another thinker, Felix Guattari. Deleuzian approaches focus on affect and move away from the spectator/viewer as a

Figure 3.10 *Holy Motors* (Leos Carax, 2012): In the Motion Capture Room

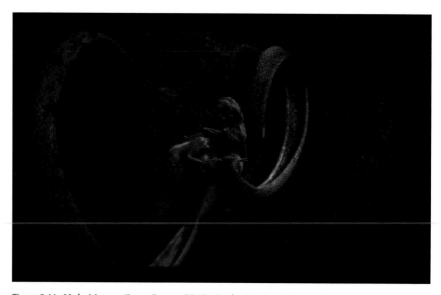

Figure 3.11 *Holy Motors* (Leos Carax, 2012): In the Motion Capture Room

subject. In place of a subject, the viewer becomes a constellation of forces that is perpetually in flux. Deleuzian approaches use a complex specialized vocabulary – terms such as lines of flight, time-images, assemblages, the real and the virtual, and bodies-without-organs are just a handful of the theory-specific terminology one might see in a Deleuzian account. This new and often abstract vocabulary is necessary for shifting our thinking away from dominant paradigms that tend to think of subjects as already formed and relatively stable entities. Instead, a Deleuzian philosophy asks us to think in terms of forces and to reframe subjectivity as always becoming rather than being, always transforming outside of itself rather than remaining fixed in its boundaries.

Deleuzian approaches are generally interested in the forces that traverse both film and viewer and that work against larger macro-systems, such as stable characters, identities, positions, or narrative logics. In a Deleuzian framework, we never exist as a static entity but are always becoming, always being altered in conjunction with machines, air, stones, animals – and, importantly, media. This is a major point of diversion from a phenomenological approach. Whereas the latter sees the relation between viewer and film as intersubjective, Deleuzian approaches are interested in a level below or in excess of subjectivity. In other words, they critique the notion of the self or the human as a coherent stable structure that gives fixed meanings to the world and objects in the world based on her perceiving consciousness. Identities – political, gendered, or otherwise – are a result of trying to fix or stabilize the flow of forces in the world into larger coherent and stable systems. In reality, what interests a Deleuzian theorist is the micro-level: the affects and intensities that traverse and alter what is in the world so that nothing ever *is* one thing once and for all, but rather we all are always becoming. If we bring film into this equation, it becomes part of the affective intensities that do things in the world – we become with the film in a human-machine assemblage. These micro-forces are not merely philosophical abstractions; rather, they represent what Deleuze and Guattari called "lines of flight"; that is, revolutionary paths out of the prison-like nature of identities – be that the identity of the self, the state, the church, or otherwise. This is particularly where Deleuzian philosophy gets taken up as a feminist methodology.

As Dijana Jelača writes, a Deleuzian framework,

> can be returned to a feminist political project that sees "woman" as a figure who is always both becoming and becoming undone, yet is nevertheless important to retain, in all her conceptual instability. This figure [of woman] is a site of political struggle over not only contested meanings, but also of continued material inequalities that persist even after the concept of "woman" is theoretically deconstructed as a phantasm. . . . By strategically retaining the temporary stability of the notion of "woman" (while remaining mindful of the pitfalls of essentialism), we can recognize the continued vitality of feminism as a political project that challenges the status quo rather than descending into relativism.
>
> (2017: 450)

In this framework, womanhood and feminism are not static but are both perpetually becoming. In other words, while the idea of women as a category, like that of lesbian and gay, trans, or disabled, may be useful and necessary politically, Deleuzian frameworks allow us to also understand these categories as always being situational and in flux. Since one of the key concepts here is that of affect, let us examine more closely its meaning in its theoretical usage.

Affect is connected to the sensory and to sensation. *Unlike* emotion, it is difficult to label affect as signifying or being any one thing. Emotions or feeling-words are attempts to give meaning to the bodily sensations we experience. For example, we may label the bodily sensations we experience during a horror film as "fear" or "tension." While these labels may be partially accurate, from a Deleuzian perspective, they freeze the dynamic and unnamable reality of affect with a sign that fixes it in time and in terms of what it "means." Affective approaches tend to favor flux and movement over fixed meanings, definitions, or identities. They are interested in the reality of what escapes definition or coherent representation – much as key dimensions of Mr. Oscar's motion capture performance elude our ability to describe them with language. One way of thinking about affect is in terms of excess – there are always aspects of any experience that are missed by our attempts to represent them or to label them. Affect attempts to account for that which exceeds our attempts to label or master the world around us. In another sense, the notion of excess can help us to account for the tension between real and materially productive categories – such as "man" or "woman," "straight" or "gay" – and their actual inadequacy when it comes to accounting for our experiences and capabilities, which always exist in excess of any one identity category. This is one reason why some feminists have found Deleuzian frameworks useful. They provide a way to move beyond or below the level of identity categories – categories which have often been limiting and hurtful – and to creatively think around concepts like race or gender in ways that don't privilege these categories as coherent sites of static meaning.

An example of a Deleuzian approach to film form can be found in the writing of Martine Beugnet (2007). She has argued for what she terms "a cinema of sensation." Focusing in particular on the work of French female filmmakers such as Catherine Breillat, Claire Denis, and Agnès Varda, Beugnet has looked at how formal techniques such as the close-up, when used in particular ways, can turn the image into a sensory experience that privileges exploration and sensation over identity, visual mastery, and fixed meaning.

Take for example this image (Figure 3.12) from another Claire Denis film, *Trouble Every Day* (2001, France):

Figure 3.12 A haptic image in *Trouble Every Day* (Claire Denis, 2001)

In this image, the camera moves across a body exploring it as a landscape. In fact, it is difficult for the viewer to know exactly what they are looking at. As Kristin Lené Hole writes of this scene,

> Tufts of hair that could be a woman's pubic area, a belly button, or an armpit fill the screen. Flesh is exposed such that it is made strange to the eye – a landscape or a palpitating organism that is encountered without a sense of visual mastery or possession. The viewer is exposed to an image that does not allow an easy perspective. This means that the she must remain open to the image as it is slowly revealed in all its viscerality.
>
> (2016: 142)

This connects to the discussion of haptics in the previous section. Rather than an identity, for example "This is woman. This is a woman's breast," the viewer is asked to be comfortable with not knowing exactly what they are seeing, with experiencing the image in its materiality, its tactility, and its formlessness. This is very different than the dominant perspective and style of filmmaking (see also the image comparison in Figures 3.3 and 3.4). For Beugnet, who uses elements of both phenomenology and Deleuzian theory in her writing, one of the reasons this is significant is that when we move below the level of concrete form, or the body as a totality, we move outside of identity categories that are often limiting and/or oppressive, such as "male" or "female." She writes,

In contrast with the body caught in action in medium or long shot, filming in close-up makes it possible to evoke a body that is temporarily freed from its function as social, cultural and even gender signifier – a body that escapes the conventional order of male/female dualism.

(2007: 96)

Here we see a theoretical interest in the way that the film can act at a level below that of identity, to open up different affective connections that don't privilege pre-established categories. While this example examines the way that certain camera techniques can privilege sensation over meaning, there are other possibilities for what a Deleuzian approach might do or look like in practice.

Take, for example, Sally Potter's film *Orlando*, which is based on Virginia Woolf's novel of the same name. It is a painterly, sensual film about a character that lives over 300 years and changes sex from male to female. In the course of the film we see Orlando take on many identities that go beyond simply biological sex – from queen's chosen heir, to lover, to poet, diplomat, mother, and author. The film reveals sexual and gendered identity as performative, fluid, and mutable – subject to restrictions and norms based on cultural and historical context. In that sense, the film shows gender and other forms of identity as always *becoming* rather than *being*. Categories like "love," "politics," and "man" are revealed as fleeting solidifications of the dynamic flux of life. Barbara Kennedy, in her book *Deleuze and Cinema: The Aesthetics of Sensation* (2000) also locates the Deleuzian dimensions of the film in its aesthetic style. In an early scene in the film, which mostly occurs on ice as figures skate in various patterns of alliance and separation, the (young male) Orlando falls in love with a Russian diplomat's daughter, Sasha (Figure 3.13).

Kennedy writes that characters such as Sasha,

work outside any notion of gendered subjectivities or identity. They work through a materiality of the brain/body at a deeper level, in the proto-subjective, in the affective realms. The film's style articulates those 'affective intensities' in the ways it moves and vibrates . . . Sasha, then, rather than being 'read' as a character, with a narrative trajectory . . . functions in locomotion, not as fixed locus of identity, [but rather] as an abstract force.

(136)

As is evident here, one way a Deleuzian theorist might approach film is to analyze not what it means, or what characters represent, but rather to describe the sensations and affects the film produces. Deleuze tends to be less

Figure 3.13 Orlando attempts to capture Sasha, a force rather than "a fixed locus of identity" (*Orlando*, Sally Potter, 1992)

interested in what things are than in what they do. This approach would be less interested in "characters" as stable entities than in the forces they represent onscreen, the ways in which they both solidify as figures of intensity, but also keep moving and becoming through various encounters, contexts and situations, never remaining fixed in their signification. One powerful visual illustration of this occurs in *Orlando*, when she runs through a maze from the 18th century and in the process transforms into a woman of the mid-19th century (Figures 3.14 and 3.15). She is a force moving through the world, changing before our eyes, remaining, in this instance, "woman" but showing how "woman's" meaning alters through time – from powdered wigs and pastel frippery to a dark muted dress and natural, less ornate hair. Just as her sex has altered in previous moments, here in the space of the labyrinth the visual signifiers, and with them the meanings, of gender have altered.

In the film's final scene, Orlando sits under a tree in contemporary London as her daughter runs through the park filming video of what she sees. Here the images alternate between the video, blurry and dynamic, and Potter's camera. Orlando looks up to see a queer angel floating above, singing in falsetto to the dance music on the soundtrack: "Here I am!/Neither a woman, nor a man/We are joined, we are one/With a human face/We are joined, we are one/With a human face/I am on earth/And I am in outer space/I'm being born and I am dying." The lyrics articulate a queer notion of Deleuzian becoming.

Figure 3.14 Orlando travels through the maze of time (*Orlando*, Sally Potter, 1992)

Figure 3.15 Orlando travels through the maze of time (*Orlando*, Sally Potter, 1992)

Moreover, with the entrance of contemporary video technology in the final scene, the film comments on the convergence of gender and shifting screen technologies as mutually implicated in the politics of representation.

A Deleuzian method would involve, like phenomenology, thick description, which includes attention to form: what are the sounds, colors, and tones the film offers and how do they combine to generate particular sensations, or affects? Films that focus less on dialogue and feature elements such as dance or more rhythmic compositions are good examples of the kinds of texts that may be more fruitfully read through a Deleuzian framework than other approaches. It should be noted that many thinkers use a variety of approaches together, mixing Deleuzian and phenomenological traditions, or using notions of affect but connecting them to other paradigms, such as psychoanalysis (which we will see in the section on trauma ahead). The case studies included in this chapter give examples of how these approaches can be applied and lead to fruitful readings of films.

ACTIVITY

Stage a dialogue between three thinkers: one who takes a phenomenological approach, one who takes a Deleuzian approach, and one who takes a psychoanalytic approach. Write a script in which they debate the meanings of a film or a particular scene in a film. This could be videotaped or performed in front of the class. How does each perspective highlight different dimensions of the film experience?

CASE STUDY: *UNDER THE SKIN* (JONATHAN GLAZER, 2013, UK)

As a parable for the posthuman condition, *Under the Skin* can be approached as a genre study of **becoming-woman**. According to Deleuzian arguments, identities never simply exist – they are always in the process of becoming. Womanhood, then, is not a given, natural category, but rather a skin-deep assumption of identity that – in *Under the Skin* – conceals an uncontrollable alien mass underneath.

In the film, a nameless, mysterious alien arrives on Earth and takes the shape of a young, attractive woman (played by Scarlett Johansson). The opening sequence firmly places us within the film's alien form – always somewhat outside of the grasp of our full understanding. As atonal music plays in fast-paced, dramatic rhythm, we see a series of puzzling images – a mysterious circle suddenly becomes a pulsating human eye (Figure 3.16) – and hear the sound of a woman's voice uttering sounds and then words. The film's opening therefore depicts the process of becoming-posthuman, the synergy of organic and inorganic matter, as well as the entrance into language as a signifier of

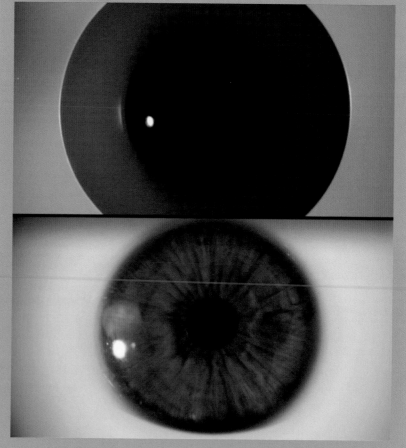

Figure 3.16 Becoming posthuman (*Under the Skin*, Jonathan Glazer, 2013)

subjectivity. The sequence and its accompanying sound are abruptly cut by the title card, after which the film cuts to an outdoor shot of a waterfall – its first conventional frame, nevertheless accompanied by eerie music that suggests threat and an alien atmosphere.

The alien woman spends her days and nights driving around Glasgow in a white van, luring and seducing unsuspecting men with her feminine traits, and then leading them, enthralled and oblivious to the danger, into a black pool of nothingness, into which they eventually dissolve. The film frequently features phantom ride sequences in which the camera embodies the alien's point of view, as she cruises the streets in search of unsuspecting male victims. She is a vigilante loner on a mission, whose motivation is never explained, but is most assuredly both otherworldly, and at the same time an embodiment of a radical feminist threat. This hybrid positionality makes the alien a liminal figure who can be fully empathized with only when she is rendered in the traditional framework of a female victim towards the end of the film. It is productive to read the alien's character in terms of the concept of the **posthuman**, which sees traditional humanist frameworks of anthropocentric understandings of identity, bodily integrity, and subjectivity as inadequate to fully account for our experiences of the world. The posthuman body is located at the intersections of "postmodern relations of power and pleasure, virtuality and reality, sex and its consequences" (Halberstam and Livingstone 1995: 3). The notion of the posthuman challenges the idea of identity as a stable entity persisting through space and time, even challenging the human as a fixed category.

In the film's early stages, it appears that the posthuman femme fatale in the form of a she-alien does not harbor any anthropocentric motivational drives. The film form echoes this alien perspective – as the familiar is frequently made unfamiliar and strange through the alien's point of view and by the use of framing that emphasizes the strange aspects of everyday occurrences. As she moves through space and observes the mundane, the spectator is aligned with the alien's perspective and compelled to perform a phenomenological shift in perception, not taking for granted the familiarity of that which is considered ordinary.

The alien's affectively detached subjectivity persists uninterrupted in a non-anthropocentric (i.e. not centered on the human) moral vacuum until she encounters a man who is socially ostracized because of his severe facial disfiguration. Something in their exchange affectively moves the alien, and compels her to arrive at empathy, perhaps through an encounter with the structures of humanist ableism heretofore unknown to her, which render some humans as inhuman as she is. After leading the man into the black pool, she stops by a mirror – and intently examines her own reflection, enacting a mirror stage of sorts (discussed in Chapter 2). She then releases the man (he is later captured by the alien's male helper nevertheless). The encounter with the disabled other is therefore also an arrival at subjectivity and the emergence of ethics. She appears to realize that not all her victims are the same. It is also the first time she understands and connects with a human being, perhaps identifying the alien dimensions of the disfigured human, who is, in many ways, as alienated and rendered inhuman as the heroine is under her skin.

The film privileges the sensory, haptic experiential domain over traditional narrative plot or exposition. When the alien flees into the forest towards the end of the film, she runs into a ranger who engages her in small talk. Now the roles are completely reversed – the ranger, appearing nonchalant, casually asks her if she is there on her own, in an echo of the questions she posed to her victims. Indeed, he later attacks her, and the threat of sexual violence becomes real. In the ensuing physical struggle, her skin starts to peel off, exposing the alien who resides under the humanoid layer of skin. The skin then, functions as a temporary humanoid container of an alien form. What is under the skin? Something shape-shifting and material, yet elusive, made out of inorganic matter but nevertheless still shaped in female form: the feminine alien posthuman. Yet, the alien is not able to escape the fate of a brutalized woman, even when her human female identity is revealed to be only skin-deep. The more human she becomes, the more susceptible to the masculinist violent threat she appears to be. As the skin starts to peel off, the alien examines her human face (Figure 3.17) in a kind of posthuman mirror stage where one encounters the self as the ultimate other, and rather than it being an entrance into identity, it becomes an entrance into the impossible experience of one's own death. As the alien, shed of human skin, is set on fire by the male attacker, she crawls outside of the forest and dies, surrounded by the tranquility of an indifferent landscape. The film's final shot has the camera facing upwards into the white sky from which snow is slowly

Figure 3.17 The alien posthuman examines her female face (*Under the Skin*, Jonathan Glazer, 2013)

falling. Organic and inorganic forms are fused in what serves as a cinematic study of the feminine as alien posthuman entity.

If the skin is typically understood as the surface limit of our human bodies, and by extension, our beings – albeit one that expands and contracts in unexpected ways – the alien's humanoid skin appears to conceal, to use a Deleuzian vocabulary, a literal **body without organs**.

Deleuze and Guattari use the concept of bodies without organs to theorize structures that run deeper than their surface appearances – bodies without organs denominate shapes "traversed by gradients marking the transitions and the becomings, the destinations of the subject developing along these particular vectors" (1984: 21). At the same time, in the sequences in *Under the Skin* that depict men who descend into the black pool, their bodies dissolve from the inside, to the point where only skin without matter is left. They become skin without organs. In one alien sequence, a red mass is seen floating away after one such bodily dissolve. In the posthuman, alien framework of *Under the Skin*, feminine skin does not cloak a human body, but rather an alien form whose attempts at becoming-human end in brutal death. Becoming-woman is a process imbued with giving humanoid shape to, and thereby effectively concealing, alien forms that reside under the skin (for more, see Jelača 2018).

Watch and Discuss: *Under the Skin*

1 What is the significance of the film's title? How does it relate to issues of embodiment?
2 What is the significance of the opening scene?
3 How does language relate to "her" experience of the world? How does her relationship to language change throughout the film?
4 Does the film reveal anything about gender? As the protagonist becomes more interested in exploring "humanity," how does her experience of gender roles change?
5 What happens when she meets the man with neurofibromatosis?
6 How do we know that the scene where she orders a cake is significant in terms of the formal choices the director makes? Why do you think this is a significant scene, and how does it relate to sensory experience?

DISABILITY AND THE BODY

Turning to issues of disability in relation to the body and cinema has generally meant evaluating how bodies labeled as "disabled" are represented onscreen (it should be noted here that this chapter is focusing on the body, therefore intellectual or less "visible" forms of disability are outside its purview, although no less important to examine in terms of their media representations).

The study of representations of disability in film studies began somewhat later than analyses of race and gender, developing in the 1980s alongside the emergence of disability studies as a field. Paul Longmore's pioneering essay on the topic, "Screening Stereotypes" (1985), examines major tropes of disability in mainstream cinema, including the portrayal of the disabled person as a sympathetic "monster" or a "crippled" criminal, and the figure of the disabled war veteran learning how to cope. Longmore writes, in part, from an activist perspective, critiquing the narrative arcs of many films that reduce disability to an individualized problem of overcoming, or, in some cases, as a problem to be logically solved by suicide or assisted death. Another serious critique of representations of disability is that narratives featuring disabled characters often use them as catalysts for the development of able-bodied protagonists in the narrative.

Clint Eastwood's *Million Dollar Baby* (2004, US) serves as a more recent illustration of some of these narrative tropes at work. The film was a critical success, garnering both a best director and best lead actress Oscar (the latter for Hilary Swank). In the film, the character of Maggie convinces Eastwood's character, Frankie, to coach her in boxing, even though she is a woman and therefore, in his world, not champion boxing material. After achieving great success in the ring, Maggie becomes a quadriplegic after breaking her neck during a fight. Eventually Maggie decides her differently embodied life is not worth living and convinces Frankie to help her commit assisted suicide. Despite the film's positive critical reception, the disability community heavily criticized the film for depicting death as the best option for someone living with a spinal injury. Maggie, a strong and tenacious woman, suddenly loses all will when she becomes quadriplegic and is represented as having no reason to live with a body that doesn't function as it used to. Maggie's character arc fits the trope of the suffering isolated disabled body that is better off dead. She also acts as a catalyst for the emotional and personal growth of the white able-bodied male character, Frankie. As some scholars have pointed out, Maggie's body is not only marked as disabled but also heavily classed (her Appalachian working-class background is a large part of her characterization) and, of course, gendered. Jay Dolmage and William DeGenaro (2005) argue that Maggie's desire to overcome her class is always, like her disability, represented in individualizing terms, as something she can will herself to overcome through hard work. Maggie's working-class mother is represented as obese, which metonymically stands in for laziness, a lack of taste, and greed, all of which serve to perpetuate the myth of class as linked to innate personality traits. Maggie's class ascendency is also displayed through her fit, powerful body. Dolmage and DeGenaro write, "So, for Maggie, class is something to be overcome, and something that she *can* overcome. But disability – also imagined in the film as a personal and corporeal failure – is something that Maggie *cannot* overcome. The difference lies in individuality." That is, the individual cannot independently overcome disability – and the film denies any possibility of community for the non-conforming body.

This isolation is precisely what Martin Norden argues defines the representation of disability in mainstream cinema, or what he calls "the cinema of isolation" (1994). Norden writes that:

> In the case of people with physical disabilities, the movie industry has perpetuated or initiated a number of stereotypes over the years as a part of the general practice of isolation – stereotypes so durable and pervasive that they have become mainstream society's perception of disabled people and have obscured if not outright supplanted disabled people's perception of themselves . . . its more common representations include extraordinary (and often initially embittered) individuals whose lonely struggles against incredible odds make for what it considers heart-warming stories of courage and triumph, violence-prone beasts just asking to be destroyed, comic characters who

inadvertently cause trouble for themselves or others, saintly sages who possess the gift of second sight, and sweet young things whose goodness and innocence are sufficient currency for a one-way ticket out of isolation in the form of a miraculous cure.

(3)

By contrast, representations from within the disabled community itself have been dramatically different. The short documentary film *Self Preservation: The Art of Riva Lehrer* (Sharon Snyder, US, 2004) is notable for the way that it both challenges dominant stereotypes and representations of disability, while also discussing the very history of representations of disability through its subject matter, an artist whose monumental and beautiful paintings focus on notable members of the disability rights community. Her subjects, many of whom are present as talking heads in the film, speak alongside art historians, critical disability scholars, and the artist herself about the paintings *as art*, but also as offering a major counterpoint to controlling representations of disability. The film, like the artwork, challenges the notion that disability is a source of otherness, of lack, of weakness, or of isolation, instead depicting the ways in which different forms of embodiment shape the singularity of the person and their experience and vision of the world. As Nicole Markotíc writes of disability and cinema in general, "representing the experience of 'loss' rarely represents the experience of disability. Films that focus on the absence of an ability almost always manage to convey the opposite experience to that of disabled people" (2008: 7). As one talking head in *Self Preservation* – disability rights and queer scholar Eli Clare – notes, in many medical textbooks the disabled body is portrayed with the eyes blacked out, dehumanizing the disabled subject and making them incapable of looking back. What is noticeable about Lehrer's work is that the disabled gaze is returned. There is a refusal to dehumanize the bodies on the canvas and to make these bodies the object of an unchallenged gaze. This is a strategy the documentary itself echoes in its representation of these formidable subjects, including, first and foremost, Lehrer herself.

Films made from a disability-positive perspective by people with disabilities (PWDs) or their allies, "tend to occupy the farthest economic crannies of the independent film market" (Mitchell and Snyder, 2008: 20) and, as self-representations, illuminate the experiences of non-normative bodies drastically differently than do mainstream cinematic representations that largely favor able-bodied subjects. Some notable entries into this canon include *Born Freak* (Paul Sapin, 2002, UK), which documents the struggles of Mat Fraser – an actor and comedian whose arms were affected by thalidomide at birth – to understand his body against and within the history of the "freak show." *Austin Unbound* (Eliza Greenwood, 2011,

US) documents the top surgery of transman Austin Greenwood, who also happens to be deaf. *Double the Trouble, Twice the Fun* (Pratibha Parmar, 1992, UK) takes as its subject the sexuality of gay and lesbian PWDs. This is just a small sample of documentary-format films that have attempted to offer alternative representations of disability to those of dominant culture. All of these films insist on the subjectivity, sexuality, and often humor, of their subjects and refuse a pathologizing gaze.

There are also an increasing number of higher-profile narrative feature films that provide for a challenging and non-traditional view of disability, from *The Sea Inside* (*Mar adentro*, Alejandro Amenábar, 2004, Spain), and *Rust and Bone* (*De rouille et d'os*, Jacques Audiard, 2012, France/Belgium), to the blockbuster *Mad Max: Fury Road* (George Miller, 2015, US), whose female protagonist, Imperator Furiosa, represents a radical feminist warrior whose physical disability does not prevent her from being the most powerful and in-control character in the film (Figure 3.18). Moreover, the highly provocative film *The Tribe* (*Plemya*, Myroslav Slaboshpytskyi, 2014, Ukraine), which is entirely in Ukrainian sign language and without subtitles, focuses on a deaf and mute subculture of delinquent teenagers, and presents an uncompromising vision of grit and violence that does not romanticize disability or use it as an excuse. Rather, by depicting the narrative strictly from the deaf and mute protagonists' point of view – exemplified by the privileging of their language over spoken language or subtitles – the film

Figure 3.18 Imperator Furiosa, a feminist warrior (*Mad Max: Fury Road*, George Miller, 2015)

asks viewers to actively engage in attempting to understand the narrative, rather than being passively presented with it. It also positions the hearing spectator as an outsider, mirroring the experience of deafness in oral culture. Additionally, a graphic scene of an illegal abortion presents one of the most visceral bodily experiences depicted in recent cinema. The film offers an uncompromising look at the life of petty crime with a bleak future for a youth subculture brought together through physical difference from the norm.

In its insistence on challenging normative notions of bodily identity, critical disability theory has developed a kinship with queer theory in scholarship and filmic practice. Robert McRuer has coined the term **crip theory** (2006), to describe the intersection of queerness and disability as critical analytic frameworks. Crip theory reappropriates the word "crip" from a term of derision and slander to one that celebrates difference from the able-bodied and often heterosexual unmarked norm, as has been done historically with the term "queer." Both queerness and disability have functioned to mark bodies as other to the norm, and in the process reinforce the unmarked, "desirable" heterosexual able-body as norm. The concept of crip, like that of queer, critiques a politics of normalization or inclusion in favor of maintaining the troubling and non-normativizing force of these categories. Queering disability is also a way of insisting on the sexuality of bodies marked as disabled, or on the disabled body as a desiring body, as seen in aforementioned films like *Double the Trouble, Twice the Fun*, and the bigger budget narrative film *Rust and Bone*.

McRuer argues that earlier accounts of representations of disability, such as Norden's, can no longer account for the contemporary representational landscape. He argues that we are seeing a cultural shift towards neoliberal models of "flexible" heterosexual able-bodied subjectivity.

These new flexible forms of dominant subjectivity are able to tolerate or even affiliate with non-normatively abled, gendered, and sexed others. In fact, these "other" bodies often help in the maintenance of the hetero-ableist subject. He writes:

> In many cultural representations, disabled, queer figures no longer embody absolute deviance but are still visually and narratively subordinated, and sometimes they are eliminated outright. . . . Flexibility again works both ways: heterosexual, able-bodied characters in such texts work with queer and disabled minorities, flexibly contracting and expanding, while queer, disabled minorities flexibly comply.
>
> (18)

McRuer's filmic example is *As Good as It Gets* (James L. Brooks, 1997 US), in which Jack Nicholson's OCD-afflicted character is able to shed his disability, and with it, his character flaws, through his entry into a heterosexual relationship, all of which is facilitated by a gay and recently crippled neighbor, who absorbs the difference that the male protagonist sheds along his narrative trajectory. In more contemporary films, then, McRuer argues, forms of disability are not presented in terms of inflexible simplistic notions of good and evil, or as rendering characters monstrous but sympathetic outsiders, but rather disabled (and queer) characters are made to function as support for the character arcs of able-bodied heterosexual characters (or characters who are moving towards more normative forms of subjectivity).

The cinematic framing of differently abled bodies continues to be a fraught cultural issue that reflects deeper attitudes towards disability and its intersections with gender, race, class, sexuality, and national identity. This is precisely why the issue is closely aligned with feminist politics that similarly seek to critique the ways in which certain attitudes towards gender are standardized and naturalized. It is no coincidence, then, that one of the most openly feminist characters to be produced in mainstream Hollywood action cinema – the aforementioned Imperator Furiosa – is not only a powerful woman whose bodily difference does not prove a limitation to her, but who is also a crusader for women, the weak, and the environment.

ACTIVITIES

1 Watch the film *Rust and Bone*. Does its representation of sexuality challenge dominant ideas about the disabled body as asexual? According to Nikolaidis (2013), the film starts out by emphasizing the links between able-bodied/male and disabled body/female only to deconstruct this binary in the second half of the film. In what ways does the film reinforce and then challenge the links between gendered constructions and socially constructed notions of ability?

2 Watch the short film *G.I.M.P. Boot Camp* (Danielle Peers, 2008, US) on Vimeo. How does the film parody dominant tropes about and attitudes towards disability? How does it foreground cultural fears of "becoming disabled"? How does it represent queerness vis-à-vis disability?

TRAUMA

As a scholarly field, **trauma studies** arose through the merging of literary theory, memory studies, psychoanalysis, and Holocaust studies. The field has sought to address the question of how **trauma** is an experience not fully accessible to our consciousness, therefore frequently expressed through recurring dreams and involuntary flashbacks rather than articulated through conscious recall or linear storytelling. The implications of this insight to subsequent studies of literary works and cinema brought about an understanding that trauma is often expressed through non-verbal forms, incomplete or seemingly illogical narratives, temporal disorientations, and silences and memory gaps. In the modern-day meaning of the concept, generally deployed in trauma studies, trauma is understood to be a psychic wound, or a wound of the mind. However, the word's origins in ancient Greek suggest that its initial meaning primarily referred to a physical wound. This transformation in the concept's meaning from a physical to a psychic wound runs the risk of obfuscating the role of the body when it comes to the understanding of trauma in contemporary trauma studies. This tendency can be countered by focusing on trauma's effect on the physical existence of those who suffer from its consequences (or rather, on the ways in which trauma is remembered, expressed or repressed *within* the body). Thereby, the dichotomy between the body and mind is at least partially destabilized. Studying trauma within cinema involves, in part, asking questions about how the inability to fully experience and therefore represent trauma shapes film narrative and film form. How can the unrepresentable be represented? Recent years have seen a rise in the scholarly works that examine the role of cinema in the collective traumatic memory of different catastrophes and conflict zones from around the world, from German cinema in the aftermath of World War II (Elsaesser 2014), media representations of 9/11 (Kaplan 2005), the ongoing occupation of Palestine as represented in film (Gertz & Khleifi 2008), to documentaries about incest and the Holocaust (Walker 2005), and trauma in post-Yugoslav cinema (Jelača 2016). Many of these scholars deploy feminist frameworks to critically examine how trauma is gendered and how gender is traumatic. To that end, Kaplan notes "the implicit gendering of trauma studies, such that traumas of (and perpetrated by) men have been the main focus" (2005: 19). At the same time, **feminist approaches to trauma** do not focus solely on women's experiences; rather, they examine the larger structures that make gender a structuring aspect of traumatic experience and its aftermath, whether one looks at survivor or perpetrator trauma (the latter being a controversial concept that some theorists dispute). For example, in her work, Jelača examines in the post-Yugoslav film context,

> how trauma not only displaces the stability of the categories that
> might have precipitated it, but also becomes constitutive of the new

ways of approaching the difference between Self and Other, be it in gendered or ethnic terms, or at those points where the nexus of the two creates our understanding of what it means to survive.

(102)

She further argues that the insertion of queer trauma within post-Yugoslav cinema challenges the engrained heteronormativity of national traumas of different ethnic groups in the region. For instance, in Želimir Žilnik's *Marble Ass* (1997, Serbia), set in the troubled context of 1990s Serbia, the protagonists are two trans sex workers who imply that their aim in selling sex is to heal the wounds of a society ravaged by conflict and ethno-national upheavals. By addressing ethno-national trauma through a queer lens, the film troubles the heteronormative premises on which the national body is based. This is an example of how film and video can play a central role in addressing cultural traumas, while also challenging the very conceptions of gender and ethnicity that have shaped the traumatic conflict.

When it comes to cultural expressions of trauma, the tension between the individual and the collective is a prominent feature. By the nature of its impact, trauma is an intimate experience. However, the scale of some catastrophes – such as the Holocaust, the nuclear bombing of Hiroshima and Nagasaki, or slavery – inevitably makes them into objects of collective traumatic memories, be they ethnic, national, racial, or organized around some other axis of group identification. **Postcolonial trauma studies** have emphasized moving away from approaches to collective trauma that privilege the white European subject as the preeminent victim of trauma (Saadi Nikro 2014). This entails not only the decolonizing of trauma studies (and, by extension, of trauma itself), but also an undoing of stable or singular parameters of subjectivity. In this respect, the works by Rea Tajiri and Mona Hatoum discussed earlier in the chapter are rich examples of transnational or intercultural films whose form and content are shaped by traumas of war, separation, and forced relocation. These films bring us back to the body, or the fact that some bodies – marginalized groups such as racial minorities, women, or gender non-conforming individuals – are more vulnerable or susceptible to trauma than others. If trauma is experienced in a sensory rather than fully rational manner, then affect is central to its mechanisms of impact. Earlier in this chapter, we discussed affect as a pre-cognitive bodily experience, largely involuntary or devoid of our conscious control. To that end, cinema can be approached as a medium that can tap into trauma's pre-cognitive affective impact, through a disassociation of image and sound, or temporal and spatial disorientations. Indeed, film has long been interested in trauma and traumatic memory, whether in the genre of war cinema (American films about the Vietnam War, for instance, provide a rich body of work for analyzing trauma) or in documentaries that address painful intimate or collective memories (such as Joshua Oppenheimer's films about the Indonesian mass killings of 1965–1966, *The Act of Killing* [2012, Denmark/UK] and *The Look of Silence* [2014, Denmark/ Indonesia]).

Recent years have seen a rise in films that focus on **climate trauma** (Kaplan 2015), or on the ways in which climate change and the looming threat of Earth's demise through an ecological cataclysm have a traumatic effect on its inhabitants. This strain of trauma studies is closely related to the field of **ecofeminism**. Kaplan examines how many films that tackle ecological themes present an experience of "pre-trauma" – or trauma effects being experienced before any traumatic event takes place. She analyzes *Take Shelter* (Jeff Nichols, 2011, US; Figure 3.3) as one such example of a film in which the main protagonist is haunted by hallucinations (or premonitions) and nightmares of a cataclysmic environmental disaster before it has occurred. Another example of a climate trauma film is Todd Haynes' *Safe* (1995, US/UK), which depicts the slow decline of a suburban housewife, Carol White, who suffers from a mysterious environmental disease. Through the depiction of the disease, suspected to be multiple chemical sensitivity (sometimes also referred to as "20th century disease"), which severely affects the body's immune system, the film functions as a critique of both environmental pollution and traditional gender roles (since the chemicals that Carol develops an intolerance to are largely found in housecleaning and beauty products). In the film, the intertwined traumas of gender and climate change are decidedly physical in nature, and slowly chip away at the body's ability to fend for itself.

Some theorists of trauma and memory have looked at the transgenerational transfer of trauma, most notably Marianne Hirsch, who coined the term **postmemory** (2008) to refer to the inheritance of the traumatic experience of survivors, which, through cross-generational transfer, becomes an indirect, or vicarious experience of the second generation. Postmemory is frequently inherited through images (family photographs or home videos) and silences, more so than through detailed or linear storytelling, since the latter is not an adequate mode of expression for traumatic recall and loss. Relating transgenerational traumatic memory back to the body, and particularly woman's body, we can look at an example such as *The Milk of Sorrow* (*La teta asustada*, 2009, Peru/Spain), by Peruvian director Claudia Llosa. The film's protagonist, Fausta, suffers from a rare condition: she appears to have inherited, through her mother's milk, the bodily memory of her mother's brutal rape while pregnant "during terrorism," which is how the protagonist refers to the violence between Maoist guerillas and government paramilitary forces in Peru in the 1980s and 1990s. As Fausta's uncle explains to the doctor: "Her mother transmitted her fear through her breast milk." "Both matter-of-fact and poetic, naïve and resonant," observes Patricia White, "the myth he offers is indicative of the film's tone, through which horror is uncomfortably, figurally displaced" (2015: 191). Among ordinary people, the uncle says, this condition is referred to as "the milk of sorrow," which implies that its occurrence is more widespread than the doctor, or the medical establishment more generally, allows for. The doctor attributes Fausta's symptoms to a potato growing inside her vagina (Fausta has placed it there to protect herself from rape, which her mother has told her was a common practice among women "during terrorism"), and dismisses the uncle's explanation about the physical transference of intergenerational trauma from the mother's body to the daughter's. Fausta's symptoms also include frequent bleeding and fainting. The mother and daughter communicate through song, even after the mother's death. They sing to each other about the trauma of the mother's brutalization, which Fausta says she observed from within the mother's belly. Magical realism, fantastical elements and song here replace traditional narration, as trauma is reflected through alternative modes of expression. The film tackles the systemic and often unacknowledged violence against indigenous women, whose bodies simultaneously conceal and reveal grave physical and psychic wounds. White argues that "the conceit of *la teta asustada* [whose literal translation is 'frightened teat'] is offered as both alternative genealogy that binds mother and daughter over and against sanctioned state narratives, and a crippling legacy that Fausta must overcome" (191). With this, the film can only indirectly address the traumatic effects of the violence against indigenous peoples, and women in particular. "Without historical footage, analysis, or statistics, the film attempts to engage the imaginary and the extent of crimes against women. The mother's actual body in its mummified state stands in for the racialized and class-specific nature of these crimes," concludes White (192). The film therefore speaks to the experience of bodily postmemory, depicting the transgenerational trauma of indigenous women.

CASE STUDY: *PAN'S LABYRINTH* (GUILLERMO DEL TORO, 2006, SPAIN/MEXICO)

A traumatic expression is less about the truth of what happened, and more about the consequences it leaves on the psyche by dislocating normative forms of linear (and literal) expression. Janet Walker has called this "the traumatic paradox": "Far from belying the truth of an event, a fantasy (used here to mean an imagined scene that is the distorted representation of a wish) may be inextricably, but obliquely, connected to and produced by real events of the past" (2001: 212). This seeming paradox can be observed in a film such as *Pan's Labyrinth* (Guillermo del Toro, 2006, Spain/Mexico), in which the central protagonist – a young girl named Ofelia – is simultaneously living in the traumatic setting of the Spanish Civil War, and in the fantasy world in which she is a long-lost princess of an underground kingdom, who has to fulfill three tasks in order to fully return to its realm (Figures 3.19 and 3.20). When approached as a trauma text, the film very pointedly positions fantasy as a way for Ofelia to process the traumatic events taking place in the real world: her mother's marriage to a sadistic fascist general, violent clashes between warring sides, the torture of guerilla rebels, and her mother's death during childbirth. In emphasizing the brutal patriarchy of the domestic sphere, the film also structures its trauma narrative around issues of gender. In the end, Ofelia herself is shot and killed by her stepfather (her newborn brother is saved), but even in her death, the fantasy world carries on, and the film's final moments see Ofelia returned to the underground kingdom as a princess, seated next to her biological parents. These moments indeed serve as a form of wish fulfillment, but this time it is a wish fulfilled for the spectator rather than the dead child. A child's death is so traumatic and unthinkable that the film offers the spectator a fantastical happy ending as a reparative scenario that replaces the brutal reality of a child's violent demise.

Figure 3.19 The reality in *Pan's Labyrinth* (Guillermo del Toro, 2006)

Figure 3.20 The fantasy in *Pan's Labyrinth* (Guillermo del Toro, 2006)

Watch and discuss: *Pan's Labyrinth*

1 What is the relationship between reality and fantasy in *Pan's Labyrinth*, and what does it suggest about trauma?
2 How does gender figure into the film's treatment of trauma and violence? Identify specific scenes to support your answers.
3 How does the film reflect the tension between the personal and collective trauma of war?
4 What is the role of children's fairytales in the film?
5 Find instances where the film overtly links trauma to the body.
6 How does the film represent trauma visually (as opposed to through language)? How is trauma experienced and reflected through the senses: touch, sight, smell, taste, and hearing?

DISCUSSION QUESTIONS

1 Can you think of any horror films in which it is a male character who is the most terrified or displays the most "abject" fear onscreen? Can you think of examples of male melodramas, where

the spectacle of the male body suffering or being "victimized" is the main source of identification for the viewer?

2 Can you think of a film that you have watched recently in which certain sensory impressions had a strong impact on you, and were as significant to you as what the characters were saying or how the plot was progressing?

3 What could a phenomenological approach capture or address that may be missing from a psychoanalytic approach or an approach based on an abstract or ideal spectator (see Chapter 2 on spectatorship)?

4 Can you think of any films that would work well with a Deleuzian analysis? What makes them well positioned for such an approach? Think in terms of their narrative and their formal aesthetic and stylistic choices.

5 Consider your own experience of seeing disability represented in film or television shows. Are PWDs major or minor characters? Complex or one-dimensional? Does their disability define them or relate to their main function in the narrative?

6 Is trauma a significant theme or concept shaping contemporary cinema? If so, what are the major events that are linked to trauma in recent films (and/or television shows)?

KEY TERMS

affect

ambiguous transcendence

becoming-woman

body genres

body without organs

climate trauma

crip theory

Deleuzian approaches

ecofeminism

feminist approaches to trauma

haptic image

idealism

intentionality

intersubjectivity

phenomenology

postcolonial trauma studies

posthuman

postmemory

thick description

transcendent consciousness

trauma

trauma studies

the traumatic paradox

REFERENCES

Barker, J. M. (2009). *The tactile eye: Touch and the cinematic experience.* Los Angeles: University of California Press.

Beugnet, M. (2007) *Cinema and sensation: French film and the art of transgression.* Edinburgh: Edinburgh University Press.

Deleuze G., & Guattari, F. (1984). *A thousand plateaus: Capitalism and schizophrenia.* Minneapolis: Minnesota University Press.

Dolmage, J., & DeGenaro, W. (2005). "'I cannot be like this Frankie': Disability, social class, and gender in *Million Dollar Baby.*" *Disability Studies Quarterly, 25*(2). Online Access.

Elsaesser, T. (2014). *German cinema – Terror and trauma: Cultural memory since 1945.* New York: Routledge.

Gertz, N., & Khleifi, G. (2008). *Palestinian cinema: Landscape, trauma and memory.* Edinburgh: Edinburgh University Press.

Halberstam, J., & Livingston, I. (Eds.). (1995). *Posthuman bodies.* Bloomington: Indiana University Press.

Hirsch, M. (2008). "The generation of postmemory." *Poetics Today, 29*(1), 103–128.

Hole, K. L. (2016). *Towards a feminist cinematic ethics: Claire Denis, Emmanuel Levinas and Jean-Luc Nancy.* Edinburgh: Edinburgh University Press.

Jelača, D. (2016). *Dislocated screen memory: Narrating trauma in post-Yugoslav cinema.* New York: Palgrave.

Jelača, D. (2017). "Film feminism, post-cinema, and the affective turn." In K. L. Hole, D. Jelača, E. A. Kaplan & P. Petro (Eds.), *The Routledge companion to cinema and gender.* London: Routledge, 446–457.

Jelača, D. (2018). "Alien feminisms and cinema's posthuman women." *Signs: Journal of Women in Culture and Society, 43*(2), 371–400.

Kaplan, E. A. (2005). *Trauma culture: The politics of terror and loss in media and literature*. New Brunswick: Rutgers University Press.

Kaplan, E. A. (2015). *Climate trauma: Foreseeing the future in dystopian film and fiction*. New Brunswick: Rutgers University Press.

Kennedy, B. (2000). *Deleuze and cinema: The aesthetics of sensation*. Edinburgh: Edinburgh University Press

Longmore, P. K. (1985). "Screening stereotypes: Images of disabled people." *Social Policy, 16*(1), 31–37

Markotíc, N. (2008) "Punching up the story: Disability and film." *Canadian Journal of Film Studies, 17*(1), 2–10.

Marks, L. U. (2000). *The skin of the film: Intercultural cinema and embodiment*. Durham: Duke University Press.

McRuer, R. (2006). *Crip theory: Cultural signs of queerness and disability*. NewYork: New York University Press.

Merleau-Ponty, M. (1962). *The phenomenology of perception*. London and New York: Routledge.

Mitchell, D. T., & S. L. Snyder. (2008). "'How do we get all these disabilities in here?': Disability film festivals as new spaces of collectivity." *Canadian Journal of Film Studies*: 11–29.

Naficy, H. (2001). *An accented cinema: Diasporic and exilic filmmaking*. Princeton: Princeton University Press.

Nikolaidis, A. (2013). "(En)Gendering Disability in Film." *Feminist Media Studies, 13*(4), 759–764.

Norden, M. F. (1994). *The cinema of isolation: A history of physical disability in the movies*. New Brunswick: Rutgers University Press.

Saadi Nikro, N. (2014). "Situating postcolonial trauma studies." *Postcolonial Text, 9*(2), 1–21.

Sobchack, V. (1991). *The address of the eye: A phenomenology of film experience*. Princeton: Princeton University Press.

Walker, J. (2001). "Trauma cinema: False memories and true experience." *Screen, 42*(2), 211–216.

Walker, J. (2005). *Trauma cinema: Documenting incest and the Holocaust*. Berkeley: University of California Press.

White, P. (2015). *Women's cinema, world cinema: Projecting contemporary feminisms*. Durham: Duke University Press.

Williams, L. (1991). "Film bodies: Gender, genre, excess." *Film Quarterly,* 44(4), 2–13.

Young, I. M. (1980). "Throwing like a girl: A phenomenology of feminine body comportment, motility, and spatiality." *Human Studies, 3*(2), 136–156.

Chapter four
STARS
Gendered texts, circulating images

STUDYING STARS

What do we study when we study movie stars? As Richard Dyer argues in his pioneering work on star studies, stars can tell us a lot about our cultural ideas of the person, or how we define the "individual" in society. Different stars represent different attitudes towards dimensions of experience such as work, consumption, love, and family. Stars can also be sites of negotiation around contradictory tensions or social demands. As Dyer argues:

> Stars are also embodiments of the social categories in which people are placed and through which we make our lives – categories of class, gender, ethnicity, religion, sexual orientation, and so on. And all of these typical, common ideas, that have the feeling of being the air that you breathe, just the way things are, have their own histories, their own peculiarities of social construction.

(1986: 18)

This quote draws attention to the ways in which stars reflect and partici-pate in the naturalization of ideas about categories such as gender and race that are in fact culturally and historically constructed. For example, stars may reflect the myth that a woman's success and happiness are intrinsically linked to normative beauty standards or lighter skin color (see the section on Bollywood stars ahead). Or, they may support notions that the self is largely defined by the things one buys or consumes. In this way stars' mediated identities represent "texts" that we can use to analyze the changing and contradictory meanings of various identity categories. On one hand, stars often conform to dominant norms relating to gender and sexuality, and white celebrities dominate the Hollywood star system. On the other hand, stars can also work to challenge the norms of gender, sexuality, and race. For this reason, they are significant objects of feminist inquiry.

While traditionally the term **star** has been used in film studies, the concept of **celebrity** has broader reach. Whereas stars are known for their successful careers as actors (or musicians or even athletes), celebrity tends to refer simply to the fact that one is famous, whether or not one has demonstrated talent in a particular field. With the rise of digital social media and the phenomenon of reality TV, celebrities have proliferated in contemporary culture. One is a celebrity often simply because they've been successful at marketing their lifestyle or persona in a way that has garnered interest from the public (and subsequently become "famous for being famous"). For example, while we may consider someone like Jennifer Lawrence an indisputable "movie star" in the traditional sense of the word, known because of her acting accomplishments (which have increased public interest in her personal offscreen life), a celebrity like Kim Kardashian is famous for being Kim Kardashian. First brought to attention by a "leaked" sex tape, Kardashian (and her family) have gone on to become major celebrities through reality TV shows, product endorsements/fashion lines, exploiting their personal lives and promoting themselves as "influencers." The emphasis in celebrity tends to be "on the person's 'private' life rather than career, if indeed they are seen as having a 'career' at all" (Holmes & Redmond 2010: 4). While this may imply that celebrities are talentless fame-seekers, the boundaries between stars and celebrities are increasingly less fixed in our contemporary moment. We have developed a culture of celebrity where the consumption of celebrity gossip and related products is a significant facet of contemporary life. As Su Holmes and Sean Redmond (2010: 4) argue, "what generally unites the work on stardom and celebrity is the agreement that celebrity or fame does not reside in the individual: it is constituted discursively," that is to say through public discourse and representation. While celebrity may better apply to certain more contemporary figures discussed in this chapter, because of our focus on film and the film studies tradition, we will employ the term star throughout.

When we talk about stars, it is important to distinguish between the "real" person and the star as a text. That is to say, the star is a negotiated set of meanings that alters through time. The **star text** is composed of many factors including the roles that the star has played onscreen; material promoting the star from studios or other institutional channels; press coverage, including celebrity tabloid magazines and interviews; and the media and dialogue contributed by fans in digital forums. In contemporary culture, digital technology has offered many more opportunities for fans and audiences to contribute to a star's meaning in the cultural landscape, and stars themselves have begun to harness fans to develop a social media base that furthers their own careers. For example, many Hollywood stars today use Twitter, Facebook, and Instagram to directly communicate with their fans, whereas before, such communication was conducted solely through the stars' publicists. The direct interaction with the fans that new media makes possible produces a significant shift in how stars are perceived, particularly in terms of how accessible or relatable they seem. Different facets of a star's text will take precedence over others at different points in their career. For example, a star like Jennifer Aniston was originally best known for her role as Rachel in the 1990s sitcom *Friends*. However, she is arguably better known today for the media coverage of her perceived romantic successes and failures, and the media speculation about her desire to bear children, than she is for her actual film roles. Additionally, offscreen knowledge of a star may shape audience perception of the characters she plays. In the studio era, Bette Davis' much-publicized battles over her contract at Warner Brothers were a crucial part of her star image that informed the way that audiences read the strong, often difficult, female characters she portrayed in many films (Figure 4.1). Both Aniston and Davis bring extra-diegetic dimensions of their images related to love, family, and work into their onscreen roles.

Figure 4.1 Bette Davis in *Jezebel* (William Wyler, 1938)

Approaching the star as a text is a way of conceptualizing the star as a signifying system, a manufactured and mediated image, as opposed to a real person. Of course, however fabricated their images may be, discourses of authenticity are crucial to many stars' constructions. Take for example, the regular feature in *US Weekly* magazine, entitled "Stars: They're Just Like Us." In this weekly segment, stars are shown doing things that presumably "ordinary" people (i.e. non-stars) do, such as shopping for pet food, walking the dog, or buying ice cream with their children. Captions over paparazzi photos have taglines such as "they feed their children" or "they text while walking." While these images display our cultural obsession with star images (we want to see their private lives made public), they also obscure the fact that these ostensibly private moments may themselves be staged media events, curated to counter public discourse about a star, or calculated to put a star back into the public eye at a strategic moment in their career. These features are also notable for their mixing of discourses of the ordinary and extraordinary. One of the dichotomies that stars embody then, is that of the everyday versus the exceptional: they are simultaneously perceived as both "like us" and something more – more talented, more successful, often more beautiful, and more charismatic.

Dyer refers to the meanings a star has as a **structured polysemy** (1980: 63). In other words, the star can evoke diverse and often contradictory significations simultaneously. In fact, stars are part of the system through which capitalism and other dominant ideologies manage their own conflicts and internal contradictions. However, these meanings are *structured*, that is to say, there are limits to what a star can mean based on the available discourses surrounding them. Pop star Beyoncé's recent visual album *Lemonade* (2016, US) is a strong example of the star's ability to encapsulate multiple meanings within one text. In it, Beyoncé negotiates her glamorous superstar image with discourses of authenticity and the private sphere, in part by making overt links to her rural Southern roots in the lyrics and imagery of the film, by including lyrics that are thought to be autobiographical (in particular, relating to her husband's infidelity), and by including home movies and "personal" footage of her family and wedding. These elements all serve to construct *Lemonade* as an authentic document that gives us insight into the star's personal life. At the same time, the visual album draws on highly stylized imagery that operates in various registers – from urban edginess, rural settings, mystical symbolism, political rhetoric regarding race (for example, the #blacklivesmatter movement and imagery referencing Hurricane Katrina in the video for "Formation"), and lyrics and music that are the result of collaborating with many popular musicians in genres outside Beyoncé's typical area. In this sense, *Lemonade* reflects a public and more nuanced image as well. The visual album's overt references to both the patriarchal discrimination against black women and police brutality toward African-Americans more generally makes the work an example of

intersectional feminism. As the term itself suggests, intersectional feminism seeks to uncover oppression constituted through the intersection of factors such as gender, race, and class. With *Lemonade*, Beyoncé's larger-than-life star persona takes her personal narrative of marital betrayal as a mere starting point in offering a broader critique of the difficult social conditions that African-Americans, and particularly black women, face on a daily basis. She also ties this contemporary narrative to the past, by using visual motifs such as Southern Gothic aesthetics, or references to *Lemonade*'s important cinematic predecessor, Julie Dash's *Daughters of the Dust* (1991, US) (see Figures 4.2 and 4.3).

Because of Beyoncé's global superstardom, *Lemonade* is generally interpreted through the lens of her star text, and moreover, she is perceived as the sole authentic author of it, even though she shares the project's songwriting and directorial credits with many other people. In other words, cultural debates about *Lemonade* inevitably center around the persona of its star, and on the question of what she wanted to convey through her work, both personally and politically. *Lemonade*, then, also illustrates how in star images, discourses of the private intersect with larger political issues, such as the value of black womanhood and black female sexuality. At the same time, as bell hooks notes in her critique of *Lemonade*, its feminism is still packaged as a product to be sold to the fans, and does little to address the economic privilege of the wealthy pop star at the center of it all.[1] One of the contradictions of *Lemonade* then, is that despite the ways it gives visibility to lives and issues that are marginalized by dominant ideologies, it is

Figure 4.2 Beyoncé's *Lemonade* (Beyoncé, 2016)

Figure 4.3 *Lemonade's* visual foremother *Daughters of the Dust* (Julie Dash, 1991)

nonetheless inextricably bound up with the dominant capitalist system as a product that is meant to sell an image to anyone who will buy it. In this sense, a marginalized subject position becomes an economic opportunity with a public always looking for something new and different.

While we have been largely addressing how stars function as texts or images, it is also crucial to remember that stars are workers and are products that are branded, marketed, and bought – that is, they are also labor and forms of capital. However, while they are workers, their status as capital – i.e. as valuable commodities that help to sell films and other products – often gives them more flexibility and privilege than the average laborer. Some stars travel across borders throughout their careers, even working in different languages across varied national cinemas. The flow of bodies from non-Western cinemas towards Hollywood, and the kinds of roles international stars are able to play in Hollywood, as opposed to their home cinemas, often reflect larger geopolitical flows of capital and power, as well as racist stereotypes and tropes.

Transnational stars are stars who have success in multiple national or international cinemas, and typically have made films in more than one language over their career. So, for example, Penelope Cruz and Aishwarya Rai are stars who are properly transnational in their career trajectories, having worked across industry borders and in multiple languages. John Wayne is an interesting case – perhaps the most internationally famous American movie star of the 1950s and 1960s, he never worked in an industry outside Hollywood and certainly not in a language other than English. Yet his stardom was so iconic on a global scale that we can talk about the transnational aspects of his star text. As an example of his global popularity, in a 1953 poll conducted by the Hollywood Foreign Press Association, Wayne was voted the most popular film star in the world by fans in more than fifty countries (Meeuf 2014). Despite Wayne's deep association with myths of the "settling" of America's Western frontier and a brand of rugged laconic American masculinity, Soviet leader Nikita Krushchev declared Wayne his favorite movie star at the height of the Cold War (ibid). However, since Wayne never worked outside of his national industry or in another language, perhaps he is best understood as an **international star**, rather than a transnational one, because his star persona never really challenged the stability of a collective national identity. Regardless of his cross-cultural popularity, he is always perceived as American first and foremost. Transnational movie stars, on the other hand, tend to destabilize the notions of pure, singular, or fixed national identities.

As noted, a key term that helps us understand the construction of stars is the concept of intersectionality. Intersectionality looks at the ways in which identity categories do not have meaning in isolation from one another. Rather, they are all articulated onto one another. In other words, they are made meaningful *in relation to* each other. For example, black middle-class femininity may mean something quite different than Latina working-class femininity – both culturally and in the experiences of women who live within the constraining ideas of these categories. This concept will be reflected throughout the chapter's discussion of various stars, from Latin American stars of the studio era, to Bollywood stardoms, to transnational stars who circulate through China, Hong Kong, and Western borders. In what follows we will explore how stars relate to the film industry, to identity categories, and to geopolitical flows of bodies, by focusing on various periods and figures in the history of cinema.

PRODUCING STARS IN HOLLYWOOD

Different national cinemas have varying relationships to stars as cultural products. Additionally, within national contexts, the ways in which star texts circulate and are produced varies across time. The Hollywood studio system, for example, relied heavily on stars to sell films. Most stars during the 1930s and 1940s worked under contract for one of five major studios. These contracts allowed studios to control the kinds of roles that stars were offered and also to lend stars out to other studios for the financial benefit of the loaning studio. We focus here on the 1930s because this was a decade when female stars had a wider cultural influence than their male counterparts and held more power in terms of their box-office draw. Stars like Bette Davis (Figure 4.1) had famous conflicts with their studios over the kinds of roles they were offered and the lack of control they experienced over their own careers. Despite her rise to fame in the 1930s, Warner Brothers, the studio that held Davis under contract, denied her control over her public image and over the kinds of roles she was given. Earlier in the decade, Davis, like many actresses of the time, chose to deliberately off-cast herself when she was on loan to RKO in *Of Human Bondage* (John Cromwell, 1934, US). Her success in this more substantial and serious role contributed to Davis' increasing stardom, but did not result in more creative and financial power for her over her career. Davis took Warner Brothers to court in 1937, desiring to break her contract and move to London, where she would receive better roles. While she lost this lawsuit, Davis nonetheless went on to be a huge box-office draw for Warner Brothers at the end of the decade.

Katharine Hepburn is another well-documented example of an actress who was tired of the limited and trivial roles she was given by her studio, RKO. Unlike many other actors, however, Hepburn had independent wealth and was able to buy out the final years of her contract instead of accepting the roles that were given her. An analysis of Hepburn's star trajectory illustrates the fact that star images were firmly based in dominant norms of gender, class, and race. Hepburn is often seen as a feminist ahead of her time – she was intelligent, well spoken, and strong. In comparison with many other stars of the time, and because of her class background and relationships with important people in Hollywood, she had a significant amount of control over her career. However, the public often saw her as too elite for their tastes: her acting style and diction were clearly shaped by her New England roots and influenced by the finer art of the theater. She was typically received as too upper class, educated, and independent (Naremore 1988). This was reinforced by many of her film roles, which characterized her as a fast-talking, often ditzy New England or Manhattan socialite. Screwball comedies based on a battle-of-the-sexes trope, such as *Bringing Up Baby* (Howard Hawks, 1938, US) and *Holiday* (George Cukor, 1938, US), while much loved today, were failures in their time. After *Bringing Up Baby*, for instance, Hepburn was labeled as "box-office poison" (Naremore 1988). Her class position, white Protestant background, and her perceivably "aberrant" performance of gender, contributed to a lack of appeal with average audiences. As a result, James Naremore notes, Hepburn engaged in a "retreat from assertiveness," deliberately choosing more conservative scripts that downplayed her strong female sensibilities onscreen (175). Hepburn's eventual romance with Spencer Tracy, who was seen as a "man of the people," ended up reviving her career and popularity with audiences. From 1940 on, they starred in a series of romantic comedies and audience reception of their performances was influenced by knowledge of their offscreen romance (Figure 4.4). As Naremore writes of the Tracy/Hepburn collaborations, "they foster an image of 'good old Kate' – a woman who might behave like a liberationist, but who is reassuringly, almost maternally, attached to Tracy and who will, in the

Figure 4.4 Katharine Hepburn (with Spencer Tracy) in *Without Love* (Harold S. Bucquet, 1945)

last instance, subdue her rebellion for his sake" (177). Hepburn's career, then, shows how gendered norms are inflected by class and ethnicity, and offers insight into the relationship between career success and the ability to negotiate dominant cultural expectations around the performance of gender.

Also significant in terms of Hollywood in the 1930s is the history of female stars who negotiated successful forms of stardom independent from exclusive, long-term studio contracts. Although this fact has been largely neglected in the study of film history, actresses have sought financial equality and creative control over their careers from the earliest days of sound (see Carman 2016). Dominant film history narratives locate the origins of independent stardom – a system that became the norm as the 1950s progressed – in Jimmy Stewart's 1950 profit-sharing deals negotiated by his agent, Lew Wasserman. These deals are typically held up as having inaugurated a new system of star/agent-negotiated independence in the post-studio era. For example, stars began negotiating on a per-picture basis and receiving a share of box-office profits, as opposed to a flat rate or weekly salary. Yet archival records indicate that studio actresses were *already* negotiating independent contract deals throughout the 1930s. While the studio system is often construed as having been an inflexible star factory where talent had limited freedom and creative opportunities – which may seem to be supported by cases like Davis's and Hepburn's – there in fact existed a range of independent stardoms – from more successful examples, such as the careers of Barbara Stanwyck and Carole Lombard (Figure 4.5), to ones that ultimately failed, as with Clara Bow and Miriam Hopkins.

Figure 4.5 Carole Lombard in *My Man Godfrey* (Gregory La Cava, 1936)

Female stars like Constance Bennett, Irene Dunne, and Lombard negotiated for a range of provisions, including – among many other things – percentages of box-office profits (which meant tax breaks on earnings); the approval of scripts, directors, and co-stars; the right to make fixed numbers of pictures for multiple studios; top billing privileges; and control over various facets of their media personas, from choosing makeup and costume artists to off-casting themselves in roles that would enlarge or redirect their careers.

These stars also often consciously framed their independence in terms of gender. Constance Bennett maintained to the press in a 1934 article that acting was the only career "where [women] are on an absolute equality with men" (Carman 2016: 106). By contrast, Miriam Hopkins noted to the trade papers in 1935 that despite the success of women in Hollywood, the top decision makers were still men, calling out the ultimately patriarchal nature of the industry. Carole Lombard was quoted in trade articles where she described how she "lived by a man's code," including paying her share of the bills, keeping busy with her work, and being career-focused (114). Female readers of film periodicals desired to know the details of these stars' contracts and independent maneuvering, and these facets of their careers formed part of their star texts, for better or worse (Carman 2016). Barbara Stanwyck, an orphan who was a Broadway chorus girl before making it in Hollywood, was known for her professionalism and devoted work habits (Figure 4.6). Her freelance negotiations were framed by the press in terms of her work ethic and her willingness to go on her own, professionally and personally, after her divorce in the mid-30s. In a 1936 fan magazine interview

Figure 4.6 Barbara Stanwyck in *Double Indemnity* (Billy Wilder, 1944)

Stanwyck cautioned young women to develop their own lives before fall-ing in love and said, "'I am free, I am my own man. And it's dangerous because no woman can live in marriage this way'; instead, she preferred 'the romance of living'" (101). The independence of these women personally and professionally is an important corrective to the historical record, in terms of locating the origins of independent stardom and challenging the role of female stars in the studio system.

As prestigious as an independent contract could be, actresses coded as "eth-nic" (a problematic term that often, in practice, denotes anyone who is not white Anglo-Saxon Protestant) were *forced* into forms of "independent stardom," as they were unable to attain the stability of a long-term studio contract in a racist Hollywood. These stars included talents such as Anna May Wong and Lupe Vélez (Vélez is discussed in the following section). People of color are an undeniable part of Hollywood's acting history, but in the industry's first few decades, they were largely made to play support-ing roles frequently imbued with racial stereotypes, rather than allowed to be individualized stars like their white counterparts. For instance, Hattie McDaniel's most celebrated and best-known role is Mammy in *Gone With the Wind* (Victor Fleming, 1939, US), in which she plays Scarlett O'Hara's flamboyant lifelong servant (Figure 4.7). The "Mammy archetype" is one of the four controlling images of back womanhood that Patricia Hill Collins (1990) discusses in her critique of the intersections of race and gender in cultural representations of black women (the other three are the matriarch, the welfare mother, and the Jezebel). The role of a stereotypical Mammy

Figure 4.7 Hattie McDaniel in *Gone with the Wind* (Victor Fleming, 1939)

earned McDaniel an Academy Award for Best Actress in a Supporting Role. And while she became the first African-American to win an Oscar, during the award ceremony she was made to sit in the back of the theater, while her white colleagues were in the front rows. Even though McDaniel's Oscar led to a uniquely (for an African-American actor) stable long-term contract with Warner Brothers, including first-billing privileges, she was never able to escape her stereotyped casting in supporting "Mammy" roles, which severely limited her ability to challenge herself professionally and artistically.

Whiteness and **colorism** (greater discrimination towards individuals with darker skin color) continue to function as norms for many film industries. There is no current example clearer than the ongoing controversies and debates about **whitewashing** – the practice of casting white actors in roles meant to be played by actors of color in the original source. The history of such problematic tendencies is not unrelated to the practice of **blackface** and **yellowface** – where black and Asian actors, respectively, are made to exaggerate their racial features and play into troubling stereotypes about an entire race or ethnicity, or where white actors are visually altered in order to appear nonwhite and play persons of color. In recent times, such examples include Angelina Jolie playing Marianne Pearl in *A Mighty Heart* (Michael Winterbottom, 2007, US), Tilda Swinton playing the role that, in the original comic book source, was an Asian male mystic in the movie *Dr. Strange* (Scott Derrickson, 2016, US), or Scarlett Johansson playing what was originally a Japanese manga character in *Ghost in the Shell* (Rupert Sanders, 2017, US). Whitewashing is not far from the trope of a white savior, whereby white actors are featured in roles in which they, as outsiders, save an entire nonwhite, non-Western community (often from themselves) – examples include Tom Cruise in *The Last Samurai* (Edward Zwick, 2003, US) and Matt Damon in *The Great Wall* (Zhang Yimou, 2016, China/US). Through such interrelated practices that reiterate the primacy of whiteness, white Hollywood stars contribute to the ongoing global imbalance of circulating star texts, whereby normative white Western masculinities and femininities are privileged over everything else. Racially correct casting in itself, however, as Shohat and Stam (1994) argue, "is hardly sufficient if narrative structure and cinematic strategies remain Eurocentric," as the career of an actress like Halle Berry (Figure 4.8) demonstrates (190).

To date only one black woman has won a Best Actress Oscar – Halle Berry in 2002. Berry's career shows many of the limitations put on nonwhite actors in Hollywood (see Mask 2009). In *Bulworth* (Warren Beatty, 1998, US), she plays a black activist who gives a white politician a new lease on life (he has actually hired someone to assassinate him at the film's start). The white politician – Bulworth – begins rapping and living more "fully" (i.e. partying and smoking marijuana, offering uncensored commentary on the campaign trail) because of his contact with a black woman and black culture. This trope of black people being somehow more vital and creative than white people is pervasive in Hollywood films, and black forms of cultural expression, black characters, and black milieus are often used as background or support to inject life

Figure 4.8 Halle Berry in *Monster's Ball* (Marc Forster, 2001)

and inspiration into the lives of white protagonists (2016's *La La Land* [Damien Chazelle, US] is a recent example of this tendency). The ambivalent racial politics of this trope are also present in the film for which Berry won the Oscar, *Monster's Ball* (Marc Forster, 2001, US). The win put her in a controversial spotlight, as *Monster's Ball* involves steamy sex scenes between Berry's character and that of a racist white man. This latter character, played by Billy Bob Thornton, is also her husband's death row executioner. Thus, the film ends with a black woman being cared for by an explicitly racist white man who has executed her (black) husband. Given the overrepresentation of black men in U.S. prisons, the film's politics were very contentious with minority and antiracist audiences. These examples from Berry's career are exemplary of the limitations of the roles offered to nonwhite actors and the difficult choices they must make between furthering their careers and being responsible to constituencies based on race or ethnicity. However, it also needs to be acknowledged that it is difficult to turn down major roles when so few are available for women of color to begin with.

The 2016 Academy Awards were notable for being particularly politicized around issues of race (prompting a viral #OscarsSoWhite hashtag), with some minority actors boycotting and the host, Chris Rock, making an impassioned argument for more meaningful roles for nonwhite actors in his opening monologue. The limited roles offered to nonwhite actors establish parameters on their star texts, as film roles are a major component of a star's meaning. As we will see throughout this chapter, ethnic and racial stereotyping and the question of whether actors have a responsibility to avoid roles that reproduce racist stereotypes are issues that actors of color have faced from the silent era on.

ACTIVITIES

1   Choose a contemporary film star who is not discussed in this chapter. Based on their media coverage, acting roles, and any additional products they promote, does their star text confirm or challenge dominant stereotypes about gender, race, and class (or other categories)? Are there contradictions in their star text?
2   Choose a black actress and examine the roles she has played. Do her characters challenge or reproduce controlling ideas about black womanhood? Are there ways in which the star negotiates larger cultural discourses about black womanhood through her film roles or public appearances?

LATIN AMERICAN/US LATINA STARS IN HOLLYWOOD

Historically, Hollywood has been a difficult place for "ethnic" – or non-white – women to find career stability or a wide range of meaningful and non-stereotypical roles. In this section we will examine Mexican and Brazilian actresses of the studio era and end with a discussion of Latina actresses in Hollywood today. The term "Latinx" has more recently come into popular usage, as way of declaring an ethnic identity without also having to identify a binary gender category (in Spanish, most adjectives take on either a masculine or feminine ending depending on whether they are describing something designated male or female/masculine or feminine). In most of what follows, we use the term Latina for contemporary stars such as Jennifer Lopez, as it has come into popular usage around the turn of the 21st century, and is how those stars have identified. However, some have disputed its homogenizing function across a range of significantly different identities, from Chicana to Puerto Rican and beyond. That is, "Latina" can flatten significant national and cultural differences among Latin American women. However, the concept of Latina/o identity has become both a powerful tool for unity among women of the Latin American diaspora *and* a marketing category for targeting Latin American consumers, particularly as the Latin American population continues to grow in the United States. Studying Latin American stars can teach us about the ways that differences operate *within* the category of "Latina" and how opportunities have both diminished and grown for varied historical and geopolitical reasons for Latin American stars. We can also see how the trope of **tropicalism** continues to dominate the meanings of Latina star texts, even for American-born Latinas. Tropicalism,

> erases specificity and homogenizes all that is identified as Latin and Latina/o. Under the trope of tropicalism, attributes such as bright colors, rhythmic music, and brown or olive skin comprise some of the most enduring stereotypes about Latina/os. . . . Gendered aspects of the trope of tropicalism include the male Latin lover, macho, dark-haired, mustachioed, and the spitfire female Latina characterized by red-colored lips, bright seductive clothing, curvaceous hips and breasts, long brunette hair, and extravagant jewelry.
>
> (Molina Guzmán and Valdivia 2004: 211)

The cases of two Mexican stars – Lupe Vélez and Delores del Río – who acted on both sides of the transition from silent to sound film in Hollywood are illustrative of the ways in which categories like ethnicity and gender intersect with class, as well as the flexibility of American ideology when it comes to marketing its stars.

CASE STUDY: LUPE VÉLEZ AND DELORES DEL RÍO

Lupe Vélez (Figure 4.9) and Delores del Río (Figure 4.10) both came to Hollywood in the 1920s to act in silent films. Del Río came from a wealthy family and was married into the Mexican aristocracy; she was recruited to Hollywood through social connections with her then-husband. By contrast, Vélez, the daughter of a military colonel and an opera singer, came to Hollywood on her own to make it as an actress. What is evident from studying their star texts – which include the roles they were offered and agreed to play, as well as the promotional materials and publicity surrounding them – is that although both women were Mexican actresses, there were significant class dimensions to their star texts. For example, both women were cast broadly, but while del Río was often given roles playing European characters, from a French woman in *What Price, Glory?* (Raoul Walsh, 1926, US) to a Russian dancer in *The Red Dance* (Raoul Walsh, 1928, US), Vélez often played Asians, Latinas, and "Natives"; she even played a character name Princess Exotica in *The Half Naked Truth* (Gregory La Cava, 1932, US). That is to say, Vélez was seen as having a less European presence, a designation that had

Figure 4.9 Lupe Vélez in *Mexican Spitfire Sees a Ghost* (Leslie Goodwins, 1942)

Figure 4.10 Delores del Río in *Flying Down to Rio* (Thornton Freeland, 1933)

connotations of class. Vélez was given ethnically charged monikers such as "Hot Tamale" and "Hot Pepper," and eventually made her career in a series of films where she played a character nicknamed "The Mexican Spitfire." This reveals the ways in which her star image was read in terms of her coding as a passionate Latina – a standard stereotype of tropicalism. In fact, Vélez's first major role was one that del Río had turned down because of its offensive overtones, starring opposite Douglas Fairbanks in *The Gaucho* (F. Richard Jones, 1928, US). Vélez's sexuality was always read in terms of stereotypical ideas of Latina womanhood. Marketed as an exotic fiery woman, in both her film roles and the press, her well-publicized romances were described as combinations of passion and violence. Her marriage to Johnny Weissmuller, best known for his role as Tarzan, finally ended on grounds of cruelty and physical and mental violence. Yet, articles about the star often emphasized that Vélez was a force that needed to be conquered or tamed offscreen as well as on, legitimizing domestic violence in her private life. A *Photoplay* article from 1929 noted that,

> Outwardly, Lupe has changed. She curbs her tongue with people she doesn't know. To interviewers she talks in a dignified manner of her home, which she really loves, her dogs and her work. She dresses better. Gone are the little short pleated skirts and blouses cut almost to her waist. In her wardrobe hang

gowns that any Park Avenue lady would be delighted to own. In them, of course, Lupe does not look like a Park Avenue lady, merely because *she is too striking a type*.

(Rodríquez-Estrada 1997: 482)

The subtext here is that Vélez's perceived lack of class and excessive sexuality, linked to her ethnicity, make her somehow unable to occupy the category of a "Park Avenue Lady."

Delores del Río, by contrast, was seen and marketed as a high-class actress from the beginning, with publicity often focusing on her personal style, the glamorous parties she threw and the way in which she decorated her home. Despite del Río's insistence on being publicized as a Mexican actress, she was often promoted as Spanish (Rodríquez-Estrada: 485). She was viewed as more ethnically ambiguous than Vélez and, as mentioned, often played European or more glamorous aristocratic characters. The press continuously emphasized her elite origins and "strict morality," positioning her as the "right kind" of ethnic star (Beltrán 2008: 34). Del Río broke repeatedly with the studios because she desired roles she felt fit her image and were worthy of her talents. However, as Mary Beltrán argues, with the coming of sound, leading roles for Latino/a actors became increasingly rare. "Del Río's accent ultimately brought about the waning of her status and casting possibilities as a film actress," she argues (40). This may explain why del Río agreed to do a film like *Girl of the Rio* (Herbert Brenon, 1932, US). This film, which was steeped in stereotypes about Mexicans, including a Mexican villain called "Don José Tostado," provoked a formal protest from the Mexican government. While her role in *Girl of the Rio* became the subject of controversy in the American Spanish-language press, the potentially offensive stereotyping of the film went unnoted in del Río's English-language coverage, which continued to focus on her lifestyle and image (Rodríquez-Estrada: 480). This contrast between white American audiences and "hyphenated" constituencies (in this case Mexican-American audiences) is an important dimension of stars' varying reception, even within one national context. Del Río's decision to act in *Girl of the Rio* shows that her options were becoming increasingly limited in Hollywood. Furthermore, even demeaning roles such as this would soon become less common with the stricter enforcement of the Production Code, beginning in 1934. At the film's end, del Río's character is united with her white lover. The Code, which included a ban on the depiction of interracial relationships, would mean less opportunity for stars deemed of ambiguous whiteness to be cast as romantic leads opposite white actors.

The contrasting careers of Vélez and del Río show the way that class inflects ideas about ethnicity, gender, and sexuality and the ways in which options are often limited for transnational stars working in Hollywood. The two actresses also came to very different ends. Whereas Vélez committed suicide while five months pregnant in December 1944, del Río returned to Mexico where she became a successful actress in the Mexican film industry.

Discuss: Latin American Stardom

1   What do you think it means to be the "right kind of ethnic star," as del Río was viewed?
2   Who are some of the major contemporary Latinx or Latin American stars? Do their star texts share traits with or differ from cases like del Río and Vélez? Have opportunities and ideas about Latinx identity changed in the 21st century?
3   Do stars with "hyphenated identities" have a responsibility to their constituencies (for example, a Latinx star to young Latinxes)?

While it is easy to see how transnational stars are often reduced to representing caricatures or stereotypes of their home country for a – typically Western – audience, it is important to also recognize the ways in which stars consciously appropriate these stereotypes to further their Western careers. For example, Carmen Miranda (Figure 4.11) came to the United States from Brazil in 1938, slightly later than del Río and Vélez (see case study), and historically during a time when the United States was adopting a "Good Neighbor" policy with South America to promote trade and tourism between the northern and southern hemispheres.

Visually literalizing the international exchange of both goods and bodies, in Miranda's role in the Busby Berkeley musical *The Gang's All Here* (1943, US), she emerges off of a boat from Brazil, with goods like coffee, bananas and other fruits. Miranda's character in the film then, is a symbol of the fertility and abundance of Brazil, like the coffee and other agricultural products. Her fertility is linked to her alleged vivacious insatiable Latin sexuality. In the film, her character is referred to as "that gypsy" and a "South American savage" reproducing colonial distinctions between north and south as

Figure 4.11 Carmen Miranda in *The Gang's All Here* (Busby Berkeley, 1943)

representing high and low culture, purity and impurity, respectively. The film's opening number "You Discover You're in New York" is staged as a cultural encounter between Brazil and the United States, represented by cosmopolitan New York. Here, New York can usefully be read as a neocolonial **contact zone** – that is to say, a space where different cultures interact with each other, but typically with a strong power differential between the two (Shaw 2010: 290). In this film, as was the case in her real life, Miranda herself becomes part of what Brazil can offer in exchange for American capital – both monetary and cultural. Miranda, who had previously established herself as a successful vocalist and performer in South America, made frequent appearances at Brazil's World's Fair exhibit in 1939–1940, consciously marketing herself as part of the goods that the country had to offer. This is perhaps most iconically illustrated by the famous Tutti Frutti hat she wears in one of the film's song numbers (Figure 4.11). Her role in *The Gang's All Here* was typical of most of the Hollywood productions in which she was featured: Miranda was limited to non-romantic, often comical "ethnic" color roles that supported the dominant romantic narrative arc of white leads. This, again, reflects the reduction in star-making opportunities for non-American actors with the coming of sound in the studio era, as discussed in the previous case study.

Rather than simply viewing Miranda's career as a tragic capitulation to northern stereotypes of Brazil, we can read her cultivation of her star persona as a willful and conscious appropriation of those stereotypes in order to succeed internationally. This is what Lisa Shaw terms Miranda's **strategic** exoticism (2010: 288). Miranda was a successful singer and performer in Brazil before she came to the United States. Although she was born in Portugal, to Portuguese parents, she appropriated the Afro-Brazilian dress of the *baianas*, the women who sold goods in the marketplaces, in developing her star image in Brazil. Creating a more glammed-up version of the traditional costume and headdress, Miranda, who was also a talented milliner, began making her own signature hats, often adding the fruit for which she became famous. However, as a comparison of her costume and performance style in Brazil and in the United States reveals, Miranda's performance of this ethnic character became hypersexualized and hyperbolized in her American incarnation.

Her face became comically animated and her movements more rapid and frequent, detracting from her vocal performance. Her outfits became gaudier and her hats higher and more ostentatious. In her American incarnation, Miranda was an iconic embodiment of the trope of tropicalism. She quickly became a parody of herself and welcomed her parodization as it furthered her fame and career (289). In her transition to performing for an American audience, Miranda also stopped darkening her face, literally whitening the *baiana* look. As Shaw argues, "By customizing the *baiana* look Miranda effectively turned Afro-Brazilian culture into a performance of 'Latinness' rather than 'blackness', thus rendering herself acceptable to mainstream WASP audiences" (291). So, while Miranda consciously appropriated her perceived cultural difference in marketing herself to an American audience, she also paradoxically toned down that difference, representing a version of Latin identity that was whiter than its Brazilian counterpart. The documentary *Carmen Miranda: Bananas Is My Business* (Helena Solberg 1994, US/Brazil/UK) explores the complexities of Miranda's role in both promoting Brazil abroad, and yet being seen as an Americanized betrayer of Brazilian culture by many back home. Her inability to escape the caricatured roles she'd originally courted upon her arrival in America, combined with personal difficulties, took its toll on the star, who died of a heart attack at the age of forty-six. Miranda's case suggests that we need to be mindful of the ways in which stars exercise agency over their images and negotiate the racial and gendered stereotypes with which they are confronted in Hollywood.

Although diversity and ethnic hybridity have always existed in the United States, as its population continues to become ever more diverse and racially hybrid, Latin audiences have come to be recognized as an important market in themselves and Latina stars have become much more prominent. Yet, within the idea of *Latinidad* class and value hierarchies remain. Jennifer Lopez, perhaps the most prominent Latina star at the turn of the 21st century, has had tremendous success in music, acting, and in marketing her own product lines and fragrances. At $13 million per film, she went on record as the highest paid Latina actress in history (Molina Guzmán and Valdivia 2004). A major part of Lopez's promotion has focused on her buttocks, so much so that she has had them insured for $1 million. While readers who have come of age in an era of Beyoncé and Kim Kardashian may see the "butt" as a major factor in the sex appeal of many stars, in the 1990s, a curvaceous figure, including an ethnically marked posterior, was still a source of body shame and a feeling of physical inferiority for many women. Mexican-American star Selena was notable for making visible a more curvaceous figure, and notably, Lopez was cast as Selena in her biopic (*Selena*, Gregory Nava, 1997, US), linking them metonymically as Latina stars (Figure 4.12). When criticized or questioned as a non-Mexican actress (Lopez is from the Bronx and of Puerto Rican descent) playing the beloved, tragically murdered cultural icon, Lopez often defended her ability to portray Selena by invoking their shared experience of embodiment, that is, of being curvaceous women in a culture that prized very skinny, even androgynous and ethnically white female body types. Ironically, Lopez's success as an icon of beauty and feminine sexuality caused major shifts in beauty norms, including a spike in posterior plastic surgery enhancements for women who suddenly "lacked" the desired curves that were previously so disparaged.

Thus the types of bodies that stars have are important parts of their star texts, entering into popular body politics around race, class and gender. The association of stars such as Selena and Lopez primarily with the lower body is rooted in histories of imperialism and colonialism, where colonized populations were associated with the physical and irrational, or with nature, and the colonizers with culture, the mind, and civilization. The buttocks in particular can be traced through a history of racial fetishization and Afro-Latin hybridity through figures like the so-called "Hottentot Venus," an African woman named Sara Baartman, whose prominent rear curves were put on display throughout Europe as an anthropological curiosity in the

Figure 4.12 Jennifer Lopez as *Selena* (Gregory Nava, 1997)

early 19th century and whose body, even after death, was preserved as a scientific specimen. The lower stratum of the body is associated in the Western cultural imaginary with the primitive and sexual and is semiotically linked to the lower classes and to former colonial spaces such as Latin America and Africa. As Frances Negrón-Muntaner writes, "references to [the buttocks] are often a way of speaking about Africa in(side) America" (1997: 185). Further, "A big culo does not only upset hegemonic (white) notions of beauty and good taste, it is a sign for the dark, incomprehensible excess of 'Latino' and other African diaspora cultures" (189). These residual colonial systems of value are evident in comparing the media coverage of the Spanish actress Penelope Cruz with the Nuyorican Lopez. In coverage of Cruz, rarely is a single body part given prominence, other than her face (see Valdivia 2005). Furthermore, the captions on images of Cruz, while they may suggest a certain exoticism, include phrases such as "Beyond Beauty," or, in one advertisement for Ralph Lauren, a brand that is closely associated with the upper class, Cruz is labeled with a quote from William Blake, "Exuberance is beauty." This copy text highlights Cruz as having value as a person of culture and class. By contrast, Lopez's promotion as "Jenny from the Block," often photographed from behind or to emphasize her legs or breasts, reflects a notion of non-Spanish Latinas as working class, excessively embodied and defined in terms of sex appeal and "attitude." This illustrates one of the ways that differences stemming from colonial histories operate within *Latinidad* (a concept which sometimes, however problematically, encompasses Spanish stars such as Cruz). The European Cruz may appear exotic, but she is seen as cultured, beautiful, and as representing a form of perfection that extends beyond the body. Lopez is from the Bronx and represents a hyper-embodied notion of the sexual and spicy Latina. As Angharad N. Validvia writes, "within *Latinidad*, Europeanness in general and Spanish-ness in particular may very well function like whiteness does in terms of the general U.S. racial topography – that is, they stand for that imaginary prevalence of the middle class which is the unmarked standard and thus implicitly superior" (72).

What the comparison of Cruz and Lopez reminds us, as do the cases of del Río, Vélez, and Miranda, is that processes of racialization and gendering are never uniform or ahistorical. Categories like race, class, and gender are constantly shifting in meaning and significant differences exist even within these categories. Differences are always relational – they have meaning in relation to each other within larger categories of difference, such as "Latina."

BEYOND HOLLYWOOD: BOLLYWOOD STARDOM

The largest film industry in the world, Bollywood – as India's Hindi language-based film industry is known – is fueled by big-name stars. As Kush

Varia writes, "Stars are at the epicentre of Bollywood film, holding more importance than the directors, producers and all other aspects of the film-making process" (2013: 96). Because films in the Bollywood system are largely financed "through a combination of commercial interests, with success being dependent upon securing distribution deals that require some guarantee of success at the box office," films must be able to offer a crowd-pleasing package to potential funders, and stars are the surest guarantee of a film's draw (Shingler 2014: 100). Stars dominate the production schedules of Indian films, as their contracts typically allow them to shoot multiple pictures simultaneously (this is known as the "shift system") (Varia 2013: 96). In practice, this means that stars may be on several film sets for several different films throughout the day and their personal shooting schedules can constrain the production rate of individual films. This is different from the typical American system in which a star is booked for one film at a time. Despite the enormity and international popularity of Bollywood stars (and their films), they have not had the kind of box-office draw in the West that they do in South Asia. Moreover, no major Bollywood star has become a crossover success in Hollywood, with Aishwarya Rai's career being one of the most sustained attempts to develop a career in the English speaking film world (her case is discussed more ahead). Priyanka Chopra's recent success as the first South Asian lead in an American television series (*Quantico* 2015–) is also perhaps an indication that tides are shifting, at least for female Indian actors. The reasons for a lack of meaningful Bollywood/Hollywood crossover are complex, but the circulation of actors across borders, as is illustrated amply in the cases of Hong Kong action stars, Latin American performers, and even European talent, tends to be oriented *to* and not *from* Hollywood. That is to say, stars who have established their careers in industries other than Hollywood tend to move to Hollywood as the ultimate signifier of international "success," where, as we have seen, they are often offered stereotypical and more limited roles than those they were given in their home industry. Rarely do American actors become stars in Hollywood and then move to, for example, Hong Kong to try and "make it big" in another industry. This, of course, reflects larger geopolitical asymmetries. Hollywood has historically had a position of global dominance in the distribution and exhibition of films and the United States is still seen to signify wealth, modernity, and style globally. Star bodies and their circulation reflect these systems of differential privilege and power.

In the Bollywood star system, generally speaking, male stars have greater fan bases and can draw higher fees for their work (Henniker 2013: 208). Shah Rukh Khan is possibly the biggest contemporary Bollywood star (Figure 4.13). He endorses a broad variety of products internationally, as well as starring in countless big-budget films. Compared to the majority of Indian citizens, Khan has a significant amount of money, privilege, and mobility, making him part of an elite class of cosmopolitan global citizens. In the

Figure 4.13 Shah Rukh Khan plays a star and his fan (in prosthetics) in the thriller *Fan* (Maneesh Sharma, 2016)

recent film *Fan* (Maneesh Sharma, 2016, India), Khan plays a movie star, a character who references his real-life star text, from having a similar looking family and home, to engaging in rituals such as his annual birthday appearance on the high terrace of his mansion, where he greets a multitude of devoted fans on the same day every year. Khan also plays the star's fan, who, in the film, becomes so obsessed with the star that he is willing to do anything, first to help him, and then, after being rebuked by the star, to harm him. The film engages in an over-the-top manner (in true Bollywood style) with very real issues raised by celebrity culture, including the responsibilities of stars to their fans, fans' identification with and consumption of star texts, and very real differences in terms of power and privilege between stars and audiences. Despite *Fan's* arguably unsatisfactory ability to actually address these issues in a meaningful way, it provides a fascinating engagement with stardom in the Bollywood context, with applications beyond the Indian and film contexts.

Despite his international celebrity, Khan has never crossed over into Hollywood films. Not only is he virtually unknown in Western popular culture, the renowned star has also been detained at the U.S. border three times at the time of writing. Immigration officials do not recognize him as a major star in the world's largest film industry, and his Muslim name and Indian provenance have made him the target of lengthy detainment and questioning by U.S. customs and immigration. Khan, staying true to the likable and down-to-earth star persona he has cultivated, has publicly laughed off these "inconvenient" detainments. Giving a speech at Yale University after the second time that he was detained for several hours at a U.S. airport, Khan said, "Yes, it always happens. Whenever I start feeling arrogant about myself, I always take a trip to America. The immigration guys kick the star out of stardom."[2] However, after his most recent detention in August 2016, Khan tweeted that the pattern "really sucks," finally showing some frustration with the racial profiling he experiences at the border. His example reveals the complex layers of stardom and privilege based on wealth and fame. While within the Indian subcontinent, Khan is a "King" (one of his nicknames is King Khan), possessing much greater mobility than the vast majority of his compatriots, his skin color and ethnicity are a very real barrier to his westward mobility. His image can circulate across borders much more easily than his actual body can.

Khan is also notable for his status as a gay-friendly icon, despite the fact that homosexuality is a topic still somewhat suppressed in mainstream Indian culture. Although he is married to a woman with whom he has several children and is regarded as a straight sex symbol, he has never shied from taking roles that challenge dominant conceptions of masculinity – even doing an "item song" in one of his films (*Om Shanti Om*, Farah Khan, 2007, India). An item song follows a style that is typically gendered feminine and performed by a woman in Hindi films. Khan has also appeared in films that either contain subplots readable as "gay" or in films whose storyline is open to queer readings (Henniker 2013: 213). By this, we mean that the plots can be read against their obvious/explicit meaning in ways that resonate with or relate to gay experiences. For example, in several films he plays a character who must give up someone he loves, i.e. deny his desire, and suffer feeling separated from his family and peers. In *Kal Ho Naa Ho* (Nikhil Advani, 2003, India), Khan plays a character with a terminal heart condition. The knowledge that he is doomed motivates him to step aside and encourage the love of his life to marry his best friend instead. As Charlie Henniker notes, in the film's final scene, his character, who has suffered greatly because his illness and his love have been kept a secret, watches his best friend and his true love at their wedding, and is shown somewhat isolated and removed from the family and the events taking place (216). This narrative of isolation and self-denial, typical of the experience of many gay Indians, is the kind of performance that has made Khan open to gay readings both in India and within the Indian diaspora. These roles have been reinforced by public appearances in which he openly supports gay rights and playfully addresses questions about his own sexuality. The queer elements of Khan's star text are also reiterated in some of his product endorsements. For example, he was the first male star to promote Lux soap, a company endorsed only by women for seventy-five years (212). In one Lux ad, he is depicted in a feminized manner, frolicking in a large bubble bath and blowing soap bubbles from his hand into the air. His body is clearly an object of display and desire. Khan represents what Richard Dyer called a star's **charisma** – a quality that foregrounds the star's ability to contain major cultural contradictions within their star text. For Khan, this is the contradiction between his traditional family man image (he even refuses to kiss onscreen, although it has by now become acceptable in the Hindi film industry) and a more progressive approach to supporting gay rights and accepting alternate gender/sexual identities. This progressive dimension to his text needs to be read as linked to both politics *and* economics, however. Openness to being read in progressive and sexually ambiguous terms is a lucrative strategy for stars, both with gay audiences domestically and also diasporically. As Martin Shingler writes, "many of twenty-first-century Bollywood's biggest names have achieved success by appealing largely to members of the Indian diaspora. . . . Despite having a huge international fan base however, very few of these have made English-language films in Europe or America" (2014: 100). This brings us back to the uneven circulation of star bodies, which tends to reflect other patterns of geopolitical capital distribution.

Despite the large following of male Bollywood stars, male icons have not historically been the dominant source of gay readings in Bollywood. Rather, female actresses from Nargis to Rekha to Meena Kumari, among many others, have represented icons that can be read against the grain of heteronormativity by oppressed minority gay audiences. In particular, it is these stars' association with tragic melodrama, as characters who suffer secret shames and forbidden loves, and, sometimes, their own tragic biographies offscreen that have given them gay iconic status. For example, mentioning a preference for the film *Pakeezah* (Kamal Amrohi, 1972, India), starring Meena Kumari has become a way to signal gay identity in the resident and non-resident gay Indian community (Varia 2013: 107). *Pakeezah* (Figure 4.14) is the story of a courtesan, Sahib Jaan, who for various reasons cannot be with the man she loves, although he has offered to marry her and "free" her from her life as a courtesan. The two fall in love when he notices Sahib Jaan's beautiful feet. A melodramatic climax occurs when Jaan sings and dances at her former love's wedding celebration (to another woman). As her dancing becomes more frantic and ecstatic, she breaks glass and begins to dance on it, poignantly destroying her own feet in a bloody dance that externalizes her suffering and loss.

The star of the film, Meena Kumari, who was also an accomplished poet, is known as "The Tragedy Queen of Indian Cinema." Kumari herself led a tragic life – the child of actors who tried to give her up as an infant, she started acting at a young age. She married director Kamal Amrohi, who was fifteen years her senior, in a secret ceremony at the age of nineteen. Amrohi was married with children when they met, but they began a sustained, if secret, courtship after a difficult car accident severely damaged Kumari's hand. The marriage became controlling and abusive and Kumari developed

Figure 4.14 Meena Kumari as Sahib Jaan in *Pakeezah* (Kamal Amrohi, 1972)

a serious drinking problem. Production of *Pakeezah* was stopped in 1964 when the couple finally separated. Eight years later, Kumari, extremely ill from drinking-related medical problems, agreed to finish the film at the urging of Nargis and Sunil Dutt, two notable members of Bollywood royalty. The epic story of the film's making and the love and suffering behind its story and production have thus become part of the film's text itself and have given it a cult status. Kumari died from liver cirrhosis less than month after *Pakeezah's* release. She was only thirty-eight. Her tragic life of love, abuse, addiction, and suffering mirrored that of the characters she played onscreen and further reinforced the reading of her star text as connecting to themes that resonated with gay male experiences and camp sensibilities.

A remake of another classic "gay" courtesan film, *Umrao Jaan* (J.P. Dutta, 2006, India), starred Aishwarya Rai, a star who, in contrast with most Bollywood stars, has been more well known in the West, in part by winning the 1994 Miss World competition and being declared "the most beautiful woman in the world" by Hollywood royalty Julia Roberts (Figure 4.15). The original *Umrao Jaan* (Muzaffar Ali, 1981, India) starred Rekha, a gay camp icon like Kumari. Rai's star text is quite different, and she is notable for being one of the few Bollywood stars to make a sustained attempt to act in first British and then Hollywood films – although her crossover career was largely unsuccessful. Her only Hollywood film, *The Pink Panther 2* (Harald Zwart, 2009, US), never gave her the opportunity to show her acting range or to establish herself as a real star. Some have argued that

But still my heart
has brought me here.

Figure 4.15 Aishwarya Rai in *Umrao Jaan* (J. P. Dutta, 2006)

films like *The Pink Panther 2* use strategies of global marketing to reach the greatest possible audience by casting stars like Rai alongside actors like Andy García, Yuki Matsuzaki, and Alfred Molina playing Italian, Japanese, and British characters, respectively (Shingler 2014: 106). International or multi-ethnic casting, then, is one of the ways Hollywood attempts to reach the largest possible audience and maintain its global hegemony. However, as is often the case, in *Pink Panther 2*, Rai's role was reductive and lacked any depth or the material to prove her ability to work as an international star.

Rai *has* had international success, however, in modeling for companies like L'Oreal. In this, she is joined by many successful actresses including Zoe Saldana, Julianne Moore, Jane Fonda, and Eva Longoria. L'Oreal's campaign, which aims to represent a range of races and ages in its marketing, is notable for the ways it reflects larger inequities in terms of world beauty standards.

For example, one advertisement for L'Oreal's 2015 Color Riche Collection featured John Legend playing "La Vie en Rose" on a baby grand piano. He is gradually joined by various models, including Rai, all of whom wear a rose-beige colored yet distinct outfit. Despite an attempt to show diversity, the skin tones in these ads in large part tend towards the lighter end of the skin color spectrum, contributing to the West's continued problem with colorism. Furthermore, only white women are shown at a variety of ages – most of the international or nonwhite actresses are fairly young, whereas actresses like Helen Mirren (not in this particular ad for the campaign), Jane Fonda, and Julianne Moore represent a greater age range with respect to white beauty. Therefore, whiteness is implicitly reaffirmed as the "norm" in these ads – it is the "unmarked" category that is allowed differentiation, whereas nonwhite women stand in as tokens of "exotic" versions of cosmopolitan beauty. Lip service is paid to diversity, while whiteness remains protected as the standard of attractiveness. In most of the ads, the women wear outfits in the same color, such as white or black, creating a kind of uniformity against which their differences are highlighted. What this makes evident is the very limited range of what is considered beautiful by Western standards, even within a supposedly diverse beauty campaign. The women are all extremely thin, with no variety in body type or bodily shape represented in an ad that purports to promote inclusivity. In this way, diverse notions of beauty are given lip service, but thinness and whiteness are implicitly reaffirmed as the standard by which beauty is judged. Rai, for example, is noted for her green eyes and, like many Bollywood stars, her lighter skin tone. In India, she markets a skin-whitening cream for L'Oreal – a different facet to her work for this corporation that is not seen in its Western advertising.

Skin-whitening products are common in South and East Asia and reflect the ways in which beauty norms privilege lighter skin – a symbol of class privilege and wealth as well as supposedly universal (i.e. "white") norms of beauty. In fact L'Oreal's version is called "White Perfect," making the values coded into whiteness explicit in the product's title. As Goldie Osuri argues,

> individualist, consumer choice discourses not only ignore, but also completely disavow the extent to which the fair, light skinned or wheatish complexioned woman has historically been privileged through various cultural forms in the Indian cultural sphere – forms that illustrate the colour prejudice and discrimination that governs darker pigmentation. . . . Bollywood has been one of the major cultural forms through which this discursive embodied validation of light-skinned women is manifested.
>
> (2008: 114–115)

While in global marketing campaigns, such as that of L'Oreal, Rai represents the inclusion of diversity in dominant standards of beauty, it is paradoxically because the Indianness of her appearance "can be dissociated from" that of the vast majority of Indians that she is deemed attractive (116). As discursive analyses of the White Perfect ads reveal, they:

> reinforce . . . the biomedicalized intervention of Asian women's skin coded by the sign of 'Melanin-Block™.' L'Oreal's advertisements for skin-whitening cosmetics are often reinforced by constant interplay between the ideological precepts of white supremacy and the technologically mediated suppression or 'blocking' of the capacity for Asian women's bodies and skins to produce skin pigment, melanin.
>
> (Mire 2010: 7–10)

The casting of male Bollywood stars also reproduces notions of lighter skin as more attractive, powerful, and linked to financial success. Shah Rukh Khan markets a skin-whitening product for men called *Fair and Handsome*. A 2009 ad shows the actor among flashing lights on the red carpet, accosted by beautiful women, while a slightly darker skinned man looks on. Khan is shown acting in a variety of scenes that associate him with physical mobility/ability and wealth. After using the cream Khan recommends, the onlooker himself appears on the red carpet, surrounded by beautiful adoring women, his skin visibly fairer. This all suggests that there is a materiality to the star texts that circulate globally. These star texts do important ideological work, sometimes reproducing standards that privilege Western notions of beauty. Furthermore, the circulation of these skin-covered bodies is uneven. While Khan the image can circulate freely across borders, speaking to members of the diaspora both queer and straight, and promoting a fairer notion of handsomeness, in reality his physical body has repeatedly had difficulty entering the United States.

ACTIVITY

Find a recent advertisement campaign that both uses stars *and* attempts to include diversity in terms of race, gender identity, or body type in its marketing. Do a semiotic analysis of the ads in the campaign. How do the individual stars contribute to the meanings the advertisements attempt to convey?

CASE STUDY: RUAN LINGYU AND MAGGIE CHEUNG

Ruan Lingyu (1910–1935) was one of the most iconic stars of the 1930s Chinese cinema, often referred to as the Chinese Greta Garbo, or the Greta Garbo of Shanghai (Figure 4.16). Her short but intense movie career propelled her into a heretofore unseen movie stardom in China. Some of her most iconic roles include *Love and Duty* (*Liàn ài yu yìwù*, Bu Wancang, 1931, China) and *The Goddess* (*Shénnǚ*, Wu Yonggang, 1934, China). In 1935, she starred in *New Women* (*Xīn nǚxìng*, Cai Chusheng, China), which was based on the life of another

Figure 4.16 Ruan Lingyu in *The Goddess* (Wu Yonggang, 1934)

actress, Ai Xia, who committed suicide. In an example of life imitating art, Ruan Lingyu ended her own life shortly after the film's release, at only twenty-four years old. It is believed she took her own life due to the intense personal and professional difficulties she faced, which speaks to the pressures female movie stars were dealing with in the Chinese film industry more broadly. Reportedly, Ruan's funeral procession was several miles long, and remains one of the defining events of early Chinese film history. Her death has been deemed "uncanny because of its mise-en-abyme quality" (Yiman Wang 2011: 250) – that is, because it eerily mirrored the role she played in one of her last movies.

Her tragic life story received a cinematic treatment some sixty years later, in *Center Stage* (*Ruǎn Líng Yù*, Stanley Kwan, 1992, Hong Kong), in which contemporary Hong Kong movie star Maggie Cheung played Ruan (Figure 4.17). Rather than being a traditional biopic, *Center Stage* is a multi-layered meditation on stardom, cinema's history, and women's role in it. It mixes archival footage of Ruan with reenactments of scenes from her personal life and missing films, as well as with documentary-style interviews with the film's actors and people who worked with or wrote about the "real" Ruan. Maggie Cheung not only plays Ruan in the reenactment scenes, but also appears as herself in the interview scenes where she is in conversation with others about Ruan, including talking about what Ruan's legacy means to a contemporary film actress like herself.

Figure 4.17 Maggie Cheung as Ruan Lingyu in *Center Stage* (Stanley Kwan, 1992)

With all these intertextual elements (an actress both playing and talking about an actress who played another actress), the film offers illuminating insight into the pressures and complexities of female movie stardom across different eras of (Chinese) film history. In particular, Shanghai functions in Ruan's life as a place of political and personal insecurity – a vibrant, cosmopolitan city that is, at the time, besieged by the Japanese and is now viewed through the legacy of the communist revolution. These larger historical events shape her star text – both her personal life and the kinds of roles available to her (at one point a fellow actress is concerned that one of their films won't be screened because of some negative dialogue about the Japanese). Politics play a role in the more contemporary context of stardom as well – Hong Kong, at the time of the making of *Center Stage*, was preparing for a transfer of sovereignty, from being a British protectorate to being under the auspices of Mainland China (which was completed in 1997). Thus, parallels can be drawn between Ruan's Shanghai and the Hong Kong of Cheung and her colleagues on the film, in terms of the social and political instability framing their film work and star texts.

Maggie Cheung's own prolific and incredibly successful movie career propelled her into international stardom. Indeed, she can be considered a transnational movie star, having starred in many iconic and internationally lauded films such as Wong Kar-Wai's *In the Mood for Love* (2000, Hong Kong) and Zhang Yimou's *Hero* (2002, China). She has also starred in two films by French director

Figure 4.18 Maggie Cheung as Irma Vep (Olivier Assayas, 1996)

Olivier Assayas – *Irma Vep* (1996, France) and *Clean* (2004, France/ UK/Canada) – and was reportedly featured in a deleted scene from Quentin Tarantino's *Inglourious Basterds* (2009, US). Cheung speaks several languages – English and French, in addition to Mandarin and Cantonese. In *Irma Vep*, she plays a version of herself, in another instance of an actor's star text permeating the cinematic narrative itself. In this film, Cheung's cosmopolitan film festival persona intrudes into fantasies of a pure national French film culture. Cheung is hired to play Irma Vep, an iconic role from the French silent era, by a fading director positioned as a remnant of the French New Wave. Cheung's star text here intersects with questions about national cinema, Frenchness, the fetishization of Asian women's bodies, and the role of the star in the production of films in a way that is uniquely supported by what only she could bring to the film in terms of extra-diegetic significance. This is visually illustrated by a shot included in the film's marketing, an iconic image of Cheung as Vep on a Paris rooftop, with Notre Dame Cathedral in the background. Cheung, in her black latex costume, is positioned as a foreigner, an intruder on the landscape of French tradition, represented by the cathedral. Her costume as Vep puts her in stark contrast to the muted background – it is sleek, modern, and suggests darkness. Yet by the film's end, Cheung herself has moved on and away from the problems plaguing French identity – true to her cosmopolitan persona, she is heading to America to meet with Ridley Scott, leaving behind the French crew to debate the future of French cinema (she has been replaced by a white French actress).

Nodding to her fascinating screen persona that is often characterized as timeless, director Olivier Assayas described Cheung as an "up-to-date version of an old-fashioned movie star."[3] Such assessments of contemporary movie stars suggest the enduring power of movie stardom to create an illusion of timelessness, even after the stars themselves are long gone. Yet *Irma Vep* also suggests that that timelessness is a racialized quality – and for the fictional crew, it was not yet Cheung's time.

Watch and discuss: *Irma Vep*

1 How does the film characterize French film culture? Be specific.
2 Does the soundtrack provide any additional meanings in terms of the film's main themes?
3 How does Cheung as transnational star function in the film? What does she represent vis-à-vis French national cinema? What is the function of the star here?
4 What role do Cheung's costumes/clothing play in the film?
5 What do you make of Vidal's version of *Irma Vep* (the short film that we see at the film's end)?

MASCULINITIES AND STARDOM: FROM SESSUE HAYAKAWA TO HONG KONG ACTION STARS

While this chapter has largely focused on female stars, male star texts are equally informative of the politics of race and ethnicity, gender and desire as they shift between cultures and across time. One of the earliest transnational stars, the Japanese silent film actor Sessue Hayakawa was a major sex symbol for American women during the rise of the star system in the silent era (Miyao 2007). Hayakawa was catapulted to stardom by Cecil B. DeMille's 1916 film *The Cheat* (US), in which he played Tori, a dealer of "oriental" objects who lends money to a white woman – Edith – in exchange for her body (Figure 4.19). When Edith tries to pay him back and break the deal, Tori brands her with the brand he uses to mark all of his imported (Asian) goods. Edith shoots him in self-defense and at his trial Tori is ambushed by a mob of angry white men.

Figure 4.19 Sessue Hayakawa (with Fanny Ward) in *The Cheat* (Cecil B. DeMille, 1916)

Reviews declared that Hayakawa had stolen the show and women swooned over his evil and menacing character. According to Daisuke Miyao, this was a historical moment in which an obsession with Japanese design and ceramics coexisted with discourses of the so-called "yellow peril," or the threat of Japan's rise as a military and economic power (32). Japan was seen as paradoxically both cultivated and refined, *and* primitive and pre-modern, and the fear of Japanese expansion trickled over into white American attitudes towards Japanese immigrants. These discourses of yellow peril and Japanese refinement (both of which draw on facets of East Asian **orientalism**) came together in Hayakawa's performance in *The Cheat*. Orientalism refers to a history of discourses and visual representations that depicted "the East" as a place of both repression and sexual license, a feminized exoticized space that was used to define "the West," by contrast, as implicitly rational, just, morally upright, civilized, and superior. Because of his negative portrayal of a Japanese man, Hayakawa was seen as a traitor in Japan and the film was not released there. Japanese-Americans also started a campaign against the film and Hayakawa's misrepresentation of Japaneseness, which they linked to racially motivated attacks in the film's wake. As a concession, when the film was re-released in 1918 (due to popular demand) his character's background was changed to Burmese to address the Japanese backlash. Besides being exemplary of the ways in which transnational star texts are shaped by larger cultural and geopolitical discourses, Hayakawa is also notable for his very sexualized reception. Contemporary Western discourses of Asian masculinity often tend to desexualize or feminize Asian and Asian-American stars, but Hayakawa was a great sex symbol in the United States during his heyday.

Many Hong Kong action stars have found themselves limited to desexualized roles in their American careers. Hong Kong cinema has produced many successful stars that have migrated into Hollywood cinema with differing levels of success, from Bruce Lee to Jackie Chan and Jet Li. In the translation to Hollywood film roles, many Hong Kong stars find the opportunities open to them extremely circumscribed – Jackie Chan has made a career of combining comedy with physical daredevilry; Chow Yun-Fat has focused more on his Chinese career because of the limited roles available in Hollywood (and Chow is not a trained martial artist like Chan and Li); finally, Jet Li's roles have typically been based on his fighting skills and perhaps less so on his acting range or significant character arcs. As Sabrina Qiong Yu (2012) argues, Li (the only "Hong Kong" action star originally from Mainland China) has predominantly been represented in the West as a villain, a killer, or as being childlike. His best-received performances are his roles as a ruthless villain, i.e. roles where he confirms certain stereotypes about the Asian peril. Yu writes:

> Western critical readings show Chinese stars can be accepted in the West only if they conform to Western expectations, which confirms once again the logic of "cultural translation"; that is, exchange between East and West always means "the demand on non-Western people to conform to Western standards and models but not vice versa."

(123)

The success of stars like Chan and Li can be seen as representing a major challenge to Western stereotypes of the feminized passive Asian male, and as "remasculinizing" the Chinese male body. At the same time, the Western star texts of these action stars tend to be desexualized, refusing an Asian male sexuality. Chow Yun-Fat, for example, had a background as a romantic lead and heartthrob in his Hong Kong productions, but became more internationally known for his gangster roles in John Woo films. Yet, the roles offered him in Western productions have tended to be limited to stereotyped Asian villain or action roles with little opportunity for romantic development. Jet Li, in his Western roles with interracial leads, such as Aaliyah in *Romeo Must Die* (Andrzej Bartkowiak, 2000, US) or Bridget Fonda in *Kiss of the Dragon* (Chris Nahon, 2001, France), is notably denied any romantic character arc with the women who play opposite him (Figure 4.20). While this is not in and of itself a negative thing, it is noteworthy in contrast with action hero roles played by white men, which tend to include romantic interests or, at the least, obligatory steamy sex scenes. It is crucial to consider these role limitations in light of

Figure 4.20 Jet Li and Aaliyah in *Romeo Must Die* (Andrzej Bartkowiak, 2000)

larger cultural representations of and stereotypes about racialized sexual proclivities and capacities.

As we have seen throughout this chapter, stars' bodies are texts that circulate in complex ways, revealing, and also sometimes helping to shift, cultural values and prejudices around gender as it intersects with ethnicity, nationality, race, and class, among other factors.

DISCUSSION QUESTIONS

1   What can we learn from studying stars?
2   What are some of the methods used for studying stars as texts?
3   Why is intersectionality a useful concept for studying stars? Can you think of a contemporary example of a star for whom an intersectional approach is particularly illuminating?
4   How does the circulation of transnational stars reflect uneven processes of globalization and/or larger geopolitical inequities?
5   What is strategic exoticism? Do you see it at work in any contemporary star texts?

blackface

celebrity

charisma

colorism

contact zone

international star

intersectional feminism

orientalism

star

star text

strategic exoticism

structured polysemy

transnational stars

tropicalism

whiteness

whitewashing

yellowface

NOTES

1 bell hooks, "Moving beyond pain," www.bellhooksinstitute.com/blog/2016/5/9/moving-beyond-pain

2 "Bollywood star Shah Rukh Khan detained at US airport again," www.theguardian.com/us-news/2016/aug/12/bollywood-star-shah-rukh-khan-detained-at-us-airport-again

3 Melissa Anderson, "Maggie cheung stiches together eras and selves," www.villagevoice.com/2016/12/07/maggie-cheung-stitches-together-eras-and-selves/

REFERENCES

Beltrán, M. (2008). "When Delores del Río became Latina: Latina/o stardom in Hollywood's transition to sound." In A. N. Valdivia (Ed.), *Latina/o communication studies today*. Bern: Peter Lang, 27–50.

Carman, E. (2016). *Independent stardom: Freelance women in the Hollywood studio system*. Austin: University of Texas Press.

Dyer, R. (1980). *Stars*. London: BFI.

Dyer, R. (1986). *Heavenly bodies: Film stars and society*. New York: St. Martin's Press.

Henniker, C. (2013). "Pink rupees or gay icons? Accounting for the camp appropriation of male Bollywood stars." In R. Meeuf & R. Raphael (Eds.), *Transnational stardom: International celebrity in film and popular culture*. Basingstoke: Palgrave Macmillan, 207–226.

Hill Collins, P. (1990). *Black feminist thought: Knowledge, consciousness, and the politics of empowerment*. London: Harper Collins.

Holmes, S., & S. Redmond. (2010). "A journal in celebrity studies." *Celebrity Studies, 1*(1), 1–10.

Mask, M. (2009). *Divas on screen: Black women in American film*. Champaign: University of Illinois Press.

Meeuf, R. (2014). *John Wayne's world: Transnational masculinity in the fifties*. Austin: University of Texas Press.

Mire, A. (2010). "Pigmentation and empire." *The new black magazine*, www.researchgate.net/publication/228644290_Brain_Brow_and_Booty_Latina_Iconicity_in_US_Popular_Culture

Miyao, D. (2007). *Sessue Hayakawa: Silent cinema and transnational stardom*. Durham: Duke University Press.

Molina Guzmán, I., & Valdivia, A. N. (2004). "Brain, brow, and booty: Latina iconicity in US popular culture." *The Communication Review, 7*, 205–221.

Naremore, J. (1988). *Acting in the cinema*. Berkeley: University of California Press.

Negrón-Muntaner, F. (1997). "Jennifer's butt." *Aztlán, 22*(2), 181–195.

Osuri, G. O. (2008). "Ash-colored whiteness: The transfiguration of Aishwarya Rai." *South Asian Popular Culture*, 6(2), 109–123.

Rodríquez-Estrada, A. (1997). "Dolores del Río and Lupe Vélez: Images on and off the Screen, 1925–1944." In E. Jameson & S. Armitage (Eds.), *Writing the Range: Race, class, and culture in the women's west*. Norman: University of Oklahoma Press, 475–492.

Shaw, L. (2010). "The celebration of Carmen Miranda in New York, 1939–41." *Celebrity Studies*, 1(3), 286–302.

Shingler, M. (2014). "Aishwarya Rai Bachchan: From Miss World to world star." *Transnational Cinemas*, 5(2), 98–110.

Shohat, E., & R. Stam (1994). *Unthinking eurocentrism: Multiculturalism and the media*. London: Routledge.

Valdivia, A. N. (2005). "The location of the Spanish in Latinidad: Examples from contemporary U.S. popular culture." *Letras Femininas*, 31(1), 60–78.

Varia, K. (2013). *Bollywood: Gods, glamour, and gossip*. New York: Wallflower Press.

Wang, Y. (2011). "To write or to act, that is the question: 1920s to 1930s Shanghai Actress-writers and the death of the 'New Woman'." In L. Wang (Ed.), *Chinese Women's Cinema: Transnational Contexts*. New York: Columbia University Press, 235–254.

Yu, S. Q. (2015). *Jet Li: Chinese masculinity and transnational film stardom*. Edinburgh: Edinburgh University Press.

Chapter five
DOCUMENTARY
Local realities, (trans) national perspectives

As a mode of filmmaking, documentary has been at the forefront of telling women's stories on a global scale, as well as a significant domain where female directors have consistently had the opportunity to hone their authorial voices. Paula Rabinowitz has argued that "documentary circulates between the public and private, personal and political spheres by becoming simultaneously an aesthetic and archival object – part-fiction, part-truth; or if you will, at once base and superstructure, economic practice and cultural form" (1994: 6). That is to say, the documentary is both an artistic object and an attempt to document a reality. It is an art form actively invested in addressing and depicting (directly or indirectly) the larger political and economic systems in which it is made. Furthermore, documentary raises key questions about representation, truth, and memory that have been central to feminist political and intellectual projects. This chapter critically interrogates questions around the politics of representing "others," and of the inextricability of power and knowledge in documentary representation. We also probe the relationship that poetic modes, experimentation and "speaking nearby" have with feminist documentary, and how women have used documentary forms to challenge dominant discourses and power inequalities.

In her exploration of the politics of documentary filmmaking, Paula Rabinowitz has asserted that "gender is a central category within documentary rhetoric, though one often ignored, suppressed, or resisted, because it is not always clear who occupies what position when" (6). This assertion can be observed in Barbara Kopple's landmark documentary *Harlan County, USA* (1976, US), which documents a coal miners' strike that took place in Kentucky in 1973 (Figure 5.1). While the coal miners are largely men, their wives and other female family members are shown to be as important to the protest and the morale of the strikers, and as active in the day-to-day logistics (evocative of the 1954 narrative film *Salt of the Earth*, discussed in Chapter 1). The activities of the women in the film bring overt attention to the intersections of gender politics and social class, where poverty unites men and women in a fight for a better life, while simultaneously revealing the double bind that women find themselves in: they are oppressed both across gender and class lines.

In a slightly different way, gender and sexuality play a critical role in Jenny Livingston's *Paris Is Burning* (1990, US), a documentary about a subculture of queer men of color who engage in "vogueing" competitions in New York City clubs ("vogueing" is a dance style that Madonna subsequently popularized – or co-opted – in her song and accompanying David Fincher-directed music video "Vogue" [1990]). While Livingston's documentary gave visibility to a marginalized group, it has also "been criticized in some circles for adopting a kind of pedagogical approach" (Halberstam 1999: 126). The debates around whether the film's gaze is objectifying or empowering illuminate the difficulty of positioning documentary as either an a priori progressive political tool, or as an inevitably objectifying mode of representation.

In the sections that follow, we explore how issues of gender have been at the forefront of many socially engaged documentaries, regardless of whether

Figure 5.1 Women on strike in *Harlan County, USA* (Barbara Kopple, 1976)

they were framed as overtly feminist. After an overview of the larger categories in which women documentarians have worked – including biographical, autobiographical, and experimental forms – we examine questions of documentary ethics, the problematization of what is "real," and finally, transnational feminist documentary.

FEMINISM AND THE POLITICAL DOCUMENTARY

Even though it is frequently at the forefront of the interaction between cinema and social justice, documentary has received less scholarly and critical attention than narrative fiction film, due at least in part to narrative cinema's wider mainstream reach and artistic standing. However, documentary filmmaking has gained increased cultural prominence in recent times, perhaps best illustrated by Michael Moore's Palme d'Or win in Cannes for *Fahrenheit 9/11* (US) in 2004, the first and (still) only documentary that has done so. Similarly, Joshua Oppenheimer's *The Act of Killing* (2012, UK/Denmark) and *The Look of Silence* (2015, Denmark/Indonesia), both about the aftermath of the Indonesian genocide that took place in the 1960s, have become two of the most critically lauded social justice films of the past decade. As a prominent vehicle for social change, documentary lends itself to being utilized as a medium for feminist politics and interrelated forms of struggle against different forms of systemic discrimination, whether they are based on gender, sexuality, race, class, ethnicity, or other identity categories. When it comes to women documentary filmmakers, Laura Poitras has, in recent years, achieved mainstream recognition with her political documentaries, most notably with *Citizenfour* (2014, US), about the NSA whistleblower Edward Snowden, which won an Academy Award for best documentary. **Political documentary**, it could be surmised then, has become a dominant strain of documentary filmmaking in the 21st century, one that has brought documentary film newfound mainstream recognition and prominence. Rabinowitz argues that political documentary "foregrounds sexual, class, racial, and gender differences within its address. These differences construct a spectator whose position is located within history, essentially remaking the relationship of truth to ideology by insisting on advocacy rather than objectivity" (7). In other words, political documentaries explicitly ask the viewer to engage with the inequalities and issues presented onscreen and take an active stand. Rather than presenting an "objective" account of an issue, they foreground their partisan position and explicitly encourage politicization and position-taking from their audience. In that vein, Jehane Noujaim's *The Square* (*Al midan*, 2013, UK/Egypt), takes a close look at the events surrounding the political crisis that has engulfed Egypt since 2011, and focuses on the protesters overtaking Cairo's Tahrir Square in a citizens' bid to fight for democratic changes. Egyptian-American filmmaker Jehane Noujaim, who was raised in Kuwait, Cairo, and Boston, returned to Cairo to make a film about the protests. Her documentary archives the ensuing violence, casting an intimate look at local activists and their sacrifices (Figure 5.2). At the same time, the film received some criticism with respect to its perceivably unfavorable depiction of Muslim Brotherhood, and in particular for appearing to feed into Egypt's ongoing political divisions rather than suggesting possible ways to resolve them.[1] The controversy highlights the difficulties of making political documentaries about current events that are still in flux, because the complexities of the situation on the ground often make it impossible to provide a comprehensive or ethically sound narrative.

With respect to the painful and ongoing legacies of colonialism, illuminated through postcolonial and decolonizing frameworks, we can trace the deployment of documentary as an overt political vehicle for social change in concepts such as **Third Cinema**, or "films of decolonization," as Octavio Getino and Fernando Solanas refer to political documentary in their manifesto "Toward a Third Cinema" (1970: 108). Critiquing the fantasies and phantoms that permeate neocolonial First Cinema (embodied by Hollywood), Getino and Solanas argue that "the cinema of the revolution is at the same time one of destruction and construction: destruction of the image that neocolonialism has created of itself and of us, and construction of a throbbing, living reality which recaptures truth in any of its expressions" (123). Their four-hour documentary *The Hour of the Furnaces* (1968, Argentina) is an example of revolutionary Third Cinema (Figure 5.3), or **Third Worldist Cinema**, as Shohat and Stam refer to the "cinematic counter-telling" that "began with the postwar collapse of the European empires and the emergence of independent Third World nation states" (1994: 248). *The Hour of*

Figure 5.2 *The Square* (Jehane Noujaim, 2013)

Figure 5.3 *The Hour of the Furnaces* (Octavio Getino & Fernando Solanas, 1968)

the Furnaces is an unrelenting depiction of the West's imperialist neocolonial domination on a transnational stage, conveying interrelated stories of oppression from many corners of the world, including Argentina, Eastern Europe and the United States. The film is a provocative political call to arms and a revolutionary pamphlet, embodying Getino and Solanas' argument that cinema needs to be used as a weapon in anticolonial struggle.

And while Third Cinema pushed many geopolitical boundaries, it has been critiqued for the fact that its anticolonial filmmaking remains largely in the hands of male authors, and frequently elides or diminishes women's role in the anticolonial struggle. Ranjana Khanna thus proposes the concept of **Fourth Cinema**, "a woman's cinema of decolonization" (1998: 24),

> which moves beyond the guerrilla cinema where the camera is a weapon, is a revolutionary cinema of the cocoon, where the metaphor of the birth of a nation is not repressed into denial of the *feminine*, where film could give a voice, silence and image to women in the revolution, where this uncanny could become reified on the screen.
>
> (26)

179

Here Khanna proposes an alignment of feminist political projects with decolonizing practices that is overt rather than implicit, and that straightforwardly shows how equal rights for women need to be recognized as inherently tied to decolonial struggle rather than subordinated to it.

Trinh T. Minh-ha, a filmmaker and theorist whose work will be discussed in greater detail later in the chapter, also points to the imbalance of gender representation in revolutionary struggle when she notes that "the socially oriented filmmaker is thus the almighty voice-giver (here, in a vocalizing context that is all-male), whose position of authority in the production of meaning continues to go unchallenged, skillfully masked as it is by its righteous mission" (1991: 36). Movements like Third Cinema did indeed feature women filmmakers, such as Sarah Maldoror, Sara Gomez, and Assia Djebar (whose film *The Nouba of the Women of Mount Chenoua* [1976, Algeria] is used by Ranjana Khanna as an example of Fourth Cinema). They were "legendary women involved in postcolonial cinemas of liberation or Third Cinema in the 1960s and 1970s" (White 2015: 172). Their work, however, remains overshadowed, or at least less prominent, than that of their male counterparts, whose voices continue to frequently be positioned as "the almighty voice-givers" of the decolonizing movement.

Political documentary is only one subset of the variety of documentary work created by feminist documentarians. In the following sections, we will also explore poetic and expressive uses of the documentary that range from memoir to ethnography. This boundary between political and personal documentary, however, is less clear in practice. When approached through the popular feminist mantra that the personal is political, personal documentaries can be read as sites of political encounter in their own right. Through a range of modalities, forms and themes, documentary has continued to prove itself one of the central and most complex sites of feminist filmmaking – a site that simultaneously challenges many ingrained assumptions about identity, authorship, objectivity, and the ethics of cinematic storytelling, as well as sometimes (inadvertently) reiterating existing global power hierarchies. To that end, documentary, in opposition to its narrative counterpart, can be seen as more inherently political, even when it is decidedly personal, or when it challenges the notion of "reality" as such – perhaps especially then.

GENDER, HISTORY, AND THE DOCUMENTARY

Some of the earliest women film pioneers were documentary filmmakers: Thea (Terezie) Červenková (Czechoslovakia); sisters Adriana and Dolores Ehlers (Mexico and the United States); sisters Isabel, Phyllis, and Paulette McDonagh (Australia); Yuliya Solnstseva (Russia); Esfir Shub (Russia); Carmen Toscano Escobedo (Mexico); Elena Sánchez Valenzuela (Mexico); Gudrun Bjerring Parker (Canada); ethnographic filmmakers Osa Johnson,

Margaret Mead, and Zora Neale Hurston (all three from the United States); and Laura Boulton (United States and Canada) (some of these filmmakers are also discussed in Chapter 1).[2] The prevalence of documentary forms in early cinema is in part due to its status as an emerging technology. In early cinema, the distinction between narrative and documentary film was not as clear-cut as it is understood to be today, since the capturing of movement on film was perceived as always partially fantastical, even when it depicted "real life."

As the 20th century progressed, the development of documentary as a mode of filmmaking became increasingly linked to the **newsreel** and **propaganda film**. Leni Riefenstahl (Figure 5.4) was one of the most formally innovative documentary filmmakers in this tradition, whose crowning achievements were Nazi Germany's defining cinematic manifestos: *Triumph of the Will* (1935, Germany) and *Olympia* (1938, Germany). Her work gestures to the impossibility of equating documentation with truth or ethical objectivity, and women's filmmaking with inherently progressive political leanings. Riefenstahl's formal work as a documentarian adopted many innovative techniques and shot compositions, such as the use of tracking cameras, aerial shots, and underwater shots, as well as high and low camera angles to imply power or status and animate objects. Riefenstahl was also a master editor: she used techniques such as the dissolve to impart meaning on her subject matter without resorting to traditional newsreel documentary techniques (for instance, talking heads or voiceover narration). Her work was internationally recognized: *Triumph* won the grand prize at the Venice Film Festival in 1935 and the top prize at the world exhibition in Paris, 1937. For this film,

Figure 5.4 Leni Riefenstahl at work. From *The Wonderful Horrible Life of Leni Riefenstahl* (Ray Müller, 1993)

Riefenstahl had a crew of 172 people working under her, including thirty-six camera operators and assistants. Her films were so innovative because they relied on the power of images, rather than on verbal cues, to tell their stories. This is also why they were so ideologically dangerous – because they did not seem to have an explicit narrative, they were easily absorbed as "truth." That is to say, Riefenstahl appeared to be merely documenting a reality that she was in fact manipulating cinematographically and in the editing room. This appearance of non-guided documentation made the constructed nature of the films' messages about Aryan superiority and the greatness of Hitler as a leader much more difficult to pinpoint. The audience was not directly told, for example, that Hitler was like a god, but his person was animated by low angles tracking around the stage where he spoke, imparting a sense of larger than life magnitude to his person. Cuts between Hitler and seemingly unending crowds subconsciously linked the leader to the will of the masses and made his reign seem preordained. In the documentary *The Wonderful Horrible Life of Leni Riefenstahl* (Ray Müller, 1993, Germany), Riefenstahl, who lived to be 101 and who commissioned Müller's documentary, argues that in the case of the rally at Nuremberg seen in *Triumph of the Will*, she was simply documenting an event. Riefenstahl contends that she did not create propaganda, because she did not use techniques such as the voiceover to tell people what to think about the images onscreen – rather, she wanted the audience members to make up their own minds. With this, she insists on divorcing aesthetics from politics and problematically implies that the visual and formal elements of the documentary cannot be imbued with ideological messages in their own right. Identifying first and foremost as an artist, she maintains that she represented events aesthetically, but was not concerned with the politics of her work. Riefenstahl, then, is a difficult figure for feminist film history – both a woman film pioneer and a filmmaker whose work supported and legitimized a regime responsible for mass genocide on an unprecedented scale. This is an uneasy position that film history in general, and feminist film studies in particular, has struggled to meaningfully address. We will return to questions of the ethics and responsibility of the documentarian towards her subjects in the section on ethics below.

While women filmmakers have had a difficult time getting opportunities to make fiction films, many film critics and scholars agree that female documentarians are continuously represented in strong numbers. In 2008, Melissa Silverstein observed that, "while no one has exact figures, anecdotally most experts in the documentary community believe that women directors make up at least 50 percent of the directing ranks."[3] Silverstein attributes this, in part, to the lower cost of making documentaries, which in turn contributes to the perception of documentary film's lower prestige in the industry. This may also be why documentary has been at the forefront of addressing queer and trans themes, in films such as the aforementioned *Paris Is Burning*; *Choosing Children* (Debra Chasnoff & Kim Klausner, 1985, US); *Common*

Threads: Stories from the Quilt (1990, US) and *The Celluloid Closet* (1995, France/UK), both directed by Rob Epstein and Jeffrey Friedman; *Southern Comfort* (Kate Davis, 2001, US); *Tongzhi in Love* (Ruby Yang, 2008, US); *Fig Trees* (John Greyson, 2009, Canada); *Call Me Kuchu* (Katherine Fairfax Wright & Malika Zouhali-Worrall, 2012, US/Uganda); *How to Survive a Plague* (David France, 2012, US); and *That B.E.A.T.* (Abteen Bagheri, 2012, US/UK).

Moreover, many notable women filmmakers started their careers in documentary before earning broader recognition and turning to fiction films, including contemporary filmmakers such as Sabiha Sumar in Pakistan, Chou Zero in Taiwan, and Kawase Naomi in Japan. Hungary's Márta Mészáros made a number of politically charged documentaries in the 1950s and 1960s, before making her narrative feature debut *The Girl* (*Eltávozott nap*, Hungary) in 1968. And yet, even her fiction films – particularly the *Diary* series – continued to play with documentary footage, both archival and staged, where "the boundaries between documentary and fiction were crossed and re-crossed" (Cunningham 2004: 163). Catherine Portuges observes that: "[T]he trajectory of [Mészáros'] film career underscores her

Figure 5.5 A sequence that reveals fiction to be more real than documentary reality (*Diary for My Children*, Márta Mészáros, 1984)

conceptual and visual ability to link the personal with the political in order to depict individuals and the ways in which their efforts shape history, perhaps as much as they are constructed by it" (2004: 191). For instance, in *Diary for My Children* (*Napló gyermekeimnek*, 1984, Hungary), Mészáros sets the story between 1947 and 1953 (a time of iron-fisted Stalinist oppression in Hungary), and focuses on a young girl, Juli, who is disillusioned with the political situation in her country. The film frequently features documentary footage, seen, for instance, when Juli sits in a movie theater that is showing a pamphlet propaganda film about Stalin. Although Mészáros' film does not offer overt commentary on this footage, Juli's face clearly reflects the film's political stance towards such use of documentary film. At one point, the propaganda film shows children adoringly looking at a portrait of Stalin and Lenin. When we again cut to Juli's face, the juxtaposition of the children's adoring faces in the documentary, and Juli's serious, unamused expression makes it overtly clear that the documentary footage hardly represents any true reality as such (Figure 5.5).

ACTIVITY

Stage a debate around the following question:

Can a filmmaker like Leni Riefenstahl be comfortably recognized for her paradigm-shifting formal achievements if those achievements were used in the service of a fascist and genocidal political regime?

These intricate links between the personal and political prove to be particularly important to women's documentary filmmaking on several different levels. One level is the insertion of the filmmakers' autobiographical stories in their documentary work, discussed in one of the sections ahead. Another level is the female documentarians' insistence on politicizing the personal stories of others, or rather, conveying large-scale historical events through the intimate experiences of those whom history often forgets. Such an approach can be seen as a political intervention and a gesture that gives visibility to other histories that speak back to the grand narratives that dominate official history. An example of such an approach to documentary can be observed in Chantal Akerman's *From The East* (*D'Est*, 1993, Belgium; Figure 5.6), a documentary that mines the dramatic events around the disintegration of the Soviet Bloc through the decidedly non-dramatic use of still camera, and through silent and intimate depictions of ordinary people and their everyday lives. The film is comprised of lingering long takes of everydayness – for example, a street seen through a kitchen window, still shots

Figure 5.6 *From the East* (Chantal Akerman, 1993)

of busy street corners or deserted rural crossroads, or a tracking shot that follows an elderly woman walking down a sidewalk. *From the East* does not have any commentary or dialogue – its subjects are silent and simply carry on with their lives, performing routine everyday tasks. The documentary's time of filming (the years immediately following the collapse of communism in Eastern Europe) indicates that it captures a time of historically tumul-tuous transition, but the life it depicts is anything but. With this stylistic choice, Akerman calls attention to the mundane orderliness of daily life even in the context of great historical shifts perceived as "upheavals." The subjects do not speak, but they frequently look straight at the camera in long silent shots, while seated in everyday milieu, at a kitchen table or on a living room sofa. By silently facing the camera, they leave it to the viewer to imagine their story and fill in the gaps.

In an essay accompanying the film's DVD, Akerman refers to "my own style of documentary bordering on fiction," and suggests that, even though the time of making this documentary was undoubtedly important, "I will not attempt to show the disintegration of a system, nor the difficulties of enter-ing into another one, because she who seeks shall find, find all too well, and end up clouding her vision with her own preconceptions." Akerman is here actively aware of the inherent biases that might inadvertently inform her approach to the "Second World" (as socialist Eastern Europe has frequently been referred to), and therefore refrains from making a documentary along the expected route with respect to this great historical and political shift. Another reason for undertaking this project is personal – Akerman grew up in Belgium, but her parents were Holocaust survivors who came from Poland. Linking the personal back to the political, she notes: "And yet, even if the personal reasons are real, I don't want to make a 'back to my roots' kind of film because, as I said, she who seeks shall find, find all too well, and manipulate things a little too much in order to find them." Here again, the political and the personal converge, particularly around the filmmaker's conscious effort to avoid the pitfalls of either grand political narratives or stereotypical personal stories about (re)discovering one's roots. We further discuss the convergence of the personal and political when it comes to feminist documentaries in the section on autobiographical documentary.

ACTIVITY

If you could create a documentary about an important woman in your personal life, who would that be, and what techniques would you deploy? How would you negotiate issues of objectivity and your personal investment in your subject? Produce a brief video essay describing your concept, the approach you would take, and why.

DOCUMENTING THE LIVES OF WOMEN

Biographical documentary film can act as a reparatory counter-narrative where narrative cinema is unable to do historical justice. For example, Liz Garbus' *What Happened, Miss Simone?* (2015, US) is an insightful and provocative documentary about legendary singer and activist Nina Simone, which places particular emphasis on the singer's outspoken political views against systemic racism and colorism in the United States. Only a few months after the film's release, a narrative film about Simone, Cynthia Mort's *Nina* (2016, US), caused a controversy due to its simplistic (and reportedly inaccurate) representation of the singer, and because of the fact that Simone was played by a lighter-skinned actress, Zoe Saldana, whose skin appears to have been darkened for the role, thereby evoking the problematic practice of blackface (Figure 5.7). The narrative film, therefore, troublingly played into the very double standards of colorism placed on black femininity that Nina Simone herself spoke out against. Where the narrative film failed Simone's legacy, the documentary *What Happened, Miss Simone?* offered a

Figure 5.7 Nina Simone in *What Happened Miss Simone?* (Liz Garbus, 2015), and Zoe Saldana as Nina Simone in *Nina* (Cynthia Mort, 2016)

reparative script, allowing the singer to speak on her own terms (through archival footage), and retaining a sense of the complicated subjectivity that made Simone such a compelling figure in the first place.

Indeed, a number of documentary films have sought to act as reparative biographies of notable figures from women's history or contemporary culture. Examples include films such as *Anna May Wong: In Her Own Words* (Yunah Hong, 2011, US), about the Chinese-American actress who was typecast into stereotypical roles in Hollywood movies for most of her career, Frieda Lee Mock's *Maya Lin: A Strong Clear Vision* (1994, US), about the artist Maya Lin, and *Anita* (2013, US), about the scholar and feminist icon Anita Hill. And while films such as *Regarding Susan Sontag* (Nancy Kates, 2014, US) or *Amy* (Asif Kapadia, 2015, UK) seek to expose the less familiar aspects of well known, if misunderstood public figures, a documentary such as *Finding Vivian Maier* (John Maloof, Charlie Siskel, 2013, US) introduces as its subject a heretofore unknown woman who worked as a nanny her whole life while taking street photographs as a hobby. Thousands of undeveloped photo negatives were discovered by chance only after Maier's death, revealing her to be an incredible artist whose work no one saw while she was alive. The documentary reconstructs Maier's life story from fragments and from the photographs she obsessively took (including many self-portraits), and therefore serves as a reparative script that establishes Maier as one of the most talented photographers of her generation. Documentary film is, therefore, an important medium for conveying the complexities and hidden transcripts of women's history, whether the woman in question is a figure already well known but reduced to a simple narrative, or overlooked by dominant historical narratives.

ACTIVITY

Watch a biographical documentary about a female figure and discuss whether its content can be considered feminist. Does the film

> challenge any preconceived notions about the person (if she is already
> well known)? If the subject is not well known, how does the film argue
> for her importance? Does the film address a gap in history or give a
> voice to someone who has been absent from the historical record?

PERSONAL, POLITICAL, AUTOBIOGRAPHICAL: EXPERIMENTING WITH THE DOCUMENTARY FORM

Within the documentary mode, **experimental documentary** represents a particularly engaging form of filmmaking because it challenges the boundaries between documentary, fiction, and experimental poetics (see also Chapter 6). One subgenre of documentary filmmaking in which formal experimentation became a prominent way of telling (or challenging) personal stories is **autobiographical documentary**. Indeed, nowhere is the focus on the feminine and feminist more pronounced than in autobiographical works in which female documentarians mine deeply personal and often painful stories about their own lives and intimate family histories. Jim Lane (2002) argues that the autobiographical documentary arose as a reaction to the direct cinema of the 1960s. Autobiographical documentary runs counter to direct cinema, which, as discussed ahead, adopts a policy of non-interference, where they director is seen to merely record rather than influence the events they capture on film. By contrast, autobiographical documentary actively reinserts personal biases and subjective frameworks as central to the filmmakers' approach to depicting reality. In this way, it challenges the notion of objectivity altogether, as well as the neat separation of filmmaker from her subjects.

Women autobiographical filmmakers explicitly utilize the feminist credo that the personal is political (Erens 1988). Examples of autobiographical films include Michelle Citron's *Parthenogenesis* (1975, US) and *Daughter Rite* (1979, US), Amalie Rosenfeld Rothschild's *Nana, Mom and Me* (1974, US), and Joyce Chopra's *Joyce at 34* (1974, US). These filmmakers' turn to autobiographical documentary "significantly parallels the historical rise of the second wave women's movement" (Lane 2002: 146). Citron herself has argued that the feminist investigation of the relationship between the filmmaker and the audience is particularly well explored in autobiographical film because "with the autobiographical act the personal moves into the cultural, the private becomes the social" (1999: 271). Contemporary female documentarians have continued the tradition of autobiographical film – examples include Sarah Polley's *Stories We Tell* (2012, Canada), Alex Sichel's *A Woman Like Me* (2015, US), Kirsten Johnson's *Cameraperson*

(2016, US; see also Chapter 1), Petra Epperlein's *Karl Marx City* (with Michael Tucker, 2016, Germany), and Chantal Akerman's *No Home Movie* (2015, Belgium).

As a form of storytelling that blurs the relationship between subject and object, autobiography lends itself well to feminist political projects. As Michelle Citron notes, "the autobiographical act is historically significant for women, and all others, who have traditionally lacked either a voice or a public forum for their speaking" (272). Moreover, autobiography is a paradox, because "it allows for more authenticity by giving voice to that which we both consciously *and* unconsciously know" (282, emphasis in the text). And with a focus on oneself as both an object and subject, autobiography resolves the ethical dilemmas about objectivity, truth, and reality, even if only provisionally. This is why, frequently, autobiographical documentary does not rely on realist forms of representation, but rather mixes genres and blurs fact and fiction, calls attention to the unreliability of memory through reenactments and performances, and offers inconclusive glimpses into family histories rather than complete, linear stories. Each of the following two case studies provides an opportunity to explore the intersection of the personal and the political in autobiographical and experimental documentary modes.

CASE STUDY: DOCUMENTING MOTHERHOOD AND FAMILY HISTORY IN *FINDING CHRISTA* (CAMILLE BILLOPS & JAMES HATCH, 1991, US)

As has been asserted by many feminist thinkers, motherhood is one of the most strictly policed categories through which images of women are disseminated and consumed in popular culture. The cultural markers of good versus bad mothers are usually treated as unequivocal indications of ethical versus unethical personality traits and actions. In both narrative and documentary films, mothers are rarely exempt from a gaze shaped by normative understandings of race, ethnicity, sexuality, and social class.

Camille Billops and her partner James Hatch's documentary *Finding Christa* is a film that challenges the standard tropes of the adoption autobiography genre: remorse, loss, and guilt as defining traits of mothers who give their children up for adoption. In this autobiographical documentary, Billops depicts the story of her own decision to give up her daughter Christa for adoption when the girl was four years old, as well as her reunion with the now-adult daughter two decades later. *Finding Christa* offers a non-judgmental representation of a black woman who chooses *not* to be a mother to the child to whom she gives birth. This non-judgmental exploration marks a radical difference from most mainstream adoption narratives and from dominant depictions of African-American mothers, and makes *Finding Christa* a poignant, rare example of a counter-image to pathologizing images of black maternity (for more on the controlling images of black women, see Hill Collins 2000). As Dijana Jelača (2013) notes, the documentary examines affective responses to family trauma and adoption, as well as to the construction of identity, illuminating the taboo topic of biological mothers who decide to give their children away. Through this, the film tackles culturally charged discourses of motherhood, family, home space, marriage, and heterosexual relationships that have traditionally confined female subjectivity, particularly with the double bind of race and gender for women of color. *Finding Christa* offers a powerful counternarrative about women making sense of their difficult past, and the ways in which that past is actively utilized (in often deliberately contradictory ways) in negotiating the present.

Centered around the story of Billops reconnecting with her biological daughter Christa Victoria (Figure 5.8) years after having given her up for adoption, *Finding Christa* offers insight into the mechanisms through which the more contradictory and subjective workings of memory can subvert the notion of authentic or objective family history. When Christa was four years old, Billops, a single mother whose fiancé left her after she became pregnant, decided to give her daughter up for adoption and dedicate herself to her art instead. Two decades later, Christa contacts her biological mother, and this first contact is what initiates Billops's decision to make a documentary about Christa's search, as well as about her own rediscovery of her identity as a mother. Probing the limits of objective documentation, *Finding Christa* repeatedly questions the validity of its own accounts of the family's past by presenting us with many overlapping voices whose versions of events do not necessarily add up into a coherent whole. This meta-language of perpetual self-questioning is emphasized by the film's use of reenactments and dream sequences as tools for fictionalizing, and therefore destabilizing, the realist foundations of the documentary genre within which it operates.

Figure 5.8 Billops' daughter Christa as a baby (*Finding Christa*, Camille Billops, 1991)

In *Finding Christa*, the question of the narrator's reliability is open-ended. The film begins and ends, and is occasionally interspersed with, the voiceover of Christa, yet one cannot definitively say that the daughter's disembodied voice marks her as an authoritative narrator. On the contrary, since Christa was not present for many of the events recounted in the film (most notably, Billops's life after giving Christa up and before their reunion), she cannot be narrating them as her own experience. Christa's haunting voiceover serves as a reminder that she is provided with vicarious memories of events that were often not an organic or lived part of her experience. In a way, Christa's disembodied voice symbolically illustrates her restless search for an embodied identity that would connect her to her birth mother and with it, her biological family history (a search that Christa's adoptive mother Margaret implies is essential for the daughter's peace of mind).

The film reveals that the family is never merely private, and never independent of the larger societal structures that limit possibilities and subjectivities alike, particularly through the categories of race, gender, or class. By putting the motif of adoption front and center in her exploration of the larger structures that inform and influence familial formations (and black familial formations in particular), Billops denaturalizes family altogether by exposing it as a highly contested entity whose existence is dependent on a system of inequality split along gendered, classed, and racialized lines.

In the film, Billops says:

> I had obviously done something that was absolutely unacceptable to the tribe. Somehow, when women want to change their lives, it's unacceptable, but when men leave . . . you know. So, now I see it as a feminist statement, but, of course, I didn't at twenty-seven years old.

Here Billops tellingly implies that at the time she was deciding to give Christa away, she did not have a feminist framework available to help her rationalize, or even defend, her own actions – it was simply not a part of the available cultural discourses about women and their choices the way that it became some years later. By denaturalizing the link between the mother and child – stating quite unapologetically that she chose herself over the child – Billops does the work of disrupting the smooth enamel that typically glosses over the taboo of the more restrictive aspects of maternal attachments to children.

Finding Christa's documentary style intersects with narrative cinema, and occasionally, with elements of performance art and theater. This hybridity points to the performative nature of familial roles, but also to the notion of documentary's (in)ability to tell a complete and objectively rendered story. The (un)reliability of memory is a trope around which the documentary genre often builds its claim of representing a realistic and objective portrayal of events. And even though *Finding Christa* is identified as an autobiographical documentary, it also actively deconstructs many documentary conventions. In conventional documentary filmmaking, talking heads are most often tasked with the role of constructing a neat and reliably truthful narrative. This, in turn, serves to mask the subjective aspects of the interlocutors', as well as the filmmaker's, authorship in interpreting the events in question. This is where *Finding Christa* diverges from the documentary norm, as the author's subjectivity is never masked, but always front and center – a central framing device for conveying the events at hand.

Watch and discuss: *Finding Christa*

1 What are some of the most provocative elements of the film's treatment of motherhood?
2 How does the film frame the roles of the biological and adoptive mothers differently?
3 How is race positioned in the film? Is it overtly addressed?
4 Almost paradoxically, *Finding Christa*'s most heartfelt emotional moments arise from its dramatized, potentially fictional reenactments. How might these reenactments trouble the notions of truth, memory and objectivity?
5 Think about the representation of black motherhood more generally, and particularly in fiction films – for example, in *Precious* (Lee Daniels, 2009, US). What prevailing negative stereotypes can you detect? How do films like *Finding Christa* challenge such negative racial stereotypes?

CASE STUDY: DOCUMENTING THE PAIN OF WOMEN IN TWO FILMS BY JASMILA ŽBANIĆ

Jasmila Žbanić is one of the highest-profile women filmmakers to emerge from Eastern Europe in recent years. Her films consistently tackle the role of women in society, particularly through the lens of the volatile changes that war and postwar reality bring about. A few years after the war in her native Bosnia-Herzegovina had ended, Žbanić distinguished herself with documentary work that sought to articulate the intimate and often unacknowledged losses of women during the times of social and political upheaval. Her documentaries opt for the intimate over the collective, depicting women's stories that, while perhaps indicative of broader tendencies, are always decidedly local and grounded in the intricacies of the particular contexts they represent.

In her short documentary *Red Rubber Boots* (*Crvene gumene čizme*, 2000, Bosnia-Herzegovina), Žbanić follows Jasna P.'s efforts to find the remains of her two young children, who were taken away from her and killed during the war. Mixing footage of teams digging up mass graves and collecting scattered human remains with close-ups of Jasna's face as she talks about her experience in voiceover, the documentary poignantly conveys the human story and intimate tragedy that hides behind the statistics of how many people died or went missing in the war. The mother (Figure 5.9) talks about her inability to dream about her children, as even in her sleep, she only dreams about their absence and about her efforts to find them. In one silent sequence, Jasna shows the camera pictures of her missing children. Knowing that they are dead, the mother's only goal is to find the remains of her children so that she can reach closure and begin her grieving process in earnest by giving them burial rites. The red rubber boots referenced

Figure 5.9 A mother's anguish in *Red Rubber Boots* (Jasmila Žbanić, 2000)

in the film's title are the boots that the woman's four-year-old son was wearing when he was taken away. She hopes that if she can find the boots in one of the mass graves, it would be a reliable indication that her son's remains are there as well. The importance of identifying a seemingly ordinary children's item, such as red rubber boots, in order to confirm a young child's violent demise emphasizes the film's unspeakably tragic overtones. By the end of the film, Jasna P. is still searching for the remains, so there is no closure for her grief. Every time a search is unsuccessful, it appears that Jasna loses her children all over again, as reflected on her dejected face. In its understated and non-sensationalist way, the film explores the impossible loss brought on by necropolitics, a concept within which "the ultimate expression of sovereignty resides, to a large degree, in the power and the capacity to dictate who may live and who must die" (Mbembe 2003: 11). In the film, the ultimate power extends beyond life and death, and stipulates who may be allowed to grieve and whose life and death may or may not be acknowledged. In that sense, Žbanić's film represents a key intervention into the regional necropolitics that feed the ongoing ethno-national divides and politicization of victimhood in the post-conflict region of the former Yugoslavia.

In another short documentary, *Images From the Corner* (*Slike sa ugla*, 2003, Bosnia-Herzegovina), Žbanić reconstructs a painful episode from the wartime siege of Sarajevo, when one of her schoolmates was gravely wounded in a shelling attack. Žbanić, who provides a voiceover in this film, recalls that a picture of her wounded schoolmate lying on the street corner where the grenade fell was taken by a foreign journalist, and went on to become an internationally recognized, award-winning photograph depicting the plight of Sarajevo's citizens during the war. However, Žbanić refuses to show the image in her documentary, and instead wonders how this lasting depiction of the wounded woman's pain serves to perpetuate her suffering, and moreover, how the fact that the journalist took photographs during the moments of her agony implies that he did nothing to help the wounded girl. In one poignant scene, the lens of Žbanić's still photography camera rests on the empty corner where the event took place, while we hear the sound of two rolls of film being used (the number of images the photographer reportedly took). With this sequence, Žbanić viscerally illustrates the duration of time that it took the photographer to shoot the images, and with it, the duration of time that the girl lay wounded while her pain was an object of the Western journalist's award-winning lens. Žbanić condemns as inhumane the journalist's privileging of documentation over relief. The film is also a condemnation of the Western media's focus on the spectacle of suffering when it comes to "remote" conflicts.

Watch and discuss: *Red Rubber Boots* and *Images From the Corner*

1 Which documentary tradition would you say the two films belong to – for example, direct cinema, autobiographical cinema, women's biography, political documentary, or transnational feminist documentary?
2 How do the films blend some of these strains of documentary filmmaking?
3 How does the idea of absence shape both of these films? What does this suggest about documenting traumatic historical events?
4 Building on question 3, what is the effect of Žbanić's refusal to show the famous image of her friend after the grenade attack? What does it suggest about documentary's access to the real?
5 How does the fact that Žbanić is a member of the communities she documents shape the content or form of her films? In your opinion, does it make her films more or less objective?

FEMINIST DOCUMENTARY ETHICS: THE LIMITS OF DOCUMENTING REALITY

Where are you right now, as you read this textbook? How would your behavior or mentality shift if someone were filming you for a documentary, as you studied? Would it alter your behavior? Would it heighten your self-awareness? How would you behave if the documentary were about the difficulties of teaching documentary ethics at a college level? Now imagine that the film is about the relationship between information retention and body language while studying. Would this change how you see yourself being filmed? The documentarian and her equipment are variables that inevitably alter the reality they attempt to film. In the case of this thought experiment, do you think your awareness of being filmed would alter the "objective" reality of you as a reading subject?

From its inception, documentary has been fraught with questions around the achievability of an objective representation. This is perhaps most evident in **ethnographic film**, which positions the documentary filmmaker as an objective researcher studying (through filming) either foreign or familiar cultures, and therefore acting as an observer who stands aside and supposedly does not interfere with the way of life being studied. However, one of the earliest ethnographic films, *Nanook of the North* (Robert Flaherty, 1922, US), notoriously staged many of its scenes of Inuit life for the camera. Flaherty renamed the film's protagonist Nanook, and cast one of his own Inuit lovers in the role of Nanook's wife. "Nanook" was asked to pretend to encounter objects of technology – such as the phonograph – as if he had never seen them before. While this film is still heralded as an important document of a way of life that was changing with time, it was highly manufactured. In addition to the issues of truth/fiction that *Nanook* raises, it also brings up questions about the power dynamics inherent in documentary, particularly when people from marginalized communities or underprivileged economic and geographical contexts are used as subjects in a film that is meant for a Western, privileged audience. These questions of documentary film's ability to capture the real and the politics of looking at and representing others are endemic to feminist documentary work and theorizing.

As decidedly political forms of filmmaking, the burgeoning direct cinema and *cinéma vérité* movements of the 1960s provided training ground or inspiration for many feminist documentarians. **Direct cinema** deploys a detached observational technique that seeks to convey an unmediated and objective reality without the interference of the filmmaker. Direct cinema is closely related, but not entirely identical, to *cinéma vérité*. Both styles give primacy to observational aspects of documentary filmmaking and aim at objectivity, but *cinéma vérité* allows for occasional filmmaker interventions and interactions with the subjects being depicted, acknowledging that the presence of the camera changes the reality being depicted, whereas direct cinema typically tries to remove any interference between the audience and the subject depicted onscreen. In many ways, the more formally experimental documentary work of many feminist documentarians arose as a response to the ways in which direct cinema, *cinéma vérité*, and other traditions, such as the ethnographic film, masked the power dynamics inherent in representing subjects. Formally experimental documentary called for more engagement around questions of truth and the politics and ethics of representation (see the case study in this chapter on *Portrait of Jason*).

In North America, along with the rise of the women's liberation movement, or second wave feminism, women filmmakers made a number of **feminist documentaries** that often functioned as political pamphlets and calls to action. Some examples include Joan Churchill's *Sylvia, Fran and Joy* (1973, US), Martha Coolidge's *Old-Fashioned Woman* (1974, US), Liane

Brandon's *Betty Tells Her Story* (1972, US), and Madeline Anderson's *I Am Somebody* (1970, US; Figure 5.10). If the 1970s "mark a decisive moment in the production of feminist codes" (Rabinowitz 1994: 161), during which women activists took film cameras and deployed *cinéma vérité* aesthetics in order to "authenticate women's lives on screen" (ibid), the relationship between feminist documentary work and the documentation of reality has always been a complicated one. Patricia Zimmerman observes that "the political sea changes of the antiwar, the women's, and civil rights movements called for films that critiqued institutions to mobilize audiences to action, an epistemology alien to the refined, almost mythical distance of *cinéma vérité*" (1999: 74).

Indeed, one of the central debates in feminist theory at this time was around the use of realism as a documentary mode. Julia Lesage notes of the appeal of *cinéma vérité*: "Many of the first feminist documentaries used a simple format to present to the audience (presumably composed primarily of women) a picture of the ordinary details of women's lives, their thoughts – told directly by the protagonists to the camera" (1978). However, as Linda Williams and B. Ruby Rich observe, "the use of the documentary as a form of social evidence has rested on the misconception that film can be equated with 'truth'" (1981: 18). Further complicating the relationship between the filmmaker, the protagonist and the camera, Trinh T. Minh-ha argues that "[t]here is no such thing as documentary – whether the term designates a

Figure 5.10 *I Am Somebody* (Madeline Anderson, 1970)

category of material, a genre, an approach, or a set of techniques" (1991: 29). She adds that, "[o]n the one hand, truth is produced, induced, and extended according to the regime in power. One the other, truth lies in between all regimes of truth" (30). Here, Minh-ha highlights the ways in which power – often in the form of capital investment – shapes the representation of truth in documentary form. Truth is somewhere much less accessible than onscreen – it exists between "regimes of truth." Documentary conventions are part of these truth regimes.

This sentiment is echoed in Minh-ha's documentaries *Reassemblage: From the Firelight to the Screen* (1983, US) and *Surname Viet Given Name Nam* (1989, US; Figure 5.11), in which the theorist/filmmaker poses probing questions about the limits of representing an other, as well as about the unstable boundaries between fact and fiction. Aside from her influential writing, Minh-ha's films are feminist theories in their own right – or, more accurately, embody a feminist film *praxis* – merging theory and practice and challenging the spectator to engage with an intersectional and postcolonial framework for making sense of the world. In her films, Minh-ha attempts to disrupt both form and content. For example, in *Reassemblage*, a film shot while Minh-ha was doing fieldwork in Senegal, she attempts to disrupt our conventional ways of viewing the other through her manipulation of the

Figure 5.11 *Surname Viet Given Name Nam* (Trinh T. Minh-ha, 1989)

audio and visual tracks. *Reassemblage* has an audio track that is purpose-fully *not* synchronized to the images onscreen. Instead, the sound often ends abruptly, so the viewer sees the image suddenly without the intervention of a narrator or diegetic sound, foregrounding the constructed nature of the representation for the viewer. The soundtrack features a collection of spoken quotes and commentary on the politics of ethnography, again reflex-ively drawing attention to the film as a constructed reality. These musings are interrupted by the insertion of music, quotations and anecdotes from the culture represented onscreen. The film repeats the phrase, "Don't speak about. Speak nearby," while the screen displays images of people going about their daily lives. This phrase, "speak nearby," reminds the viewer of the impossibility of mastering or assigning one "truth" to the images onscreen. While this film foregrounds its "reassembled" nature, it asks us to consider that all films, in particular the ethnographic film, are assembled artifacts: they represent a simplified narration of a messy plotless reality. The ethical documentarian can therefore only speak *nearby* instead of *about* her subjects, acknowledging both her power as holder of the camera and giver of meaning to the images she collects.

In *Surname Viet Given Name Nam*, Minh-ha explores the experiences of Vietnamese women after the Vietnam War, again using montage in both audio and visual tracks to disrupt the viewer's simple consumption of oth-erness onscreen. Of particular interest is her disruption of the authority of talking heads – here she has Vietnamese women who have immigrated to the US reenact, in highly stylized form, interviews conducted with Vietnamese women still living in Vietnam. The interviews are translated and performed in often difficult-to-decipher English. Later, the immigrant women speak about their own experience in Vietnamese, but English text overlays the images, only representing parts of what the women are saying and often moving too fast for the viewer to read. Here, Minh-ha reminds the viewer that truth is elusive and is always mediated – translated even – by the format of the documentary film.

This is very different from the anthropologically based approach of fem-inist filmmaker Ngozi Onwurah in *Monday's Girls* (1993, UK/Nigeria). Onwurah, a Nigerian-born filmmaker who relocated to the United King-dom as a child, here focuses on a tradition called the *Iria*, held by the Wakirke people in Nigeria. This ceremony is an initiation into womanhood for Wakirke girls that involves inspecting their bodies to ensure that their "purity" is intact, followed by weeks spent being pampered and fed in the "fattening" room before being released back into the community to much fanfare and celebration. This ceremony is presided over by the elder women of the community, foremost among them the Monday of the film's title. Onwurah tracks this ceremony through two main protagonists – a village girl who sees the celebration as a privilege and honor, and another who has moved to Lagos and returns for the ceremony, ultimately to reject it and return to the city. While this film offers insight into women-centered rituals – too often ignored by male-authored ethnographic work – and offers the women themselves a voice to assess their own relationship to the traditional culture, it does so in a much less formally innovative and more accessible mode than Minh-ha uses in her work. Sound is synchronized, and the viewer is offered multiple, apparently balanced perspectives. Onwurah's film here is a useful comparison to Minh-ha's work, as it raises the question of whether a documentary need be experimental in form, as well as progressive in content. Must documentary foreground its own representational nature in order to do ethical justice to the subject it purports to represent?

In her films and written work, Minh-ha challenges the notion that documentary is by default closer to "**the real**" than fiction film, and that it therefore presents an unambiguously ethical tool. Perhaps more so than any other cinematic mode, documentary has been scrutinized in feminist film studies for its fraught relationship to **objective reality**. Can film ever adequately convey such a thing as an objective reality, particularly if the latter does not exist outside of one's subjective perception to begin with? What is more, the emphasis on representing the world objectively and "as is" runs the risk of eliding the inherent power imbalance between the filmmaker and those being filmed. With regards to this, Minh-ha observes that "[t]he silent common people – those 'who have never expressed themselves' unless they are given the opportunity to voice their thoughts by the one who comes to redeem them – are constantly summoned to signify the real world" (37). This statement highlights the inherent power dynamic in even well intentioned attempts to represent the other. Often, those doing the representing come from places of more geopolitical privilege than the objects of their documentary gaze, and are usually making films for an outside audience. Yet, these attempts at representation are often taken as *the* truth of the other – for example, Western audiences can believe that they know the truth about an issue, such as cliterodectomy or sex trafficking, by watching a documentary made by a filmmaker who enacts an objectifying outsider's gaze on the topic.

ACTIVITY

Choose a female documentary film "pioneer" and research her work. Does her choice of subjects reflect a perspective shaped by issues of gender or race? Does her work challenge or reproduce some of the problematic tendencies in documentary filmmaking, for example, a fascinated interest in "others" documented for a Western gaze?

INTERROGATING REALISM

In 1975, Eileen McGarry's essay "Documentary Realism and Women's Cinema" challenged the notion that reality exists in an entirely pure form outside of the filmmaker's intervention into it. In documentary filmmaking, she claims:

> Certain *decisions about reality* are made: the choice of subject and the location of shooting (not to mention the preconceptions, no matter how minimal, of the film workers), the presence of the film workers and their equipment (no matter how *unobtrusive*), all participate in, control and encode the pro-filmic event within the context of the technology of cinema and the dominant ideology.
>
> (50)

Reality, therefore, cannot ever exist in a pure form, outside our preconceived notions about meaning and knowing. The question of **realism** – as a form that attempts to convey reality *as it exists*, with as little subjective intervention as possible – has been a stumbling block for many feminist filmmakers and theorists (we further discuss realism in Chapter 7). In discussing Chick Strand's influential feminist work *Soft Fiction* (1979, US), Paula Rabinowitz observes that it "dwells between the borders of ethnography, documentary, avant-garde, and feminist counter-cinema" (165). Moreover, "films like [Strand's] and [Minh-ha's] depict the historicity of cinematic engagement by calling attention to the performances of documentary film's subjects and objects" (167). The focus on performance reveals the tension between authenticity and artifice, the real and the fictional. Moreover, if our social identities, and particularly gender, are performative (Butler 1990) – which is to say, they arise from a limited set of options and socially constructed scripts that define the norms of femininity and masculinity – how might a deliberate focus on the artificiality of identity provide a subversive counterpoint?

In attempting to convey the stories of ordinary, typically silenced women objectively and without formal or narrative interventions, wouldn't feminist documentary inadvertently reiterate a patriarchal emphasis on realist observational detachment as the only form of reliable storytelling? Indeed, Claire Johnston's "Women's Cinema as Counter-Cinema," probes these questions and argues against the *vérité* techniques deployed in notable 1970s feminist documentaries (such as Kate Millett and Susan Kleckner's 1971 documentary *Three Lives* [US]). Johnston argues:

> Any revolutionary strategy must challenge the depiction of reality; it is not enough to discuss the oppression of women within the text of the film; the language of the cinema/the depiction of reality must also be interrogated, so that a break between ideology and text is effected.
>
> (1999: 215)

This has to be done because reality is not an objective fact, but rather a construct. Johnston adds that, "the danger of developing a cinema of non-intervention is that it promotes a passive subjectivity at the expense of intervention" (37).

Such a break between ideology and text can be detected in Michelle Citron's *Daughter Rite* (1978, US; Figure 5.12), a landmark film that challenges documentary's focus on reality by mixing the author's poetic voiceover with home movie footage from her childhood and improvised reenactments of two women playing her sisters, themselves reminiscing about their mother. These formal strategies point to the unreliability of intimate memory. The film blends three varied film forms – documentary, fiction, and experimental film – in order to trouble the boundaries between them. As B. Ruby Rich notes, "*Daughter Rite* is a classic, the missing link between the 'direct cinema' documentaries and the later hybrids that acknowledged truth couldn't always be found in front of a camera lens."[4] And while the film challenges the conventions of direct cinema, it also "functions to redeem documentary, in that its form is accessible, related to the lives of women, a meaningful tradition and a still powerful taproot into the emotions as well as the intellects of viewers" (Williams & Rich 1981: 21). Citron herself has asserted that "in documentary film or videomaking every shot is charged with ethical implications and choices" (1999: 271).

Because *vérité*-style documentaries deploy conventions of realism – a camera running in real time on unstaged events, a lack of voiceover narration or

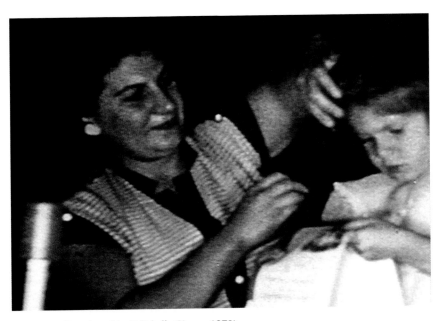

Figure 5.12 *Daughter Rite* (Michelle Citron, 1978)

talking heads, and the absence of stylization – they often hide the construction of reality in which they participate. Yet, as Alexandra Juhasz (1999) observes, to entirely dismiss documentaries which are overtly political in content but do not challenge film form or the notion of objective reality is to negate a history of **realist documentary** filmmaking that played a crucial role in championing the fight against gender inequality and related forms of oppression. Diane Waldman and Janet Walker convincingly argue that:

> While often accused of falling into the realist illusion that documentary film represents real women, feminist documentary practices and studies have in fact looked for ways to avoid that illusionist pitfall while at the same time acknowledging the political stakes in representing the images and voices of women who are not professional actors and whose documentary representation seeks to build consensus with actual women for the audiences of these films. Feminism's political grounding has mitigated any facile reduction of documentary to its fictive properties by retaining the paradox of the "reality fiction" as a *paradox*, and moreover, as a paradox in which there is much at stake.
>
> (1999: 11–12)

To that end, the documentary *Year of the Woman: A Fantasy by Sandra Hochman* (Sandra Hochman, 1973, US) can serve as a poignant indication of how much is indeed at stake. Appearing in the same year as Claire Johnston's landmark essay, Sandra Hochman's documentary "fantasy" drew critical attention upon its (very brief) initial release only to be locked away in a vault for the next forty years, because it was "too radical, or too weird for distributors to touch"[5] (the film finally received wide release in 2015). Even in today's terms, the documentary appears radical and radically strange, and it seems that its very strangeness prevented such an important chronicle of its time from being more widely seen during the decade whose complexities it tackles. Filmed in a style that openly articulates the observation that "feminist filmmakers have thought long and hard about the politics of people filming people" (Waldman & Walker 1999: 13), Hochman's film inserts its filmmaker and her perspective into the texture and shape of the narrative being conveyed, long before that became a stylistic documentary norm through the mainstream and critical success of documentary filmmakers such as Michael Moore. Moreover, the documentary is framed as a sci-fi fantasy that sees Hochman switch between present and future, and between Earth and Mars. With a close-up of her face looking at the camera, Hochman introduces herself in the voiceover at the beginning of the film: "I'm a poet, a spy, a fool. I'm everywoman, living through an invisible revolution that would change our world in ways we still do not know." Hochman deploys guerilla filmmaking to depict the role of women at the Democratic National Convention in 1972, and by interrogating men in powerful positions – from politicians to journalists to clergy – on their stance regarding women's rights. The film features numerous prominent female activists of the time, including Gloria Steinem, Betty Friedan, and Shirley MacLaine. Florynce "Flo" Kennedy, in particular, is prominently featured, as a feminist activist who engages in a decidedly intersectional critique of patriarchy. Sometimes Hochman's female interlocutors wear improvised homemade eyewear in order to symbolize women's constrained optics (Figure 5.13). At other times, they narrate their dreams or enact fantasies, such as a mock welcoming party for Indira Gandhi, who is being greeted by a "cross section of the American public," mainly consisting of women sitting on a beach and wearing face masks. Hochman impersonates Gandhi's voice to declare: "The strangeness of it all. It's even stranger here than it is in India." The group then proceeds to enact for the imaginary guest a dance titled "an American woman's anxiety number." In a fantasy sci-fi scene, we are transplanted into the future on Mars, a hundred years after women have staged a revolution and taken over. The man being interviewed in this imaginary future complains that no one is having fun anymore in the world led by women. He also notes that the difference between men and women was eliminated on Earth in light of the revolution. This scene, which links social justice to cosmic relevance, is followed by footage of Vietnam veterans demonstrating against the war. The

Figure 5.13 Sandra Hochman talks to Florynce ("Flo") Kennedy in *Year of the Woman* (Sandra Hochman, 1973)

focus is again political and intersectional, as antiwar efforts are linked to feminist goals and vice versa. In the film, Hochman interviews largely uncooperative male interlocutors who often express disdain over her disruptive feminist agenda. Upon hearing that her goal is to have women take over the world, Hollywood star (and Shirley MacLaine's brother) Warren Beatty responds with: "But aren't women really worse male chauvinists than men? I mean, most of them."

The film resists a traditionally realist framework, opting instead for a subjective prism of storytelling through the voice of its director and through dream sequences, as well as voiceover segments by a girl posing as Hochman's younger self. At one point in the film, over the footage of the Convention's women's caucus meeting, Hochman narrates the story of going through an illegal abortion. Other times, Hochman talks to Liz Reney, a glamorous actress, author and stripper whose appearance on the Convention floor draws a lot of attention from the male delegates. As Reney charms her admirers, Hochman says in the voiceover: "Isn't sexism a bitch? Liz, exploited and exploitive, playing a game, like myself. Little girl grown up, hiding behind a mask, all-knowing dumbbell. I know you. All guts and scared to death. Anything for a laugh. Cuckoo!"

Generally, the voiceover serves as a meta-commentary that humorously and cynically accompanies Hochman's visual documentation. She, for instance, shows herself walking the Convention floor with a crocodile mask on her face, while in the voiceover she worries what her mother's reaction would be to seeing her like this. She decides to stop worrying since her film "luckily . . . will never be on television." "The funny thing is, I never have so much fun as when I make trouble," Hochman concludes. This is followed by a dramatic encounter between the women activists and representatives of the media gathered to cover the Convention. The journalists and their crews are all men. The women accuse them of not doing anything to meaningfully cover women's issues, although they have the power to change things. The power of media and representation is here acutely positioned as a key issue. At the end, the film returns to the sci-fi fantasy scenes of the future, where humorist Art Buchwald observes from Mars that men have staged a counterrevolution back on Earth. "There it is," says Buchwald looking through the telescope, "a man is going into the White House." When Hochman complains that she does not like this ending, she and Buchwald discuss an ending she would be happier with. "You're your fantasy, Sandra," he notes. Here the film overtly shows the mechanics of its own making, by offering alternative endings and staging its own projections of the future. This is also where the norms of documentary filmmaking are again challenged, as the entire Convention is depicted through the highly intimate perspective of its filmmaker, who deploys fictional elements to call further attention to the politics of representation.

CASE STUDY: *PORTRAIT OF JASON* (SHIRLEY CLARKE, 1967, US)

Shirley Clarke started out as a dancer, eventually applying her sense of movement and rhythm to experimental film in the 1950s. A key member of the New American Cinema Group, Clarke came from a relatively privileged background as the child of white wealthy New Yorkers. However, Clarke felt herself an outsider. She said:

> For years I'd felt like an outsider, so I identified with the problems of minority groups. . . . I thought it was more important to be some kind of goddamned junkie who felt alienated rather than to say I am an alienated woman who doesn't feel part of the world and who wants in.
>
> (quoted in Butt 2007: 52–53)

Clarke made two narrative feature films dealing with black subcultures and drugs before making her documentary *Portrait of Jason* in 1967, a film that is often read as a critique of the direct cinema tradition that was flourishing at the time. As Irene Gustafson says, "It is [Clarke's] test of [direct cinema's stalwart advocates'] most cherished and problematic faith – that the camera can both capture an authentic moment and represent the complete subject" (13). Of her two fiction feature films, *The Connection* (1963, US) is particularly relevant as a precursor, as it is *about* a documentary filmmaker filming a group of junkies waiting for a heroin delivery. Although a scripted fiction film, it is shot in a *vérité* style. In the film, the junkies mock and challenge the character of the filmmaker, who naïvely believes he can capture their "reality" on film and wants to make a spectacle of their suffering.

In *Portrait of Jason*, Clarke focuses on the story of Jason Holliday (Figure 5.14), a black gay scenester and aspiring cabaret performer who held various jobs, from houseboy to hustler, in the past. The film is edited down to 105 minutes from around twelve hours of footage shot consecutively in Clarke's apartment in the Chelsea Hotel. Clarke and her lover Carl Lee are often heard offscreen asking Jason questions or encouraging him to retell stories – an approach that challenges direct cinema's stipulation about filmmakers not interfering with the world they are documenting. As the film progresses, Jason becomes progressively drunker and higher on drugs, and the

Figure 5.14 Jason Holliday in *Portrait of Jason* (Shirley Clarke, 1967)

off-camera questions become more intense and intrusive. In fact, the end of the film hears Carl Lee, a black heterosexual man, encouraging an inebriated and exhausted Jason to "orgasm" for the camera. The film raises uncomfortable questions about the power differential between filmmaker and subject, especially when the former holds forms of racial, sexual, or class privilege over those s/he films. Commenting on a story Jason tells about a white boss asking him to come out and join the guests at a Halloween party, where he'll be just another "spook," one critic comments, "It's also hard not to wonder if [Jason] saw Clarke, who was seated off camera and peppering him with questions, as another of those white women he served. It's natural to ask if Clarke thought the same."[6] Jason's increasingly drugged out performance raises additional questions about the reliability and the ethics of what is being filmed and, later, viewed.

At the same time, the film provides a fascinating look into the life of a self-identified performer whose very performance on camera raises questions about the ability of documentary to capture the authentic truth of its subject.

Jason's first words are: "My name is Jason Holliday.

My name is Jason Holliday.

My name is Aaron Payne."

By stating his name twice, only to reveal that he has been presenting a constructed self to the camera, Jason destabilizes the viewer's sense of witnessing a "true self" onscreen. In addition to performing different (female and white) characters from films that he enjoys, Jason is obviously a supreme performer of his own life. He often alludes to the fact that he is performing and talks about the film they are making as a film that will be about him. For this reason, Gavin Butt explicitly links his performance to queer black survival: "Jason is able to *survive* homophobic and racist society precisely through appropriating the fictions of symbolic culture; through his campy appreciation of, and identification with, such forms of mass-produced artifice and song" (2007: 45). Melissa Anderson argues that, "Ultimately, there are no 'truths' revealed about Jason; what is disclosed instead is the theatricality of both Jason's performance in front of the camera *and* the film itself" (1999: 58). *Cinéma vérité* – which means "cinema truth" – is revealed as an impossibility through Jason's refusal to be an authentic self before the camera. His queer and racialized performance refuses to fit into any models of essential identity. As noted, Clarke herself set out on this project to interrogate the limits of realism as a documentary mode. She has said that, "[t]here is no real difference between a traditional fiction film and a documentary. I've never made a documentary. There is no such trip" (quoted in Anderson: 56).

Watch and discuss: *Portrait of Jason*

1   Note the moments in the film when Jason explicitly draws attention to his performance or his awareness of being captured on film. What do they say about the project of "fly-on-the-wall" style documentary filmmaking?
2   What types of Hollywood performances does Jason reference or impersonate? How do the meanings of these performances shift when performed by a black, gay body?
3   Do you find the film to be a racist and/or homophobic representation? What would you say are the major ethical quandaries the film raises?
4   The film includes a number of blurry or out-of-focus shots. Do they say something about the film's content? That is, is there a way in which they comment on identity or Jason's identity in particular?
5   What is the effect of the black frames that stand in for Jason's image while the film is being changed?

BEYOND NATION: TRANSNATIONAL FEMINIST DOCUMENTARY

In our increasingly globalized world, the politics of national borders, as well as the impossibility of stable national collectivities, have in the past two decades ushered in a closer scholarly attention to **transnational cinema**, whether it is reflected through documentary or fiction film modes. Critiquing the stability of national (and nationalist) frameworks, as well as the hegemony of the global north, is increasingly seen as a feminist issue due to the fact that women are disproportionally affected by neoliberal forces of globalization, whether through migration (legal and undocumented), labor exploitation, and/or sexual violence in conflict zones. Likewise, **transnational feminist thought** has developed in opposition to Western hegemonic understandings of women, gender, and equality. In 1981, Cherrie Moraga and Gloria Anzaldúa edited a volume entitled *This Bridge Called My Back: Writings by Radical Women of Color*, which is considered one of the pivotal publications establishing **Third World feminism**. The book illustrated the framework of **intersectional feminism**, which focuses on identity as composed of multiple, intersecting vectors of meaning. In 1987, another influential book, Anzaldúa's *Borderlands/La Frontera*, declared that "[a] borderland is a vague and undetermined place created by the emotional residue of an unnatural boundary. It is in a constant state of transition" (3). For theorists like Anzaldúa, borders function as metaphors for the identities of those people who do not neatly fit into any one dominant category, and are, as a result, marginalized socially and culturally, or relegated to the borderlands of discourse. Anzaldúa goes on to critique the notion that the only legitimate residents of borderlands are those who embody the privilege of whiteness. Her autobiographical study of invisible borders does not focus only on race, but also gender, sexuality and nationality as important points of both separation and connection. Along similar lines, Chandra Talpade Mohanty identifies "the urgent political necessity of forming strategic coalitions across class, race and national boundaries" (1988: 61). Noting that "feminist scholarly practices exist within relations of power – relations which they counter, redefine, or even implicitly support" (62), Mohanty critiques Western feminism's hegemonic construction of the Third World woman as "ignorant, poor, uneducated, tradition-bound, religious, domesticated, family-oriented, victimized, etc." (65). Mohanty identifies this as a colonialist move and adds that:

> The "status" or "position" of women is assumed to be self-evident because women as an already constituted group are placed within religious, economic, familial and legal structures. However, this focus on the position of women whereby women are seen as a coherent group across contexts, regardless of class or ethnicity, structures the world in ultimately binary, dichotomous terms, where women are

always seen in opposition to men, patriarchy is always necessarily male dominance, and the religious, legal, economic and familial systems are implicitly assumed to be constructed by men.

(78)

As an alternative to these hegemonic Western discourses around women and feminism, Inderpal Grewal and Caren Kaplan (1994) call for transnational feminist alliances in order to explore how "we come to do feminist work across cultural divides" (2). In their use of the term "**scattered hegemonies**," they seek to illuminate how, in postmodernity and under the globalized hierarchies of uneven economic flows, "transnational linkages influence every level of social existence" (13). Rather than one hegemonic ruling order, then, globalization produces multiple and conflicting power imbalances, specific to times and places, and open to contestation. The term transnational refuses the global-local, center-periphery binaries, opting instead to look for "the lines cutting across them" (13).

Mohanty's point about the "inherently political nature of feminist scholarship" (1988: 78) can be extended to feminist documentary filmmaking, which may similarly uphold or confront problematic binary discourses about women and feminism. Often, as is the case with *Born Into Brothels* (Zana Briski & Ross Kauffman, 2004, US; Figure 5.15), Western filmmakers inadvertently reiterate problematic stereotypes about First World and Third World divisions, in which Third World women and children are portrayed as helpless victims in need of being saved by Westerners and/or Western feminism. Another example may be observed in *Warrior Marks* (Pratibha Parmar, 1994, UK), a documentary that purports to criticize the practice

Figure 5.15 *Born Into Brothels* (Zana Briski & Ross Kauffman, 2004)

of female genital circumcision taking place in different African countries. The film does so through the didactic tone of moral outrage of its U.K.- and U.S.-based creators Prathiba Parmar and Alice Walker (the author of *The Color Purple*, discussed in Chapter 2). Inderpal Grewal and Caren Kaplan therefore find that "the Walker-Parmar film assumes that a Euro-American multicultural agenda travels freely across national boundaries," which in turn, "results in a neocolonial representational practice" (2003: 257). What this means is that the film fails to interrogate reductive assumptions about non-Western others, and seeks to erase the contextual differences among women's experience by subsuming them under the umbrella of global sisterhood. "This form of **global feminism**," continue Grewal and Kaplan, "as Chandra Mohanty and others have pointed out, can result in imperializing and racist forms of 'knowing' those constituted as 'others'" (257).

Such pitfalls, however, can be avoided. In her analysis of documentarian Kim Longinotto's work, Patricia White finds that "Longinotto has long been a practitioner of transnational feminism" (2006: 120), and moreover, that she avoids problematic structures of casting a Western gaze on non-Western subjects precisely because "her subjects, methods, and emphases are transnational rather than global(izing)" (121). What this entails is the destabilizing of the national positioning of the filmmaker and her subjects, as well as close attention to local dynamics and complexities rather than an uncritical focus on universalizing themes that privilege sameness. Longinotto's film *Sisters in Law* (co-directed with Florence Ayisi, 2005, Cameroon/UK; Figure 5.16), for instance, depicts the efforts of two Cameroonian

Figure 5.16 *Sisters in Law* (Kim Longinotto & Florence Ayisi, 2005)

women to change domestic abuse laws. In comparison with a film like *Born Into Brothels*, here, the Western filmmaker is using her camera to film local women empowering themselves and each other in a sustainable way *without* the intervention of Western aid. In the film, Longinotto's "unobtrusiveness grants voice and presence to the women on-camera" (White 2006: 122). It is a nod to the conventions of direct cinema, then, that makes possible a transnational framing of the feminist documentary in question by allowing the filmmaker to step aside and let her subjects speak for themselves.

Recently, films like *India's Daughter* (Leslee Udwin, 2015, UK/India; Figure 5.17) have been received as vehicles that overtly aim to support or incite meaningful social change when it comes to sexual violence and gender-based discrimination in different parts of the world. *India's Daughter* recounts the story of the brutal gang rape and murder of a young woman, which occurred in New Delhi in 2012. The crime galvanized Indian society and led to mass civilian protests and violent clashes with the police. The unrest led to a national conversation about sexual violence and the stigma that victims often endure through blame and shaming. However, the film caused controversy when it came to light that it features an interview with one of the rapists/murderers, since some people found it problematic that a rapist and murderer would be given a platform to tell his side of the story. As a result, the film was banned from being shown on Indian television. Moreover, one of the women who speaks in the film, an activist associated with the All India Progressive Women's Association, Kavita Krishnan, subsequently said in an interview that the film's title reinforces patriarchal assumptions about women as the nation's mothers and daughters who should behave themselves. Moreover, Krishnan suggests that the film leans on the white

Figure 5.17 *India's Daughter* (Leslee Udwin, 2015)

savior framework and that its exploration of the impoverished socioeconomic position that the attackers come from "ends up profiling Indian men from poor and deprived backgrounds as potential rapists. It doesn't show you that men from such backgrounds may not be rapists – many of them are not."[7] These critiques make explicit the complicated intersection of race, class, gender and ethnicity, and reveal that the politics of representation are fraught with the relationships of power between the filmmaker, her subjects, and the audience, and further complicated by their geopolitical locations.

Transnational feminist documentary therefore operates in the context of **post-Third Worldist culture** (which negates the simplistic dichotomy between First World and Third World). Ella Shohat describes post-Third Worldism as a "perspective that assumes the validity of antiracist and anticolonialist movements, but also interrogates the multiple fissures in the 'Third World' nation and U.S. sixties national power movements" (2001: 10). "'Third World' feminists and/or womanists," Shohat continues, "have criticized the facile harmony of a Western-based global sisterhood that has on the whole been blind to the privileges it has derived from its comfortable station on the neoimperial pyramid" (11). Women documenting their lives in the non-Western world face a struggle on several fronts – they are both critiquing representations of the nation that have excluded women and sexual, religious, and racial minorities, while also forging their own distinct feminist visions that are not subsumed by Western feminist narratives.

CASE STUDY: *SONITA* (ROKHSAREH GHAEM MAGHAMI, 2015, IRAN)

The documentary *Sonita* follows Sonita Alizadeh (Figure 5.18), a teenage girl who is a refugee from Afghanistan, and who lives with her sister and niece in Tehran, Iran. They are threatened with eviction because they cannot afford to pay their modest rent. Moreover, facing a growing financial strain, Sonita's family looks into selling the girl into an arranged marriage in order to make money. Sonita spends her days composing rap verses and dreaming of performing in big concerts. She pastes her own face on a picture of Rihanna singing in front of a huge crowd. The girl is, technically speaking, stateless, because she does not posses any documents – either Afghani or Iranian – which would legally establish her national identity. Her first name means sparrow, "a migrant bird," as she says. When she is asked by the instructors at the center for street children to make

Figure 5.18 *Sonita* (Rokhsareh Ghaem Maghami, 2015)

her own imaginary passport with a name and identity, she writes "Sonita Jackson." To the question of why Jackson, she answers with: "It sounds foreign." She dreams of being a U.S. citizen, and a child of Michael Jackson and Rihanna. In reality, she is being pressured to return to Afghanistan and get married so that her brother can collect the dowry. Sonita's idols illustrate the wide-reaching influence of globalized Western popular culture, as well as Western beauty standards – she plans to pay for her mother's laser treatments, and wants her to look like a blond, Western white woman.

Midway through the film, the tone of the documentary shifts and the heretofore unseen filmmaker becomes a part of the story. In one scene, Sonita takes the camera and turns it around, deciding to ask the director some questions in return. In another, the girl asks the director to find a way to pay the money to Sonita's family in order to buy her freedom, money that Sonita offers to pay back with the earnings she plans to make from her music. Echoing the tenets of *cinéma vérité*, and facing a moral dilemma, the director responds with: "Sonita, dear, I must record the truth. It's not right for me to interfere like this in your life." When the girl's mother comes from Afghanistan to take her back, it becomes clear that Sonita's options are increasingly limited, and that she is facing a real possibility of having to go back and be forcibly married. In one scene, the children's center worker, the film's director and the sound technician discuss Sonita's situation and what they can do about it, thereby breaking the unspoken rule of "objective" documentary representation achieved through non-interference. Then Sonita goes missing and the film briefly shifts to documenting the filmmaker's desperate efforts to locate her. When Sonita is found again, the filmmaker appears to pay $2,000 to buy her freedom. She makes a song and a video, which get some recognition internationally. But the children's support center has to sever ties with her because women are not permitted to sing in Iran. The end of the documentary sees Sonita arriving to the United States after she receives a scholarship, with hopes of a better future.

The director's interference in paying $2,000 in order to secure her documentary subject's freedom garnered some criticism and controversy because it appeared to have broken one of the key rules of documentary ethics – that the filmmaker should not interfere in the lives of her subjects. Ghaem Maghami responded by stating: "I can't film people who are suffering for something I can afford, when they are giving their life, their story, to me." Asked about the perceived destruction of objectivity that such interference brings about, the director adds:

> It's always a lie. You are never a fly on the wall. You are always an elephant in the room. You change everything with your presence. I don't believe objectivity is important, or even happens. Human stories are always subjective and personal. The film-maker decides, creates.[8]

Watch and discuss: *Sonita*

1 What do you think of the filmmaker's decision to interfere with the real-life events that her film was documenting? Do you think it is more important to capture objective reality, or does the filmmaker have a responsibility to interfere if she can protect a person who would otherwise face a dire situation?
2 Does the film reproduce an othering or objectifying gaze on its subject? Why or why not?
3 Consider whether *Sonita* can be seen as an example of what Trinh T. Minh-ha calls "speaking nearby." Elaborate on your answer.

ACTIVITY

In small groups or individually, choose a topic for a documentary. What informs your decision? Are you interested in a current issue or in representing events from the past? If the latter, are there present concerns motivating your choice of a historical subject? What would the major sources for your documentary be, and how would you represent your material formally? How would you choose to mitigate the power dynamics present or to foreground issues of representation, if at all? How would you approach the notion of the documentary's objectivity?

DISCUSSION QUESTIONS

1   Are realist approaches to documentary inherently problematic? What might be some of the limitations of more experimental approaches or documentaries that blend fact and fiction?

2   Can you think of any documentary films, feminist and otherwise, that adhere to realism, or, on the other hand, actively subvert it? How does this shape your understanding of or relationship to the information they present?

3   With respect to films like *Year of the Woman* and *Finding Christa*, do you find that playing with fiction, enactments and dream sequences undermines the activists' political agenda or aids it? In what ways are women's relationships to history and politics performative and/or fantastical?

4   What was the most recent documentary you saw? Think about its formal and stylistic aspects. Would you say it represents an example of ethnographic documentary, *cinema vérité*, direct cinema, or another strain of documentary filmmaking? How does the film's style reflect the filmmaker's attitude towards the subject matter?

5   What do you think it means to "speak nearby" rather than *about* a topic?

6   Can biographical documentaries do the work of filling the gaps in women's history? What might be the limitations of this task?

KEY TERMS

autobiographical documentary

biographical documentary film

cinéma vérité

direct cinema

ethnographic film

experimental documentary

feminist documentaries

Fourth Cinema

global feminism

intersectional feminism

newsreel

objective reality

political documentary

post-Third Worldist culture

propaganda film

the real

realism

realist documentary

scattered hegemonies

Third Cinema

Third World feminism

Third Worldist cinema

transnational feminist documentary

NOTES

1 Max Fisher, "*The Square* is a beautiful documentary. But its politics are dangerous," (www.washingtonpost.com/news/worldviews/wp/2014/01/17/the-dangerously-one-sided-politics-of-oscar-nominated-documentary-the-square/)

2 For more names and information about these filmmakers, see website Women Film Pioneers Project: https://wfpp.cdrs.columbia.edu/

3 Melissa Silverstein, "The success of women documentary filmmakers," www.alternet.org/story/88642/the_success_of_women_documentary_filmmakers

4 *Women Make Movies*, "Daughter rite," www.wmm.com/filmcatalog/pages/c356.shtml

5 Douglas Rogers, "The troublemaker," www.theguardian.com/film/2004/apr/16/gender.usa

6 Manohla Dargis, "One man, saved from invisibility," www.nytimes.com/2013/04/14/movies/shirley-clarkes-portrait-of-jason-back-in-circulation.html?_r=0

7 Tinku Ray, "A women's rights activist has mixed feelings about *India's Daughter*," www.npr.org/sections/goatsandsoda/2015/03/10/392111392/an-anti-rape-activist-is-disturbed-by-indias-daughter

8 Homa Khaleeli, "*Sonita*'s director: Why I paid $2000 to stop a rapper being sold into a forced marriage," www.theguardian.com/film/2016/oct/24/sonita-director-interview-rokhsareh-ghaem-maghami

REFERENCES

Anderson, M. (1999). "The vagaries of verities: On Shirley Clarke's *Portrait of Jason*," *Film Comment*, 35(6), 56–59.

Anzaldúa, G. (1987). *Borderlands: La frontera*. San Francisco: Aunt Lute Books.

Butler, J. (1990). *Gender trouble: Feminism and the subversion of identity*. New York: Routledge.

Butt, G. (2007). "'Stop that acting!': Performance and authenticity in Shirley Clarke's *Portrait of Jason*." In K. Mercer (Ed.), *Pop art and vernacular cultures*. London: Iniva and Boston: MIT Press, 36–55.

Citron, M. (1999). "Fleeing from documentary: Autobiographical film/video and the ethics of responsibility." In D. Waldman & J. Walker (Eds.), *Feminism and documentary*. Minneapolis: University of Minnesota Press, 271–286.

Cunningham, J. (2004). *Hungarian cinema: From coffee house to multiplex*. London: Wallflower Press.

Erens, P. (1988). "Women's documentary filmmaking: The personal is political." *New Challenges for Documentary*, 554–565.

Getino, O., & Solanas, F. (1970). "Toward a Third Cinema." *Tricontinental*, 14, 107–132.

Grewal, I., & Kaplan, C. (Eds.). (1994). *Scattered hegemonies: Postmodernity and feminist practices*. Minneapolis: University of Minnesota Press.

Grewal, I., & Kaplan, C. (2003), "Warrior marks: Global womanism's neocolonial discourse in a multicultural context." In E. Shohat & R. Stam (Eds.), *Multiculturalism, postcoloniality, and transnational media*. New Brunswick: Rutgers University Press, 256–278.

Halberstam, J. (1999). "F2M: The making of female masculinity." In J. Price & M. Shildrick (Eds.), *Feminist theory and the body: A reader*. New York: Routledge, 125–133.

Hill Collins, P. (2000). *Black feminist thought: Knowledge, consciousness, and the politics of empowerment*. London: Routledge.

Jelača, D. (2013). "Between mothers and daughters: Adoption, family, and black female subjectivity in *Finding Christa* and *Off and Running*." *Camera Obscura: Feminism, Culture, and Media Studies*, 28(2(83)), 77–107.

Johnston. C. (1973) [1999]. "Women's cinema as counter-cinema." In S. Thornham (Ed.), *Feminist film theory: A reader*. New York: NYU Press, 31–40.

Juhasz, A. (1999). "Bad girls come and go, but a lying girl can never be fenced in." In D. Waldman & J. Walker (Eds.), *Feminism and documentary*. Minneapolis: University of Minnesota Press, 95–115.

Khanna, R. (1998). "*The Battle of Algiers* and *The Nouba of the Women of Mount Chenoua*: From third to fourth cinema." *Third Text*, 12(43), 13–32.

Lane, J. (2002). *The autobiographical documentary in America*. Madison: University of Wisconsin Press.

Lesage, J. (1978). "The political aesthetics of the feminist documentary film." *Quarterly Review of Film Studies*, 3(4), 507–523.

Mbembe, A. (2003). "Necropolitics." *Public Culture*, 15(1), 11–40.

McGarry, E. (1975). "Documentary, realism and women's cinema." *Women and Film*, 2(7), 50–9.

Minh-ha, T. T. (1991). *When the moon waxes red: Representation, gender and cultural politics*. London: Routledge.

Mohanty, C. T. (1988). "Under western eyes: Feminist scholarship and colonial discourses." *Feminist Review*, (30), 61–88.

Moraga, C., & Anzaldúa, G. (Eds.). (1981). *This bridge called my back: Writings by radical women of color*. Albany: SUNY Press.

Portuges, C. (2004). "Diary for my children, 1982." In P. Hames (Ed.), *The cinema of central Europe*. London: Wallflower Press, 191–202.

Rabinowitz, P. (1994). *They must be represented: The politics of documentary*. London: Verso.

Shohat, E. (Ed.). (2001). *Talking visions: Multicultural feminism in a transnational age*. Cambridge: MIT Press.

Shohat, E., & Stam, R. (1994). *Unthinking eurocentrism: Multiculturalism and the media*. New York: Routledge.

Waldman, D., & Walker, J. (Eds.). (1999). *Feminism and documentary*. Minneapolis: University of Minnesota Press.

White, P. (2006). "Cinema solidarity: The documentary practice of Kim Longinotto." *Cinema Journal, 46*(1), 120–128.

White, P. (2015). *Women's cinema, world cinema: Projecting contemporary feminisms*. Durham: Duke University Press.

Williams L., & Rich B. R. (1981). "The right of re-vision: Michelle Citron's *Daughter Rite*." *Film Quarterly, 35*(1), 17–22.

Zimmerman, P. (1999). "Flaherty's midwives." In D. Waldman & J. Walker (Eds.), *Feminism and documentary*. Minneapolis: University of Minnesota Press, 64–83.

Chapter six
FEMINISM AND EXPERIMENTAL FILM AND VIDEO

Women have been experimenting with the film medium since its early days (see Chapter 1 on female authorship for overviews of some early women experimental filmmakers). Alternative and poetic cinematic modes have offered opportunities for women, and for those who do not align with dominant national, gender, racial, and sexual identities, to express personal vision and experience in ways counter to dominant film language. Additionally, the fact that experimental filmmaking tends to be more accessible and to rely on alternative systems of distribution and exhibition has in many ways made it more available to artists who are from marginal or excluded groups. For example, experimental work can be made alone, in the privacy of one's home, and using cheap, accessible technology. It is often shown in small venues, from friends' garages to temporary micro-cinemas, and nowadays can simply be posted to online platforms. The fact that experimental modes of exhibition and distribution can or have to rely less on institutionalized channels means that those who are consistently marginalized through dominant institutions can often exhibit their work in less formal and possibly more oppositional contexts and spaces. It can also mean that women's and other work within these channels may remain to some extent marginalized.

Early female film pioneers like Alice Guy Blaché and Germaine Dulac (see Chapter 1) explored experimental form, in addition to more commercial work, while Maya Deren continues to be one of the major figures associated with the emergence of the **American avant-garde**. Shirley Clarke (discussed in Chapter 5) was central to the filmmaking, distribution, and community organizing that occurred around the emergence of the American avant-garde, and other figures like Marie Menken, Gunnvor Nelson, and Joyce Wieland were also central members of the emerging experimental American film scene in the postwar period. Yet, in dominant accounts of the avant-garde and counterculture traditions, women's contributions have historically been ignored. This is no doubt in part because the avant-garde and underground cinema that emerged in the 1950s and 1960s in America came to define a canon of experimental filmmaking premised on the idea of the filmmaker as visionary genius. This is a category that has traditionally been gendered male or seen as the exclusive domain of the male creative virtuoso. As Robin Blaetz argues, "With some major exceptions, the women's work was more or less plugged in to a structure built around the notion of the romantic artist, and women's films seemed to be peripheral to a tradition that had been defined as male" (2007: 2–3). A tradition of women's often hybrid and less orthodox experimental work has always existed. William Wees argues that the emergence of a new generation of experimental feminist filmmakers in the 1980s, "rejected [the male avant-garde's] Romantic, Emersonian, Great-Man Theory of individual creation as well as its perpetuation of a canon of great films and filmmakers, and they were well aware that, with the exception of Maya Deren, all the 'giants' were men" (2005: 22). Once we take into consideration the contributions of female filmmakers, it challenges the heroic male narrative of the American avant-garde, as well as the traditional categories that have been used to classify experimental work.

Laura Mulvey argued in her foundational polemic, "Visual Pleasure and Narrative Cinema" (1975) that the goal of feminist filmmaking should be to destroy pleasure, since the pleasure of narrative cinema was based in a dominant film language that perpetuated a male gaze and positioned women as spectacles, there for male enjoyment. As we have mentioned in previous chapters, Mulvey was arguing for the destruction of a particular kind of male-centered pleasure catered to by classical Hollywood. Her scholarship was accompanied by a filmmaking practice, where she attempted to give her theory audiovisual form. Her film *Riddles of the Sphinx* (with Peter Wollen, 1977, UK), for example, contains a long middle section composed of 360-degree pans of various locations. The soundtrack is a mix of synthesized music and the questioning voiceover of the female protagonist who attempts to negotiate work and leisure, motherhood and pleasure and to understand her life in the context of patriarchal capitalism. While the soundtrack privileges a female perspective and consciousness on the world, the 360-degree shots remove the cinematic gaze from a human perspective and their mechanized rotation refuses to privilege any one character or action within the frame. This film, then, moves away from the representation of the female as object of desire: instead, her consciousness and multi-dimensional thoughts provide the framework through which we understand unfetishized images of women in everyday life, and particularly, depictions of motherhood as a major issue for contemporary women, related to the full realization and integration of the self.

Mulvey's practice, however, is not the paradigm for all women's experimental work. While many feminist experimental works are quite pleasurable to watch, they consistently use their medium to question our habitualized way of seeing the world or digesting audiovisual information: "Women's experimental film practice often challenges masculinist avant-garde aesthetic dogmas by juxtaposing narrativity and non-narrativity, deploying narrative pleasure alongside narrative disruption, providing viewers with identification as well as critical distance, and so on" (Petrolle & Wexman 2005: 3). In fact, examining a history of experimentation through the work of women or non-binary identified artists reveals that the complicated relationship between pleasure and politics is intrinsic to experimental filmmaking (see for example the discussion of Carolee Schneemann's work in Chapter 3). Both feminism more broadly, and experimental work in particular, ask larger questions about representation and invite us to look at the world, or the screen, differently, through a gaze that does not reproduce hegemonic ways of seeing.

One of the problems with documenting feminist experimental work involves basic questions of how the term feminist is defined (these questions are also intrinsic to discussions of female authorship as introduced in Chapter 1). Is any experimental work by a woman automatically "feminist," where being feminist is defined in political terms? Maya Deren, one of the previously mentioned "giants" of the American avant-garde and virtually the only woman filmmaker initially included in that group, does not necessarily make films that are in any obvious way political. Her best-known film, for example, *Meshes of the Afternoon* (with Alexander Hammid, 1943, US) is an exploration of dreams and the unconscious, which is often described as poetic or lyrical. In the film, Deren performs a character who falls asleep and enters a world of veiled women with no faces, altered laws of gravity, multiplying selves, mysterious objects and garden paths with no clear destinations. The film's oneiric imagery has been interpreted as offering a feminist critique, but the political content of the film is in no way obvious. Consider *why* this film might be considered feminist, or at least important to women filmmakers, as well as why it might not be. As another example, Jodie Mack, a contemporary experimental filmmaker, works primarily with textiles as her visual landscape. Her work involves the editing together of shots of various colorful and patterned fabrics to create beautiful compositions and juxtapositions and often uses stop-motion effects to amplify rhythm. Mack's work has no explicit political content. Yet, she is an important contemporary filmmaker in a traditionally male-dominated field, who takes a realm traditionally associated with women and craft – that of textiles – as the basis of her work (see Figure 6.1).

Is Mack a feminist filmmaker? These filmmakers ask us to stretch our understanding of feminism beyond the terms and frameworks that render it obvious. Since so much of experimental work focuses on abstractions and form, requiring an explicitly political content would eliminate many of the important and innovative contributions of women to the field. Furthermore, as has been mentioned in previous chapters, how do we define what a "woman" is? The problematic assumption that the identity of women is a unifying category across race, class, and other axes of identity has long been critiqued within feminist theorizing and continues to be problematized as we develop ever more sophisticated notions of gender and identity. For this reason, we include women's, trans, and non-binary work here under the rubric "feminist." Rather than answering the question of what makes or does not make experimental work feminist, we've included a large sample of work that offers a range of what might be considered under this label.

This chapter first examines one of the fundamental divisions within subcategories of experimental film – that between structural film and more expressive or lyrical traditions. We then look at another major category of experimental work – the diary film. After this, we trace various strategies that feminist

Figure 6.1 *Harlequin* (Jodie Mack, 2009)

filmmakers have used in their work: appropriating and recontextualizing images, rewriting male texts, telling culturally or politically marginalized stories and exploring identities, and, finally, creating histories where official records do not exist. Of course, these categories are highly porous, and most films occupy several of these categories at once. These strategies are meant as tools with which to begin thinking about what motivates certain forms of experimentation and what might constitute feminist work.

STRUCTURALISM AND SELF-EXPRESSION IN THE AVANT-GARDE TRADITION

Experimental films often raise questions about the relationship between form and content. One of the things that has traditionally distinguished much of women's film content from some of its male counterparts is that while the latter may engage in purely formal or structural experimentation, women's experimental film has tended to challenge the idea that one can meditate purely on form without a related examination of some content/context to the work. Many important feminist examples of **formalism** are also examinations of the politics of identity and place (formalism, like structural film, explores and foregrounds the form and formal dimensions of the work and its medium). We can see in a feminist counter-trajectory, "how formal innovation enables women to enlarge discourses about women's subjectivity" (Petrolle & Wexman 2005: 3). Therefore, the structuring opposition between **expressive work** that depicts the personal visions and impressions of the filmmaker, and **structural film**, which is more focused on form and the medium itself, is revealed as a false dichotomy in the work of many feminist filmmakers.

Structural filmmakers, in the canonical avant-garde sense of the term, are concerned with the material base of the film – for example, they may be interested in playing with the process of projection or development itself; with working over the material of the celluloid film by scratching it, painting it, or taping things onto it; or exploring an isolated element of the medium like color, shape, or camera movement. This can also be called formalism and is particularly connected with American avant-garde filmmakers working from the 1960s forward. For example, Michael Snow's film *Wavelength* (1967, Canada) is a 45-minute slow zoom across a room towards a picture hanging on the wall. Paul Sharits, another structural filmmaker, made many films experimenting with the properties of color and was interested in the structural basis of the medium, including the flicker effect and the sound of the projectors. Sharits would even burn film to explore the material celluloid base of the medium. His film *Bad Burns* (1982, US) is an example of the structural impulse in experimental filmmaking. The film is based on out-takes from an installation in which film got caught in the projector. Sharits then used this accident to create a new film print, which replicates the jerky motion of the film going through the original projector. The (original) image of the film burning becomes an abstract meditation on light, color, and projection itself. The viewer can see the film sprockets, which along with the flicker of the projector become part of the aesthetic experience that the film creates through exploring the basic structural elements of the medium.

This film is described at length here to illustrate the ways in which structural or formal concerns are often viewed as somehow separate from content – or from commentary on subjectivity, politics, and identity. However, what we can see in the work of many women experimental filmmakers who work in this tradition is that an exploration of the medium and of form need not be inherently divorced from commentary on the experience of existing in a world. Even Sharits's work relies on a repressed image – the original image that becomes an abstraction in the film is of a woman being menaced by a lit match that is being waved closer and closer to her face by someone offscreen. Thus, the secondary or even tertiary images of burning film and sprockets overlay an image that reflects a certain sadism and gendered politics of looking. In this sense, *Bad Burns* arguably reveals that even in purportedly apolitical or "neutral" texts ideological dynamics can be located beneath the surface.

To give two counter examples of feminist filmmakers who employ structural principles but connect them to social issues or larger problems of subjectivity, we turn to the work of Su Friedrich and Nazli Dinçel. Su Friedrich began making films in the late 1970s (Figure 6.2). She is known for blending experimental aesthetics with documentary, autobiographical, and narrative

Figure 6.2 Su Friedrich inserts herself into her film in *Sink or Swim* (1990)

forms. Her films often tell highly personal stories in humorous ways, linking them to larger political and historical contexts. Friedrich combines found footage and home movies with original images, and scratches text onto her film stock. Her soundtracks employ a similar mixture of diegetic sound, pop and classical music, silence, and narration. Friedrich has said of her early work that she:

> was reacting against both psychodramas and structural films, and trying to do something different. But mostly I was just pissed off and thought, "Some of these films are really boring, and some of them have potential but they're really badly crafted, and *where are all the women?*"

(Cutler 2007: 315)

In *Sink or Swim* (1990, US), Friedrich tells the story of her relationship with her father – a distant and often cruel linguist and anthropologist who eventually left the family (Figure 6.3).

The film is organized by the letters of the alphabet, starting with Z and ending with A – each letter is given a title word which then offers an interpretative frame for the images and narration that follow. The film ends with the alphabet song, which poignantly includes the line "tell me what you think of me," given additional meaning through the film's exploration of the ways in which Friedrich's distant and difficult father impacted her sense of self. Through the use of the alphabetical organizing principle, Friedrich

Figure 6.3 A letter to her father in Friedrich's *Sink or Swim* (1990)

establishes a structural constraint on the film. The alphabet also echoes some of the film's content, given her father's role as an academic with many publications relating to linguistics (ironically, he also wrote extensively on kinship structures, even as their family was in the process of dissolving).

The film is narrated through the voice of a young girl. Drawing on various Greek myths and other stories in the narration, the personal experience of the narrator is translated into a third-person story – the events are related as happening to "the girl" or "the woman," which highlights a certain innocence on the part of the child as well as the constructed nature of memory and personal history. As William Wees (2005) notes, the use of third-person narration shifts the tone of the work away from some of the dominant American avant-garde autobiographical films such as Jerome Hill's *Film Portrait* (1970), Bruce Baillie's *Quick Billy* (1970), and many of Jonas Mekas's works, including *Walden* (1964–1969) and *Lost, Lost, Lost* (1949–1975). Effectively, these first-person stories tend to build up the idea of the romantic artist whose unique personal story is inextricably linked to the expressive and formal dimensions of their work. Wees notes that Friedrich's choice to narrate her own story as though it is happening to "a girl" distances herself from the narrative and gives the viewer more leeway for interpretation. It "encourages a view of the autobiographical 'self' as a social subject and, in cinematic terms, as an *effect* of the film's form and content rather than its *cause*" (2005: 32–33). Thus, her work moves away from centering the artist as genius, whose work is born of nothing but their own auto-generating insights, and places the filmmaker firmly into a social world in which the sense of self and abilities for self-expression are both constrained and enabled by a web of external forces and relations and are mediated by the unreliability of memory and language.

Nazli Dinçel is a Turkish-born filmmaker who moved to the United States at the age of seventeen. Dinçel has continued to prefer celluloid as her medium of choice and tends to heavily work the surface of her 16mm films. Like Su Friedrich, Dinçel often scratches text directly onto the surface of her film (Figure 6.4). Her manifesto elaborates that she "relates the tedious acts of physically animating the text onto her imagery with the traditional female roles in her Turkish upbringing as intricate cooking or rug making."[1] In addition to scratching and painting on film stock, she also sews into the film itself.

Her series of films entitled *Solitary Acts* (2015, US) use this structuralist experimentation with the medium itself to explore issues of sexual identity, in both dark and humorous modes. For example, *Solitary Acts #5* includes a series of frames in which Dinçel has scratched words into the surface of the film, such as "eating." These frames are intercut with scenes of Dinçel heavily, almost grotesquely, applying lipstick and kissing herself in the mirror. The scratched-out text describes her masturbating with a carrot and

Figure 6.4 *Solitary Acts #6* (Nazli Dinçel, 2015)

then eating it in the bathroom. Her grandmother accuses her of making a bad Muslim because she is eating in the bathroom. In this film Dinçel thus touches on multiple facets of subjectivity, generational inheritance, self-exploration, and the complex relation between desire and the environment in which desire is produced and explored. Dinçel's work is concerned with the body – in *Solitary Acts #4*, we see graphic close-up depictions of masturbation. Her decision to literally explore the material body of the film thus mirrors her interest in the physical and bodily as her thematic content. It makes sense that Dinçel chooses to continue to work in film and to hand process her work, since she is so thematically concerned with tactility and the body, and the celluloid medium is equally a tactile handled surface. As articulated in her manifesto:

> The tediousness of the making of her text is a form of meditation. Over-working a subject matter is a form of healing. The context is exhausted in the making of the films. The repetition of re-photographing, scratching, cutting, typing the text on the film systematically becomes a form of flesh memory because of the amount of time spent doing it."[2]

The film as a surface shaped by desire, aggression, creativity, and frustration is thus a metaphor for the filmmaker's own body and is a surface on which to represent very personal and intimate experiences. Again, Dinçel's work demonstrates that structural experiments in form are not mutually exclusive of personal and political explorations.

CASE STUDY: VERA CHYTILOVÁ'S *DAISIES* (1966, CZECHOSLOVAKIA)

Vera Chytilová's 1966 film *Daisies* is a key film of the movement known as the Czech New Wave. The only female director working in the New Wave, Chytilová was also the most experimental filmmaker of the group. *Daisies* uses a playful episodic structure to tell the story of two women (they are often referred to as "Marie I and Marie II," although they adopt various pseudonyms throughout the film) who engage in various forms of rebellion and bad behavior. The film experiments with montage, lens filters, and visual distortions to tell a story that seems to allegorize the two women's descent into "badness" and their brief attempt at reform and redemption.

As with many films of the Czech New Wave, *Daisies* was significantly delayed as censors tried to find a reason to forbid its release. They protested the wastage of food in the film, as the two women are shown consuming to excess and eventually having a food fight that destroys a banquet laid (presumably) for communist party officials. The film was eventually released and then quickly banned after the Prague Spring protests of 1968. Chytilová herself was effectively banned from filmmaking for seven years.

The film offers a strong critique of the construction of feminine desire – it begins with the Maries' declaration that they are virgins, followed by an archetypical scene in which they dance around a tree suggesting the Garden of Eden, the tree of the knowledge of good and evil and the forbidden fruit, which the Maries willingly consume. Apples then become a repeated motif throughout the film, as the protagonists go on to flirt with and use a series of suitors. Food is central to the Maries' flirtations and sexual refusals – they trick men into buying them lavish meals only to abandon them at the train station. When a piano-playing butterfly collector professes his love to one of the women, she replies by asking him if he has anything to eat, and, in another scene, the women graphically chop up sausages, pickles, and other phallic food objects while listening to suitors declare their love over the telephone (Figure 6.5).

In fact, the Maries consistently substitute food for sex. In one scene with an elderly suitor, even the orgasmic soundtrack that overlays a montage of food being placed on and disappearing from a table

Figure 6.5 The Maries cut up some sausage in *Daisies* (Vera Chytilová, 1966)

suggests the sexual gratification they receive from consumption. That the meal is finished with a collective cigarette further solidifies the erotic nature of their desire for food. Thus, in the film, food comes to stand in as a metaphor for unrestrained female sexual appetites. The Maries are literally *vagina dentata* – their mouths consuming orifices that threaten the patriarchal world in which they exist. In yet another scene the women take a bath of milk, dipping bread into the bathwater as they wash. One Marie cracks an egg into the mixture, asking, "That's what I don't understand. Why do they say 'I love you'? Why don't they say, for example, 'egg'?" To which the second responds, "What a good idea!"

Food also stands in at many moments in the film as an ambivalent object that represents norms of beauty and the pressure that women feel around body shape and diet. The gendered cultural codings of food and eating are played with throughout the film. The women, young, thin, and attractive, never seem to gain weight as a result of their consumption. At one moment, as the two women strut up the stairs, a hall of mirrors effect takes over and the women's bodies appear to expand and contract as they move. Here, the tensions and fears surrounding female hunger and bodily norms are given visual expression.

One scholar has described the film's power as lying, "in its seeming ability to confirm misogynist views while inciting deep acrimony toward the patriarchal order" (Lim 2001: 62). Many feminist scholars see the film's subversive qualities in its parodic repetition and citation of feminine scripts and the women's variations within these repetitions. For example, one of the women feigns a small (i.e. feminine) appetite: when looking at the menu she declares, "that's much too large" about an item. However, she then proceeds to order an exorbitant amount of food and eat all of it, while questioning the astonished man at the table about why *he* isn't eating more and whether *he* is on a diet.

In the film's final sequence, the two Maries sneak into a dumbwaiter, which takes them up several floors. On their way up, they pass a cultural event in progress, and they end up at a door, behind which they discover a huge dining room. Inside, there are tables laden with dishes both savory and sweet, and one covered in bottles of alcohol. The viewer can infer that the banquet has been laid for party officials. The two women enter the room and cautiously approach the food. Quickly abandoning their tentative approach, they wildly and carelessly sample all the food, eventually moving from place setting to place setting, as they gorge themselves on various dishes. They end their feast with mouthfuls of cake and a food fight and then proceed to put on a mock fashion show, using the table as their runway. One woman drapes herself in a curtain she rips from the window and the other turns her slip into a cocktail dress. They dance across the table squishing food under their black heels, eventually swinging from the chandelier until it comes crashing down. This scene is followed by a mock scene of reform in which the women promise to be good and work hard, and attempt to piece the banquet setting back together again. By the scene's end the women lie side by side looking like trussed up slabs of meet – here femininity is explicitly linked to a form of visual and physical consumption (Figure 6.6).

In contrast to much mainstream narrative film, in which beautiful female characters are on display for the viewers' visual consumption, these women are displayed actively consuming, at the same time as they themselves are available for visual consumption.

The discussion has so far focused on the film's wide-ranging feminist critique, but the film's experimentation must also be situated

We're really happy!

Figure 6.6 The Maries try to make things right again in *Daisies* (Vera Chytilová, 1966)

within the context of socialist aesthetics and socialist ideology in general. The film's exploration of consumption, the Maries' behavior throughout the film and their attempts to reform, including their trips to the countryside, must be understood within the context of socialist Czechoslovakia. Chytilová's experimental aesthetics are even more radical within the ideological context of 1960s Czechoslovakian culture. One of the likely reasons why the authorities found the film subversive is the juxtaposition of this excessive female gluttony and corporeal enjoyment with the dominant ideological notions of socialist life as productive, sparse and modest. When Marie I and Marie II claim they want to "be good" at the end of the film, and attempt to clean up the mess they have made in the lavish dining room, they manage to only clumsily put things back together by unevenly gluing broken plates and partially reconstructing their own torn-up clothes. Yet much as they humorously try, they are incapable of becoming proper in non-threatening ways. This scene, among many others, ridicules acceptable norms of women's behavior, in the socialist context and more broadly.

Watch and discuss: *Daisies*

1   Consider this film within the socialist context of its making. In what ways does it challenge the dominant Soviet aesthetics of

socialist realism? This may involve doing some research around the basic tenets of socialist realist aesthetics.

2   In what ways does *Daisies* challenge socialist ideals about industrious citizens and workers? How might it challenge the idea of gender equality under socialism, or the notion that the "woman question" had been answered with the change in society's economic base?

3   How, specifically, does the form offer a critique of gender norms? Is its critique narrative, formal, or both?

4   What is the significance of food in the film? How is food as a trope related to the film's larger themes/critiques?

THE DIARY FILM

Because experimental filmmaking doesn't necessarily require a crew or great technical and financial resources (and its financial accessibility has grown with the advent of digital production), it has historically been easier for women and other marginalized groups to access. The issue of accessibility is perhaps best illustrated by the work of Sadie Benning, who, while still a teenager in the 1990s, made films about her identity, her world, love and lesbianism all using a Fisher Price PixelVision video recorder (an affordable technology that used standard cassette tapes and recorded in black and white). Benning used the dubious quality of the images produced by the toy machine to shape the aesthetic of her project. Commenting on themes such as coming of age and being young, the technology itself reflects the transitional moment between childhood and adulthood that the filmmaker documents. It also denies the viewer mastery over the images, seemingly locating them in a space of memory and representation that foregrounds their constructed nature.

Films that record daily life experience are known as **diary films,** and form a subgenre of experimental film. In fact, a female filmmaker, Marie Menken (1909–1970) is often credited with the invention of the diary film (Petrolle & Wexman 2005), although it is also associated with her male contemporaries, such as Jonas Mekas and George Kuchar. Menken's 16mm films often recorded the creative worlds of her friends, such as her early *Visual Variations on Noguchi* (1945, US), which takes as its subject the sculptures of her friend Isamu Noguchi, or another friend's garden in *Glimpse of the Garden* (1957, US). But her films did not simply record the world as she saw it; Menken's light and portable 16mm camera often danced with and around her subjects, transforming them into moving sculptures (*Noguchi*), meditations on light (*Lights*, 1966, US), or affective impressions of life in the city (*Go! Go! Go!* 1962–1964, US). Her soundtracks vary from experimental scores (*Noguchi*) to birds chirping (*Glimpse of the Garden*), to silent works (*Go! Go! Go!* and *Lights*), which leave the movement within and between frames the driving rhythm of the work.

Anne Charlotte Robertson (1949–2012) is an overlooked and important figure in the diary film tradition. While Robertson made a variety of films, her longest-running project was called *Five Year Diary*. Started in 1981, the project lasted until 1997, long past the five years of the series' title. Each episode runs around twenty-seven minutes, or the length of eight camera rolls, and the series totals thirty-eight hours in running time. Robertson suffered from various mental health issues, including bipolar disorder, and film was one of the ways that she recorded her experiences and gave them order and meaning (Figure 6.7). Shot on Super 8mm, her films mix images found and new (often of herself, her family, her garden, and the food she makes) with layered soundtracks that include music, voiceover narration, and sounds from sources such as television shows. She also recorded cassettes that could be played along with the films to further layer the soundtracks. At screenings, she would often speak while her films were running and occasionally play a radio, adding another layer of personal intimacy to her work (she was also known to bake food for her own screenings). Robertson's films are often sad, but also affirmative and funny. Each episode of the five-year diary begins with a brutally honest synopsis of her life at the point of shooting. For example, *Reel 76 "Fall to Spring"* (1991, US) begins:

Figure 6.7 Robertson in one of her diary films (Reel 78)

I was 34 years old. I was on vacation from graduate school in film-making. I was in therapy with a psychiatrist and taking an anti-depressant drug. I had moved home with my mother in June after 14 years alone in Boston. I had just bought my first silent Super8 camera, top of the line Nizo 801. I was on vacation in rural New York at my grandmother's house.

Episodes often speak to one another, sharing themes, but also function as self-contained texts. One of these themes is the rise and fall of her crush on Tom Baker, best known for his role as the fourth Dr. Who (Figure 6.8). Robertson obsessively records and sends him regular audio messages on cassette, and footage of Baker speaking and his film appearances are interlaced with comments on Robertson's own addictions to alcohol and cigarettes, footage of visits with her family, and ongoing narration about Robertson's burgeoning commitment to Roman Catholicism.

Robertson's struggles to survive and willingness to be vulnerable and even abject in her self-representation offer an important perspective on a woman's experience and struggles with mental health and addiction. The diaries provide ample evidence of her creative expressive talents, which find their strongest outlet in the documentation of her daily reality. Although Robertson periodically mentions having to go to screenings of her work in various

Figure 6.8 Footage of Tom Baker is intercut with images of gardening and of Robertson chain-smoking in Reel 71 "On Probation" (1990). The soundtrack here is a mix of narration, including Robertson discussing her successes in the avant-garde world, layered with the repeated refrain of "I love you, Tom."

cities throughout her diary films, her role within the art world is never her focus. She dramatizes her own psychic life, her obsessions, failures, and dreams through her skillful editing and combination of sounds and images.

Hong Kong artist Yau Ching, whose work includes feature-length experimental documentaries and fictional and experimental shorts, deconstructs the diary film in her series of three "letters" (*Video Letters 1–3*, 1993, Hong Kong). Her work often deals with issues connected to Hong Kong, including sexuality in the Hong Kong context, Hong Kong's relationships with China and Britain, and Hong Kong as one space, among others, that Ching traverses and works in as a global citizen. Ching's short *Video Letters* include grainy footage, often of her face in close-up, in some cases interspersed with quotes from her own writing and from other sources that are layered with a visceral sound montage. The films are letters without a clear recipient or a coherent message; often even the image is difficult to fully comprehend (Figure 6.9). In this way, they speak to Ching's border-crossing transnational experience as an artist and Hong Kong citizen and deny the viewer a vision of the filmmaker as unified expressive subjectivity. As Ching states of these *Video Letters*:

> Because I have always been on the move, departing a city and waking up in another country, I find myself writing letters all the time – to

Before the British Empire
retreated from its colonies

Figure 6.9 Yau Ching's *Video Letter #2 (or, call me an essentialist)* [1993]

238

people I miss, people I met on the road, people I look forward to meeting. . . . When I grew tired of words (which happened very often), I began writing them in video. Since I was travelling, writing letters in unknown lands, I also have very limited access to technology. I write my video letters with Fisher Price Pixelvision, Super-8, and Hi-8. When I could not find editing facilities I edited them with the camera. They became records of my desires desperately in need of an outlet. . . . When shown in public, they re-invent new meanings in different contexts. They become letters to anyone who can relate to them.[3]

Ching's insistence on the accessibility of formats like Super-8 is also true of the diary form itself: a personal genre of filmmaking, it has been – and continues to be – a way that women and feminists make private worlds public.

FEMINIST STRATEGIES

Instead of organizing the rest of the chapter through categories such as "animation" or "activist video works," we offer a list of possible ways to understand experimental feminist work through the strategies it employs. This list is by no means exhaustive and the categories are porous. Some films could be included under any of the following strategies, and many are exemplary of several of them. The strategies included here are: appropriating and recontextualizing images, rewriting male texts, telling culturally and politically marginalized stories and exploring identities, and finally, creating a history where official records do not exist.

Strategy 1: appropriating and recontextualizing images

Experimental filmmakers have always used **found footage** in their work. While in the past this might have meant discarded home video footage or old prints of Hollywood or exploitation films, nowadays found footage may be recorded off of television, or appropriated from the internet in the form of YouTube videos or memes. Soviet filmmaker Esfir Shub, who we discuss in more detail in Chapter 1, pioneered the use of found footage by inventing the so-called "compilation film" – movies made entirely out of previously existing footage. An example of this approach is her experimental documentary *The Fall of the Romanov Dynasty* (1927, USSR).

Reappropriating footage has been a major feminist strategy for interrogating the representation of gender, the female body, and dominant histories and narratives.

For example, Ja'tovia Gary's film *An Ecstatic Experience* (2015, US) takes a performance of the black actress and civil rights activist Ruby Dee reciting a slave narrative for television in 1960 and combines it with archival footage of a rural African-American church service from the 1950s. She also incorporates the words of Assata Shakur, a black rights activist and Black Panther member currently living in Cuba under political asylum. Gary scratches on the emulsion of the original footage, creating an aura around Dee as she recites this traumatic testimony (Figure 6.10). One function of the scratched celluloid is to remind the viewer that they are watching a mediated representation. Though taken from the actual testimony of an enslaved woman, this is a narrative being performed by the actress for American television audiences. The image's multiplication on the screen further reminds us that we are watching a reenactment, while adding to the rhythm and visual appeal of Gary's film.

In this case, the found footage serves multiple and complex functions – it acts as a recorded trace of a history that is largely excluded from dominant media representations. In the footage of Dee, Gary also unearths a rare representation of black womanhood from the midcentury media. The film thus highlights not only silence around the history of slavery, but the invisibility of black women in the media. This is further emphasized by the title, which references one of the first feature films made by an African-American woman, Kathleen Collins' *Losing Ground* (1982, US). It also suggests the mediated access we have to black history. The narrative's juxtaposition with black religious and political culture raises questions about the relationship

Figure 6.10 Manipulated footage of Ruby Dee in Gary's *An Ecstatic Experience* (2015)

between rebellion, redemption, and revolution. Found footage here represents a traumatic working with and through of history for the filmmaker. At the same time, the performance of the slave narrative in melodramatic form raises questions about the representation of traumatic history and its vicarious cultural transmission across the generations.

In the 1980s and 1990s, before the emergence of digital filmmaking, feminist artist Joan Braderman spoke back at popular culture by using green screen technology to project herself into various television shows and Hollywood movies and opened a dialogue with what was happening onscreen. In Braderman's *Joan Does Dynasty* (1986, US) and *Joan Sees Stars* (1993, US), the artist uses the popular television melodrama *Dynasty* and, in the latter video, a variety of classical and postclassical Hollywood films, as her backdrops and interlocutors (see Figure 6.11). Braderman offers a humorous yet biting feminist critique of, for example, *Dynasty* – highlighting the ways in which its plot and characters reflect the failures of 1970s feminism and yet offer alternative fantasies in their place. Over a loop of *Dynasty's* arch antagonist Alexis saying "Get out of my sight, you has-been" while smoking a cigarette through shiny red nails, her hair immaculately coiffed and her face surround by large pearl earrings and a multiple strand pearl necklace, Braderman exclaims:

> God, I love it when she says things like that! Centuries of women's oppression, a huge passionate movement against it, and where are we in 1986? Engaged by twisted pleasure while this monstrous victim of fashion delivers verbal karate chops while issuing bursts of smoke through her shiny blood red key light lips.

Figure 6.11 *Joan Does Dynasty*: Braderman on top of Alexis and Dex (Joan Braderman, 1986)

Moving on to Alexis's relationship with a much younger hunk, Braderman explores the potential subversiveness of this relationship, all while lamenting that it is linked up to capitalism – it is Alexis's wealth that tells women they can have a younger man, contrary to most dominant cultural messages. Speaking of Dex, the young lover character, she narrates:

> He marks for us, the viewers, one of the pseudo-progressive trajectories of this show. That even if you're old and bitchy, if you have enough money, the right make-up man and Nolan Miller to design your clothes you can still get laid over 50 – and by a cowboy with great thighs no less. Here Alexis, the one-toned but canny performance and energy center of the show, the phallic woman, daughter of noir cynicism, power, and sexual charisma, becomes both active subject and object of desire in the narrative.

Braderman, then, uses video to speak back at popular culture, performing a semiotic and historical analysis of the images she receives, rather than passively consuming them. Similarly, in a different geopolitical context, Yugoslav experimental multimedia artist Sanja Iveković reappropriates archival footage of socialist life in *Personal Cuts* (*Osobni rezovi*, 1982, Yugoslavia) and intercuts it with a close-up of her own face covered in hosiery. With each cinematic cut between archival footage (of President Tito and his wife Jovanka, of dancing socialist youth, or of women's shoes displayed in a store), Iveković cuts a new hole in the material that covers her face (Figure 6.12).

Figure 6.12 Sanja Iveković's *Personal Cuts* (1982)

With this technique she draws attention to the parallels between film cutting and the cuts to the hosiery that make her face more and more visible, but also displaces the seemingly mundane images of socialist life from their original context in order to make them strange and expose them in a new light. The practice of reappropriating existing footage has become more common today in terms of the ways that digital technology makes possible **participatory culture**, illustrated in the ability of consumers to easily record, alter, and remix popular culture to "speak back" to it – therefore effectively blurring the line between the author and the consumer (see also Chapter 8).

A more contemporary example, Hannah Piper Burns, similarly uses popular culture as her source material, critiquing its promises and deconstructing its vision of gender, often by recontextualizing media images or making them strange through editing and the use of a soundtrack. For example, her installation *Active Ingredients* (July 2015, US) was a video that participants watched while receiving a skin treatment of "live snails," which crawled over the skin of reclining viewers/clients (snail extracts are popular in some contemporary beauty products). The video that accompanied the treatment was comprised of footage from various skin care commercials. The images create a cosmic otherworldly vision of skin care technologies that promise results that seem to best belong in the realm of science fiction (see Figure 6.13).

The video then acts as a way to speak back to corporations that make vast amounts of money by preying on women's (socially constructed) insecurities

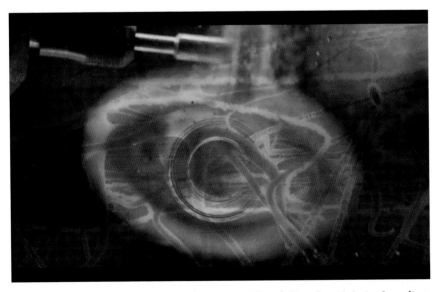

Figure 6.13 The semiotics of skin care advertising in Hannah Piper Burns' *Active Ingredients* (2015)

about aging and being beautiful. It critiques those norms as well through the ridiculous promises of these products – highlighted in their fantastical mise-en-scène – and the unachievability of the ideals they promote. *Active Ingredients* is also exemplary of the ways in which experimental visual work often blurs boundaries between film and other forms of art, from installation to performance (and this can even be thought of in relation to Robertson's aforementioned live narration and baking at screenings of her Super 8mm films). Part of the meaning of the work comes from the viewer's understanding that it is part of a larger performative installation, even when the work is viewed alone, long after the installation is over.

In *Outer Darkness* (2015, US), Piper Burns edits footage from the popular reality show *The Bachelorette*. The imagery is recontextualized through editing and a soundtrack that evokes at times dark sacred rites and at others emptiness and melancholy, giving the popular TV series an ominous and mysterious cast. The video explores the feelings that the media creates and circulates. In its focus on the male candidates (the face of the bachelorette, the supposed object of desire, is effectively edited out), it centers the show's performance of masculinity. It uses repetition to cast a critical eye on its subject matter. For example, close-ups of male contestants' faces at the "rose ceremonies" (the part of the show when the bachelorette decides who she will continue to see by giving them a rose) are edited together such that their repetition reveals the strangeness of dominant representations of masculinity. The repeated shots of faces of male contestants expressing their pride and disappointment, their experiences of competition and desire, become a meditation on canned versions of masculinity, romance, and emotion, all filtered through the lens of reality TV. The offscreen death of the main contestant becomes the narrative arc of the video, and raises questions about the "reality" behind the fantasy world of reality television, further calling into question the naturalness of the gender performances we have witnessed.

Moving from television to other forms of media content, Jennifer Chan, a Canadian artist, uses the internet as a source of found images, from YouTube posts to advertisements to stock photos. Her film *Boyfriend* (2015, Canada), edits together K-pop, Mandarin Justin Bieber covers, images of Japanese sex doll cartoons, and various YouTube videos in which Asian and Asian-American/Canadian men discuss dating, love, and relationships. Sometimes these images, a mix of user-generated content and slick commercial footage, are layered on top of each other or made to move across the screen in ways that detach them from their original viewing context (see Figures 6.14 and 6.15).

Often, they are overlaid with brightly colored bubble fonts that declare sentiments such as "I'm a gentleman who can give you everything." The film compiles these images and sounds to create a complex constellation of ideas around the politics of gender, ethnicity, and sexuality, particularly

244

Figure 6.14 One moment in Jennifer Chan's *Boyfriend* (2015)

Figure 6.15 Another moment in Jennifer Chan's *Boyfriend* (2015)

around Asian/Asian-American masculinity. Chan's work, then, is interested in exploring the construction of masculinity in terms of representation and self-representation through the internet as a source of information, exploration, and identity construction.

American Natalie Bookchin is another contemporary experimental media artist whose work uses the internet – in particular, YouTube – as a source of found footage. Her four-channel installation *Testament* (2009, US) is a meticulously edited collection of various confessional YouTube posts, each with a distinct theme. Bookchin's work identifies the way in which platforms like YouTube generate new genres of self-representation and modes of belonging. For example, in *My Meds*, Bookchin edits together numerous posts of individuals discussing the various medications they take, how often and when. In *Laid Off*, she focuses on posts in which people talk about how they have just been fired. In editing together the clips, many patterns and consistencies are revealed through the ways in which people narrate their experiences and construct their stories about an event like job loss. "Being Fired" stories become a new genre with common narrative arcs and patterns of confession. This raises all kinds of questions about the authenticity of the self: in what ways are our identities shaped by, and do they reflect back ways of speaking and being that are already mediated by the representations of others? How does our consumption of media, such as YouTube videos, play a role in the very construction of the narratives we use to make sense of our experience? The videos explore issues at the heart of the neoliberal economy, from job loss, to the use of pharmaceuticals to address a variety of physical and psychological symptoms. Finally, the videos reveal a diversity of ethnicities, genders, and ages within each YouTube genre that suggest certain utopian dimensions to the internet – in some sense the internet is a space where similarities in experience are revealed across identity categories that may be seen as typically dividing us (Figure 6.16).

Existing footage can also be utilized to explore the construction and dissolution of imagined communities. For example, in Samira Alkassim's *Far From You* (1996, Egypt), the filmmaker uses footage of legendary Egyptian

Figure 6.16 Natalie Bookchin's *Laid Off* (2009)

singer Umm Kulthum to talk about the lost dream of pan-Arab socialism. Kulthum, who also starred in Egyptian feature films, became a symbol of Egyptian nationalism, particularly through her association with the rule of Gamal Abdel Nasser. Nasser advocated for a pan-Arab nationalism, forms of socialist economics, advancements in the position of women in Egyptian society, and an end to colonial influence. Alkassim mixes footage from Kulthum's concert and film performances, often accompanied by dialogue from the films that relates to her characters inciting a fiery passion in some man. For example, in an early scene, a man claims he must jump into a fountain because of the fire Kulthum's character has generated. But what Alkassim is truly interested in is the passion for another Egypt and a different, perhaps lost, form of Arab identity that Kulthum represents. For example, Alkassim's original narration states, "The flame she ignited merged with [Nasser's], from the war, from their deaths and their funerals, the cinders smoldered for decades in spite of the changes of the 70s. Even Sadaam [Hussein]'s ban on the pro-Nasser song she sang only served to reinscribe the memory."

The narrator notes that Kulthum's life spanned the emergence of the Egyptian film industry, the rise and fall of Nasser, and many other significant historical and political events in the Middle East. The singer's music dominates the soundtrack – footage and still images mix with shots of the Egyptian landscape seen through colored filters. The images often include major landmarks, from mosques to the pyramids to the Sphinx. Kulthum's voice then, is rendered as monumental within the film as these symbols of cultural greatness and sources of national pride. The color filters create a sense of timelessness, making it difficult to place the images in a particular historical moment. It effectively challenges their indexicality – that is their link to a specific place and moment in time in the "real" world – just as we are not given dates and film titles for the performances of Kulthum we see. As the soundtrack says, "Making black and white film cohere with color stills of the same places implies multiple perhaps synchronous ways and times of viewing. One involves time's duration and the other time's deferral." These themes of time freezing and of the endurance of the past in the present are central to the narration and the images presented. Kulthum becomes a symbol of a promise perhaps not lost, but deferred. Her status as idea and as appropriated memory is further emphasized by the grainy and degraded quality of her images, which the filmmaker further manipulates by showing them in negative or surrounding them with a bleached-out frame (see Figure 6.17). These strategies of visually mediating the found footage create an even greater sense of the distance between filmmaker, viewer, and the original source material. This is further thematized in the narration:

> Longing fills the void with remembrance and desire. Scavenging through the ruins we build a memory – real or imaginary, authentic or appropriated.

Figure 6.17 Umm Kulthum's worked-over image in Samirah Alkassim's *Far From You* (1996)

Loitering in space, hearing beyond the forms of language, time is deferred, no longer appearing to move. Enveloping us in structures of space and time she fills the distance between worlds with the pleasure of listening to the invisible language of a place.

Echoing these themes of acoustic memory, the narration highlights Kulthum's inability to read music and commitment to learning music orally. Formally, the film gives the voice the last word by ending with a black screen while the soundtrack continues.

ACTIVITY

Watch Dara Birnbaum's film *Technology/Transformation: Wonder Woman* (1978, US) on YouTube. Birnbaum is an early progenitor of using found sources and reediting them to create new interpretations that challenge the original meanings. How have **new media** increased the opportunity for these kinds of interventions (see also Chapter 8)? Find recent examples on YouTube of appropriating and reediting found images for feminist and/or anti-oppressive purposes. Analyze how they use their sources to generate alternate meanings from those intended by the original source.

Strategy 2: rewriting male texts

Another tactic often used in feminist film and video work is the rewriting of traditionally male stories and texts. For instance, Jennifer Montgomery made an all-female version of the 1972 John Boorman feature film *Deliverance* (US). The original film has an all-male central cast and involves a scene in which one of the men visiting the countryside is brutally raped by a local resident. Montgomery revisits this story with a cast comprised of experimental feminist filmmakers including Peggy Ahwesh, Su Friedrich, Meredith Root and Jackie Goss. *Deliver* (2008, US) explores the dominant constructions of masculinity espoused by the original film – a tale of survival and male violence. By re-telling this very male-centered story with women, the film reveals many dimensions of gendered experience, including questions of the possibility of rape between women, women's entitlement to and feeling of ownership over land, and so on. The film is relocated from Georgia to upstate New York, to a river appropriately called Beaverkill. As Montgomery says of her film's title, *Deliver*, it "refers to the re-birthing experience of surviving extreme physical challenges, the product-obsessed nature of the film industry, and, of course, the fact that it is only women who can, biologically, truly deliver".[4]

Another film that takes on a male text is Sally Potter's *Thriller* (1979, UK), which revisits Puccini's opera *La Bohème* to explore the silenced story of the woman (Mimi), whose death in the opera becomes an occasion for male heroism and noble sentiment. In the opera, four male artists and intellectuals live in a Paris apartment. One of them, Rodolfo, falls in love with a woman named Mimi when she asks him for help lighting her candle. Eventually the two separate, as Mimi is dying of tuberculosis and Rodolfo is ashamed that he is too poor to buy her medicine. Dying, Mimi and Rodolfo are reunited at the opera's end, and Rodolfo is overcome with emotion as she takes her last breath.

In *Thriller*, Potter shifts the terms of the original opera, focusing on Mimi's experience and casting a black actress as Mimi. This highlights the whiteness of the original opera in general and evokes global flows of bodies and capital (Mimi works as a seamstress) – all while deconstructing dominant narratives and the limited positions they offer women. The film foregrounds the classed dimensions of Mimi's character – a seamstress who dies in poverty of tuberculosis – as opposed to the heroic "poverty" of the white male artists (who presumably choose poverty so they can live their "bohemian" lifestyle), and opens up the possibility of lesbian desire between Mimi and her foil in the opera, Musetta.

Peggy Ahwesh's *She Puppet* (2001, US) appropriates a male narrative of a different kind. The film is an example of feminist **machinima** – art made using video games as material. *She Puppet* was created from recorded footage of the video game *Tomb Raider*, which features the very voluptuous character of Lara Croft (Figure 6.18). Croft's large chest and curvaceous rear end often occupy the frame in close-up low angled shots and the only noises she makes are sexualized groans and grunts. Presumably, her character offers an abundance of viewing pleasure to straight male players, who often see Croft in front of the camera even though they are playing "her." Croft, as a "she puppet" who explores mostly empty worlds, becomes an exploration of mortality, futility, and alienation in Ahwesh's film. Ahwesh describes the film as a meditation on the personas of the alien, the orphan, and the clone. Croft's character is made to wander aimlessly in spaces devoid of purpose, shooting at brick walls or dying over and over and over again in various meaningless scenarios. In one scene, a tragic sounding aria plays as she mesmerizingly floats underwater, her repeated death from a school of fish rendered poetic and Zen-like. Footage from the game is accompanied by voiceover narration read by several narrators, sometimes in heavily accented English, contributing to the film's themes of alienated identities and feeling like a stranger in strange lands. The text is taken from Fernando Pessoa's *The Book of Disquiet*, Joanna Russ's feminist science fiction novel *The Female Man*, and the musician Sun Ra, and includes lines such as "We are who we are not and life is swift and sad." In one scene, Croft approaches the bodyguards meant to protect her, but their programming renders them incapable of actually physically or verbally connecting with her. They can kill her enemies, but they cannot offer her any companionship

Figure 6.18 *She Puppet* (Peggy Ahwesh, 2001)

on her existential quest. That the depth of the character suggested by the narration is often coincident with imagery emphasizing her buttocks and chest or eroticizing her death only further highlights the dehumanization of the female figure in the game. The overall effect is one of alienation and sadness, transforming a sexualized video game character into a rumination on existence and exile.

Naomi Uman's film *Removed* (1999, US) takes European softcore porn from the 1970s as its source material. Uman meticulously removes the images of naked women from the celluloid frame using bleach and nail polish remover (like Ja'Tovia Gary, Nazli Dinçel, and Su Friedrich, she directly manipulates the celluloid). In addition to refusing the status of the woman as "to-be-looked-at-ness" through this act, Uman also makes visible the extent to which the entire frame relies on the female body and its erotic display (Figure 6.19). The removal of the naked woman (and in some scenes of the many images of naked women that are plastered on the wall) effectively removes the focus of the gaze in every scene, leaving instead a ghostly absence that suggests the absence of actual female desire and agency in the construction of the film. In other words, the removal of the title refers not just to the filmmaker's practice of removing the image of the woman but also to the removal of real female pleasure from the dominant construction of sexuality. The film ends with scratched leader (essentially an imageless screen) over which we hear the original porn film's soundtrack. This emphasizes acoustically what we've seen visually – the soundtrack is dominated not by woman's speech but by her

Figure 6.19 In *Removed* (Naomi Uman, 1999), the pornographic frame becomes almost meaningless with the removal of the female form

simulated pleasure – heavy breathing and groaning mix with a stereotypical porn score. Uman's use of bleach and nail polish remover as tools also situates her art practice as a gendered act of interrogation – using tools associated with gendered cleaning and beauty regimens suggests women's reality outside the fantasy space of the pornographic text.

Removed also illustrates the porousness of the feminist strategies we have articulated here – it intervenes in a male text, it appropriates preexisting footage, and it also illustrates a feminist use of structural principles.

Strategy 3: telling culturally and politically marginalized stories and exploring identities

Experimental form is also well suited to exploring marginalized identities or telling stories that operate outside of dominant cultural codes. Ghanaian-American filmmaker Akosua Adoma Owusu's short *Reluctantly Queer* (2016, Ghana/US), for example, explores a Ghanaian man's queer identity and relationship with his mother within the context of same-sex politics in Ghana. Owusu's films generally draw on many of the strategies articulated here, but several, including *Reluctantly Queer* and *Ajube Kete* (2005, Ghana), which follows a day in the life of a West African girl as she does chores and is discussed by adults around her, are explicitly focused on telling under-represented stories using the experimental short form.

In her short film, *Why I Never Became a Dancer* (1995, UK), British artist Tracey Emin uses film to reclaim an experience of shame from her adolescence. Over footage of various streets and buildings, presumably of Emin's hometown of Margate, England, Emin narrates her experiences as a young teen sleeping with a number of older men, who she describes as "pathetic." She describes her own early experience of sexual curiosity and excitement and the way that various sexual encounters provided a form of escape and relief from boredom. Eventually, she becomes bored with sex and takes up dancing. Entering a disco competition in 1978, she recalls how a group of men began to yell at her as she danced – a humiliating scene of what we would now call "slut shaming" is recounted by the narrator. The men, most of whom had slept with her earlier, call her a slag (a term with the same connotations as "slut") and she runs off of the dance floor. The soundtrack then transitions to the upbeat and euphoric disco track "You Make me Feel (Mighty Real)" by Sylvester. The narrator calls out, "Shane, Eddy, Tony, Doug, Richard . . . this one's for you," addressing some of the men who'd slept with her as a much younger girl and then humiliated her at the competition. The image then shifts to a video of the artist (some twenty years after the events recounted in the film) dancing to the disco track in a large sunny studio. The circular motion of the camera combined with the exuberance of the song and the joy of the artist's dancing body give the film a feeling of elation and freedom from the humiliation of the past. Emin thus uses the film form to narrate her own experience of sexuality and shaming and to reclaim her love of her body and its pleasures.

Nigerian-born and British raised Ngozi Onwurah has similarly used film to explore feelings of shame around the body, particularly in relation to race. Her early film *Coffee Coloured Children* (1988, UK) explores her experience of shame at her skin color as a child of a white mother and absent black father growing up in a white community. She recounts horrific stories of feces being rubbed on the door of their home, while showing images of Onwurah and her brother scrubbing their bodies with Vim cleaner to try to efface their racial difference (Figure 6.20). The soundtrack includes music that provides an ironic counterpoint to the narration and images – songs with lyrics like, "What we need is a big melting pot," which celebrate a multiracial world whose premise Onwurah critiques using her own experiences of racism. Children's rhymes like "Eeny Meeny Miny Mo" and "Baa Baa Black Sheep" become insidious in this context. But the film promises a different future: the past is exorcized through imagery of water and fire and the filmmaker vows to give her unborn daughter a life of pride and dignity. Similar themes are addressed by Tracey Moffatt in her experimental explorations of the experiences of Aboriginal women in contemporary Australia,

Figure 6.20 *Coffee Coloured Children* (Ngozi Onwurah, 1988)

including the trauma of having their heritage systemically and violently suppressed (see Strategy 4).

The motif of scrubbing the skin to efface difference, or as an act of externalizing internalized self-hatred is also a repeated motif in the film *Sally's Beauty Spot* (1996), by Canadian artist Helen Lee. Here, the narrator similarly negotiates feelings of shame over a black beauty spot on her chest. This "mark" is intricately linked to an exploration of Asian-Canadian femininity. Like many of the films previously discussed in this chapter, the film combines original footage with images from popular culture – here the intertext is the 1960 film *The Tale of Suzie Wong* (Richard Quine, UK/US), which the narrator states fascinated her as a child. The film tells the story of a white businessman who takes a year in Hong Kong to explore his proclivity for painting. He meets a Chinese sex worker and she begins to pose for him. As the narrator states, "They fall in love, of course." *Suzie Wong* represents a rare Western media representation of Asian femininity at the time, whose orientalist messages Lee explores by juxtaposing scenes from the film with staged images of interracial couples kissing. The film is also an exploration of the norms of beauty as they constellate around the problem of the black beauty spot, which comes to be an overdetermined symbol of racial and sexual otherness.

Other filmmakers have used experimental forms to interrogate the experience of transgender identity and its own limitations. Vika Kirchenbauer's film *Like Rats Leaving a Sinking Ship* (2012, Germany) explores transgender identity over a montage of images whose location in time and space is vague. Fairgrounds, store windows, pedestrians, bandleaders and many other subjects are combined with black screens to create the visual track of the film. Some of these are home movies of the past, some appear to be found footage, and others shot for the film. The film's use of black screens throughout, accompanied by narration, both refuses the medicalized or voyeuristic gaze and privileges nonvisual, sensory ways of experiencing the world, a motif that is sometimes reinforced by the film's images (Figure 6.21).

The narration track is particularly powerful, juxtaposing throughout what read like medical and psychiatric evaluations of the transgender subject ("Difficulties Falling asleep. Bowel movements and urination are normal. No allergies."), with more poetic subjective and diaristic narrative. The narration examines the pathologization and medicalization of transgender identity from both sides of the patient/doctor relationship. However, the patient's own discourse continually undermines the categories of male and female on which diagnoses of transgender identity so stubbornly rely. For example, the narrator states:

> Freaks and abnormals need to suffer. Nothing else would make any sense to them. But there's a liberty in having no past, no home to return to, no memory to get absorbed in. And the flattering joy of breaking the laws of what we call nature. By choice, not by destiny.

Figure 6.21 *Like Rats Leaving a Sinking Ship* (Vika Kirchenbauer, 2012)

The narration continually challenges the psychiatric establishment by contrasting the performance that the patient must give in order to be diagnosed as transgender with the much murkier reality of choosing a life that exists somewhere beyond binary gender – and finding pleasure in that life. The film's title is explained in the narration:

> Rats are glorious deserters and we must admire them. You'll sink. I won't. But "thanks for everything," they'll say and jump right into the ocean. Rats don't want to be captives, trying to keep the cause afloat.

By analogy, nor is the filmmaker invested in keeping normative gender roles and the society they support intact. As the narrator says at the film's end, describing a pleasurable day spent in bed listening to the bustle of the world outside, "Fuck you, world. I owe you nothing." This defiance connects the work to other acts of reclaiming discussed in this section, such as Emin and Onwurah's films.

ACTIVITY

Historically, there has been a strong link between dance and experimental film in the work of many female artists. Filmmakers like Maya

Deren and Shirley Clarke started as dancers before they worked in film and a sense of rhythm and movement inflects their films and cinematography. Yvonne Rainer also drew on her dance background as a focus for films like *The Lives of Performers* (1972, US) and *Film about a Woman Who . . .* (1974, US). Mexican filmmaker Pola Weiss Álvarez (1947–1990) is considered a major progenitor of the screendance form, whose work spans a dark period in modern Mexican history. Other filmmakers, such as Sally Potter, Babette Mangolte, and Amy Greenfield all incorporate and use dance and rhythm to shape their films.

Screen some of the works of these and other screendance filmmakers on Ubuweb, Vimeo, or YouTube. How does dance shape the content and the form of their work? What do you think the links between dance and filmmaking might be? Is there anything that might point to a feminist impulse behind the desire to document dance worlds and bodies in motion?

Strategy 4: creating a history where no official record exists

Closely connected to and often overlapping with the previous strategy of telling marginalized stories and exploring identities is the impulse to create histories where no official record exists. This may involve experimenting with documentary forms to uncover untold stories, or, in some cases, fabricating histories where the archives are silent.

Hermine Freed's *Art Herstory* (1974, US) is a humorous look at women's exclusion from the art world, except, of course, as models. Made on video, Freed uses television studio technology (like Braderman would later) to place herself directly into the position of various iconic female subjects in the history of art (Figure 6.22). Her comical commentary as she sits in the position of the Madonna and of classical nudes draws attention to the historical (and continued) exclusion of women from the art world and invites the viewer to imaginatively engage with the silent faces of the women whose images make up the canon of painting.

Barbara Hammer's *Nitrate Kisses* (1992, US) explores the lost and silenced history of LGBTQ communities and individuals in the 20th century. The film combines footage of a film from the 1930s, *Lot in Sodom* (James Sibley Watson & Melville Webber, 1933, US), with other images from lesbian and gay history. The emulsion is degraded and manipulated in some cases.

Figure 6.22 Hermine Freed inserts herself into a canonical art image and assumes the gaze with her camera in *Art Herstory* (1974)

Hammer combines historical explorations of case studies such as gay folks living under the Third Reich in Germany and the potential lesbianism of author Willa Cather, who destroyed her personal papers before she died, with four contemporary scenes of gay and lesbian couples of different ages, races, and sexual dispositions making love. This creates a contrast between a repressed past and a defiant insistence on LGBTQ sexuality and desire in the present. The title refers to the volatile stock of nitrate film – and therefore, metaphorically the volatility of historical records or evidence – and also to the burning desire to have a history and be recognized within history, even if that history is often one of pain and oppression. That the film was made during the AIDS crisis makes its assertion of lesbian and gay desire as positive and in need of recognition even more powerful and defiant.

Cheryl Dunye's film *The Watermelon Woman* (1996, US) is an experimental mockumentary of sorts – a style that Dunye has termed "the Dunyemen-tary." It deals with issues of lesbian invisibility similar to those raised by Hammer, while compounding them with issues of the historical invisibility of black actresses in classical Hollywood. Dunye herself plays an aspiring film-maker who finds herself in a budding interracial relationship. She becomes obsessed with a studio era actress who was credited only as "The Water-melon Woman" and limited to Mammy roles. As she delves into the past to discover who this enigmatic woman was, she discovers that "the Water-melon Woman" was in an interracial relationship with a white female direc-tor (modeled on Dorothy Arzner). The film offers humorous forays into the character Cheryl's own black lesbian community and into that of Fae Richards (the Watermelon Woman), exploring intergenerational differences and lineages. At the end, the film reveals that "the Watermelon Woman" was a fictional construction. That Dunye and her real-life partner played the parts of Fae and her director girlfriend in the images from the "past" suggests a complex layering of identifications across time and media and refers to the autobiographical dimensions of the desire for history that shapes the film. It suggests that in the absence of a "real" recorded history – i.e. that of queer black women working in film – sometimes a history must be invented. It also proposes that *all* of our explorations and narrations of history are shaped by the desire for continuity and connection with the past, even when they are based on historical record. In foregrounding the story of a mysterious black supporting actress from the studio era, *The Watermelon Woman* also raises important questions about film history. Namely, it questions film history's erasures and the absence of so many non-dominant subjects from the film canon. It asks us to consider the consequences of this for the ways that film history is organized and taught and for how we conceive the possibilities for women – and nonwhite women in particular – working in and with film.

A final film that illustrates the ways in which experimental modes have been used to draw attention to repressed or untold histories is Tracey Moffatt's *Night Cries: A Rural Tragedy* (1989, Australia). This striking film offers little in the way of narrative explanation. Clearly shot on a sound stage, the film focuses on the relationship between an elderly white woman and her Australian aboriginal caretaker (Figure 6.23).

Figure 6.23 Tracey Moffatt's *Night Cries* (1989)

The film deals with the so-called "stolen generation" of aboriginal youths taken from their parents by the Australian government to be raised by white families as part of the colonization project. Thus, the ambivalence of the unspoken relationship we witness in the film is that of the mother-daughter bond, overlain with the politics of race and colonial violence. The haunting soundtrack includes winds blowing, cries and whispers, and the absence of dialogue between mother and daughter. The film's expressionist color palette and lighting highlight the un-naturalness of the relationship we are witnessing and are counterpointed with campy images of an aboriginal singer, fully Westernized in appearance and musical style, who encourages us to dial up God on the telephone. This singer, Jimmy Little, a popular performer of the 1950s, was seen as a successful example of assimilation. Here his peppy image is rendered disturbing through its juxtaposition with scenes of private pain. This repressed history of aboriginal children taken from their parents is given visibility through Moffatt's film. Rather than a melodramatic narrative structure, using stylized imagery and sound design and experimental contrasts through editing enables Moffatt to evoke the affective legacy of the past without pinning down its meaning.

CASE STUDY: DISPLACEMENT AND TRAUMA IN THE FILMS OF TWO MIDDLE EASTERN FILMMAKERS

Experimental film has been used to explore the difficult realities of life in the countries of Palestine, Lebanon, and Syria, which have complex modern histories of civil wars, refugee migrations and displaced populations, and shrinking national borders. In Chapter 3, we discussed Mona Hatoum's video *Measures of Distance*, a letter of sorts to her mother in war-torn Lebanon, mediated by displacements of time and place. Mounira al Solh's *Now Eat my Script* (2014, Lebanon; Figure 6.24) also takes as one of its themes the lives of refugee populations in the region. Her narrator silently (through titles) describes herself observing refugees from her window as she sits, pregnant and trying to write, distracted by hunger, a desire for sex, and memory. The refugees she sees in the street below remind her of her family's own journey to Damascus from Beirut during the civil war in Lebanon. During a slow high-resolution tracking shot over the pieces of a slaughtered animal, al Solh raises questions about trauma and the capacity to represent it for others and for the self in images

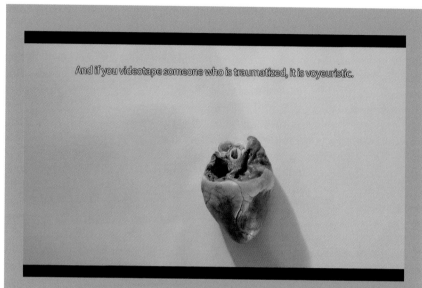

And if you videotape someone who is traumatized, it is voyeuristic.

Figure 6.24 *Now Eat My Script's* narrator raises questions about the representation of trauma (Mounira Al Solh, 2014)

and in writing. By not offering narration on the audio track, the text itself becomes part of the image and therefore foregrounded as a representation, mediated by memory and the filmmaker's consciousness of its representational status.

This is also indicated by shifts in the narrator's (written) voice, from talking about a woman in the third person, to using "I" to invoke the same woman. Focusing first on a car, packed with all the earthly belongings of a refugee family, and then on the internal organs of a slaughtered animal, al Solh offers the viewer graphic details of certain objects, while refusing to show typical media images of suffering or violence in the region. Instead, she questions the banality of these images and their abstraction from the complex reality of everyday life for refugees and citizens (many of whom are former refugees, like the narrator) in Beirut, from which she writes. In this way she refuses a tokenizing Western gaze on her region, while asserting the humanity – from hunger to horniness to distractedness – of people living their daily reality in the midst of great political and social upheavals.

This contrast between living in the midst of great tragedy and the banality of the everyday is a theme threaded throughout the narration of Basma al Sharif's *We Began by Measuring Distance* (2009, Egypt).

The film deals with the complex history of contemporary Palestine – a history that remains in many ways effaced, either lost in the shuffle of shifting refugee populations or overwritten by dominant media images of suffering. Al Sharif offers a meditation on the distance in time and space between media representations of the region and the actual lives of the people these images represent. It also meditates on the distance between Palestine and the places (often European cities) where decisions about the fate of Palestinians are made. The protagonists awake (according to the narration) to find that their surroundings have frozen over and they grow more and more unsettled. The soundtrack repeats the phrase "more and more" as the English words "more and more" dominate the frame. This creates a disconcerting feeling highlighting the "un-settledness" of the Palestinian population literally (i.e. they have been displaced) and metaphorically (they can not feel at ease within the heavily patrolled current Palestinian lands).

Al Sharif uses an absurdist humor throughout her exploration. For example, to kill boredom, and presumably relieve anxiety, the protagonists begin measuring apples to discover they're oranges and then move on to measure distances between the cities where major agreements about the Palestine-Israel situation have been reached (Figure 6.25). From Rome to Geneva to Madrid to Oslo, they end up measuring the distance between Gaza and Jerusalem, which keeps

Figure 6.25 Measuring the distance between the cities in which major decisions about Israel and Palestine have been made in Basma al Sharif's film

changing, the number becoming smaller and smaller, and turns into the numbers of years passing. She says, "We measured the distance between Palestine and Israel and found that Rome was not built in a day," suggesting perhaps the imperial tendencies of Israel but also the absurdity of both clichés and of quantitative data in trying to understand the complex geopolitical situation of modern Palestine. Abstractions of number cannot measure the "distance" of people from their lost history, land, displaced and dead friends and family members, and from the Palestine they once knew.

The protagonists escape to the "virgin forest," a description of which is read over undersea images. The fantasy of a world without ethnic and religious conflict – but also of access to space that is not occupied – are expressed in the fantasy of the untouched forest. But slowly, accompanied by a whimsical soundtrack, images of jellyfish become bombs exploding through their juxtaposition in the frame. Sharif ends the film with worked-over images of violence, children and women fleeing as we hear sounds of fear and grief. These images, however, are denied to the viewer in their typical voyeuristic context. Instead, one particular woman's expression of agony is emphasized by slowing down the film and layering it with a more complex soundtrack, divorcing the sound and image from a clear referential relationship. Moments earlier the narration states: "We began to get the distinct feeling that we had been lied to. That we unfortunately

and that our measurements
had left us empty handed

Figure 6.26 An image of suffering separated from its diegetic sound and drastically slowed down in Basma al Sharif's film

had not rested at all and that our measurements had left us empty-handed" (Figure 6.26).

Watch and discuss: *Now Eat My Script* and *We Began by Measuring Distance*

1 Why do you think these filmmakers use an experimental form rather than making a more conventional dramatic film?
2 What do you think the role of humor might be in works that address such serious issues?
3 Why do you think these filmmakers avoid showing us the images we are used to seeing from the region? Why doesn't al Solh in particular show us any images of people?
4 Compare and relate these films to Mona Hatoum's earlier work, *Measures of Distance* (see Chapter 3). How do issues of distance and mediation shape the form of all of these films?

DISCUSSION QUESTIONS

1 Why might experimental film language be more suited than dominant narrative cinema to articulating experiences not typically represented within mainstream culture?
2 Does formal experimentation necessarily alienate audiences of popular culture, or could it be assimilated into the mainstream so as to become more widely recognizable as a film form?
3 In watching the experimental work discussed in this chapter, or in other experimental films you have seen, are there additional feminist strategies not mentioned here that you see as important or worthy of inclusion?
4 What criteria can we use to assess whether an experimental film is a "feminist" film?
5 Are there any advantages to experimental filmmaking often having to find alternative methods and practices of distribution and exhibition from those of the mainstream? What are the drawbacks?

KEY TERMS

compilation film

diary films

expressive work

formalism

found footage

machinima

new media

participatory culture

structural film

NOTES

1 Nazli Dinçel, "Manifesto," www.nazlidincel.com/manifesto/

2 Nazli Dinçel, "Manifesto," www.nazlidincel.com/manifesto/

3 Yau Ching, "Video Letters 1–3," http://yauching.com/en/art/video/videoletters/

4 Jennifer Montgomery, *Deliver*, VDB website, http://www.vdb.org/titles/deliver

REFERENCES

Blaetz, R. (Ed.). (2007). *Women's experimental cinema: Critical frameworks*. Durham: Duke University Press.

Cutler J. (2007). "Su Friedrich: Breaking the rules." In R. Blaetz (Ed.), *Women's experimental cinema: Critical frameworks*. Durham: Duke University Press, 312–338.

Lim, B. C. (2001). "Dolls in fragments: *Daisies* as feminist allegory." *Camera Obscura*, 16(2 (47)), 37–77.

Mulvey, L. (1975). "Visual pleasure and narrative cinema." *Screen*, 16(3), 6–18.

Petrolle, J., & Wexman, V. W. (Eds.). (2005). *Women and experimental filmmaking*. Champaign, IL: Illinois University Press.

Wees, W. (2005). "No more giants." In J. Petrolle & V.W. Wexman (Eds.), *Women and experimental filmmaking*. Champaign, IL: Illinois University Press, 22–43.

Chapter seven
NARRATIVE FILM
Gender and genre

INTRODUCTION

Narrative film is a difficult term to define because one could argue that nearly all films have narratives and therefore, most films could by default be considered narrative films. Yet the term itself is typically used to describe fiction films, in juxtaposition to documentary or abstract experimental work. Laura Mulvey's much cited essay "Visual Pleasure and Narrative Cinema" (1975), for instance, deploys the term specifically in order to scrutinize classic Hollywood fiction film. In the most general sense, narrative cinema is a term used to create a distinction between documentary filmmaking on the one hand, and fictional stories on the other. However, documentaries themselves frequently play with the notion of what the real world outside of fiction is (see Chapter 5). On the other hand, narrative or fictional film can often be based on true events and, in a sense, be received as historical documentation of an event that really happened. Due to the broadness of the term, we will define narrative film more narrowly for the purpose of this chapter, in order to chart a trajectory of feminist, as well as female-centric, film narration, and in order to examine representations of women in the so-called fiction film while remaining cognizant of the notion that in cinema, fact and fiction are often blurred. We offer notable examples of how, within different genres of narrative film, gender operates in illuminating and complicated ways. The chapter will focus on a select group of prominent film genres – melodrama, horror and sci-fi, porn, and action film – that articulate a complex relationship between film form and (implicit or explicit) gender norms. But before that, we briefly turn to **mainstream drama** as one of the most prevalent film modes that is often pitted as the opposite of genre cinema.

MAINSTREAMING REALISM

The debate about how film should depict reality is a long-standing one (see our discussion on reality, truth and documentary in Chapter 5). With respect to narrative cinema, Soviet film pioneer Sergei Eisenstein famously believed that reality should be constructed, even manipulated, through and in film by using the technique of **montage**, which consisted of brief, often dramatically juxtaposed shots cut together in fast sequences. Film theorist André Bazin, on the other hand, held the opposite view: he believed that cinema should reflect seamless **realism** through long takes, wide shots, and deep focus, without the director reminding the viewers of the technology being used to depict the cinematic story through frequent cutting and editing. Various filmmakers have since adopted one approach or the other, or drawn on both, in using film to tell stories. As we have seen throughout previous chapters, feminist filmmakers frequently challenge the notions of both cinematic neutrality and realism, playing with mixed methods and filmmaking techniques in order to bring critical attention to cinema's close proximity to patriarchal mechanisms of control, but also to cinema's potential as a tool for reflecting and constituting subversive feminist politics. It needs to be noted that realism is a set of culturally and historically specific conventions, and does not merely translate into a seamless representation of reality. What may appear realistic to us is in fact always highly mediated. For example, Peter Jackson's decision to film *The Hobbit* trilogy at the frame rate of forty-eight frames per second (double the usual speed), although it may be closer to how things "really" look in everyday life, was alienating for some viewers because it seemed "too real." Undoubtedly, we are already getting used to higher frame rates and our ideas about what looks realistic will shift, as they have historically, with, for instance, the transition from black and white to color films. Indeed, as discussed in Chapter 5 on documentary, conventions of representing the real are an important consideration in feminist analyses of the cinema. And even though we may be fully aware that realist narrative films are constructions of reality in their own right, they often become our cultural memories of historical events, which is why there is so much at stake in how they represent the world. Genre films are frequently juxtaposed to realist narrative cinema as "unrealistic" by comparison, and are often seen as representing less culturally esteemed forms of entertainment, even though in recent years some genre films (such as Jordan Peele's *Get Out* [2017, US]) have received broader mainstream recognition.

In the most general sense, mainstream drama typically seeks to reflect a seamless cinematic reality that does not attempt to deconstruct or call overt attention to the process of filmmaking as an exercise in the (re)production of reality. In other words, mainstream drama invites the viewer to disappear into the film's world and forget that they are watching a film to begin with. Mainstream drama's narrative imperatives are commonly premised on offering closure and normativity, which distinguishes it from art cinema's conventions that frequently embrace ambiguity. However, this does not necessarily mean that mainstream cinema always upholds the status quo. Quite the contrary, as we have seen in the theory of women's cinema as counter-cinema proposed by Claire Johnston (see Chapter 1), predictable, easily readable dominant film language in and of itself may be precisely what makes mainstream cinema most susceptible to subversive or aberrant encodings and readings. To that end, mainstream drama is a good case in point because, throughout film history, there have been a number of films that can be classified within this broad category that articulate women's experiences in implicitly or explicitly feminist or oppositional terms. This palatable film form designed to appeal to broad audiences can often be the most effective way of introducing said audiences to critical perspectives on patriarchy and women's position in society on a transnational scale. Notable examples of engaged dramas that deploy mainstream film language include Jane Campion's Palme d'Or winner *The Piano* (1993, New Zealand), the Oscar-winning *A Separation* (Asghar Farhadi, 2011, Iran), *A Brand New Life* (Ounie Lecomte, 2011, South Korea), *The Virgin Suicides* (Sofia Coppola, 1999, US), *Pariah* (Dee Rees, 2011, US), *Girlhood* (Céline Sciamma, 2014, France), *The Fits* (Anna Rose Holmer, 2015, US) and *Mustang* (Deniz Gamze Ergüven, 2015, Turkey/France).

On the other hand, mainstream cinema does not rely on the realist mode alone, as evidenced by the currently dominant and most commercial framework of mainstream moviemaking: the superhero movie. In this particular strain of films, comic book hero narratives draw on a mix of supernatural, sci-fi and action movie elements in order to create an all-encompassing spectacle enhanced through elaborate CGI visual effects. Unsurprisingly, the vast majority of superhero movies are focused on male superheroes and directed by men. A rare exception to this general trend is *Wonder Woman* (Patty Jenkins, 2017, US), which focused on the origin story of its titular female superhero. The film has been lauded for its feminist and female-centric narrative arc that does not objectify women, strip them of their agency, or cater to the male gaze (Figure 7.1). Moreover, it earned the distinction of highest intake at the U.S. box office for the summer of 2017, signaling that audiences are more than willing to embrace female-driven narratives when it comes to mainstream movie fare.

Figure 7.1 *Wonder Woman* (Patty Jenkins, 2017)

The concept of **genre** has a complicated relationship to mainstream culture. Barry Keith Grant defines genre as "those commercial feature films which, through repetition and variation, tell familiar stories with familiar characters in familiar situations" (1986: ix).[1] While some genres such as comedy, the war film, melodrama, and the Western are undoubtedly perceived as mainstream, others, such as film noir, horror, and sci-fi, operate on a more complicated terrain both inside and outside mainstream culture in equal measure. Moreover, while some genres – such as the war film and historical drama – predominantly aim for traditional understandings of film realism, others actively challenge realism as such. The latter group includes horror, fantasy, and sci-fi, where the viewer is actively invited to suspend disbelief in order to be immersed in the cinematic world. Annette Kuhn describes genre through the lens of the cinema audience: "[G]enre films can be understood in terms of expectations: expectations on the part of audiences that films will provide the security of generic conventions whilst promising the pleasure, and limiting the risk, of the new, the unexpected" (1990: 2).

Most importantly where film feminisms are concerned, genre has a complicated relationship to gender, and exploring that relationship further may help us understand "how narrative and cultural forms imply a specific sexual politics" (Fischer 1996: 6). As we noted in Chapter 3, Linda Williams' influential essay on the topic of gender and genre (1991) identified three **body genres** that seek to provoke an excessive physical reaction in the viewer: melodrama (crying), horror (fear) and porn (arousal). We will discuss each of these genres in greater detail in separate sections later, but here it is important to recount Williams' theoretical insight. Regarding the "body genre" and its perceivably "low" cultural capital, Williams observes that, what may especially mark these body genres as low is the perception that the body of the spectator is caught up in an almost involuntary mimicry of the emotion or sensation of the body on the screen along with the fact that the body displayed is female.

(4)

In other words, they are "low" genres because the viewer is compelled to mimic the excess of affective bodily response of a female figure on the screen, be it excessive fear, crying, or sexual ecstasy. However, according to Williams, this does not entail a simplistic understanding of identification, because "the subject positions that appear to be constructed by each of the genres are not as gender-linked and as gender-fixed as has often been supposed" (8). This is the case because these genre films and the excessive bodily affect that they seek to evoke in the viewer operate on the plane of fantasy, and fantasy by definition does not allow for fixed identity positions – rather, it is "the place where 'desubjectified' subjectivities oscillate between self and other occupying no fixed place in the scenario" (10). What that means is that these genres and their effect on the viewer cannot be interpreted merely at face value. Underneath the surface, more complicated structures take hold, as we discuss in greater detail with each separate genre case.

MELODRAMA

As one of the preeminent examples of **woman's film**, melodrama – or the "weepie" – has been a source of great interest for feminist film scholars. "A woman's film is a movie that places at the center of its universe a female who is trying to deal with emotional, social, and psychological problems that are specifically connected to the fact that she is a woman" (Basinger 1993: 20). Moreover, woman's film is typically targeted almost exclusively at female audiences. To wit, **melodrama** is a genre generally featuring female protagonists who go through various personal trials and tribulations, from family problems largely to do with motherhood, to unrequited love, loss and grief. This female-centred approach was part of the genre's interest for feminist film scholars – the woman's picture was perhaps the only studio era genre that addressed women in terms of their socially defined position in the family and society. Molly Haskell (1974) was one of the first critics to recognize that in melodrama, woman's role (and her worth) is closely tied to sacrifice, typically to family, and particularly to her children. This is especially the case in the subgenre frequently referred to as **maternal melodrama**, where the conflict between the mother and child is central to the narrative arc. Noting that the connection between melodrama and mothers is an old one, Tania Modleski observes that melodramas (particularly in their iterations as soap operas) invite identification with multiple characters and points of view rather than with a single one. "The subject/spectator of soap operas, it could be said," Modleski adds,

> is constituted as a sort of ideal mother: a person who possesses greater wisdom than all her children, whose sympathy is large enough to encompass the conflicting claims of her family (she identifies with them all), and who has no demands or claims of her own (she identifies with no one character exclusively).
>
> (1982: 84)

Linda Williams adopts this argument as a way to interpret the influential melodrama *Stella Dallas* (King Vidor, 1937, US) through an oppositional lens, arguing that, rather than the film merely reaffirming a patriarchal stance about women's sacrifice, its multiple points of view invite us to see:

> the contradictions between what the patriarchal resolution of the film asks us to see – the mother 'in her place' as spectator, abdicating her former position *in* the scene – and what we as empathetic, identifying female spectators can't help but feel – the loss of mother to daughter and daughter to mother.
>
> (1984: 18)

As noted earlier, the genre of melodrama openly seeks to evoke a strong emotional response in its audience. The question often posed by feminist film scholars is such: as a paradigmatic mainstream genre, can melodrama – which often trades on stereotypical gender roles and constructions of femininity – be effectively utilized to subversive ends? Moreover, where might we locate the ruptures within the genre that allow for counter or aberrant readings? Theorists like Modleski and Williams locate these ruptures in multiple points of view that allow the (female) spectator to critically scrutinize patriarchy even as the female protagonist on the screen succumbs to its limits. E. Ann Kaplan identifies two main strains of melodrama: those she calls "complicit" with the dominant patriarchal order (she also refers to them as maternal melodramas), and, on the other hand, those she calls "resisting" (or the maternal woman's film) (1992: 12). Sometimes, however, it is difficult to draw a strict boundary between the two general types and say that some melodramas are exclusively reactionary while others are definitively subversive (for more discussion around the complications of designating texts as either entirely problematic or affirmative, see Chapter 2).

Melodrama reached the height of its cultural prominence in 1950s Hollywood, with filmmakers such as Douglas Sirk directing canonical films of the genre including *All That Heaven Allows* (1955) and *Imitation of Life* (1959) (see Figure 7.2). However, examples of melodrama can be found in every decade of Hollywood cinema. For instance, Sirk's *Imitation of Life* (Figure 7.2) is actually a remake of John M. Stahl's 1934 film of the same

Figure 7.2 The female household in *Imitation of Life* (Douglas Sirk, 1959)

name. Furthermore, the aforementioned version of *Stella Dallas* from 1937, with Barbara Stanwyck in the main role, was a remake of a 1925 version. More recent examples of melodrama can be found in the work of Todd Haynes, who frequently uses authentic-seeming period settings (typically the 1950s) in order to queer the genre or mine its unspoken racial overtones – examples of this include *Far from Heaven* (2002, US), the miniseries *Mildred Pierce* (2011, US) and *Carol* (2015, US). In *Far from Heaven*, a white 1950s Hartford housewife discovers that her successful businessman husband is sexually attracted to men. Amid the fallout, she develops a romantic relationship with her gardener, who is African-American. What she discovers is that her white upper-middle class community treats the implication of an interracial relationship more severely than they do (male) homosexuality. Haynes's film is a simultaneous homage to Douglas Sirk's melodramas – *All that Heaven Allows* in particular – and a studious deconstruction of the genre's implicit blind spots.

In today's globalized culture, few genres can remain solely identified with a single national film industry. Lucy Fischer notes that the study of melodrama has indeed been predominantly focused on and associated with Hollywood, but that the genre can be found in many other film industries – she offers the examples of Ingmar Bergman's *Persona* (1966, Sweden) and, following Judith Mayne's lead, Vsevolod Pudovkin's *Mother* (1926, USSR) as instances in which the genre of maternal melodrama could be identified in equally illuminating measure. The films of Spanish director Pedro Almodóvar also often draw on the maternal melodrama, but his camp sensibilities refuse to portray the mother as a blemish-free victim. As an openly gay director, he frequently illustrates that his interest in women is not grounded in biological essentialism. As Marsha Kinder says:

> In his films, being a woman isn't determined biologically, but cultur-ally. It means identifying with a set of characteristics that anyone can choose. To borrow from (gender theorist) Judith Butler here, for the women in his films – whether they're male, female or transsexual – gender is a performance.[2]

The mother in Almodóvar's *What Have I Done to Deserve This?* (1984, Spain), for example, is addicted to no-doze pills, sleeps around, murders her husband with a hambone, and pimps her young gay son off to the dentist (Figure 7.3).

The film's colorful camp sensibility is characteristic of Almodóvar's work, and his use of melodrama was itself a critique of the dominant represen-tational modes in Spain at the time. Working in the wake of the Francisco Franco dictatorship, he appropriates Hollywood forms to celebrate imper-fect femininity, alliances between women, and to highlight suffering that is based not on loss (of husband or child) but on gendered economic factors.

In another national context, Patricia Erens's work on Japanese *haha-mono* film identifies the centrality of child-mother relations akin to melodrama at work in the genre.[3] Japanese filmmakers such as Mikio Naruse (active

Figure 7.3 Carmen Maura (a frequent collaborator of Almodóvar's) takes a break from her chores to sniff some glue in *What Have I Done to Deserve This?* (Pedro Almodóvar, 1984)

1930–1967) and Kenji Mizoguchi (active 1923–1956) frequently focused on women's lives in their films, exploring the social constraints and limitations women faced in Japanese society. Mizoguchi was particularly interested in the experiences of geisha and contemporary sex workers, a theme also addressed in Naruse's *When a Woman Ascends the Stairs* (1960, Japan), which sympathetically tells the story of Keiko (played by the legendary Hideko Takamine), who must work as a bar hostess in order to live. The film's repeated motif of the stairs, which Keiko must climb each night to enter the bar, visually manifests the constraints she faces, her only source of income being her body (Figure 7.4). Keiko, painfully at times, puts on a smile to please her male clients night after night, although she dreams of other business opportunities.

Insightful re-appropriations of, or challenges to, the standard Hollywood language of melodrama can also be found in the works of New German Cinema director Rainer Werner Fassbinder. Douglas Sirk was a major influence on Fassbinder, who played with Hollywood genres in his work – from the melodrama to the gangster film and the Western – simultaneously imprinting them with his own unique style. A prolific filmmaker, he made some forty-three films and television series before dying of a drug overdose at the age of thirty-seven. Fassbinder typically focused on female characters and used Hollywood genre tropes to illuminate various social issues in contemporary Germany. *The Marriage of Maria Braun* (1979, West Germany) was the first film in Fassbinder's Federal Republic of Germany trilogy, which includes *Lola* (1981, West Germany) and *The Longing of Veronica Voss* (1982, West Germany). Each of the films focuses on a woman who exploits her own

Figure 7.4 The repeated motif of the stairs in the film visually represents both the material constraints and hurdles that Naruse's protagonist faces in *When a Woman Ascends the Stairs* (Mikio Naruse, 1960)

femininity to get ahead in the "new" Germany. *Maria Braun* is most often interpreted as an allegory for postwar Germany, with Maria standing in for the nation as a whole. Maria, married amidst the explosions of the end of World War II, works her way up in the world financially during the period of Germany's "economic miracle" (Figure 7.5).

Maria's husband, Hermann Braun, is lost at war and eventually returns to find her with an American soldier. Shocked at Hermann's return, Maria inexplicably kills her new lover and Hermann takes the blame for it, sending him to jail and prolonging their reunion. The film follows Maria as she finds another lover and moves up economically, like Germany, in the postwar period. At the film's end, Maria and Hermann are finally reunited only to perish in an explosion similar to the one that started the film. While at the beginning of the film a picture of Hitler goes flying off the wall, the film's final explosion is followed by images of the Chancellors, or West German heads of state, shown in negative, leading up to the time of the film's production (one Chancellor, Willy Brandt, who Fassbinder approved of, is noticeably absent from this lineup; Figures 7.6 and 7.7).

In this way, the film suggests continuity between past and present, and the persistence of fascism in 1970s West Germany. Fassbinder argued that because West Germany had been forced into democracy, rather than having fought for it, traces of fascism were still evident in everyday German life. He said:

> We didn't learn much about German history in Germany, so we have
> to catch up with some basic information, and as a filmmaker I simply

Figure 7.5 Mirrors are a common framing device in both Sirk's and Fassbinder's work (*The Marriage of Maria Braun*, R.W. Fassbinder, 1979)

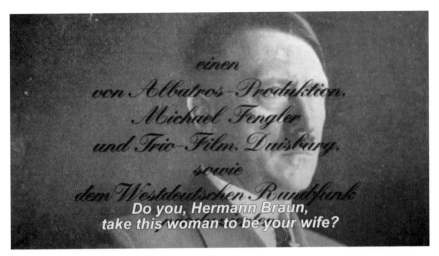

Figure 7.6 From Hitler to Helmut Schmidt in *Maria Braun* (R.W. Fassbinder, 1979)

Figure 7.7 From Hitler to Helmut Schmidt in *Maria Braun* (R.W. Fassbinder, 1979)

used this information to tell a story. That means nothing more than making reality tangible. I see many things today that arouse fear in me. The call for law and order. I want to use this film to give today's society something like a supplement to their history.

(in Kaes 1989: 88)

Fassbinder also uses the film's audio track to emphasize the return of the (repressed) past: actual radio broadcasts of Chancellor Konrad Adenauer

275

insisting that Germany will not re-arm in the postwar period are followed later in the film by broadcasts in which he states the necessity of Germany re-arming itself. The explosion that ends the film is accompanied by historical broadcasts of the 1954 World Cup soccer game in which Germany beat Hungary. The announcer screams hysterically "Germany is world champion!" (or "master" [*Weltmeister*]), which takes on an ominous meaning in light of the country's recent Nazi past. In this way, Fassbinder uses form – here sound design – in order to politicize the genre.

Melodrama is often characterized by an excess of emotion, and here emotions and contradictions that the film cannot contain are displaced onto the excess of mise-en-scène and sound, from swelling dramatic music, to objects being kicked or broken, to lurid color schemes. The legendary melodrama director who was highly influential for Fassbinder, Douglas Sirk, was a master at using elements of mise-en-scène in particular to distance the viewer. In his films, conversations take place in rooms filled with unnatural colored lighting or faces are obscured dramatically by shadows in a way that draws attention to the film as a film. Fassbinder was greatly inspired by Sirk's use of form to push back on the genre, taking it much further in his work, in part because he *could*, as he was working outside of the Hollywood system and had funding from various state sources that allowed him creative freedom.

Fassbinder's film *Ali: Fear Eats the Soul* (1974, West Germany), for example, uses shot/reverse shot editing to draw attention to form. The film is an homage to Sirk's *All that Heaven Allows*, but, as is typical of Fassbinder, uses the story of a romance across age differences to comment on contemporary Germany. The couple in Fassbinder's film are Emmi, a middle-aged cleaning lady whose husband has passed away, and the much younger Moroccan *Gastarbeiter*, Ali. *Gastarbeiter*, or guest workers, were (and are) foreign workers who come to Germany on temporary visas to do typically low-paying jobs. They are usually treated as second-class citizens, excluded from German society at the same time as they are economically necessary to it. When Emmi first meets Ali, she enters a bar and sits down (Figures 7.8 and 7.9).

By lingering on each take for an uncomfortable amount of time, drawing out the shot/reverse shot through long static camera takes, Fassbinder draws attention to the form of the film itself and asks the viewer to consider the politics and power relations embedded in what they are seeing. The scene in question works to foreground the politics of looking, including the themes of voyeurism, exhibitionism, and their role in forms of fascism and racism. The film also implicates the viewer in these politics by making her aware of the ways her own gaze is sutured into this combination of shots. To drive the point home, when everything goes wrong for Ali and Emmi in the film, they decide to take a vacation to escape from it all. The viewer, like the characters

Figure 7.8 Emmi enters the asphalt bar (*Ali: Fear Eats the Soul*, R.W. Fassbinder, 1974)

Figure 7.9 The reverse shot implicates the viewer in the look and in the process of creating and enforcing group boundaries (*Ali: Fear Eats the Soul*, R.W. Fassbinder, 1974)

in the diegetic world, is denied any visual access to this vacation. The film asks us to consider the power and objectifying potential of our own desire to see the lives of others (be they thriving, or, as is often the case in melodrama, suffering). Both *Ali* and Sirk's *All that Heaven Allows* end with images of their protagonists at their lovers' bedsides (Figures 7.10 and 7.11).

Figure 7.10 Cary at Ron's side in *All that Heaven Allows* (Douglas Sirk, 1955)

Figure 7.11 Emmi and Ali in *Ali* (R.W. Fassbinder 1974)

But whereas Sirk's character Ron is the victim of a dramatic fate (he falls off a cliff trying to get his love interest's attention at the film's darkest moment), Ali's illness is the result of his material conditions of labor. We are informed that his ulcer is likely to return and that this is a common health condition for guest workers. Ali and Emmi are in a hospital, a drab institution, whereas Ron and Cary end Sirk's film in a pastoral cabin. Here, Fassbinder more explicitly links the personal to the political and the public to the private than does Sirk.

These examples are meant to highlight the ways in which melodramatic form can be pushed to force critical consideration of its subject matter and to say something about the moment in which it is made. Melodrama, like many film genres, raises ideological contradictions within its plot that it cannot resolve. Often, the ending is a tacked-on attempt at resolving much larger issues that cannot be eradicated under current economic and political conditions (Sirk referred to this as the film's "emergency exit"). To the extent that the ending of many films in this genre does seem tacked on, melodrama may be able to subvert its own conservative tendencies, calling into question the "realism" of the solutions it offers to intractable problems.

Popular Indian cinema (also referred to as Bollywood) is characterized by its melodramatic structure. As Rosie Thomas observes, Bollywood films "are centrally structured around contradictions, conflicts, and tensions primarily within the domains of kinship and sexuality" (1995: 159). As a result, "it is an expectation of Hindi film as a genre – in accordance with the conventions of melodrama – that these conflicts are resolved within the parameters of an ideal moral universe" (159). At the same time, this does not mean that melodramatic elements are merely copied from Western conventions. In fact, as Vijay Mishra points out, "there is no exact match between Indian film and Western melodrama. What happens [in Indian film] is that melodramatic features are selectively used to stage any number of quite serious and in themselves nonmelodramatic moments" (2002: 36). Similarly, film scholars have observed that many Nollywood (Nigerian film industry) films adopt the tropes of melodrama such as an excess of tears, happiness, enjoyment, and tragedy, in order to address locally specific issues and topics that resonate with female audiences. In that respect, Moradewun Adejunmobi traces the differences between Old and New Nollywood (where changes in production conditions and the economy influenced a shift sometime around 2010) with respect to melodrama in particular:

> If Old Nollywood's melodramas represented individual responses to structural constraints, New Nollywood's alternative palette of stories offers portraits of individuals endowed with initiative in a world without constraints. The central conflicts are often the product of happenstance and/or serendipity rather than social destiny.
>
> (2015: 39)

Whether that makes the melodramas of New Nollywood potentially less subversive – because they elide structural obstacles faced by women and opt instead to focus on luck and chance – is a question worthy of further examination.

279

CASE STUDY: *SINKING SANDS* (LEILA DJANSI, 2011, GHANA)

Sinking Sands, a film set in Ghana, is directed by Ghanaian-American director Leila Djansi. In their book *Female Narratives in Nollywood Melodramas* (2016), Elizabeth Johnson and Donald Culverson categorize *Sinking Sands* as part of the Nollywood film industry, even though, as they note, technically it belongs to so-called Ghallywood (the Ghanaian film industry, which Johnson and Culverson call a sub-category of Nollywood). Since Nollywood is the more dominant of the two industries, Ghallywood films are often made with direct or indirect support from Nollywood infrastructures.

The story of *Sinking Sands* revolves around Pabi, a schoolteacher who was orphaned as child. She marries Jimah, but soon after their wedding, a domestic accident results in severe facial disfigurement for Jimah. Subsequently, he becomes depressed and increasingly violent toward Pabi, who sacrifices her ambitions of becoming a school principal in order to take care of him. As the violence intensifies and results in marital rape, regular beatings, and attempted forced abortion, Pabi questions her feeling of obligation to take care of Jimah, and turns to thinking about what is right for herself (and her unborn child). Ultimately, she leaves Jimah and starts life on an uncertain but empowering path of independence as a single mother.

Female camaraderie is a prominent feature of the film's narrative arc, emphasized through mentions of Pabi's foster mother (who dies in the beginning), and particularly through the figure of Pabi's school principal and mentor, Mrs. Dodou, who continues to be supportive of Pabi throughout the difficulties she is facing (Figure 7.12). When Pabi tells the principal that she has turned down a fellowship to become a school principal because she has to sacrifice her career in order to help her husband, Mrs. Dodou asks if it is worth helping her husband by losing herself. Later on, as Pabi becomes increasingly disillusioned about Jimah ever changing for the better, Mrs. Dodou shares the story of her own struggles as a young woman who suffered domestic violence at the hands of her alcoholic husband. When the husband died, she was blamed for his death by the family. As a result, Mrs. Dodou relates, she decided to only rely on herself, go back to school and be independent for the rest of her life – similarly to how Pabi ends up at the end of the film. Through this camaraderie, and through the parallels between the stories of Pabi and Mrs. Dodou, the film taps into the structural and

Figure 7.12 Female camaraderie in *Sinking Sands* (Leila Djansi, 2011)

systemic obstacles faced by women more broadly, rather than leaving Pabi's story merely individualized and therefore isolated.

In one of their final confrontations, in which Jimah informs Pabi that he does not want the child she is carrying, she angrily suggests she will leave him and asserts: "All I am now is your glorified house help and sex toy." The film's openly feminist message against domestic violence and in favor of female independence offers a poignant take on the genre of melodrama as a way to illuminate the complexities faced by women who experience the social burden of having to place their lives and best interests secondary to those of their husbands.

Watch and discuss: *Sinking Sands*

1   Where can you identify the elements of melodrama in this film?
2   How does the genre of melodrama serve the main story and its message against domestic violence?
3   Is melodrama well suited for the film's feminist interventions?
4   Who do you think is the target audience for this film?

ACTIVITY

Watch one of the classic Hollywood melodramas mentioned in this chapter and see whether you can discern any subversive elements in it. Who does the film invite you to identify with? Is the film's stance towards women critical of patriarchy or aligned with it? Make sure to also consider the time period of the film's making, and how the film's impact may have been different in its historical context from how we receive it today.

HORROR AND SCI-FI

Horror film is a genre that, as its name purports, seeks to evoke excessive horror and fear in its audience. **Sci-fi** – short for science fiction – is a genre that trades in fantasy based on (pseudo)science and speculative, futuristic narratives that envision the intersections of humanity, extra-terrestrial life, and technology. Although they are two separate genres, horror and sci-fi often overlap: many horror films have sci-fi elements in them and vice versa, as many sci-fi films can also be classified as horror films. For instance, the original *Alien* (Ridley Scott, 1979, US) is a sci-fi and horror blend in equal measure, making it difficult to classify the film solely within one genre. And even such sci-fi classics as *Metropolis* (Fritz Lang, 1927, Germany) contain frequent horror-like sequences, particularly with respect to the threat imposed onto its female protagonist, Maria (the iconic scene in which the evil inventor, Rotwang, chases and taunts Maria through dark tunnels, for instance, establishes many memorable horror genre tropes). These overlaps between horror and sci-fi are an important reason why we discuss the two genres in the same section, while remaining cognizant of the fact that there are many examples of films in which the delineation between the two is very clear and unambiguous.

Alien is an illustrative hybrid example to discuss here because in this sci-fi classic, we find a familiar trope of horror cinema: **the final girl**. The term final girl was originally coined by Carol J. Clover (1992), who noticed a telling pattern in horror movies, particularly in the subgenre of **slasher** horror (films involving serial murders), in which it is nearly always a girl who escapes the grips of the psychopathic serial killer in the end (Figure 7.13). This pattern can be observed in such well-known horror films as *The Texas Chain Saw Massacre* (Tobe Hooper, 1974, US), *Halloween* (John Carpenter, 1978, US) and *Scream* (Wes Craven, 1996, US). Juxtaposing the final girl to Marion Crane, the female victim in the iconic shower scene of Hitchcock's *Psycho* (1960, US), Clover notes: "Like Marion, the final girl is the designated victim, the audience incorporate, the slashing, ripping, and tearing of whose body will cause us to flinch and scream out in our seats. But unlike Marion, she does not die" (59). Importantly, the final girl ultimately acts as

Figure 7.13 Jamie Lee Curtis as final girl in *Halloween* (John Carpenter, 1978)

her own savior, as her male companions prove less capable in fighting off the killer. This is what happens in *Alien* as well: while all of Ellen Ripley's crew members – male, female, and android – are killed off one by one by the alien xenomorph that has infiltrated their spaceship, Ripley becomes the lone survivor who manages to outlast and dispose of the creature in the end.

The final girl is an important trope of genre cinema because she complicates the standard framework of dominant film language within which man is supposedly the bearer of the look and woman embodies to-be-looked-at-ness. "When the final girl . . . assumes the 'active investigating gaze,'" argues Clover, "she exactly reverses the look, making a spectacle of the killer and a spectator of herself. . . . The gaze becomes, at least for a while, female" (60). Importantly, Clover observes that the final girl is always somewhat "boyish" – that is to say, she does not exhibit traditional feminine traits to the extreme, or at least not to the extent of her female friends who perish at the hands of the killer. Libidinal pleasure plays an important role here, since the final girl is often the one who is sexually less available than other female victims. This trope, however, is rendered more complicated in horror films such as *It Follows* (David Robert Mitchell, 2014, US), in which a mysterious, supernatural threat is passed on through heterosexual intercourse. Here the final girl is the one who initially contracts the virus through casual sex, and then faces the dilemma of having to pass it on to someone else through intercourse in order to survive. Contrary to the previous archetype of the final girl being sexually unavailable, here both the threat and her survival are premised on sexual availability. Nowadays, horror films are more self-conscious about the tropes that Clover identified – so much so that there is even a film titled *Final Girl* (Tyler Shields, 2015, US).

Another archetype often associated with women in both horror and sci-fi is the trope of what Barbara Creed (1993) calls **the monstrous-feminine**. The trope focuses on female monstrosity and is often closely aligned with deviant motherhood – in films as varied as *Psycho*, *Carrie* (Brian De Palma, 1976, US) and the *Alien* series. The monstrous-feminine figure is an active agent rather than a passive onlooker and, in psychoanalytic terms, presents a clear castration threat – or a threat to the phallocentric patriarchal order (see Chapter 2). She is threatening because of her female body, sexuality and ability to reproduce. Recent cinematic iterations of the monstrous-feminine can be found in films such as *A Girl Walks Home Alone at Night* (Ana Lily Amirpour, 2014, US), *Under the Skin* (Jonathan Glazer, 2013, UK) and *Ex Machina* (Alex Garland, 2014, US) (see Chapter 3 for a discussion of *Under the Skin* and Chapter 8 for a discussion of *Ex Machina*). In all these films, the monstrous-feminine is a threatening figure to the men she encounters, and the primary agent of the films' respective narrative arcs. In *Teeth* (Mitchell Lichtenstein, 2007, US), the protagonist, Dawn, discovers that she has a *vagina dentata* – a vagina with teeth, which bites off male sexual organs whenever Dawn is forced into nonconsensual intercourse. In this horror film, the psychic threat of castration is again pushed to its logical extreme in the form of a penis-biting female sexual organ. Similarly, in *Jennifer's Body* (Karyn Kusama, 2009, US), Jennifer becomes a man-eating demon after being assaulted and brutally violated by a group of men. This film, with its female director, Karyn Kusama, and female screenwriter, Diablo Cody, offers a tongue-in-cheek reversal of some of the standard horror tropes by focusing on female camaraderie, the female gaze, homoeroticism, and a pointed critique of patriarchal violence towards women.

One of the most influential horror subgenres in the world is **Japanese horror** (or **J-horror**). As a genre, horror gained particular prominence in Japanese cinema after World War II, and generally developed within two major subcategories: the *kaidan*, or ghost story, which was marked by the figure of the *onryō*, or the avenging spirit, and the disaster movie, frequently featuring the figure of a giant monster. The former category – the *kaidan* – is of particular interest for feminist film studies because the *onryō* figure is typically female: the avenging spirit of a woman who has suffered a violent and tragic death and now comes back to haunt the living until her trauma is recognized and acknowledged (Figure 7.14). This figure is prominently featured in films such as *Ring* (*Ringu*, Hideo Nakata, 1998, Japan), which was subsequently remade in Hollywood in 2002. In the film, the avenging spirit is that of a young girl, Sadako, who was murdered by her father because of her powerful psychic abilities, which, as Jay McRoy (2008) observes, made her extremely threatening to the male-centric dominant order. And since the only way to avoid certain death by the hands of Sadako's avenging spirit is to continue to copy the cursed videotape through which she now haunts

Figure 7.14 The *onryō* comes back to haunt the living (*Ring*, Hideo Nakata, 1998)

the living, McRoy points out that "to break a contemporary cycle of literal (within the film's diegesis) and figurative (socio-cultural) fear, tragically and historically repressed women must forever be acknowledged, their silenced voices perpetually recognized if never fully understood" (87–88).

The role of women in science fiction films can be traced back to the days of silent cinema. For instance, what is considered the first Soviet feature-length sci-fi film, *Aelita, Queen of Mars* (Yakov Protazanov, 1924), features a female protagonist as an alien queen (played by the iconic Yulia Solntseva, who we discuss in Chapter 1), and Fritz Lang's *Metropolis* (1927, Germany) prominently features a female cyborg created by an evil scientist, Rotwang, in order to resurrect Hel, a dead woman with whom he was in love. In these sci-fi films, the fate of the alien/cyborg woman is usually determined by the men around her. Indeed, Mary Ann Doane finds that sci-fi films often fortify "conventional understandings of the feminine" (1990: 163). "A certain anxiety," she adds, "concerning the technological is often allayed by a displacement of this anxiety onto the figure of the woman or the idea of the feminine" (163).

Christine Cornea (2007) notes that one of the most influential modern representations of women in sci-fi films is *The Demon Seed* (Donald Cammell, 1977, US), which sees a female psychologist, Susan, imprisoned, raped and impregnated by a computer with artificial intelligence named Proteus (Figure 7.15). Susan gives birth to a human-machine hybrid to be raised and controlled by Proteus, clearly indicating that "the female here becomes a mere vessel for the reproduction of a masculine consciousness" (148).

Figure 7.15 Susan is violated by a computer with AI in *Demon Seed* (Donald Cammell, 1977)

Besides offering a reflection on the anxieties around the emergence of computer technology and its potential impact on human bodily sovereignty, Cornea finds that the film also signals "an impending re-masculinization of the genre" at least partially related to the fact that in the 1970s, "the feminist movement was in full swing and the film can be seen to engage with the reactionary responses that the movement endured" (95). Indeed, the 1980s and 1990s saw a vast majority of sci-fi/action films focused on excessive masculinity, with notable exceptions such as James Cameron's *The Terminator* (1984, US) and *Aliens* (1986, US).

Besides the monstrous-feminine, motherhood in the sci-fi genre – as in horror – is a prominent trope through which women are depicted. In *The Terminator*, Sarah Connor is pursued by a cyborg who comes from the future to kill her in order to prevent her from having a child she has yet to conceive, and who will end up leading the human rebellion against the machines some decades later. Moreover, many interpretations of the *Alien* franchise, particularly the James Cameron sequel, see it as a battle between two mothers – Ripley, who is looking to save the little girl she finds on the destroyed space colony, and the alien queen. In *The Demon Seed*, not only is Susan made to give birth to a hybrid human/inhuman child conceived through rape, she is also forced to relive the trauma of losing her biological daughter to leukemia. Interestingly, the trope of the dead child that haunts the mother is featured prominently in two contemporary sci-fi films with female protagonists – *Gravity* (Alfonso Cuarón, 2013, US) and *Arrival* (Denis Villeneuve, 2016, US). These two films are also notable because their mainstream box-office success proved the commercial viability of female-centric sci-fi films, which are still far less common than male-centric ones.

CASE STUDY: *A GIRL WALKS HOME ALONE AT NIGHT* (ANA LILY AMIRPOUR, 2014, US)

Iranian-American director Ana Lily Amirpour's feature debut, *A Girl Walks Home Alone at Night* is a hybrid genre film with overtones of horror, Western, and film noir. The film also draws on a tradition of comics and graphic novels in its story construction and visual design. The story takes place in Bad City, a place that looks like an archetypal Midwestern American town, yet all its inhabitants speak Persian, which is the only language heard throughout the film. This hybridity plays with the audiences' expectations regarding both national space and national cinema (the film could also be categorized as diasporic or accented cinema).

The film's title plays with our expectations as well – it evokes a sense that the girl in question is in a vulnerable, potentially dangerous situation. However, in the film the girl herself represents a threat on multiple levels. She is a chador-wearing vampire who exacts vigilante justice upon local drug dealers and violent addicts (Figure 7.16). At one point in the film, she aids a female sex worker, whereby a notion of camaraderie between two female social outcasts is highlighted.

As a covered Muslim girl who also happens to be a vampire, the nameless girl represents a highly provocative figure. Namely, dominant Western discourses around the covered body of Muslim women position them as subjugated and passive, and as victims of patriarchal and traditional Islamic values. This trope has been critiqued by many Islamic feminists, but it nevertheless persists, and the veil continues to be simplistically treated as an indication that the woman wearing it is being denied her basic rights and agency. Moreover, the figure of the covered Muslim woman often taps into Western anxieties about the terrorist threat hidden underneath, a theme that multimedia artist Shirin Neshat addresses in her work, for instance. Therefore, to have a covered Muslim girl be an active protagonist, as *A Girl Walks Home Alone at Night* does, is already a provocative intervention into existing discourses about Islam, women, and feminism. But to add the supernatural aspect of her also being a vampire exacting vigilante justice is to further complicate the relationship between gender and genre in particular, because the female protagonist is here in a double bind: othered as a covered Muslim girl, and as a nonhuman, supernatural figure.

Figure 7.16 The girl embodying a double threat (*A Girl Walks Home Alone at Night*, Ana Lily Amirpour, 2014)

While the vampire subgenre has always drawn on themes of eroticism and death, and explored the slippery border between desiring the other and consuming them, the film also elliptically suggests larger geopolitical dimensions to the theme of vampirism. Oil derricks pepper the landscape around Bad City, as technological vampires sucking resources and money from the earth. In a film that invokes the Middle East, and Iran in particular, with its chador-wearing Farsi-speaking protagonist, the references to oil can be read in terms of larger geopolitical forces that drive ideological oppositions such as the "West" versus "Islam." The film's references to the Western genre take on different dimensions from this perspective. *A Girl Walks Home Alone at Night* asks us to think about the drive for fossil fuels and its economic dimensions as vampiric activities. Furthermore, it indirectly asks us to consider these issues in terms of their connection to the figure of the covered Muslim woman, as she represents a significant image used in the West's political struggles to control strategic areas. The notion of the chador-wearing girl as in need of rescue is something the film directly challenges and subverts, insisting on her individual humanity and strength, and asking viewers to consider who *really* feels vulnerable in the encounter with "the girl."

Watch and discuss: *A Girl Walks Home Alone at Night*

1   How would you classify this film with respect to genre? What might be the director's reason to play with genre hybridity this way?
2   Consider the relationship between genre and gender in this film. What are some of the most provocative elements of the film?

PORN

In the broadest possible sense, **porn** (short for **pornography**) is a genre in which individuals are depicted engaging in sexual activities with various levels of explicitness. Its main purpose is to arouse the viewer and assist them in achieving sexual climax. As such, porn film is a vast genre with many different subcategories, and has arguably the lowest cultural standing among the so-called "low" or body genres. Usually, it is divided into two broad categories: **hardcore** – which features graphic, direct visual representations of sexual intercourse, and **softcore** – with a less graphic visual representation of intercourse, focused more on the erotic rather than the pornographic. While it is sometimes stereotypically assumed that softcore aligns with a more female-directed depiction of sexuality, and hardcore with its male counterpart, that assumption is easily challenged through the diverse approaches to spectatorship and libidinal desire that we discussed in Chapter 2, which complicate the standard stereotypes about fixed viewing positions and normative gender identities along masculine/feminine lines. In the context of the Women's Liberation movement, some feminists dismissed pornography as unequivocally problematic, patriarchal and demeaning to women (Dworkin 1979; MacKinnon 1985). Their argument was that pornography was a major obstacle to women's sexual and legal equality. In what has become known as the "sex wars," feminists debated whether visual forms like pornography and rape and violence against women were linked. Such a moralizing approach to porn often has the counter-effect of denying female spectators a libidinal investment in the genre, or shaming them for having one. This argument has been made by the anti-censorship feminists who hold that censoring graphic sexual content, even when it depicts women in a demeaning light, is counterproductive and does nothing to resolve the deeper underlying causes of patriarchal power structures (Burstyn 1985).

More nuanced feminist approaches to porn as a genre have sought to avoid a priori judgment and have instead focused on how the genre participates in not only reflecting or framing, but also constituting human sexuality in complex ways. Noting that it is first and foremost a commodity "produced, bought and sold," Annette Kuhn looks to address how pornography, "as a regime of representation, addresses a particular audience in a particular context, producing meanings pivoting on gender difference: and how in this process it constructs a social discourse on the nature of human sexuality" (1985: 23–24). And while she acknowledges that much of pornography rests on the objectified images of women, she also points out that this does not automatically imply that porn is not pleasurable for female spectators, since "women can and do derive pleasure from images of women, a fact which betokens the unfixity of sexual identity and the fluidity of our engagement with certain types of image" (31). This again refers us back to the complicated channels of identification and pleasure derived through spectatorship (as discussed in Chapter 2).

One of the most influential feminist studies of porn is Linda Williams' *Hard Core: Power, Pleasure, and the "Frenzy of the Visible"* (1989). In the book, Williams takes an anti-censorship stance and looks at mainstream hardcore film through a feminist lens that deconstructs some of the key elements of the genre. That includes the dominant focus on male orgasm and in particular the so-called **money shot**, or the graphic visual depiction of male ejaculation, which in mainstream hardcore porn signals the climax of the sexual act. The focus on the money shot effectively negates the importance of female orgasm in mainstream heterosexual porn. Noting that it became a genre staple during the 1970s, with films such as *Deep Throat* (Gerard Damiano, 1972, US), Williams finds that "while undeniably spectacular, the money shot is also hopelessly specular; it can only reflect back to the male gaze that purports to want knowledge of the woman's pleasure the man's own climax" (1989: 94). In this sense, Williams finds that the money shot enacts a perversion (which she uses as a neutral term) in which the focus on the tactile is abruptly and strategically switched to a focus on the visual at the moment of sexual climax. Ultimately, rather than being a realist representation of a heterosexual encounter, Williams sees the money shot in porn functioning as a fetish, and fetishes are "short-term, short-sighted solutions to more fundamental problems of power and pleasure in social relations" (105). As for the importance of this analytical insight regarding the money shot for feminists, Williams argues:

> The money shot could thus finally be viewed as that moment when the phallic male libidinal and material economy most falters, most reverts to an absolute and unitary standard of value. But the import of this statement should not be that pornography is hopelessly and monolithically phallic; instead it should be that pornography

is insistently phallic *in this particular way, at this particular time,* because of pressures within its own discourse to represent the visual truth of female pleasures about which it knows very little.

(117)

And because mainstream pornography might reflect very little about female pleasures, the remainder of this section turns to the sub-genres of porn that actively seek to circulate and address non-patriarchal, as well as non-heteronormative, sexual practices and libidinal investments. One such subgenre is **feminist porn** produced and circulated by **sex-positive** feminists – feminists who advocate for embracing open explorations in sexuality – in order to destigmatize porn made for women and by women. The editors of *The Feminist Porn Book*, Tristan Taormino, Constance Penley, Celine Shimizu and Mirelle Miller-Young, emphasize that feminist porn "uses sexually explicit imagery to contest and complicate dominant representations of gender, sexuality, race, ethnicity, class, ability, age, body type, and other identity markers" (2013: 9). Moreover, "it explores concepts of desire, agency, power, beauty, and pleasure at their most confounding and difficult, including pleasure within and across inequality, in the face of injustice, and against the limits of gender hierarchy and both heteronormativity and homonormativity" (9–10).

Another important topic that is explored under the umbrella of feminist porn is the question of female authorship of porn, as well as racial imbalances that often privilege white bodies, or excessively fetishize or essentialize the nonwhite ones. "Not only does black-cast pornography tend to be organized around a view of black sexual deviance and pathology," observes Mireille Miller-Young, "but black porn actors tend to be paid rates half to three-quarters of what white actors earn" (2013: 107). This is why it is important to support and highlight porn industry workers who turn against this dominant trend, such as Vanessa Blue (Figure 7.17), an African-American porn performer who decided to take things into her own hands and start directing porn films herself. As Miller-Young points out, "moving behind the camera . . . is a kind of mobility that allows sex workers greater agency to traverse the barriers placed around them in the porn business" (106). Adding that sex-positive feminist approaches to porn need to remain mindful not just of porn as text, but also of the labor involved in producing it, she notes that this labor cannot be extracted from the global flows of capital, since feminist porn is a for-profit industry as much as other types of porn are. Because of that, Miller-Young adds that "theorizing a feminist pornography then means thinking about a dual process of transgression and restriction, for both representation and labor" (107). And for porn industry workers of color, an added layer of difficulty is countering "the stultifying power of race in pornography's structural and social relations" (ibid).

Figure 7.17 Vanessa Blue, porn performer turned director, as Domina X

Similarly focused on the industry aspects of feminist porn, Lynn Comella notes that it cannot be addressed outside of the broader cultural frameworks that produce and circulate it. She calls these frameworks a "sex positive synergy" (2013: 82) which is crucial to the establishment of networks that create and uphold sex-positive spaces – both literal and representational – for women's sexuality. Sex-positive porn for women depends on producers who are willing to cater to such a vision, and on distribution that makes such porn available to women. For instance, Comella discusses retailers such as Babeland, whose emphasis is on providing sex-positive products and making their potential customers feel comfortable in a non-threatening and non-judgmental environment. Certainly, the digital age and the advent of online porn sites have made porn more easily accessible, including sex-positive subgenres such as feminist porn, **lesbian porn, queer porn, trans porn** and others. Moreover, porn production has been influenced by new technologies as well, which have made it easier to produce otherwise underrepresented content, whether professionally or on an amateur level. For instance, Bleu Productions, Reel Queer Productions, and Blue Artichoke Films are independent production houses that focus on making sex-positive, often artistic-leaning porn in order to offer a fresh take on erotic and pornographic representations of sexuality, and Pink Label and GoodDykePorn are sites that offer a platform for queer, lesbian and trans-centric porn. In the form of a manifesto on the GoodDykePorn website, the members claim: "In the spirit of do-it-yourself projects, the dykes on this site are taking matters into their own hands and doing dyke porn for themselves." In its dedication to sex-positivity, the website is self-described as "inclusive to all variations of the gender known as woman (past, present and future women) as well as appearances by men both cisgender and transgender."[4] Moreover, the website permissions4pleasure.com offers a comprehensive list of **ethical porn,** i.e. porn that is mindful of the ethical stances of its intended sex-positive, feminist audience.

ACTIVITY

Survey a sex-positive, feminist porn site and identify the language that its community uses to define their mission. What can you infer about their politics, as well as their approach to feminism and sexuality from their mission statement?

CASE STUDY: SEXUAL ASSAULT AND THE MAINSTREAM PORN INDUSTRY

One of the biggest scandals to affect the mainstream porn industry in the United States in recent years has been a series of allegations of sexual assault made by several porn actresses against James Deen, arguably the most famous male porn star of his generation and a winner of numerous awards in the porn industry. It should be noted that this scandal shook the porn industry well before the #MeToo movement that triggered a broader conversation on sexual harassment and assault in the entertainment industry starting in 2017. Before the accusations against Deen surfaced, he enjoyed an affirmative status with many sex-positive feminists for his proclaimed views on equality in the industry, and his refusal to film sex scenes that felt "rapey" (although he was not willing to self-identify as a feminist in interviews). In her critical piece on Deen's heretofore unchallenged status as a "feminist idol," journalist Amanda Hess notes that it was, in fact, his female fandom that performed the labor of validating him as a feminist, rather than Deen doing it single-handedly:

> The idea that Deen himself is a feminist icon is another side effect of a media narrative that warped his fans beyond recognition and erased all the truly subversive work they did to make him a star. Credit for the community they created was transferred to Deen himself.[5]

Deen was first accused of assault by his former girlfriend, porn star Stoya, in 2015, with several other female performers quickly following suit. The women accused the actor of taking advantage of his status in the industry to assert his power over them and instigate nonconsensual sex behind the scenes of film productions, and beating them during the filming of some sex scenes, among other violations. Deen vehemently denied all allegations and accused the women of defamation. However, he quickly lost his status as a "feminist idol," with many sex-positive websites and organizations condemning his alleged actions and removing his films from their databases. One website noted that "Deen is the closest thing to a Male Feminist the mainstream porn world has – which makes the accusations against him all the more jarring,"[6] while some media outlets dubbed him "the Bill Cosby of porn."[7] The story took a tragic turn when one of Deen's accusers, actress Amber Rayne, died of an apparent drug overdose in 2016. And while the scandal triggered an important discussion regarding power imbalances and the problem of sexual assault within the porn industry, James Deen's career appears to be largely unaffected by the fact that several women have accused him of sexual assault.

Research and discuss

Survey some of the media coverage of the James Deen scandal and its aftermath. Has the mainstream porn industry made any significant effort to address the problem of sexual assault within its ranks? Are there any specific initiatives that tackle gender inequality and the pressures that women face in the porn industry?

ACTION FILM

Action films came to be the dominant Hollywood film genre in the 1980s and into the 1990s, characterized by their tendency to depict the virile hyper-masculinity embodied by movie stars such as Sylvester Stallone, Arnold Schwarzenegger, and Jean-Claude Van Damme. In these films, women were often relegated to the margins of the screen, playing the stereotypical role of damsel in distress in need of rescue. The 1980s, a period connected to the rise of conservative leadership in the West and a backlash against the second wave of feminism, is arguably reflected in these gendered scripts. The conventions of the genre, with a few notable exceptions, catered to exaggerated reactionary, patriarchal dichotomies when it came to gender roles. At the same time, many action films have homosocial and homoerotic undertones, as hypermasculine men engage in battle together, or against one another. For instance, one of the top grossing movies of the 1980s, *Top Gun* (Tony Scott, 1986, US), is often interpreted as a story of suppressed homosexual desire between its two male antagonists – Maverick and Iceman – whose unfulfilled desire for one another leads to conflict. The male-centred action film, in general, tends to eschew a focus on the female body in favor of the spectacle of the sculpted male form, suggesting a broader (homo)erotic dimension to its consumption.

Despite being less frequently featured than their male counterparts, female action heroes are nevertheless an important element of the genre. Is their existence further proof that the genre rests on the patriarchal dichotomies of gender in particular, or do they trouble the binary? As Jeffrey A. Brown points out:

> Even within feminist film theory the modern action heroine has emerged as an extremely fruitful but difficult character to interpret. On the one hand, she represents a potentially transgressive figure capable of expanding the popular perception of women's roles and abilities; on the other, she runs the risk of reinscribing strict gender binaries and of being nothing more than sexist window-dressing for the predominantly male audience.
>
> (2004: 47)

Regarding the rise of the Hollywood action film and its accompanying hyper-masculinity, Yvonne Tasker finds that "the appearance of a muscular cinema, rather than signalling a radical break with the past, inflects and redefines already existing cinematic and cultural discourses of race, class, and sexuality" (1993: 5). Additionally, Tasker notes, it is important to investigate how "popular cinema affirms gendered identities at the same time as it mobilises identifications and desires which undermine the stability of such categories" (5). Tasker does so by critically examining the subtext that underlies the fetishism of the muscular body, but also by focusing on female action warriors, such as the aforementioned Ellen Ripley from the *Alien* series (Figure 7.18). She also discusses the figure of the black female warrior,

Figure 7.18 Ellen Ripley in *Aliens* (James Cameron, 1986)

or the "**macho goddess**," in the so-called **Blaxploitation movies** (a subgenre of exploitation films featuring African-American characters and aimed at African-American audiences) of the 1970s, exemplified by actresses such as Pam Grier and Tamara Dobson, but also the iconic performer Grace Jones. Here again, there are no easy conclusions as to whether the "macho goddess" is subversive or merely reflective of racial stereotypes:

> The "macho" aspects of the black action heroine – her ability to fight, her self-confidence, even arrogance – are bound up in an aggressive assertion of her sexuality. Simultaneously it is this same stereotypical attribution of sexuality to the black woman which generates anxiety around her representation.
>
> (21–22)

Blaxploitation movies were strongly influenced by the Hong Kong martial arts cinema, which in the 1970s also frequently featured female action heroes, particularly in the *wuxia* swordplay films. Hong Kong action cinema is an internationally popular genre with roots in literature that extend back thousands of years. It was initially dominated by the *wuxia* style, which centers on historical themes, swordplay, and mysticism. **Kung fu films**, which emphasize hand-to-hand combat and are often set in contemporary settings, eventually took primacy, particularly over the course of the 1970s. Kung fu films also tended to privilege male martial artists, and women were largely marginalized in the genre. The global popularity of the martial arts genre has resulted in international popularity of kung fu stars such as Bruce Lee and Jackie Chan. More recently, *wuxia* style martial arts films have also displayed global reach, and brought women martial artists back into prominence, as exemplified by the success of works such as *Crouching Tiger, Hidden Dragon* (Ang Lee, 2000, China/Hong Kong/Taiwan/US). Internationally prominent auteurs have tried their hand in the genre as well, including Wong Kar-wai with *Ashes of Time* (1994, Hong Kong) and *Ashes of Time Redux* (2008, Hong Kong), and Hou Hsiao-hsien with *The Assassin* (2015, China). The latter film features a female protagonist as an assassin facing ethical dilemmas about taking the lives of others.

The kung fu genre is often perceived as trading in realism more so than the mysticism-rooted *wuxia* tradition (Teo 2009). Some scholars attributed the rise in female action heroes in Hong Kong cinema since the 1970s to the rise of the Women's Liberation movement in the West. Yvonne Tasker cautions against this interpretation, because it positions Western feminisms as the primary reference point for understanding the images of women on film in non-Western parts of the world. Moreover, martial arts heroines typically trouble the standard masculine/feminine binary. For instance, Michelle Yeoh's protagonist in *Wing Chun* (Yuen Woo-ping, 1994, Hong Kong), called Yim Wing Chun, is a martial arts master who "dresses like a man" (as pointed out by other characters in the film) but is at the same time feminine as well, and the film never downplays the fact that she is a woman. She faces pressure from her family to become more gender-conforming, get married, and live a traditional life, which she ignores. At other times she is mistaken for a man, as well. In the martial arts tradition, gender typically does not play a defining role in the style of fighting. However, in the Wing Chun martial arts tradition depicted in Michelle Yeoh's star vehicle, the legend suggests that it was indeed a woman who first mastered the form and passed it on to others (Yim's master who taught her kung fu is a woman, as well). In the film, the role of gender is overtly evoked every time Yim faces commentary regarding the fact that she is a female kung fu fighter. Before she skillfully overcomes one male antagonist, for instance, he arrogantly announces that it is "generally known" that men are better at kung fu and women are better at child rearing. In addition to challenging these gendered stereotypes, the film focuses on female camaraderie, as Yim and her aunt share a strong bond and support one another. They take in a young, home-less widow, Charmy, and protect her from the bandits looking to assault her because of her beauty. Charmy and Yim form a close connection that frequently has homoerotic overtones, even when they are both interested in male romantic partners. And when Yim shares her backstory, we learn that she turned to kung fu because it was a way to get out of a forced marriage to a man she did not like. Becoming a kung fu fighter made her unappealing to most men and gave her agency and power to defend herself and other women in her life. When she overcomes her greatest adversary in the end, he surrenders to her by starting to refer to her as his "mother" – as does the rest of the bandit group. This surrogate motherhood becomes the greatest confirmation of her triumph over men.

Prominent crossover examples of the martial arts genre influencing American cinema are Quentin Tarantino's *Kill Bill: Vol. 1* (2003, US) and *Kill Bill: Vol. 2* (2004, US). Their story follows The Bride, a former assassin who comes back from a coma and goes on a vigilante revenge mission against those who attempted to take her life. The films contain numerous references to Hong Kong martial arts films, including the Bruce Lee starring *Fists of Fury* (Lo Wei, 1972, Hong Kong) and cult favorite *The Five Deadly Venoms* (Chang Cheh, 1978, Hong Kong). Similarly, Tarantino's *Jackie Brown* (1997, US) is an homage to Blaxploitation movies and stars the genre's iconic actress, Pam Grier. These examples of appropriation show that action genre conventions and their interactions with gender and race travel transnationally yet might function differently in each particular geopolitical and historical context.

In the new millennium, female action heroes are still outnumbered by their male counterparts, but nevertheless continue to assert their power onscreen. Prominent examples include the *Lara Croft* movies, *The Hunger Games* series, *Mad Max: Fury Road* (George Miller, 2015, US), *Atomic Blonde* (David Leitch, 2017, US) and the aforementioned *Wonder Woman* (Patty Jenkins, 2017, US). Female directors of action cinema continue to be a rarity with notable exceptions, including the first woman to win an Academy Award for directing, Kathryn Bigelow. Her films such as *Blue Steel* (1989, US), *Point Break* (1991, US) and *Strange Days* (1995, US) frequently play with action genre conventions, including conventional gender tropes and male camaraderie, but also female power and agency.

CASE STUDY: *CLEOPATRA JONES* (JACK STARRETT, 1973, US) AND *CLEOPATRA JONES AND THE CASINO OF GOLD* (CHARLES BAIL, 1975, US)

The two Blaxploitation movies featuring the character of Cleopatra "Cleo" Jones follow its heroine (played by Tamara Dobson) as she fights illegal drug trade and, in the first film in particular, attempts to stop its devastating influence on urban black communities. She is a karate-trained special agent working for the U.S. government, and an extremely imposing, stylish, and physically striking woman who takes things into her own hands in her fight for the underdogs. As Jennifer DeVere Brody points out, "she occupies the paradoxical position of being both handmaiden to the black revolution and hired handgun for the U.S. government" (1999: 93). Both films retain a kind of cult status (as genre films frequently do), and are tellingly referenced in other works, such as Cheryl Dunye's *The Watermelon Woman* (1996, US), where one character recommends renting the video of *Cleopatra Jones* (see Chapter 6 for more on *The Watermelon Woman*).

Cleopatra's main antagonist in the first movie is a powerful, white, drug kingpin matriarch who goes by Mommy, and is played by the legendary Hollywood actress Shelley Winters. The sequel, which more overtly references the martial arts genre's influences on Blaxploitation, sees Cleo arrive in Hong Kong, where she teams up with a female sidekick, Mi Ling Fong, to fight the Dragon Lady, another kingpin of an illegal drug empire (Figure 7.19). Just as in the first film, this main opponent, the Dragon Lady, is a white woman, creating an interesting juxtaposition of the Cleo and Mi Ling Fong pairing – an

Figure 7.19 Mi Ling Fong and Cleo, partners in fighting organized crime (*Cleopatra Jones and the Casino of Gold*, Charles Bail, 1975)

African-American and an Asian woman – against the criminal empire of their white female antagonist.

The character of Cleopatra Jones falls firmly within the category of "macho goddesses" who frequently appeared in this type of genre cinema. She is a strong, powerful and independent black woman whose representation at the same time rests on the stereotype of black femininity as uncontrollable and dangerous, especially for white people. Indeed, most of Cleo's antagonists are white, as the films' subtext clearly explores the racial undertones of America's (as well as the international) drug trade, police brutality, and systemic discrimination. Moreover, the fact that Cleopatra Jones's main enemy in both films is a white woman offers possible commentary on the standard criticism that the second wave of feminism primarily catered to issues concerning middle-class white women. In that sense, these two Blaxploitation films can be interpreted as a reaction against such perceived exclusions when it comes to feminist political projects. However, the films' politics are not inherently and in all respects progressive: the two white female antagonists are both coded as lesbians, perpetuating the homophobic stereotype of queer criminality.

Even within the subgenre of Blaxploitation that centers on female action heroes (or "Blaxploitation sheroes"), the two *Cleopatra Jones* films are a departure because they "work more along the lines of (male) action films" (Brody 1999: 96) with focus on the dominance, power and independence of the main protagonist. Brody adds that, rather than dismissing the female-driven Blaxploitation subgenre as simplistic and unrelated to the lived experiences of black women (as some film scholars have done), we could understand it as complicating audience identification processes by depicting powerful female figures otherwise rarely seen on the big screen. "Given that all action movies are in part fantasy projection," Brody adds, "these films might recall the fantasies of power many black women desired" (100). In *Cleopatra Jones and the Casino of Gold* in particular, Brody finds that "realness" is depicted in "queer phantasmic terms" (100), particularly through the "buddy" homoerotic aspects of Cleo and Mi Ling Fong's relationship. It should be noted that Mi Ling Fong's character actively goes against the problematic stereotype of a passive and submissive Asian woman – she is a skilled fighter and an active spy who is on equal footing with the powerful Cleopatra Jones. While in the first film Cleo is positioned as distinctly heterosexual, and an object of heterosexual male desire, in the sequel her sexuality is rendered more ambiguous, as her friendly banter with Mi Ling Fong often takes on flirtatious sexual overtones. Their transnational pairing offers an intervention into globalized discourses around gender, sexuality, and power, and highlights the agency of two women of color who stem from very different cultural backgrounds and yet join forces in order to fight white (implicitly colonial) power. In that sense, the film provides a "low cultural," genre-based treatment of the themes that would, a decade later, become prominent through the paradigm of intersectional feminism.

Watch and discuss: *Cleopatra Jones and the Casino of Gold*

1 From today's perspective, does the film's treatment of nonwhite female action heroes appear subversive or provocative?
2 How does the homoerotic relationship between Cleo and Mi Ling Fong complicate standard heteronormative, male-centric frameworks in action cinema?
3 Can you identify some of the film's references to the Hong Kong martial arts genre?

DISCUSSION QUESTIONS

1 How might a feminist approach to making a mainstream drama film differ from making a genre film (for example, a horror movie)?

2 Many horror films are centered on domestic spaces or the nuclear family. Can you think of any recent or historical examples that fit this paradigm? Do any of the concepts discussed here relate to the way gender factors into these films?

3 What are some examples of contemporary "women's films"? Are the messages of these films empowering to women or more conservative?

4 Consider another film genre or subgenre not discussed in this chapter (for example, screwball comedy, film noir, gangster film, etc.). How do the dynamics between male and female characters in this particular genre either uphold or subvert gender stereotypes? Do factors such as class and race shape the iconography and tropes of the genre?

5 How does the action movie genre uphold or exaggerate traditional gender norms? In what ways might it complicate them or even subvert them?

6 Consider the role of violence in the horror films you have seen. Does it mainly serve to perpetuate gendered stereotypes (of who commits violence and who is on its receiving end), or does it sometimes complicate the picture?

7 How might issues of race or ethnicity intersect with gender in the dominant sexual stereotypes drawn on in pornography? How can we address the issues raised by consuming fantasies that may conflict with our lived politics around issues such as sexual equality and anti-racism?

KEY TERMS

accented cinema

action films

Blaxploitation movies

body genres

ethical porn

feminist porn

the final girl

genre

hardcore (porn)

horror film

J-horror

Kung fu films

lesbian porn

macho goddess

mainstream drama

maternal melodrama

melodrama

money shot

the monstrous-feminine

montage

porn/pornography

queer porn

realism

sci-fi

sex-positive

slasher

softcore (porn)

trans porn

woman's film

wuxia swordplay films

NOTES

1 As quoted in Stephen Neale, *Genre and Hollywood* (2000: 7)

2 Neva Chonin, "Auteur and provocateur – All about Almodóvar," www.sfgate.com/entertainment/article/Auteur-and-provocateur-all-about-Almod-var-2489499.php

3 As cited in Lucy Fischer, *Cinematernity* (1996: 20)

4 www.gooddykeporn.com/

5 Amanda Hess, "James Deen was never a feminist idol," www.slate.com/articles/double_x/doublex/2015/12/james_deen_stoya_rape_accusations_the_porn_star_was_never_a_feminist_idol.html

6 EJ Dickson, "The James Deen rape allegations reveal a huge problem with 'male feminism'," https://mic.com/articles/129345/there-s-a-huge-problem-with-the-concept-of-the-male-feminist#.QhPTp5fMH

7 Hillary Hanson, "What to know about the sexual assault allegations against James Deen," www.huffingtonpost.com/entry/james-deen-rape-explainer_us_566063f8e4b079b2818d68f4

Adejunmobi, M. (2015). "Neoliberal rationalities in old and new Nolly-wood." *African Studies Review*, 58(3), 31–53.

Basinger, J. (1993). *A woman's view: How Hollywood spoke to women, 1930–1960*. New York: Knopf.

Brody, J. D. (1999). "The returns of *Cleopatra Jones*." *Signs: Journal of Women in Culture and Society*, 25(1), 91–121.

Brown, J. A. (2004). "Gender, sexuality, and toughness: The bad girls of action film and comic books." In S. Inness (Ed.), *Action chicks*. New York: Palgrave Macmillan, 47–74.

Burstyn, V. (1985). *Women against censorship*. Vancouver: Douglas and McIntyre.

Clover, C. J. (1992). *Men, women, and chain saws: Gender in the modern horror film*. Princeton: Princeton University Press.

Comella, L. (2013). "From text to context: Feminist porn and the making of a market." In T. Taormino, C. Penley, C. Shimizu & M. Miller-Young (Eds.), *The feminist porn book: The politics of producing pleasure*. New York: The Feminist Press, 79–96.

Cornea, C. (2007). *Science fiction cinema*. Edinburgh: Edinburgh University Press.

Creed, B. (1993). *The monstrous-feminine: Film, feminism, psychoanalysis*. London: Routledge.

Doane, M. A. (1990). "Technophilia: Technology, representation and the feminine." In M. Jacobus, E. F. Keller & S. Shuttleworth (Eds.), *Body/politics: Women and the discourses of science*. London: Routledge, 163–177.

Dworkin, A. (1979). *Pornography: Men possessing women*. New York: Plume.

Fischer, L. (1996). *Cinematernity: Film, motherhood, genre*. Princeton: Princeton University Press.

Haskell, M. (1974). *From reverence to rape: The treatment of women in the movies*. New York: Holt, Rinehart and Winston.

Johnson, E., & Culverson, D. (2016). *Female narratives in Nollywood melodramas*. London: Lexington Books.

Kaes, A. (1989). *From Hitler to Heimat: The return of history as film*. Cambridge: Harvard University Press.

Kaplan, E. A. (1992). *Motherhood and representation: The mother in popular culture and melodrama*. New York: Routledge.

Kuhn, A. (1985). *The power of the image: Essays on representation and sexuality*. London: Routledge.

Kuhn, A. (Ed.). (1990). *Alien zone: Cultural theory and contemporary science fiction cinema*. London: Verso.

MacKinnon, C. A. (1985). "Pornography, civil rights, and speech." *Harv. CR-CLL Rev, 20*, 1.

McRoy, J. (2008), *Nightmare Japan: Contemporary Japanese horror cinema*. Amsterdam: Rodopi.

Miller-Young, M. (2013). "Interventions: The deviant and defiant art of black women porn directors." In T. Taormino, C. Penley, C. Shimizu & M. Miller-Young (Eds.), *The feminist porn book: The politics of producing pleasure*. New York: The Feminist Press, 105–120.

Mishra, V. (2002). *Bollywood cinema: Temples of desire*. London: Routledge.

Modleski, T. (1982). *Loving with a vengeance: Mass-produced fantasies for women*. London: Routledge.

Mulvey, L. (1975). "Visual pleasure and narrative cinema." *Screen, 16*(3), 6–18.

Neale, S. (2000). *Genre and Hollywood*. London: Routledge.

Taormino, T., Penley, C., Shimizu, C. & Miller-Young, M. (Eds.). (2013). *The feminist porn book: The politics of producing pleasure*. New York: The Feminist Press.

Tasker, Y. (1993). *Spectacular bodies: Gender, genre and the action cinema*. London: Routledge.

Teo, S. (2009). *Chinese martial arts cinema: The wuxia tradition*. Edinburgh: Edinburgh University Press.

Thomas, R. (1995). "Melodrama and the negotiation of morality in mainstream Hindi film." In C. A. Breckenridge (Ed.), *Consuming modernity: Public culture in a South Asian world*. Minneapolis: University of Minnesota Press, 157–182.

Williams, L. (1984). "'Something else besides a mother:' *Stella Dallas* and the maternal melodrama." *Cinema Journal, 24*(1), 2–27.

Williams, L. (1989). *Hard core: Power, pleasure, and the "frenzy of the visible."* Berkeley: University of California Press.

Williams, L. (1991). "Film bodies: Gender, genre, and excess." *Film Quarterly, 44*(4), 2–13.

Chapter eight

FROM FILM TO NEW MEDIA

Emergent feminist perspectives

INTRODUCTION

Our contemporary cultural landscape is dominated by **new media**. *New media* is a term that typically refers to digital culture – from social media like Tumblr, Twitter, Instagram, and Facebook, to video games played either on computers or through game systems at home, and from streaming services like Netflix and Hulu to an incredible number of cell phone apps. Film and television were, of course, also once "new" media, although both emerged as analog technologies. The development of approaches to analyzing film and television were adapted to the study of digital media when it emerged in the late 20th century. Nowadays, film and television themselves operate largely in digital formats, and approaches to new media have expanded beyond the original frameworks offered by film and television studies. Today, new media, television, and film are almost impossible to separate – many theaters now exclusively show digitally distributed (and often digitally made) films and many spectators watch movies on streaming services through home television sets, laptops, or cell phones. In addition, movies and television shows are marketed through social media, and social media platforms such as YouTube are spaces where fandoms post user-generated content that shapes the reception and interpretation of various media texts, including movies. Your favorite television show may be watched on a streaming service such as Netflix, which now also produces its own original series and films. It may later be made into a feature film through a crowd-sourced campaign on Kickstarter (as was the case with the *Veronica Mars* movie [Rob Thomas, 2014, US]). You may follow the news through a social networking site like Twitter or Facebook, and you may post videos of yourself playing your favorite video game on YouTube. These are all examples of **convergence culture**. Old and new media forms are increasingly interconnected and one "text," such as a film series like *Star Wars*, may be found across many different facets of digital culture – from video game spinoffs to Tumblr memes created by fans to teaser trailers on YouTube to apps. Some of this content will be authorized (i.e. come from corporate sources) and other content will be unauthorized (i.e. consumed and produced by those outside the corporate structure producing the franchise). The predominance of digital media in our cultural moment can also be described as the **mediatization of culture**: we consume and produce dominant and subcultural texts primarily through digital media in the 21st century.

While in many ways digital film has become only one dimension of the larger field of new media studies, our concern here is to focus on new media primarily as it intersects with film studies and issues related to a feminist politics of access and representation. Many of the concerns and theoretical frameworks used within the history of feminist film studies connect to and overlap with those of media studies, old and new. New media often demand new frameworks of analysis and new terminology, but due to the increasing convergence between film and (other) forms of digital media, these new frameworks also help us understand the shifting contexts in which films are made, distributed, and received. Feminist theory and feminist film studies specifically have always been invested in the politics of representation: digital media multiplies the opportunities for self-representation, for political organizing and activism, and potentially for our exposure to different perspectives and non-dominant images. Feminist scholars of new media ask questions that echo those of feminist film scholars, such as how new media reinforce dominant power structures or provide opportunities for resistance or countercultural formations, whose voices are represented and dominate in digital spaces, and what the material effects of digital culture on people's lives are across identity categories and geographic borders. For example, we might argue that digital culture has increased the accessibility of mass media for marginal groups. The feature film *Tangerine* (Sean Baker, 2015, US) was shot entirely on iPhone 5 technology and focused on transgender women of color (Figure 8.1). New technologies make it increasingly affordable for the average person to produce and distribute their own material. Feminist scholars of new media are concerned with whether this positive dimension

Figure 8.1 Sean Baker's *Tangerine* (2015), shot entirely on iPhone 5 technology

of more access is realized in online spaces, for example, or whether hierarchies from the offline world persist. As we will see throughout the chapter, issues of the gaze and the politics of the spectacle will continue to play a strong role in studies of new media, and new media increasingly challenge older models of spectatorship in film theory. If spectators were ever simply passively receiving information, they are now actively and visibly engaging with the material they consume (see also Chapter 2).

Feminist thinkers ask us to look critically at the "common sense" or taken-for-grantedness of new technologies and offer us "the chances to reimagine how we use [digital] spaces and by whom these spaces are used" (Shaw 2014: 273). As Adrienne Shaw argues: "Unlike much of the popular rhetoric about technologies, quality feminist analysis does not assume tools are inherently bad or good, and always examines technologies in the context of their production and consumption" (274). In other words, rather than presuppose that the internet is inherently positive, or that a platform like Etsy or Kickstarter is either entirely good or bad, feminist analysis is always interested in how these tools are used in practice and what kinds of results they generate in the world. Do they reproduce inequality or challenge it? How, and in what contexts?

This chapter begins by looking broadly at the internet and asking questions about how the space is used and who uses it, as well as how the internet has been imagined on film. We then move on to broaden the discussion of fandoms and prosumers begun in Chapter 2 and, finally, discuss video games as they intersect with and diverge from film culture.

ACTIVITY

List the different screens on which you watch movies in a typical week. Consider their differences and similarities in terms of ease of access, viewing experience, viewing context, and any other issues that you can think of. How do newer screen forms differ from the ways film theorists have traditionally conceptualized the cinematic apparatus?

THE INTERNET

Early feminist writing on the internet sometimes framed it as space of unlimited potential. The net was seen as a place in which the prejudices and barriers to access present in the offline world would be inoperative. Exemplary in this regard was the writing of Sherry Turkle (1997), who argued that the internet would open up untold universes for users, in which the limitations of the material body would disappear, from disabilities to discrimination based on race or gender. This inherently positive framing of the internet and its potential can be labeled a **techno-utopian perspective**. As we will see, the idea of the internet as a disembodied space, in which the structural inequalities of the offline world would disappear, has not been realized. For example, the idea that the body is left behind in online spaces has been shown to be inaccurate in studies of **avatar** designs. Studies of teen Canadian girls who designed avatars on the site weeworld.com revealed that dominant norms about girlhood and femininity (including beauty standards) existed in these cyberspaces and had a controlling influence on how girls fashioned their online avatars (Morrison 2016). These avatars were personalized, i.e. players could fashion their self-representations from a variety of choices, rather than just choosing from pre-made avatars, as is often the case with video games. Girls were concerned about how others would judge and view their choice of avatar, particularly in terms of style. Style options that players may have preferred, or seen as being more expressive of who they wanted their avatar to be, "cost" more game points, so many girls could not afford them. This, of course, reproduces the relationship between appearance and consumption in the world offline. Girls are encouraged through the site to represent themselves in terms of consumer products, appearance, and exotic locales, perpetuating the messages that many gendered toys outside of the virtual space, from Barbie on, give to young girls. Furthermore, in early iterations of Wee World, there was no option to choose a disabled body for oneself. Moreover, only skinny-bodied avatars existed. In this way, personalized avatar sites such as Wee World placed real limits on who girls could "be" in the virtual space that often reflected social norms of desirability outside of the game world. As Morrison argues, "the WeeMee site both promises uniqueness and denies agency at the same time" (248). In video games, as well, there are typically very few choices for players outside of hypermasculine and hyperfeminine avatars, omitting any possibilities of gender queerness or even cis-gendered bodies that don't fit hyper-gendered physical norms (Jenson and de Castell 2015: 2). Thus, even in cyberspace, there can be real limitations on the frameworks through which the self can be represented, limitations that carry over from the offline world.

The myth of the internet as a disembodied space is also problematic in terms of race. For example, research revealed that in early – even text-based – virtual reality domains, users who did not choose to identify a race were assumed to be white. Whiteness as the default identity in these spaces replicated whiteness's status as an unmarked category more broadly in Western culture (Nakamura 1995). Furthermore, the users who experimented with adopting another race online – sometimes referred to as **racial tourism** – tended to reproduce racial stereotypes from the outside world. For example, female Asian characters (presumably played by non-Asian non-female users) in one examination were give names like "AsianDoll" or "Bisexual_ Asian_Guest" with accompanying profiles that indicated more about the orientalist erotic fantasies of their creators than about any actual women of Asian background (ibid).

And while the assumption that identity can be left behind in digital spaces is problematic, some feminist theorists have critiqued even the desirability of a concept of the internet based on disembodiment and transcendence. As Sue Thornham writes,

> if we look closely at Turkle's vision of the "virtual worlds" in which, she argues, we now live, the details – navigating virtual oceans, unraveling virtual mysteries, engineering virtual skyscrapers, even trying out virtual identities – seem both familiar and decidedly gendered. They are the imaginary adventures of the unitary male self, designed precisely to confirm that sense of unitary selfhood.
>
> (2007: 114)

That is to say, there may be something problematic in itself (and raced and gendered) in this desire to transcend the material world and the reality of our relational and embodied existence. How we conceptualize cyberspace and represent the internet and the possibilities of technology is culturally significant: these representations shape our understanding of the possible and reveal the limits of our cultural imaginary. Of course, cinema remains one of the main spaces in which these (often gendered and raced) fantasies of the techno-future are given form. For example, the famous match-on-action cut in Stanley Kubrick's *2001: A Space Odyssey* (1968, UK/US),

311

which shifts from a group of apes throwing a bone into the sky to a space-ship floating in space (Figures 8.2 and 8.3) is typically read as signifying a cut across time and space from the bone as the first technology – in the sense of a tool – to the shiny space-bound technological future. However,

Figure 8.2 The bone as a primitive technology of war in *2001: A Space Odyssey* (Stanley Kubrick, 1968)

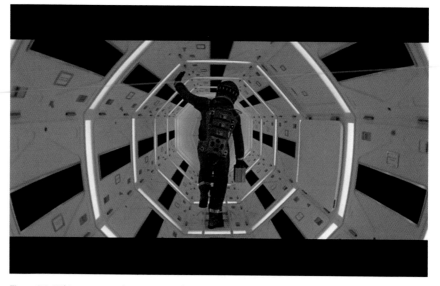

Figure 8.3 Whiteness as techno-transcendence in *2001: A Space Odyssey* (Stanley Kubrick, 1968)

the images can also be read in terms of the cultural fantasies of race and technological competence that they reflect. Moving away from the primitive blackness associated with the racist trope of the "African ape" (also evident in the attacks on civilization present in *King Kong* [Merian C. Cooper & Ernest B. Schoedsack, 1933, US] and the original *Planet of the Apes* [Franklin J. Schaffner, 1968, US]) the film associates progress with "white flight," but here instead of moving to the suburbs, white flight involves a fantasy of leaving the earth (and embodiment) altogether. This is what has been called **digital whiteness**, in which we are offered a vision of technological progress that is linked to whiteness (and maleness) as skill, transcendence, and evolution. Even ads for internet services often position cyberspace as a tool for virtual tourism, where the white Western subject can explore exotic locales, which remain comfortingly unchanging and picturesque for his or her exploration (Nakamura 2002). The digital tourist is offered unfettered access to a non-Western world that is denied the possibility of itself developing culturally, economically, and politically. In these fantasies, technology allows the world to shrink, while visually reinforcing that difference (exotic and commodifiable) will remain the burden of the non-Western other. Thus digital whiteness relies on the construction of the black body as cyberculture's primitive other. As Janell Hobson writes of *2001*:

> What remains invisible to this narrative is the way in which a primitive blackness defines the boundaries of this transcendence to ultimate white spirit and mind. From the apes of planet Earth to the blackness of deep space and the mysterious monolith to the unseeable "womb" of the Mother of the Universe (a possible black feminine figure) which carries our "star child," this "Africanist presence" frames and gives breadth to digital whiteness.
>
> (2008: 118)

By way of contrast, in the more recent reboot of *The Planet of the Apes* as a multi-part film franchise (which includes *Rise of the Planet of the Apes* [Rupert Wyatt, 2011, US], *Dawn of the Planet of the Apes* [Matt Reeves, 2014, US] and *War for the Planet of the Apes* [Matt Reeves, 2017, US]), the scientifically evolved and highly intelligent apes, lead by Caesar, rebel against the humans who had kept them in captivity, and start their own civilization. As viewers, we are invited to root for the apes in their struggle for self-determination. However, this reversal, in which we identify with and root for the simians rather than the humans, does not prevent the films from envisioning the ape community under entirely patriarchal terms, where only male apes participate in leadership and decision-making, while female apes appear to be predominantly relegated to the domestic sphere and child rearing. Again, these cultural representations matter, for they shape the ways we understand the present and future possibilities of how humans and other species are defined and changed by technology. As Sue Thornham writes of filmic representations of cyborgs and androids, "whilst the boundaries between human and nonhuman are 'enthusiastically explored' in these films, the boundaries of gender and sexuality remain firmly in place" (2007: 137). Therefore, film acts as a culturally important site where our gendered (and raced, etc.) fantasies about new media are often given narrative form. We explore this further in a case study on *Ex Machina*.

CASE STUDY: CYBORGS AND THE POSTHUMAN IN *EX MACHINA* (ALEX GARLAND, 2015, US)

In cinema, nonhuman, inhuman, and posthuman figures have been fixtures since the medium's early days, whether in F. W. Murnau's *Nosferatu* (1922, Germany), Fritz Lang's *Metropolis* (1927, Germany), or in the earliest cinema's fascination with the physiologically atypical. In recent years, the cinematic screen continues to reflect contemporary anxieties about gender, nature, and technology – for instance, in Ellen Ripley's trajectory from human to posthuman in the *Alien* franchise, in the figure of the Borg Queen in the *Star Trek* series, or in films as varied as *Blade Runner* (Ridley Scott, 1982, US), *Wall-E* (Andrew Stanton, 2008, US) and *Mad Max: Fury Road* (George Miller, 2015, US). Examining the shifts in how the posthuman is represented reveals our cultural assumptions around what it means to be human and the limits of humanness at any given time.

In *Ex Machina*, the posthuman female android, Ava, is created by an eccentric male scientist, Nathan, and is both a product and captive of his heteronormative desire. Throughout the film, she is subjected to a test of her humanness (known as the Turing test), as conducted by Caleb, a young visitor who slowly starts developing feelings for Ava. Ava, on the other hand, is driven by a powerful motivation to become more human than her sadistic human creator. Ava's struggle to become (more) human is largely framed through the traditional humanist tropes of individualism, independence, and freedom from captivity. She ultimately frees herself from imprisonment, and her quest to set herself free has lethal consequences as the men have the authority to decide her fate. Through her planning and execution of the escape, Ava ultimately passes the Turing test to which she had been subjected. Ironically, there is no human left to certify the results.

At first, Ava appears as a cyborg – with little to no skin covering her body, except for the face, and with transparent parts revealing the man-made technology that constitutes her organism. Eventually, she puts on a more human, feminine appearance: a dress and a pixie-cut wig. Later, she is seen undressing – uncovering her cyborg body in the process – while Caleb watches on the screen. The replication of the male gaze nods to the history of its dominant presence in classical cinema, but it also indicates how the conditions have changed: the object to-be-looked-at is now an inorganic machine-woman who is manipulating the male gaze in order to find her way out of confinement. Another important protagonist in the film is Kyoko, Nathan's completely silent assistant who eventually reveals to Caleb that she, too, is an AI. Kyoko and Ava eventually join forces and turn against Nathan, echoing the cinematic trope of the femme fatales who lead to the male protagonist's downfall. When Kyoko stabs Nathan in the back, she performs a crucial role in Ava's escape. While revealing her cyborg nature to Caleb, Kyoko peels off layers of skin and eventually breaks the fourth wall by looking straight at the camera with her half-human, half-cyborg face. She returns the cinematic gaze to embody a silent, defiant, hybrid entity, an alien posthuman woman who enacts revenge on a sadistic male creator (Figure 8.4).

Ex Machina's treatment of gender garnered some controversy upon its release. The director has described Ava as "genderless" and suggested that Nathan's creation of cyborgs who resemble real dolls is supposed to be seen as "creepy," or as the film's commentary on the "constructs we've made around girls in their early 20s and the way we condition them

Figure 8.4 AI Cyborg breaks the fourth wall (*Ex Machina*, Alex Garland, 2015)

culturally."[1] However, Angela Watercutter finds that "in the pursuit of that commentary, the movie ends up reenacting those same patterns." Watercutter goes on to note that "Sentient male androids want to conquer or explore or seek intellectual enlightenment; female droids may have the same goals, but they always do it with a little bit of sex appeal, or at least in a sexy package."

While pointed, this criticism misses the fact that Ava quite literally assembles herself into an organic-appearing figure of femininity, where gender is constructed in an artificial and self-controlled manner, as a mode of posthuman survival. Her assemblage of gender (re)turns to traditional feminine gender traits methodically and in calculated ways that do not merely reinstate femininity as natural or inevitable. Rather, femininity here is deployed toward ensuring posthuman female continuity, utilized to ensure the AI's seamless entrance into the world.

While most of the film is framed as a game of cat and mouse between the two men – Nathan and Caleb – it is the cyborg women's unspoken solidarity outside of the male circuit of power/knowledge that propels the film to its outcome and triggers Ava's emergence into the world. At the same time, it is important to note the continued centrality of whiteness in envisioning the posthuman, AI figure. White femininity would indeed remain the norm for cinema's posthuman women were it not for figures like Kyoko, whose actions effectively set *Ex Machina*'s key events in motion. Yet Kyoko remains completely silent throughout, an enigmatic alien – a nonwhite posthuman woman who cannot, or perhaps refuses to speak within the humanoid frameworks of expression through language (Jelača 2018).

Watch and discuss: *Ex Machina*

1 Futuristic sci-fi films offer commentary on contemporary gender politics. Viewed through that prism, what does *Ex Machina* reveal about gender and power in a technologically enhanced world?
2 Could Ava, as an AI, be considered a feminist figure in her quest for freedom? Elaborate on your answer.
3 Discuss the ways in which Ava becomes increasingly feminine as she gains agency and becomes more human-like. What do you make of this?

ACTIVITY

Watch any of the following films and discuss how they represent digital culture or the technological future. What are the pictures they offer of the relationship between race, gender, and class vis-à-vis the future? Feel free to add to the list.

Videodrome (David Cronenberg, 1982, Canada)
eXistenZ (David Cronenberg, 1999, Canada)
The Matrix (Wachowskis, 1999, US)
Blade Runner (Ridley Scott, 1982, US)
Sleep Dealer (Alex Rivera, 2008, US/Mexico)
Her (Spike Jonze, 2013, US)

Race, gender, representation

In addition to debates about embodiment and identity within new media, feminists have been invested in the questions of access or **participation** that new media raise (Portwood-Stacer 2014). Digital culture has been lauded for its potential to make information, and the power to produce and share information, available to anyone with the right technology, in the process challenging the hierarchies of older media forms and altering the relationships between producers and consumers. Again, the danger here is to see the internet or digital culture as inherently good because it enables greater participation in mass media forms than did older forms of pre-digital media. As Laura Portwood-Stacer argues, "[Feminists] have a special responsibility to recognize and publicize the differential costs of participation for subjects with varying levels of privilege to determine the conditions of their media participation" (299). Put differently, we need to, "carefully attend to how participation can reproduce power structures even while it promises to destabilize them" (Hasinoff 2014: 271).

Building on earlier feminist film theorizing of the controlling gaze, feminist scholars have been interested in the way that online platforms change our relationship to looking. Scrolling through an Instagram feed while waiting for the bus is a very different experience from sitting in a theater to see the latest *Star Trek* movie. Furthermore, we are encouraged to produce ourselves as digital content through platforms like Facebook, Twitter, and Instagram, in a way that differs radically from the historical relationship between spectator and cinema screen. The increasing visibility of our lives on social media connects to concerns about **surveillance** as it shapes contemporary culture. As Adrienne Shaw notes, "online participation is embedded

317

in systems of surveillance" (2014: 276). We are more visible than ever as producers and consumers of online media content. However, this is not an inherently good outcome, nor is it race or gender neutral. For example:

> In the mainstream press, policy and technology discussions about new media often appear to assume that publicity, visibility, connectedness, and access are de facto good things for those represented. But feminists (as well as womanists, critical race theorists, afro-pessimists, and indigenous people) are well positioned to point out that being visible or accessible to others is not necessarily liberating and that having the ability to say "no" and deny others access to one's image, words, or creative output can be a requirement for liberation.
>
> (Mann 2014: 293)

Social media are now commonly used as the basis of news media, from newscasts integrating viewer tweets about a subject, to celebrity journalists covering celebrities' self-posted content. As opposed to early feminist analyses of classical film in which women bore rather than made meaning, on many social media sites, women are both objects of the gaze and the producers and posters of that content. The selfie, for example, positions the picture-taker as both gazer and gazed, active producer of their own body as spectacle. In celebrity Twitter accounts, the viewer no longer sees the woman onscreen as existing in a separate world, unaware of being looked at (as per Mulvey's [1975] analysis). Rather:

> On Twitter . . . Users bring others – in real time – into their private (ostensibly 'real') worlds. As well, the position of viewer and of the person gazed at can change (a gazed at person becomes a viewer when he or she looks at a photograph another person posts on Twitter, for instance).
>
> (Dubrofsky & Wood 2015: 97)

In a study of the online media coverage of celebrity tweets, researchers found significant differences in terms of gender and race in tabloid discussions of celebrity "twitpics" (Dubrofsky & Wood 2015). Of a hundred media stories covering celebrity posts on Twitter during the research period, only fourteen were focused exclusively on men and only one of these referred to a picture of a male celebrity/their appearance. Women and the images they posted of themselves were the dominant focus in media coverage. During the period covered by the study, the two most discussed women were Miley Cyrus and Kim Kardashian. Although Kardashian has a background that includes Armenian, American, Scottish, English, and Dutch roots, her representation in the media has been coded as "not quite white" because of her darker skin, heavily publicized relationships with black men, and stereotypically racialized curvy body features. The study found that while Cyrus's body, and the bodies of other white celebrities, were often talked about in terms of the labor they performed on their bodies to look the way they did, Kardashian was talked about in terms that effaced any labor she performed to maintain her appearance, instead framing her body in terms of its essential uncontainable sexiness. So for example, while Cyrus "has been proudly showing off the results of her frequent working-out sessions – and controversial gluten-free diet – by flaunting her abs in midriff-baring tops and her legs in short rompers," Kardashian, "loves showing off her bikini body – even without any touch-ups! The *bootyful* reality star posted a pic of her crazy curves poured into a skimpy swimsuit boasting it was 'Photoshop-free'" (100, 102). In other words, racially loaded concepts of the nonwhite woman as excessively sexual, embodied, and animal that have deep roots in the history of imperialism and colonialism were perpetuated in 21st century coverage of American celebrity social media posts: "Kardashian's body is discussed as if it has a will of its own, divorced from any actions she might take. At the same time, her attributes are essentialized, ascribed to a body that no amount of dieting or exercise could fashion" (102–103). The fact that Kardashian is discussed in this way, despite her being predominantly Caucasian, suggests that "racialization is situated and contextual, not essential" (102). Furthermore, the fact that all of these celebrity women actively post their own images ties into discourses of **postfeminism**. Postfeminism often implies that there is no more need for feminism, and that women have achieved career and financial independence, i.e. consumer power and equality in the realm of sexual expression and desire. Paradoxically, within postfeminist discourses, women's agency and power to be sexy and authorize their own sexual subjectivity also make them implicitly responsible for their own objectification. Critique then is no longer lobbied at larger cultural scripts in which women's value is tied to their appearance, but rather is displaced onto the "liberated" women themselves, who presumably act in a post-patriarchal world. These discourses efface the ways in which women's success (particularly in the world of entertainment) is still largely tied to their ability to embody certain norms of attractiveness and sexuality.

While social media raise concerns around the ways in which raced and gendered bodies are monitored and discussed, participation has also enabled various digital campaigns that raise awareness about issues of representation. For example, the lack of Asian-American representation in mainstream American media was the subject of the trending hashtag #starringJohnCho, in which Korean American actor John Cho was photoshopped into film posters of popular films that starred white actors (Figure 8.5). This was followed closely by a #starringConstanceWu campaign to similar ends (Figure 8.6). These campaigns questioned why Asian-American actors weren't cast more often in seemingly race neutral roles. Projecting these actors into roles played by white actors was a form of social media activism, and made the visual argument that these roles could be played by Asian-American actors, thus raising questions about why better opportunities aren't given to actors like John Cho or Constance Wu (Chong 2017:130–135).

Figure 8.5 A series of photoshopped movie posters reveal a lack of racially diverse casting in Hollywood

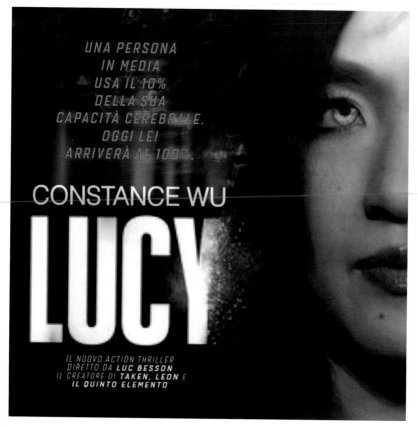

Figure 8.6 Constance Wu's presence in this *Lucy* (2014) poster asks why there aren't more substantial roles for Asian-American actresses

Thus, many of the issues around representation that were and are present in film and "older" media are given new life in new media, since there are greater opportunities to produce and distribute content that challenges, influences, and calls to task media conglomerates.

In that vein, new media such as Twitter and Tumblr have been important sites of production and criticism by women of color. Many women of color have used sites like Twitter to create an audience base and voice challenges to dominant culture. Women like Sydette Harry (@Blackamazon); Flavia Dzodan (@redlightvoices); and Lauren Chief Elk (@ChiefElk) have all become known activists through their tweeting, blogging and other forms of online activism. Lauren Chief Elk, for example, started the **hashtag activism** trend #GiveYourMoneyToWomen, which made the claim that men should pay women for the attention and emotional labor they are expected to provide as women, free of charge. The hashtag brought women together in online communities and opened up a dialogue about the kinds of gendered – and raced – (unpaid) labor that undergird patriarchal capitalism. Netherlands-based Dzodan is known for starting the phrase "My feminism will be intersectional or it will be bullshit," which went viral. In her writing, Dzodan was attacking the continued privileging of whiteness by many of those active in the feminist movement. In particular, she wrote a piece decrying the use of racially loaded language by white feminists. Since her phrase went viral, Dzodan has further discussed how her words have been turned into a variety of commodities from cross-stich decorations to mugs, buttons, and tote bags, from which she receives no economic benefits. This raises questions about the commodification of subcultural activity, which has accelerated due to digital media, a topic we will return to in the section on fandom below. The Crunk Feminist Collective[2] is an example of how black women are using digital technology to organize and agitate. Their blog brings together activists and scholars of color, many of whom are active on digital media, and uses the blog as a platform to interrogate and analyze culture. The takeaway here is that forms of social media have enabled new forms of participation in cultural politics and have been more accessible to women of color. Again, these issues of representation are not separate from those that are often central to our concerns in thinking about representation and cinema.

Perhaps the most prominent recent example of the intersection of hashtag activism with the film world and issues of gender equality has been the rise of the #MeToo movement since the fall of 2017. It began with a number of accusers coming out against powerful Hollywood producer Harvey Weinstein, revealing decades of sexual assault from the entertainment mogul. Beyond drawing attention to the presence of sexual violence in the film industry, it prompted a much broader response by women on social media who had experienced rape, assault, and other forms of sexual violence in their lives. Weinstein was only the first of many prominent men working in the media industry to have a history of sexual coercion revealed. Their downfall has caused a seismic shift in the film and entertainment industry, triggered a more open conversation about the prevalence of sexual harassment and violence in the workplace, and indicated that powerful media men are no longer untouchable authority figures whose misconduct will be tolerated. Through the ensuing #MeToo campaign, social media have also provided a major platform for women to share experiences, raise the visibility of sexual violence as an issue endemic to culture, and challenge some of the most egregious perpetrators within the establishment.

The trend of hashtag activism, which "usually involves various people repeating a single phrase accompanied by a personal variation on the theme, often including puns or other wordplay," has been argued to be well suited to historical forms of black American cultural expression and oral tradition (Mann 2014: 296). Verbally based platforms like Twitter have become sites where racial identities can be expressed through verbal marking in the service of creating visibility and community in online spaces. In other words, in spaces – such as Twitter – where a lack of visible markers exists, various forms of black cultural and oral expression are drawn on in order to create visibility and affiliation. The phenomenon of the substantial number of black Americans on Twitter in particular is known as "Black Twitter" (although they comprise 12–13% of the U.S. population, black users make up 26% of American Twitter users, according to 2018 statistics). Various versions of signifyin' – engaging in wordplay games that display wit and intelligence, which have formed a strong part of African-American cultural history – have been adapted to the medium of Twitter: "Signifyin' serves as an interactional framework that allows Black Twitter users to align themselves with Black oral traditions, to index Black cultural practices, to enact Black subjectivities, and to communicate shared knowledge and experiences" (Florini 2014: 224). Performing or doing blackness through Tweets can be read as a form of resistance to cultural invisibility or erasure. It also suggests that blackness is performed based on a shared cultural history and context, rather than being an essential identity attribute. As Sarah Florini argues:

> Signifyin' on Twitter allows Black users not only to reject colorblindness by actively performing their racial identities but also to connect with other Black users to create and reify a social space for 'Blackness.' This has the potential to sustain the visibility of race as an important social axis in U.S. culture and carve out social space for collective Black racial identities.

(235)

In this case, then, the social media platform acts as a space for community building and resistance to cultural invisibility. For example, the #blacknerdsunite thread created a trending topic that enabled the performance of humor and wordplay, while also challenging dominant cultural constructions of blackness as uneducated, unintellectual, and less technologically competent. For example: "visit the library? shoot, I WORK at the library! #blacknerdsunite" (@thefriendraiser April 12, 2010), is a tweet that challenges racialized constructions of blackness, while also participating in a form of online black community (Florini 2014). Intersecting with feminist concerns was the hashtag #NextOnNightline, which was inspired by a *Nightline* episode (2010, season 31, episode 20) that focused on why successful black women in the United States were apparently unable to find long-term romantic partners. The panel was co-moderated by someone who had questionable credentials for discussing what was a very loaded issue that intersects with historical constructions that scapegoat black womanhood (the moderator had written a book for black women about how to find and understand a man). Twitter followers used this opportunity to tweet about the intersections of race and gender. For example, "#NextOnNightline Tyler Perry discusses black feminist theory" (@CeeTheTruthy, April 22, 2010). While critiquing the choice of panelists, the tweet also depends on certain cultural knowledge as well: Tyler Perry is known for his films about black women being saved through finding the right man (Florini 2014). Spaces like Twitter, then, provide platforms to explore issues of representation and online visibility as they intersect with other media – from news programs to films.

CASE STUDY: ONLINE HARASSMENT

What has become patently evident with the ascendancy of the internet in our daily lives in the 21st century is that it is not a gender (or race) neutral space. As Sue Thornham noted in 2007, "In research studies spanning the last thirty years, the overvisibility of women as sexualized *spectacle* has been contrasted with their virtual omission from those genres seen as having a privileged relation to the real world: news, documentary, and current affairs" (84–85). Digital culture, particularly the promise of greater participation for women, people of color, and sexual minorities may have the power to change that. However, many female journalists are targeted by repeated and constant online harassment of a sexually violent and misogynist nature, a fact that has caused many women to leave the blogosphere altogether.

Comment sections on blogs, articles, and other forums arguably allow a space for free and open speech and for the possibility to correct or debate online perspectives – they can be sites of intellectual exchange, fact checking, and critique (as well as appreciation). But often, they become spaces for online bullying and hate speech. While women and men both experience aggressive commenting from time to time, it is the quantity and quality of harassment targeted at women that has made many internet spaces hostile for them. This has led to many women self-selecting out of online journalism. While some cultural pundits have argued that these women are overly sensitive and cannot handle the kinds of negative interactions that are part of participating in the public sphere, what is often at work is a refusal to recognize online harassment as harassment. As one journalist put it:

> Imagine this is not the internet but a public square. One woman stands on a soapbox and expresses an idea. She is instantly surrounded by an army of 5,000 angry people yelling the worst kind of abuse at her in an attempt to shut her up. Yes, there's a free speech issue there. But not the one you think.[3]

One of the most notorious cases of online harassment involved the online blogger Anita Sarkeesian, who in 2012 began a Kickstarter campaign to document sexist tropes in video games (Figure 8.7). She

Violent Storm (1993)

Figure 8.7 A clip from Anita Sarkeesian's *Tropes vs. Women* series illustrates the prevalence of the damsel in distress trope in video games

had previously done a similar series targeted at other media representations of women. Sarkeesian wanted to critique and document the limited possibilities offered to female players in terms of meaningful characters in games, and to call the industry to task for ignoring the desires of female game players. In response, she was targeted through a variety of death and rape threats, her image was turned into a misogynist meme, and drawings of her being raped and mutilated were circulated (all of which are documented on her blog), hate sites were devoted to her where she was often doxxed (i.e. her personal address and phone number were distributed), and a video game was even created where players could "Beat up Anita Sarkeesian." The latter shows images of her face becoming progressively bruised and bloody as players attack her photograph. Furthermore, her Wikipedia site was repeatedly vandalized with pornography, among other things, and her personal websites hacked in order to shut them down. Sarkeesian's case is one of the most well known – in part because she has been brave enough to share and document the harassment she has received – but it is hardly unique. As a milder example, game reviewer Carolyn Petit's review of *Grand Theft Auto V*, which was generally favorable except for a brief comment on the game's gender politics,[4] resulted in her receiving an onslaught of rape and death threats. Sarkeesian's case was part of a larger movement that targeted women in gaming culture, often using the hashtag #gamergate to identify their actions/membership in the larger anonymous group. Several other women were targeted in the attack. One of them, Zoë Quinn, a game designer, was the subject of a very long letter published by her ex-boyfriend personally attacking her and accusing her of sleeping with a game reviewer to get press coverage for her game (in fact, the reviewer in question never reviewed her game at all). Quinn, and her father, were also the victims of doxxing, repeated harassing phone calls, and a slew of violent and misogynist virally organized attacks. Quinn has now written a memoir, *Crash Override: How Gamergate (Nearly) Destroyed My Life and How We Can Win the Fight Against Online Hate* (PublicAffairs 2017). These issues aren't exclusive to gaming culture, of course. They raise fundamental questions about what constitutes free speech, who it protects, and whether the (virtual) public sphere is a place to which all have equal access. What is harassment? When does online commenting become harassment? What do these patterns reveal about gender in our culture?

Women journalists and bloggers experience a disproportionate degree of violent and personally directed harassment online. Women, particularly those who express any critique of patriarchal or socially unjust representations, events or experiences, are aggressively targeted by online trolls. **Trolling** has a unique history and has generated various subcultures on the internet, although because online trolls depend on anonymity for their tactics, trolls' sense of community is perhaps less personal and more ephemeral. The subculture of trolling is premised on the emotional detachment of the trolls from the subjects they meme or attack. For example, trolls have gained notoriety for turning media events, such as the rape and murder of young girls, into sexually explicit and violent memes, comments on victims' Facebook pages, and harassment of victims' families. RIP trolling is a particular manifestation of this culture, as Facebook trolls target memorial pages of the deceased (usually those whose deaths have generated media coverage for one reason or another) and then attempt to provoke mourners with their inappropriate and insensitive commentary (for example, in the case of a gay teen suicide, making explicit jokes about the method of death). Often RIP trolls target mourners who come to the page to comment without having known the actual victim, but sometimes they target the family of the victim. The aim of trolls is to generate "lulz" or to provoke others in online spaces. While trolls claim neutrality – they generally profess to being apolitical – the misogyny and racist discourse rampant on popular trolling congregation sites like 4-chan's |b|-random board reveal that the structural inequalities of the political and economic world shape participation in these virtual subcultures. However, what trolling culture reveals is perhaps less an aberration from dominant media culture, than a more extreme manifestation of behavior that is present in all major media outlets: the desire to provoke and scandalize viewers, exploitative coverage of the misfortunes of others in order to get "clicks" or people tuning into stories, and exhibiting racist and sexist behavior (Phillips 2015). However, whereas major news media benefit financially from their sensationalism, trolls do it for the lulz alone, and the overt racism and sexism of trolling behavior is often much less explicit in the mass media. For example, in a study of RIP trolling during its peak years 2010–2011,

> the disproportionate frequency with which RIP trolls descended upon news about dead white young people – specifically

murdered white teenage girls, white teenage suicides (with particular interest paid to gay white teenage suicides) and kidnapped and/or murdered white children – revealed the disproportionate frequency with which the mainstream media filed stories about these populations.

(Phillips 2015: 85)

By contrast, stories about nonwhite crime victims "rarely generated the level of moral panic typically assigned to young white victims, and so from the trolls' perspective weren't worth the time or effort" (ibid). Of course, mainstream media also get further headlines from trolls' outlandish behavior, covering stories of the threats that families have received, for example, in the wake of their loss.

Feminist new media scholars ask us to examine how behaviors like trolling reflect and support larger cultural discourses – much as feminist film scholars have been historically interested in the relationship between the representation of categories like race, class, and gender on film and the cultural milieu from which they emerge. They also ask us to probe inequalities as they emerge in digital spaces. The phenomenon by which virtual anonymity seems to engender the worst kinds of racist, homophobic, and misogynist content – be it via comments sections, trolling, or other forms of online harassment – is often naturalized on the internet, as if people can't help their behavior when they have the cloak of anonymity to cover them. Instead, feminist media scholars identify much of this activity as hate speech that should be interrogated critically and situated in the context of larger cultural discourses.[5]

Discuss

1   What can or should be done about harassment in online spaces?
2   When do you think online behavior qualifies as harassment? What should or should not be protected under the banner of free speech?
3   Do mainstream media outlets perpetuate trolling culture by covering it?
4   What are some recent examples of online harassment that have garnered public attention? Is it useful to analyze them from a feminist perspective?

ACTIVITY

Several websites have been dedicated to documenting the kinds of harassment female videogamers receive. Explore some of the following sites. What are some of the patterns that are evident? What kind of harassment do you think men may experience in these same game spaces? Are these examples of free speech or do they constitute an intimidating and exclusionary environment for female gamers? What is the purpose or effect of publicizing these comments? What can be done to alter this dimension of gaming culture?

- www.fatuglyorslutty.com
- www.notinthekitchenanymore.com
- www.bitchsandwich.tumblr.com
- www.gomakemeasandwich.wordpress.com

DIGITAL CULTURE AND FAN STUDIES

Although we discussed fandom and participatory culture in Chapter 2 as a long-standing phenomenon that predates digital culture, it bears more discussion here, as fandoms nowadays exist overwhelmingly on new media platforms. The term **prosumers** has been coined to indicate the porous distinction between producers and consumers in fan cultures. It is reported, for example, that fan generated music videos are more effective in boosting record sales than officially produced videos (Stanfill 2015: 135). Feminist scholars have been interested in the mainstreaming of geek culture and the ways in which certain forms of fan/nerd identity gain cultural legitimacy while others remain marginalized. As Kristina Busse notes, "The new geek hierarchy of positive (white, male, straight, intellectual, apolitical) and negative (person of color, female, queer, embodied, political) fan identities creates legal and economic chasms" (2015: 114). While fan filmmaking (for example, fan films inspired by *Star Wars*) has tended to be more male-dominated, women have formed the vast majority of fans who write **fanfic** and participate in **vidding**, i.e. making fan videos out of preexisting media content (Coppa 2009: 107). It has been argued that vidding, as an editing-based art form, "complicates the familiar symbolic characterization of women sewing and men cutting" (107), although as we have seen, women have historically played significant roles in film and television editing (see Chapter 1). Vidders engage in detailed and oft-repeated viewings of their favorite texts to meticulously cut and re-edit the material, often adding a new soundtrack that shapes the meaning of the images as they've been edited together. As Mel Stanfill argues:

Vidding uses positioning as argument by slowing down moments to emphasize their intensity and producing moments that do not exist in the source text by imitating the rhythms of shot-reverse shot, mixing in content from other sources (e.g. sex scenes with sufficiently similar bodies), or layering in dialogue from the source in new combinations and contexts.

(2015: 134)

Vidding creates something new out of the old.

Sometimes, this can be merely celebratory and other times it can have a deeper, even political resonance. For example, the 2007 vid "Us" by Lim positions fan activity in terms of piracy as a revolutionary act (Figure 8.8). In it, images are digitally altered and drawn over, revealing the maker's hand in reworking the content of corporate media. Many of the images, such as the one shown here of Kirk and Spock, reference characters who are popular subjects of **slash fiction** (that is, fiction in which usually straight characters are placed into gay relationships or homoerotic scenarios). Many of the images used in "Us" also reference ideas of thievery and piracy, from Jack Sparrow's image (Johnny Depp in the *Pirates of the Caribbean* franchise) to a copyright symbol projected into the sky in lieu of Batman's bat signal. The film also draws from the film *V for Vendetta* (James McTeigue, 2005, US), including its final image, which references the source material's radical democratic politics. As Alexis Lothian says of the video's final figure, drawn from *V for Vendetta*, it:

> allows us to read "Us" in a way that suggests possible links between demands for cultural commons and claims to material ones that scorn law and ownership altogether in favor of the freedom to imagine differently, dangerously, and (perhaps) unrealistically that an anarchist politics allows.

(2009: 134)

Rather than a mere celebration of a star or imagined relationship between characters, "Us" is an example of a vidding practice that is meant to draw attention to the politics around use and ownership that the practice of vidding raises. In its broad citation of film and television shows, the vid also reminds of the increasingly convergent forms that our relationships with media take.

Vidding as a practice dates back to the adoption of analog VCR technology in the home. Its emergence can be productively read in terms of feminist film theorizing of the gaze. Whereas classical feminist film theory posited women as connoting "to-be-looked-at-ness" – gazed at rather than actively looking – in many dominant Hollywood films, by contrast the VCR "enabled women to stop and look – really look – at an image in the safety of domestic space . . . without any of the physical or social dangers historically connected to the female gaze" (Coppa 2009: 112). The emergence of analog vidding

Figure 8.8 Lim's "Us": a vid that celebrates slash and piracy (2007)

thus indicated a shift in gendered practices of looking – of course women had always been spectators, but technologies that enabled women to pause, rewind, and rewatch at their leisure in the privacy of their homes arguably shifted the terms of a culture that typically privileged the male as the possessor of the desiring look, with the female body as the object of desire. In fact, fan vids often reveal the fetishization of male bodies and body parts, and are often permeated by the sexual desire of the vidder. As opposed to the woman's body being fetishized and fragmented onscreen, we see here a model of women looking, rather than being looked at, and often fetishizing the objects of *their* gaze.

Historically, feminists have used DIY culture to engage with dominant media representations: zines were a key site of feminist low-budget countercultural commentary, cheaply made and easily distributed. These cultural forms often overlap and intersect with fandoms, and digitization has brought this even more to the foreground. The popular HBO series *Game of Thrones* is an example of this overlap, as well as of the ways in which media convergence reflects the reality of our engagement with new media. The show has amassed an enthusiastic group of fans, many of whom identify as feminist (purportedly George R.R. Martin, the author of the book series on which the show is based, identifies as a feminist). Many of these fans write fanfic based on specific characters in the series. Although the series is noted for its violent and sexual content, including numerous depictions of nonconsensual sex, one episode in particular caused outrage among fans. The reasons for this are complex, but the controversy involved a character, Jaime Lannister, who was a popular subject of **shipping** fiction – many stories had been based on a fantasy relationship between Lannister and a female knight, Brienne of Tarth. Lannister had had a developmental arc that saw his character changing for the better, particularly in terms of his attitudes towards women, to which fans had responded positively. In this context, an episode depicting Lannister raping his long-term (secret) partner/sister, Cersei Lannister (Figure 8.9), sparked outrage among fans, who saw the episode as a reflection of **rape culture** (Ferreday 2015). Rape culture emphasizes the need:

> to understand rape *as* culture; as a complex social phenomenon that is not limited to discrete criminal acts perpetrated by a few violent individuals but is the product of gendered, raced and classed social relations that are central to patriarchal and heterosexist culture.
>
> (22)

Defenses of the show in online discussions, interviews with the director and actors, and other media coverage that ensued argued that *GoT* was a "fantasy" world that had nothing to do with reality. It could therefore have no relationship to rape culture because it is not "our world," it is a world of speculative fiction. This argument for the separation between the virtual and the real echoes issues raised throughout this chapter – the notion that virtual spaces (be they discussion boards or video games) have nothing to do with politics and the real world. Any mention of issues of identity or of social inequality in these spaces is often framed as an intrusion into a fun

Figure 8.9 Jamie and Cersei in a controversial *Game of Thrones* scene

and harmless space of play or entertainment. Yet, these discourses implicitly privilege a dominant perspective in their denial of issues that matter to and affect certain participants. These issues are endemic to digital culture, and of feminist concern. We will see these disputes around the purported separation between the virtual and the real come to the fore again in our discussion of video games.

What was remarkable about the *Game of Thrones* case is that the scene in question was often defended as not depicting "real" rape – the two characters were a couple and many defended the scene by saying that eventually the woman gives in or consents. These defenses of what was depicted in this "fantasy" world then in fact *do* perpetuate dominant myths identified as part of rape culture: "[S]ex in a relationship is seen as something one partner demands; the other might 'give in' and 'grant' consent. Male desire is described as overwhelming and uncontrollable: consent consists of giving in" (Ferreday 2015: 32). These sentiments were expressed in viewer comments about this issue, in which they asserted their own experiences of sex that "became consensual" as testimony to the validity of readings of the scene as "not real rape." What makes the discussion of further interest is that *Game of Thrones* has often depicted rape, but more extreme (i.e. less common) cases, such as village women being attacked by strangers raiding their town. These earlier instances of rape were not controversial among fans in the way this particular depiction of rape was. Of course it is the Jamie/Cersei depiction that is most reflective of the majority of sexual violence experienced by actual women, in which the rapist is in fact a trusted known person. These conversations thus reveal the ways in which fan discussions through new media have the potential to open up debate about major issues like rape culture and are increasingly visible in the media, becoming significant parts of the "text" of television shows (and films and video games).

As mentioned, Jamie Lannister and Brienne of Tarth had been popular subjects of fanfic.

Fanfic archives create spaces that allow for the expression of female desire and enable women to rewrite dominant narratives in ways that may subvert more normative gender roles espoused in the original script. Each archive of stories contains many variations on a basic plot, world, and characters, and often rewrites the dominant text to include queer representation (for example, creating a lesbian love story where none exists in the original film or TV series). Fanfic stories often alter the gendered power dynamics of the original text in a way that offers more options for readers who are unsatisfied with the original text. As one scholar argues,

> women can find fan fiction valuable and affecting precisely because
> it presents a multiplicity of different versions of the same character

pairing, which gives women readers the chance to imaginatively engage with a relationship repeatedly, through diverse reworkings, and experience the relationship through lenses that alternately reinforce, ameliorate, or transform dominant narratives of gender and sexuality.

(De Kosnik 2015: 122)

In fact, many archives have developed rubrics to both warn and invite readers looking for specific experiences. For example, a writer may indicate that a story has nonconsensual sex for readers who are interested in reading a story that contains nonconsensual sex and, at the same time, to warn others for whom that may be triggering. Writers can also choose not to warn as an option. Readers can avoid these types of stories if they want to know in advance what controversial content they may encounter. Conversely, some readers gravitate towards this label as they find that content warnings lessen the pleasure of the text's surprises (they function as "spoilers" of sorts for these readers). **Trigger warnings** in this context are ways to signal content both for users who may wish to avoid certain themes, but also for users who *want* to access certain kinds of taboo sexuality and/or violence (Lothian 2016). These archives are also spaces of collective storytelling and community building. The most commercially successful work of fanfic to date has been *Fifty Shades of Grey*, a story originally based on *Twilight* fanfic, which was then stripped of any details that linked it to the young adult series. In this way, it was also removed from the *Twilight* archive, and thus from its roots in collective forms of storytelling, as one (in fact, relatively mainstream) iteration on a shared theme (De Kosnik 2009).

Feminist scholars of fandom have also been invested in questions of fan labor – sometimes termed **lovebor**, because of its basis in acts of fan devotion – and how and when fan labor becomes commodified. This connects back to earlier discussions around participation: it is predominantly male-dominated areas of fan production that have the potential for remuneration, as opposed to those where women prevail. Furthermore, one of the paradoxes of fan creations is that while copyright infringement may be invoked by corporations against fans who use their material, most corporations are more than happy to appropriate fan labor for their own profit (Stanfill 2015: 135). Take for example, the hats fans designed based on the character Jayne from the popular series *Firefly*, who receives the handmade item from his mom in one of the series's episodes.[6] Fans had created replicas of Jayne Cobb's hat (Figure 8.10), exchanged them with friends, and eventually sold them on platforms like Etsy. That is, until 20th Century Fox ordered them to cease and desist and began licensing the trademark hat. This raises the issue of the structural asymmetries between producers and consumers, regardless of how productive those consumers may be.

Figure 8.10 Jayne in the hat his mother made him (*Firefly*, 2002)

As Mel Stanfill argues,

> recognizing transformative reuse as legitimate and as labor rests on the distinction not between the original and the copy but between the powerful and the disempowered. The same corporations filing takedown requests on fan transformative works are quite willing to appropriate fan labor by monetizing those works, and they often profit from appropriating other artists who never get to count as artists.
>
> (137)

Media conglomerations in effect rely on the publicity generated by fan activities and the sales generated by fan consumption, but often exploit or capitalize on this labor in a one-sided manner.

The appropriation and commodification of fan labor is also prevalent in **Korean fanfic** culture. In South Korea, fanfic typically refers to writing about two male K-pop stars that places them in homosexual erotic relationships. These stories are predominantly written by straight women in their teens or twenties (placing Korean fanfic, in terms of sexual content, in the Western slash fiction tradition). Although it originates in the world of pop music, stars who have been the objects of fanfic have moved on to perform in Korean television dramas and films. This is in part because, with the widespread practice of music downloading, entertainment conglomerates have had to find other ways to make money off of their musical artists, through acting, advertising, concerts and other tie in products (Kwon 2015: 101). Female fandoms have become a great source of content and free market research for entertainment companies. As an example, SM Entertainment held a fanfic competition in 2006. The company would own the rights to all submissions and develop the winning entry into a television show. However, the stories entered had to be heterosexual in content, therefore many authors merely changed the more feminine male character in their story into a woman (these stories typically have one character who is given more feminine qualities) (Kwon 2015). As Jungmin Kwon notes, "SME came to legally possess an immense amount of fan labor without great effort. By submitting their fanfic to SME, authors were deprived of the opportunity to self-publish their work or get contracts with other publishers" (104). However, this is an ongoing cycle – fans "queer," or otherwise alter, appropriated mainstream content, which is then reappropriated by media companies only to be reworked again by fans. Unfortunately, as indicated earlier, it is conglomerates who benefit financially from the creative labor of these young women.

The impact of Korean fanfic has influenced K-pop artists: bands members will act affectionately towards one another to incite the desire and imagination of fanfic writers. At least one male pop star has even kissed other men on two separate occasions, asserting his heterosexuality after the fact and defending his actions in terms of a desire to please his fan base. Here, consumer desire is driving the performance of the stars themselves. As Kwon (2016) argues, it was through film that media companies realized the consumer and creative power of young female fans. In particular, the release of the historical film *The King and the Clown* (Lee Joon-ik, 2005, South Korea) was a watershed moment. The film was a huge box-office success and told the story of a love triangle among three men, one of who performed an extremely feminized gender identity. The popularity of the film has ironically resulted in an increase in the production of gay male media that is targeted at young heterosexual women – its most avid consumers/commentators. These women subvert dominant scripts through their queering of mainstream culture – rejecting more patriarchal male/female relationships and showing a preference for softer masculinities and more androgynous gender presentations in their writing – and also assert their own desire and sexuality in a cultural realm where it is often denied them. However, despite the actual increase in LGBTQ visibility as a result of the media adoption of their subcultural practices, the increase in content by actual LGBTQ populations for LGBTQ populations remains suppressed in the current cultural landscape.

A closer look at the South Korean media landscape also decenters the West as the point of reference. When we talk about the circulation of culture in the West, we are almost always referring to either the popularity of Western movies, music, or other forms of pop culture in non-Western parts of the world, or Western interest in a non-Western form (for example, an obsession with Hong Kong action films that has influenced major Hollywood directors). The extreme success of Korean popular culture internationally since the 1990s is often referred to as the Korean Wave or *Hallyu*. The *Hallyu* has had a major presence within East and South Asia, from Japan to Singapore to Mainland China. This phenomena of **inter-Asian transcultural consumption** is largely driven by a female fan base and has promoted various forms of tourism from actual trips to South Korea to studying Korean language and cooking and buying Korean clothing and beauty products (Yue 2013: 121). Focusing on the circulation and understanding of digitally enabled fan practices within Asia decenters the West as the implicit reference point and sheds light on the complex local/global intersections of ethnicity, nationality, and gender, as highlighted in the case study that follows.

CASE STUDY: BAE YONG-JOON/YONSAMA AND INTER-ASIAN FANDOM

As noted earlier, the *Hallyu*, or Korean Wave, has had a strong international presence for several decades now, both within the Asian continent and far beyond. K-pop bands like Big Bang and BTS have huge international followings, and Korean dramas are subtitled into languages from around the world. An earlier example of the ascendancy of Korean popular culture in East Asia is the notoriety of actor Bae Yong-Joon, who is popularly known in Japan as "Yonsama." Yonsama is a title which functions to transform the name Yong into an appellation reserved for royalty or aristocracy in Japan (*sama*). Bae gained an international following when he starred in the hugely successful drama series *Winter Sonata* (first broadcast in Japan in 2003). The series focuses on a love relationship that was viewed by many as pure and innocent. Bae's character, Kang Jun-Sang, represented a gentle and less carnal romantic male lead (Figures 8.11 and 8.12). His portrayal proved to be of major appeal to women in South Korea, but more surprisingly, it resonated deeply with middle-aged Japanese women.

Geopolitically, the success of the show in Japan, and the huge sex symbol status of its star there were indicative of major historical shifts. While Korean popular culture had long been subordinate, and seen

Figure 8.11 Bae Yong-Joon and Choi Ji-Woo in *Winter Sonata* (2002)

Figure 8.12 Bae Yong-Joon in *Winter Sonata* (2002)

as inferior, to Japanese popular culture (which has historically had ascendancy in the region), *Winter Sonata* marked a major change. Bae Yong-Joon's fans saw his character as contrasting with prior harsher stereotypes about Korean masculinity in the region, offering a form of "soft masculinity" that had mass appeal (Jung 2010). Deemed

"Yonsama syndrome," South Korean food, culture, and tourism gained prominence in Japan as a result of fan activities. From obsessively watching *Winter Sonata* and buying Bae-related promotional material, such as posters and magazines, to traveling to South Korea to see locations from the series or to catch a glimpse of Bae on other production sets, "These consumption practices have been the stimulus behind an estimated US $2.8 billion increase in economic activity between South Korea and Japan, according to the Dai-ichi Life Research Institute" (Jung 2010: 28). These form a web of what Jung calls **transcultural consumption practices**. Conducting research with Japanese Yonsama fans, Jung found that most women saw Yonsama as radically changing their perception of Korean masculinity from one that was aggressive, violent and even "scary" to one that was "tender and gentlemanly" (45). Some of these negative perceptions can be linked to the representation of Koreans during the Japanese occupation (1910–1945) and then, later, during the South Korean economic crisis of the 1980s. Given the colonial history of the region, Koreans were depicted as the less-civilized and inferior neighbors of the Japanese.

One of the themes in the interviews given by middle-aged Japanese fans was that Yonsama held values they associated with the Japanese past – values such as politeness, elegance, and humility that they saw as being no longer present in contemporary Japan. In this sense, as the former colonial property, South Korea was in some ways seen as embodying an older form of masculinity that was part of Japan's past. While the form of masculinity was itself valued, it still functioned to place dimensions of Korean culture in a past that Japan had moved beyond (62). A deeper analysis also considers other transcultural dimensions of masculinity that stem from the Japanese occupation of Korea (in which Korean culture was essentially suppressed and assimilation to Japanese culture promoted) and Japan's regional cultural ascendency in the post-occupation period. These specific contexts promoted shared vocabularies around particular forms of masculinity, such as *bishonen* or "pretty-boy" masculinity and masculine ideals stemming from Confucianism, which inform and facilitate Bae's Japanese reception. What his case illustrates is that female fan practices and the gendered reception of international stars can result in major cultural shifts with very significant economic dimensions. It reminds us as well that fans consume stars and their (gendered) texts in ways that are (consciously or not) informed by complicated local and regional histories.

Discuss

1 Do you engage in any practices that could be considered trans-cultural consumption practices? If so, consider whether they have shifted any of your ideas about the "culture" whose media you consume.
2 Can you situate your transcultural consumption practices in any larger geopolitical or historical contexts?

VIDEO GAMES

While they are two distinct media platforms, film and video games have a lot in common, and a number of video games rely on cinematic visual storytelling in order to engage their players. Moreover, video game visuals increasingly influence mainstream action cinema. In the age of convergence, many films are made into video games and many video games – such as *Tomb Raider* – are adapted into movies. Convergence increasingly blurs the lines between films and video games, so much so that a short video game *Everything* (David OReilly, 2017) won a film festival award at VIS Vienna Shorts in 2017, therefore qualifying a video game for an Academy Award for the first time.[7] The 2015 video game *Soma* has been compared to the influential short film *World of Tomorrow* (Don Hertzfeldt, 2015, US), which is seen as the game's essential cinematic counterpart.[8] Furthermore, even independent film companies are increasingly aware of the importance of the video game market, as illustrated by Megan Ellison's Annapurna Pictures launching a video games division in 2016.

While we have discussed the online harassment experienced by many female gamers, studies show that girls/women play games in almost equal measure to boys/men. Despite this, the vast majority of game design and marketing is done by and towards men (Jenson & de Castell 2015: 1). A 2013 estimate stated that no more than 11% of game designers and only 3% of programmers were women (Jenson & de Castell 2015). Much of gaming discourse reflects a gendered bias. Terms like **casual players** vs. **hardcore players** function as gendered concepts in research and in discourse around video games, where casual players (who play games from those on Nintendo Wii to apps like Angry Birds for short interrupted intervals) are often women, and hardcore players (who invest many hours in online games that are often **MMOPRGs** – massively multi-user online role-playing games, usually played from home) are men (Jenson and Castell 2015: 1–2). As Jenson and de Castell argue: "The powerful association of masculine subjects as gamers and game designers as well as the presumption (through technologies generally) of male-competence and ability have positioned women and girls unerringly as 'less able,' 'less competent,' and as 'casual' gameplayers" (Jenson & de Castell 2010: 54). Casual games are feminized, and are labeled with dismissive adjectives such as frivolous, trivial, and a waste of time, which are often used to devalue the feminine. Studies of the language used to describe casual games also often employ homophobic language. By contrast, hardcore games are characterized as serious, demanding of skill, and worthy of time, energy, and monetary investment (Vanderhoef 2013). This gendering, and the hierarchy it implies, "reveals the way hegemonic masculinity goes beyond the mapping and categorizing of the human body in damaging and consequential ways and maps onto every other aspect of our lives, including technology" (ibid, n.p.). Of course, the larger consequences of this include the masculinization of technology and the continued lack of women entering into related fields of study.

In his study of the ways that players who identified as "hardcore" discussed casual games in online platforms, Vanderhoef found a prominent strain of comments that positioned hardcore gamers and gaming culture as under threat from the increasing popularity and cultural prominence of casual games (essentially posed as a threat to masculine values). He argues:

> The masculinity associated with gaming is a fragile defensive one that has relied repeatedly in its short history on extreme violence, the sexualization of women, and strong, male homosocial bonds for its sense of power and personal legitimacy. The introduction of a feminized, popular category of video game to gaming culture might be seen as undermining the fragile masculinity that has had to continuously defend its cultural position for several decades.
>
> (n.p.)

We can see here how the discourses that are prevalent within video game subcultures are continuous with rather than a radical break from the broader culture.

The assumption that girls and boys like and want different things when it comes to game playing leads to forms of essentialism that shape research, content design and game marketing. In this respect, studies tend to focus on female gamers as aberrations, rather than examining the supposedly "average" male gamer (Jenson & de Castell 2010, 55). As Megan Condis (2015) argues, much research into gaming:

> assume[s] that feminine and masculine approaches to play are distinct and are easily mapped onto female and male bodies. Likewise, they assume that players with female bodies require video games that feature female avatars crafted in a particular style (i.e. not sexualized for the male gaze) to fully identify with their virtual doppelganger.
>
> (200)

Of course, part of the pleasure of video games could be that players can "try on" identities that don't normally belong to them. What research *could* focus on is gender, rather than biological sex, looking at feminized versus masculinized forms of game play and not assuming that these will match up along the lines of the players' biological sex (Jenson & de Castell 2010). As one commentator has noted:

> The reality is that those men and women who currently play online games are overwhelmingly similar in terms of what they like to do with them. And stereotypical assumptions of gender motivations are either nonsignificant . . . or are dwarfed by differences in age.
>
> (Nick Yee quoted in ibid, 56–57)

Furthermore, female gamers have always found ways to resist these gendered norms and to play games despite their gender biases, just as women have historically enjoyed films that have not privileged their perspectives or experiences. Kishonna Gray (2013) has studied the way that women of color organize on Xbox Live to create spaces where they can play with others who occupy similar identity categories, or where they use the game space to protest and resist male dominance in game play. For example, "Conscious Daughters," a group/clan of black college-educated female players, entered game spaces and did nothing, either talking to male players about issues related to gender, race, and gaming, or waiting until male players asked them why they weren't playing in order to open a discussion. In this sense, their tactics reflect forms of civil disobedience, such as sit-ins, used during the civil rights movements. Another clan, mostly identified as Latina lesbians (self-described as "studs," i.e. masculine in self-presentation), the Puerto Reekan Killaz, used strategies such as "griefing" to disrupt game play. The Killaz would enter game spaces and employ tactics like killing their own team members, or finding ways to position players slightly out of the game grid so other players couldn't see them while they were firing, which would frustrate and anger other game players. In other words, they were finding ways to disrupt business as usual in the game world as a way of protesting the racism and sexism often encountered online. As Gray notes, Microsoft Xbox has not created forums to discuss issues like gender and race online, and when players have started threads related to these issues, Microsoft has deleted them: "And by deleting them, it reifies power structures along the lines of race, gender, and class" (n.p.).

ACTIVITY

Research the following video games that are either designed by women or attempt to challenge dominant gender representations in video games: *Gone Home* (Fullbright Company, 2013, designed by Steve Gaynor) *Tacoma* (Fullbright Company, 2017, designed by Steve Gaynor) and *Cibele* (Fullbright Company, 2015, designed by Nina Freeman).

- How do these games differ from or conform to your expectations?
- Do they seem to offer a more inclusive game playing experience?
- Do they fit into categories such as "casual" or "hardcore" gaming?

As was discussed earlier in relation to the fantasy of the internet as a space unfettered by material bodies, what the denial of real world identities and politics in gaming spaces often means in practice – as is evident in discussions on gaming boards and within game play – is that the default or neutral player is assumed to be a straight white male. LGBTQ gamers, popularly known as **gaymers,** have often faced pressure to not disclose or discuss their sexuality in game-related spaces, even though their sexual identity typically receives little to no representation in video games. This default privileging of the heterosexual subject position has been called **heterotextuality,** the assumption that all users are straight in the absence of any overt mention of sexual preference (Condis 2015, 207). It is well documented that the term "gay" is used pejoratively throughout gaming culture (along with many slurs for gay or lesbian). The reality of homophobia has led some game companies to, somewhat problematically, ban the discussion of sexuality in game forums. For example, Blizzard Entertainment, which makes the MMORPG *World of Warcraft* (Designed by Jeff Kaplan, Rob Pardo & Tom Chilton, 2004), banned a player's account when they attempted to create an "in-game GLBT friendly guild" (Shaw 2009: 250). The company argued that the user had violated the sexual harassment guidelines, as they saw the identification of one's (non-dominant) sexual identity as potential grounds for harassment from homophobic users. Due to legal and public backlash, the company reinstated the player's account, but nevertheless, it remains the case that to be treated as "unmarked" is to be assumed to be the default position – a heterosexual male. Similarly, BioWare's game *Star Wars: The Old Republic* (James Ohlen, 2011) forbids terms like "gay" and "lesbian" on its user discussion board, presumably to block out potential harassment and to keep the board appropriate for all ages. However, some LGBTQ users requested that this policy be reconsidered, given that it prevents queer players from forming connections and affiliations in a space that often renders them invisible, since the words they would use to identify themselves have been labeled inappropriate content. These particular discussions around BioWare's policy, which expanded outside this specific discussion board to the larger gaming community, provoked heated debate about what role identity markers such as sexuality should have in gaming culture. At stake is, of course, how "gamer" is defined and understood and who legitimately can claim that title. Thus, as Megan Condis assesses:

> What was often framed by participants [on the BioWare discussion board] as a benevolent desire to prevent political and ideological conflict from leaking into gaming and ruining its unique attractions manifested as the maintenance of a heterocentric power structure. *True* gamers and fans are assumed to be straight (or, if they are queer, it is assumed that they will remain in the closet while participating in the gaming forum), and out queer gamers and their allies are flagged as disruptive and harmful interlopers.
>
> (2015: 199)

Similar results have been found when race is considered. In his study of conversations about *Resident Evil 5* (Capcom, Kenichi Ueda & Yasuhiro Anpo, 2009) that were held *before* the game's release, André Brock found that the problematic racial context of the game was dismissed by many prospective players, who defended it as just entertainment, and therefore not subject to political critique, or argued that race was unimportant (i.e. video games were somehow divorced from issues of race, or were colorblind) (Brock 2011). In *Resident Evil 5*, the main character that is played is a white man, whose mission is to destroy all the inhabitants of an African village. The game draws on colonialist fantasies of the white man as savior entering a savage land. As Brock notes, *RE 5*, as video games often do, relies on tropes from film genres – here, the survival horror genre. The enemies are thus represented as sub- or nonhumans, their language untranslated, and "are deployed to create feelings of fear, suspense, and terror – only to be subjugated by an everyman" (432). Here we see how the study of film genres and their conventions can apply to the analysis of video games. These tropes become more problematic, of course, when the survivor/protagonist is a white man and the nonhumans are Africans, given the history of colonialism and its persistence in various neocolonial economic and cultural forms.

Richard Dyer's (1988) study of whiteness in film is also relevant to understanding the representational history that the game evokes and how whiteness, as an unmarked category, signifies in Western culture. As Brock writes, "Dyer adds that control – over the self and the spirit, over women's bodies, over land, and over others – is a hallmark of White identity. This is an important point for considering how video games enact control as an integral part of the gaming experience" (2011: 432). In *Resident Evil 5*, then, the white man's ability to control the situation, and to dominate the environment through indiscriminately murdering every "other" in his path, is central to the racialized meanings the game evokes. The game gives the white protagonist a black female sidekick (Sheva) who has special costumes

Figure 8.13 *Resident Evil 5*

that players can unlock, which serve to sexualize and/or exoticize her (Figure 8.13). She has relatively little narrative importance and thus does little to destabilize the racial and sexual dynamics of the game: "Sheva is the videogame equivalent of Pocahontas: a woman coerced into 'guiding' a White explorer across a foreign land that she is presumed to be familiar with because of her ethnic heritage" (440). Examples like this ask us to consider the meanings that are mobilized by the forms of new media we interact with and to situate them within the larger cultural, political, and economic contexts that inform and produce them. The study of representations in video games and of player reactions to these representations are not dissimilar to the kinds of frameworks that might be employed to consider representation and reception in film, despite crucial differences in the media in question. In all cases, feminist media approaches ask us to question what is being represented and why, who is doing the representing, and how those representations are received, understood, and acted upon in a given cultural and historical moment.

ACTIVITY

Watch some of Anita Sarkeesian's *Tropes vs. Women in Videogames* episodes on the internet. Do you agree with her conclusions about the predominance of certain tropes in the video game world? Why do you think her work provoked the controversy and aggression that it did from so many male gamers?

DISCUSSION QUESTIONS

1   How would you define the term "new media," and particularly new visual media?
2   In your opinion, does new media draw from cinema, and if so, in what ways?
3   What are the frameworks used in analyzing film from a feminist perspective that are relevant to understanding new media?
4   In what ways do virtual spaces reproduce inequalities from the world offline?
5   How do new media offer tools for non-dominant groups to organize and engage in new forms of activism? Do you have additional or more recent examples not discussed here?
6   What needs to happen to shift some of the misogyny, racism, and homophobia that is so pervasive in video game culture?
7   Are fan practices like vidding subversive in any way? Should they be monetized and/or regulated? How do they support the corporations they borrow from?

KEY TERMS

avatar	Korean fanfic
casual players	lovebor
convergence culture	mediatization of culture
digital whiteness	MMOPRG
fanfic	new media
gaymers	participation
Hallyu	postfeminism
hardcore players	prosumers
hashtag activism	racial tourism
heterotextuality	rape culture
inter-Asian transcultural	shipping
consumption	slash fiction

surveillance	trigger warnings
techno-utopian perspective	trolling
transcultural consumption practices	vidding

NOTES

1 Angela Watercutter, "*Ex Machina* has a serious fembot problem," www.wired.com/2015/04/ex-machina-turing-bechdel-test/

2 www.crunkfeministcollective.com/

3 Quoted in Helen Lewis, "This is what online harassment looks like," www.newstatesman.com/blogs/internet/2012/07/what-online-harassment-looks

4 Carolyn Petit, "City of angels and demons," https://www.gamespot.com/reviews/grand-theft-auto-v-review/1900-6414475/

5 Lisa Nakamura, "Glitch racism: Networks as actors within vernacular internet theory," http://culturedigitally.org/2013/12/glitch-racism-networks-as-actors-within-vernacular-Internet-theory/

6 Ellie Hall, "'Firefly' hat triggers corporate crackdown," www.buzzfeed.com/ellievhall/firefly-hat-triggers-corporate-crackdown?utm_term=.wdkLqpdwB#.tbEPE3vVJ

7 Matt Girardi, "For the first time ever, a video game has qualified for an Academy Award," https://news.avclub.com/for-the-first-time-ever-a-video-game-has-qualified-for-1798262710

8 David Sims, "*World of Tomorrow* and the copy-pasted brain," www.theatlantic.com/entertainment/archive/2016/01/world-of-tomorrow-and-the-copy-pasted-brain/425016/

REFERENCES

Brock, A. (2011). "'When keeping it real goes wrong': *Resident Evil 5*, racial representation, and gamers." *Games and Culture*, 6(5), 429–452.

Busse, K. (2015). "Fan labor and feminism: Capitalizing on the fannish labor of love." *Cinema Journal*, 54(3), 110–115.

Chong, S. S. J. (2017). "What was Asian American Cinema?" *Cinema Journal*, *56*(3), 130–135.

Condis, M. (2015). "No homosexuals in *Star Wars*? BioWare, 'gamer' identity, and the politics of privilege in a convergence culture." *Convergence*, *21*(2), 198–212.

Coppa, F. (2009). "A fannish taxonomy of hotness." *Cinema Journal*, *48*(4), 107–113.

De Kosnik, A. (2009). "Should fan fiction be free?" *Cinema Journal*, *48*(4), 118–124.

De Kosnik, A. (2015). "*Fifty Shades* and the archive of women's culture." *Cinema Journal*, *54*(3), 116–125.

Dubrofsky, R. E., & Wood, M. M. (2015). "Gender, race, and authenticity: Celebrity women tweeting for the gaze." In R. E. Dubrofsky & S. A. Magnet, (Eds.), *Feminist surveillance studies*. Durham: Duke University Press.

Dyer, R. (1988). "White." *Screen*, *29*(4), 44–65.

Ferreday, D. (2015). "*Game of Thrones*, rape culture and feminist fandom." *Australian Feminist Studies*, *30*(38), 21–36.

Florini, S. (2014). "Tweets, tweeps, and signifyin': Communication and cultural performance on 'Black Twitter'." *Television & New Media*, *15*(3), 223–237.

Gray, K. (2013). "Collective organizing, individual resistance, or asshole griefers? An ethnographic analysis of women of color in Xbox Live." *Ada: A Journal of Gender, New Media, and Technology*, (2).

Hasinoff, A. A. (2014). "Contradictions of participation: Critical feminist interventions in new media studies." *Communication and Critical/Cultural Studies*, *11*(3), 270–272.

Hobson, J. (2008). "Digital whiteness; primitive blackness." *Feminist Media Studies*, *8*(2), 111-126.

Jelača, D. (2018). "Alien feminisms and cinema's posthuman women." *Signs: Journal of Women in Culture and Society*, *43*(2), 371–400.

Jenson, J., & de Castell, S. (2010). "Gender, simulation, and gaming: Research review and redirections." *Simulation & Gaming*, *41*(1), 51–71.

Jenson, J., & de Castell, S. (2015). "Online games, gender, and feminism in." In R. Mansell & P. H. Ang (Eds.), *The international encyclopedia of digital communication and society*. Hoboken, NJ: John Wiley and Sons, Inc, 1–5.

Jung, S. (2010). *Korean masculinities and transcultural consumption: Yonsama, Rain, Oldboy*. New York: Hong Kong University Press.

Kwon, J. (2015). "Queering stars: Fan play and capital appropriation in the age of digital media." *Journal of Fandom Studies, 3*(1), 95–108.

Kwon, J. (2016). "Co-mmodifying the gay body: Globalization, the film industry, and female prosumers in the contemporary Korean mediascape." *International Journal of Communication, 10,* 1563–1580.

Lothian, A. (2009). "Living in a den of thieves: Fan video and digital challenges to ownership." *Cinema Journal, 48*(4), 130–136.

Lothian, A. (2016). "Choose not to warn: Warnings and content notes from fan culture to feminist pedagogy." *Feminist Studies, 42*(3), 743–756.

Mann, L. K. (2014). "What can feminism learn from new media?" *Communication and Critical/ Cultural Studies, 11*(3), 293–297.

Morrison, C. (2016). "Creating and regulating identity in online spaces: Girlhood, social networking, and avatars." In C. Mitchell & C. Rentshler (Eds.), *Girlhood and the politics of place.* New York: Berghahn Books, 244–258.

Mulvey, L. (1975). "Visual pleasure and narrative cinema." *Screen, 16*(3), 6–18.

Nakamura, L. (1995). "Race in/for cyberspace: Identity tourism and racial passing on the internet: The resurrection of the corpus in text-based VR." *Works and Days, 13*(1–2), 245–260.

Nakamura, L. (2002). "'Where do you want to go today': Cybernetic tourism, the internet, and transnationality." In N. Mirzoeff (Ed.), *The visual culture reader.* London and New York: Routledge, 255–263.

Phillips, W. (2015). *This is why we can't have nice things: Mapping the relationship between online trolling and mainstream culture.* Boston: MIT Press.

Portwood-Stacer, L. (2014). "Feminism and participation: A complicated relationship." *Communication and Critical/Cultural Studies, 11*(3), 298–300.

Shaw, A. (2009). "Putting the gay in games: Cultural production and GLBT content in video games." *Games and Culture, 4*(3), 228–253.

Shaw, A. (2014) "The internet is full of jerks, because the world is full of jerks: What feminist theory teaches us about the internet." *Communication and Critical/Cultural Studies, 11*(3), 273–277.

Stanfill, M. (2015). "Spinning yarn with borrowed cotton: Lessons for fandom from sampling." *Cinema Journal, 54*(3), 131–137.

Thornham, S. (2007). *Women, feminism and media*. Edinburgh: Edinburgh University Press.

Turkle, S. (1997). *Life on the screen: Identity in the age of the internet*. New York: Simon and Schuster.

Vanderhoef, J. (2013) "Casual threats: The feminization of casual video games." *Ada: A Journal of Gender, New Media, and Technology*, (2).

Yue, A. (2013). "Critical regionalities in inter-Asia and the queer diaspora." In L. McLaughlin & C. Carter (Eds.), *Current perspectives in feminist media studies*. London; New York: Routledge.

INDEX

Note: page numbers for figures are in *italics*.